# Banks
# Are Dangerous
# To Your Wealth

# BANKS ARE DANGEROUS TO YOUR WEALTH

Dr. Carol S. Greenwald,
Former Commissioner of Banks,
Commonwealth of Massachusetts

Introduction by Ralph Nader

Prentice-Hall, Inc., Englewood Cliffs, New Jersey

*Banks Are Dangerous to Your Wealth*
by Dr. Carol S. Greenwald
Copyright © 1980 by Carol S. Greenwald

Address inquiries to Prentice-Hall, Inc.,
Englewood Cliffs, N.J. 07632
Printed in the United States of America
Prentice-Hall International, Inc., London
Prentice-Hall of Australia, Pty. Ltd., Sydney
Prentice-Hall of Canada, Ltd., Toronto
Prentice-Hall of India Private Ltd., New Delhi
Prentice-Hall of Japan, Inc., Tokyo
Prentice-Hall of Southeast Asia Pte. Ltd., Singapore
Whitehall Books Limited, Wellington, New Zealand
10 9 8 7 6 5 4 3 2 1

**Library of Congress Cataloging in Publication Data**
Greenwald, Carol Schwartz.
    Banks are dangerous to your wealth.
    Includes index.
    1. Banks and banking—United States. 2. Banks and
banking—United States—State supervision. I. Title.
HG2491.G73    332.1'0973    80-18176
ISBN 0-13-055806-0

To my mother, Dorothy Friedman Schwartz

# Contents

Acknowledgments   *ix*
Introduction by Ralph Nader   *xi*
Author's Foreword   *xxi*

**I THE BANKING FRATERNITY**   *1*

1. The Banking Fraternity   *3*
2. Unarmed Robbery   *37*
3. Where Have All the Bond Buyers Gone?   *68*

**II YOUR MONEY, THEIR POWER**   *91*

4. Banks Are Dangerous to Your Wealth   *93*
5. Redlining: So You Want to Buy a House in the City   *127*
6. The Bank Branch as Hostage   *158*
7. The Great Checking Account Robbery   *186*

**III POLICING THE BANKS**   *213*

8. Who's Regulating the Regulators?   *215*
9. How to Fight Back   *257*

**APPENDIX 1**

Down Easter's Credit Guide   *269*

**APPENDIX 2**

Who to Contact for Help in Dealing With a Bank   *288*

Notes   *296*
Index   *307*

# Acknowledgments

I am deeply grateful to those people who worked with me when I was bank commissioner to change the focus of bank regulation to active promotion of consumer protection. The enthusiastic efforts of key members of the Massachusetts Banking Department—Tee Taggart, Edith Rosen, Sue Hickey, Rich Siebert, Paul Horwitz, Ed Flynn, Paul Bulman, and Will Ogburn—made the events recorded in this book a reality. Above all stands the dedicated help of my friend and deputy commissioner, Steven Weiss, who taught me about banking market structure and who was always there to encourage and inspire during these four exciting years. He is truly the unsung hero of this book.

I also want to acknowledge the friendship and help of Larry Connell, Jr., then bank commissioner in Connecticut, and of John Heimann, then superintendent of banks in New York, and of James Stone, then Massachusetts commissioner of insurance, who stood by me when I needed friends and who inspired me by their examples. And, of course, Governor Michael Dukakis, who took a great leap of faith when he appointed a young woman to be a bank regulator. I also owe a great debt to Robert Eisenmenger, senior vice president and director of research at the Federal Reserve Bank of Boston, and to Frank Morris, president of the Boston Fed, for their active support of my career when I was an economist and officer at the Federal Reserve Bank of Boston.

I am also indebted to the staffs of the House and Senate Banking Committees, Ken McLean, Bill Webber, Jerry Buckley, Elinor Bachrach, Bob Kuttner, and Lindy Marinaccio, who encouraged me in my efforts to change federal bank regulatory practices. It was out of discussions with them that many of the ideas described in this book evolved. And, of course, there is the crucial roles of key congressional leaders, Senator Proxmire, Senator Brooke, Senator McIntyre, Representative St. Germain, Representative Reuss, and Representative Rosenthal, whose congressional oversight hearings provided the national forum for taking what was done in Massachusetts and using it to change federal bank regulatory practices. These outstanding and courageous men have inspired me and everyone else who has been privileged to know them by their dedication to promoting the public interest in banking. The nation has been brilliantly served by their work.

Finally, let me acknowledge the importance of those citizen advocates Jonathan Brown of the Public Interest Research Group; Edwina Clougherty, James Carras, and Hugh McCormick of the Jamaica Plain Banking and Mortgage Committee; and Janet Selzer of the women's organization, 9 to 5; all of whom argued with me and showed me the way to serve the public. Their advice and support were critical and much appreciated.

But it was my family, who was always there with love and encouragement, that kept me from getting discouraged when the going got rough.

The views expressed in this book are, of course, entirely my own and do not represent in any way those of the board of directors or other officers of the National Consumer Cooperative Bank.

# Introduction by Ralph Nader

No regulators have been as prone to prostrate themselves before the vested interests of their regulatees as have banking regulators. The vast majority of banking regulators, both state and federal, entertain no broader mission than servicing the banking industry. Consideration of such public issues as whether banks are abusing consumers or failing to serve their communities have traditionally been considered beyond the pale of the prudent regulator.

A number of factors have shaped the protectionist mold in which bank regulators have been cast. Bank regulation as we have it today originated as a response to bank panics and failures. However, bank regulators have transformed this historical concern with bank failure into a much broader mission of opposing anything that might limit bank profits—such as vigorous enforcement of consumer protection laws or meaningful community reinvestment programs. From yesterday's experience with depositor panics regulators have derived the erroneous principle that information that casts banks in a bad light should not be made public. Worse yet, regulators have expanded this into general opposition to public disclosure of any bank activities. Nondisclosure undermines oversight and accountability and this is the cherished goal of all regulated industries and subservient regulators.

Another major force shaping bank regulation has been the tremendous political power of the banking lobby. Control over credit gives bankers great economic leverage with which to influence the political process. Financing political campaigns, influencing their many corporate customers for or against particular candidates, facilitating or blocking state and local government access to credit are the standard tools with which bankers bend politicians to their will and guarantee the appointment of compliant regulators.

Several federal laws have given unabashed legislative sanction to the notion that banking agencies are fundamentally trade associations for the banking industry. The Federal Reserve Act authorizes commercial banks which are members of the Federal Reserve System to elect two thirds of the directors of the regional Federal Reserve Banks. Similarly, the legislation establishing the Federal Home Loan Bank System authorizes savings and loans to elect a majority of the directors of the regional Federal Home Loan Banks.

Amidst this unparalleled tradition of subservience, a banking regulator willing to act to hold banks to their public responsibilities is a rarity. When Carol Greenwald sought to use her position as Massachusetts Banking Commissioner from 1975 to 1979 to advance reform, the banking industry was caught off guard Commissioner Greenwald correctly recognized that dramatic regulatory actions would mobilize public opinion in support of reform and that the banking industry would be hard pressed to justify many of its practices. To address the critical issue of bank redlining, Greenwald ordered in 1975 the banks in Boston to make public by census tract the location of their mortgage loans. To document the pervasive employment discrimination in the banking industry, Greenwald directed the banks in Massachusetts to complete an employment-practices questionnaire. The survey showed that at the largest banks minorities held only 1 percent of senior management positions, while women held only 3 percent of such positions. To encourage consumers to shop for the lowest interest rates, the Banking Department in 1977 began publishing on a monthly basis in Boston's largest newspaper "The Shopper's Credit Guide," a list of interest rates charged on consumer loans by each lender in the Boston area. Recognizing that banks can circumvent credit discrimination prohibitions by informally discouraging minorities from submitting loan applications, Greenwald began to employ testers to detect such pre-screening.

Massachusetts bankers, long accustomed to compliant regulators, reacted with frenzied protests to the new commissioner's actions. They even went so far as to refuse to consider the purchase of state bonds unless Massachusetts Governor Dukakis removed Greenwald—a demand to which the governor fortunately did not accede. This confrontation represents one of the rare instances in which bankers have been unable to work their will on politicians, although fierce opposition from the banking industry ultimately played a key role in Dukakis' defeat in the 1978 gubernatorial primary.

Although the role of reformist regulators is vital, in the long run the banking industry will be held accountable only if citizens actively inform themselves of its practices and organize to protest those that are abusive. During the 1970s the seeds of reform were sown as a growing number of citizens became aware of injurious bank practices and the complicity of banking regulators. As inflation and tight monetary policy drove market interest rates well above 10 percent, small savers took issue with banking regulations that limited their earnings on savings accounts to 5 percent. Bank redlining in many urban neighborhoods provided community organizations with a powerful organizing issue. Discriminatory credit practices became a target of the civil rights and women's movements. The collapse of the U. S. National Bank of San Diego in a riot of self-dealing and the Bert Lance affair brought to public attention the hidden world of insider deals at financial institutions.

In the early 1970s citizens' groups demanding regulatory action to halt bank abuses were stonewalled by protectionist bank regulators at both the state and federal level. However, new federal legislation, such as the Equal Credit Opportunity Act (1974 and 1976), the Home Mortgage Disclosure Act(1975), and the Community Reinvestment Act(1977) forced the federal banking agencies to change some policies. Additional pressure for reform was generated by vigorous congressional oversight led by Senator William Proxmire and Congressman Benjamin Rosenthal that documented the long-standing failure of the federal banking agencies to enforce the Fair Housing Act(1968) and the Truth-in-Lending Act(1968).

Another important impetus for regulatory change was provided by the reform actions of a handful of state banking regulators, namely Greenwald in Massachusetts, Larry Connell in Connecticut, and Donald Burns in California. Under their public-minded leadership the banking agencies in Massachusetts, Connecticut, and California took actions that were not only beneficial within these states, but also provided a fillip for reform at the federal level. By providing a model of reform in operation, these state regulators undercut traditional protectionist arguments of the banking industry, embarrassed federal bank regulators into reassessing their positions, and gave a boost to various reform measures being considered by Congress.

When the Massachusetts Banking Department in 1975 ordered Boston banks to disclose their mortgage loans, this example helped spur Congress to enact a federal disclosure statute, the Home Mortgage Disclosure Act of 1975. In 1976 the California

Savings and Loan Department adopted comprehensive regulations that prohibited geographic discrimination(redlining) by state savings and loans in California. This bold action helped prod the Federal Home Loan Bank Board, which had long argued that anti-redlining regulations were impractical, to adopt similar anti-redlining regulations for all federal and state savings and loans. When the Massachusetts and Connecticut banking departments conditioned approval of bank branch applications upon commitments by the banks to increase their inner-city banking services, here again, these positive examples provided invaluable support for congressional enactment of the Community Reinvestment Act of 1977, a key federal statute that directs the federal banking agencies to consider a bank's lending record when acting on branch or merger applications. In a similar vein, when the bank regulators in Massachusetts and Connecticut uncovered widespread violations of the Truth-in-Lending law, this helped shame the federal bank regulators into improving their enforcement program.

To appreciate fully how a reform action by one banking regulator can serve as a catalyst for similar action by other bank regulators, one must understand the unique federal-state jurisdictional structure of banking regulation. A depository institution—commercial bank, savings and loan, mutual savings bank, or credit union—may obtain either a federal charter or a state charter. Those with a federal charter are supervised exclusively by one of the federal banking agencies—the Comptroller of the Currency (Comptroller) for national banks, the Federal Home Loan Bank Board (FHLBB) for federal savings and loans and federal mutual savings banks, and the National Credit Union Administration (NCUA) for federal credit unions. Those with a state charter are supervised jointly by a state banking agency and one of the federal banking agencies. In the case of state chartered commercial banks, bank holding companies, and most state chartered mutual savings banks, the federal regulator is the Federal Deposit Insurance Corporation (FDIC) or Federal Reserve Board. For state chartered savings and loans it is the Federal Home Loan Bank Board. For state chartered credit unions it is the National Credit Union Administration.

Although holding a state charter subjects a bank to dual federal-state supervision, some banks have found state charters advantageous for a number of reasons such as less onerous reserve requirements, political leverage at the state level, or a closer relationship with state regulators. Nonetheless, in recent years many state chartered banks have converted to federal charters and this shift may accelerate due to recent federal legislation that has equalized reserve requirements for state and federally chartered commercial banks.

In the past this multiplicity of bank regulators has inhibited public-minded regulatory action, since bank regulators were afraid to step out of line with their peers. However, when there is strong citizen pressure for reform, a positive action by one bank regulator can increase the pressure on other bank regulators to follow suit. This is particularly true at the federal level where comparisons between the federal banking agencies are frequently made. As a rule, state bank regulators have been more protective of the banking industry and more derelict in their duty to the public than the federal banking regulators. Yet, it takes positive action in only one state to provide a model for reform. Citizens' groups working at the state level should become more aggressive in drawing comparisons between bank regulation in their own state and the best regulatory practices in effect in other states or at the federal level. This would greatly enhance the diffusion of banking reform at the state level.

At the federal level continuing citizen group pressure, new federal legislation, congressional oversight, and changes in agency leadership have begun to move some federal banking agencies from a posture of outright protectionism to a position that gives some recognition to responsibility to the public but still from an essentially protectionist perspective. For the first time the agencies are making efforts to discover violations of consumer protection and civil rights laws. For example, the Comptroller, the FDIC, and the FHLBB now require banks to maintain the loan application data necessary to detect discriminatory lending policies. The Comptroller and the FHLBB have agreed to collect and systematically analyze the data to see if discriminatory patterns are present. On the other hand, the agencies delay in ordering banks to reimburse consumers once Truth-in-Lending violations have been discovered by bank examiners. Nor have the agencies even begun to develop an "effects test" standard that would indicate when lending criteria with discriminatory effects are judged to violate equal credit laws.

The Community Reinvestment Act (CRA) has required the federal banking agencies to make some effort to investigate citizen group claims of bank disinvestment in the local community, but it is still too early to tell whether the agencies will take the regulatory actions needed to induce banks to turn from disinvestment to reinvestment.

Following the recommendations of community groups, the agencies have developed CRA assessment procedures that place special emphasis on evaluating a bank's record in providing mortgage, small business, and community development loans in low and moderate income neighborhoods. Prior to CRA the agencies dismissed as irrelevent community group arguments that a bank branch or merger application should be denied when the applicant bank had a poor record in this regard. However, even now, when a bank submitting a branch or merger application has a poor lending record, the agencies have been reluctant to deny the application—the remedy intended by Congress when it enacted the CRA. Instead of denying applications—to date, only two denials have occurred—the agencies have favored application approvals accompanied by vacuous commitments on the part of the applicant to improve its performance. Moreover, in keeping with their penchant for secrecy, the agencies have refused to make public their CRA assessments of bank lending records.

Central to reorientation of banking agencies, both state and federal, is the need to re-educate bank examiners. Most bank examiners have been schooled in the protectionist tradition and all too often view consumer protection and community reinvestment as a nuisance. No matter how public-minded the agency heads are, consumer protection laws will not be enforced and honest CRA assessments will not be made unless bank examiners share this commitment.

Continued advocacy by citizens groups and legislative oversight is essential if the federal banking agencies are to complete the metamorphosis from trade association to public regulator and the banking departments in most states are even to begin this process. The pressure from the banking industry is so relentless that the transition can easily be stalled or reversed. For example, with the recent departure of Greenwald, Connell, and Burns from the state banking agencies in Massachusetts, Connecticut, and California, a regulatory backslide has occurred in these states. A great value of CRA is that it has encouraged community groups to participate in bank application proceedings and thus to some extent has created a new constituency to which the bank regulators must listen.

Among the federal banking agencies the Federal Reserve Board (FRB) has been a consistent laggard in the field of consumer protection, civil rights, and community reinvestment. To give some of the most glaring examples, the FRB is the only federal banking agency that has refused to settle a lawsuit brought by civil rights groups that charged the federal banking agencies with failure to enforce the Fair Housing Act of 1968. The FRB is the only federal banking agency that has not required banks to maintain the loan application data that is necessary to detect violations of the equal credit laws. The FRB has interpreted CRA in a manner that undermines the congressional objective of encouraging banks to make greater lending efforts in credit deficient neighborhoods. In acting on challenges to bank branch and merger applications, the FRB is requiring protesting community groups to show not just a pattern of disinvestment by the applicant bank but individual violations of the equal credit laws.

The FRB's singularly pro-industry perspective stems in part from the fact that it has hoodwinked Congress and much of the public into accepting the notion that accountability and disclosure are inconsistent with its monetary function and this attitude carries over into its approach to bank supervision. Other contributing factors are the institutional structure of the Federal Reserve System—commercial bank control of the Regional Federal Reserve Banks and the shared interest of the FRB and commercial banks in managing the nation's payments system. The FRB's recalcitrance has inhibited other federal banking agencies from taking positive actions, since they are reluctant to get too far out in front of the FRB. The FRB's attitude is particularly pernicious because Congress has given the FRB authority to issue regulations interpreting most of the federal consumer protection and equal credit laws that apply to banks. Thus, the FRB's interpretative regulations apply to banks supervized by the other banking agencies as well as its own regulatees. Federal banking regulation would be greatly improved if the FRB were stripped of its bank supervision responsibility and allowed to devote full attention to its central bank function.

While consumer protection, equal credit opportunity, and community reinvestment will remain central concerns in the 1980s, other crucial issues in bank regulation must be addressed. Though these issues will most likely be treated by new legislation, the actions and attitudes of the bank regulators will play a major role in the outcomes. A key issue is the question of interest rate ceilings on deposits (Regulation Q) and home financing. There is growing recognition that Regulation Q is grossly inequitable to small savers and an ineffective mechanism to assure an adequate flow of funds to housing. Congress and the federal banking agencies are rightly working to phase out these controls. However, the thrift industry and the FHLBB now argue that savings and loans and mutual savings banks, both of which specialize in mortgage lending, cannot compete effectively for deposits in a non-Regulation Q world unless they change the type of mortgage loans they originate from the standard fixed rate, 25- to 30-year mortgage, to a floating interest rate mortgage—variable rate mortgage (VRM) or rollover mortgage (ROM). Since floating rate mortgages shift the risk of changing interest rates from lenders to borrowers, they provide great opportunity for lender manipulation of borrowers. Also, floating rate mortgage lenders may be reluctant to provide mortgage loans to less upwardly mobile persons of modest means, since such persons may have difficulty making higher monthly payments should the interest rate rise significantly. As we enter this new financial environment it is essential for Congress to enact legislation that will require thrift institutions to offer the standard fixed rate mortgage and will impose adequate disclosure requirements and interest rate change limitations on floating rate mortgages. Otherwise, banking industry operational convenience and profits will dictate the terms of the mortgage instrument to the detriment of home buyers.

A second major concern is the growing danger of a precipitous rush toward increased concentration in the banking industry. If Regulation Q and geographic restraints on branching are both phased out and electronic fund transfer system (EFTS) development accelerates, it is more than likely that a number of powerful money center banks will begin retail deposit gathering operations on a nationwide basis and squeeze out many small local banks. Several obvious reasons why large money center banks could outbid local banks for deposits are that large money center banks are permitted by the bank regulators to operate with much lower capital requirements than smaller banks and that large money center banks obtain yields from international investments that are generally higher than those available to local banks. Increased concentration in banking is of vital concern not only because of the value of competition in banking markets, but more importantly because of growing evidence that when small, local banks are replaced by branch offices of distant, giant banks, credit availability for small businesses is very often diminished. Additionally, increased concentration will augment the already excessive political and economic power wielded by giant banks and the giant corporations with which they are interlocked. As Regulation Q is phased out and geographic restraints are liberalized, it is essential that federal legislation be enacted to limit concentration in banking markets.

Another issue that must be addressed is the accountability of the managements of mutual thrift institutions. Most savings and loans and almost all savings banks are mutual institutions owned by their depositors instead of stockholders. Yet rather than design mechanisms that help depositors control management, the FHLBB and state regulators have attempted to insulate thrift managements from their depositors. Mutual thrift accountability must be revitalized by new rules that would limit each depositor to one vote, prohibit management proxies, and allow depositors at each branch office to select their own officials.

In the last several years the FHLBB has encouraged savings and loans to convert from mutual to stock ownership by means of inadequate appraisal procedures that result in windfall gains for managements and other stock purchasers. Such conversions are inequitable and destroy the potential for genuine accountability of thrift institutions; they should be stopped. Moreover, a shift from mutual to stock ownership will have an adverse impact on the long term availability of the standard fixed rate mortgage. Because stock savings and loans worry more about earnings fluctuations than mutuals, they have been much more aggressive than mutuals in campaigning for a change to floating rate mortgages. Maintaining the thrift industry on a mutual basis will greatly reduce thrift industry pressure to force floating rate mortgages on unwilling home buyers.

Finally, the need for fundamental reform of the manner in which the FRB conducts monetary policy must be considered a paramount issue of the 1980s. The FRB has become the single most important economic policy-making body in the nation. Yet, its monetary policy decisions with their critical impacts on the availability and cost of credit and the level of output and employment are reached in secrecy and implemented without meaningful public explanation. When the Federal Open Market Committee meets to establish monetary policy, the only constituency specifically represented is the commercial banking industry. It is not surprising that the FRB's attempts to fight inflation with induced credit crunches have imposed disproportionate burdens on housing, small business, farming, disinvested neighborhoods, and minority workers. Nor is it surprising that multi-national corporations have international means to circumvent domestic monetary restraint, such as direct borrowing in the Eurocurrency market and repatriation of funds obtained by foreign subsidiaries. Consumers, civil rights organizations, community groups, labor, home builders, small businesses, and thrift institutions should forge an alliance to demand reform of the manner in which monetary policy decisions are reached. As one recommendation, the FRB should be required to make public a full explanation of its monetary policy actions, including an analysis of alternative policies which includes cost-benefit estimates of impacts on housing, small business, and minority employment.

In this book Carol Greenwald provides a detailed exposure of the many abusive practices in the banking industry, such as redlining, employment discrimination, and self-dealing. She contrasts the traditional role of bank regulators as industry protectionists with her reformist actions as Massachusetts Banking Commissioner. By showing the profound effect of a shift from protectionist to public-minded regulation, her book indicates that the citizens movement should assign a high priority to the reform of bank regulation at both the state and federal level.

Ralph Nader,
Washington, D.C.

# Foreword

I decided to write this book because I wanted to share with others my outrage at banking practices and bank regulatory practices. Banking is generally treated as such an esoteric subject that the public is left feeling that it cannot understand what the issues are. I wanted to write a book that would demystify the subject in order to continue to generate pressure for change.

This book explores the changes occurring in the regulation of banks, changes which reflect a revolution in the ideological bases of banking activities. Regulation is moving away from protecting banks toward exposing them to greater competition and making them instruments of social policy. These regulatory changes are also occurring in other industries. The right of bank management to view banks as solely private institutions which grant credit as a privilege is being increasingly questioned by the public. A growing competing ideological view is that banks are quasi-public institutions and that access to credit is a right—a right, of course, carefully structured—with the duty to protect the safety and soundness of the banking system. This change fits into the general movement in American society toward greater emphasis on individual rights and consumerism.

Most people believe that banks are supposed to be safe repositories for our money, and that as long as they keep the bookkeeping straight they are doing their jobs. While these are certainly valuable services, people in fact have a right to expect more from their banks. They should be able to expect a fair return on the money they deposit. They should be able to expect fair treatment as borrowers—which means not only that banks should deal with them honestly, in letting them know exactly what the terms of a loan are, but also that banks should not discriminate against them because of their sex, their race, or their place of residence.

But there is another area of expectation we must consider. Largely because of the banks' own rhetoric, many people have come to think of banks as the economic pillars of their communities. People should be able to expect banks to use their economic power for ends the community agrees on—to promote economic development, to help create jobs, and to help make housing available to everyone.

Indeed, the promise of public benefits such as these was the rationale for giving private parties the license to take other people's money and invest it for their own (or their stockholders') gain in the first place. By the same rationale, banks have been treated very specially. A banking charter has been seen as a franchise. Competition has been limited, with entry into the field restricted by government. This has made these franchises protected, even semi-exclusive franchises.

The question is: Are our expectations being met? Is our money being used to further our individual and collective goals? Have the savings banks kept to the philanthropic concerns of their founders? Have commercial banks lived up to the economic-development aspirations of their chartering authorities? Or is our money being transformed into someone else's power?

Throughout much of the nation's history, banks and banking were among the most volatile subjects of political thought and argument. For the last forty years or so, by contrast, the everyday behavior of banks has not received the scrutiny it deserves. Sure, the old jokes about the heartless banker live on. The world of commercial banking is studied in economics classes and even in such popular works as Martin Mayer's *The Bankers.* To be sure, banks are still the targets of attack on Capitol Hill and in state legislatures. But most of the attention has gone to the stratosphere of finance: the operations of the Federal Reserve Board, the glamorous overseas operations of big banks, the concentration of power in major trust departments. These are all worthy subjects for debate, but they are hardly the concern of the average depositor.

Only recently have the more pedestrian practices of banks—those which concern the average customer—come to the center of attention. We are learning to ask questions about the return depositors receive on their savings, about the way banks have diverted needed capital from the neighborhoods where their deposits originate, about the way they discriminate against women and non-whites in lending, about the way they operate to the benefit of their management rather than to the advantage of their investors or depositors. Moreover, we are learning to ask questions about our bank regulatory agencies: Are they protecting our interests in these areas?

These matters may not be priorities in the world of high finance, but they are concerns that affect millions of people and billions of dollars. In the last five or six years, in a somewhat disjointed and disconnected fashion, all of them have become subjects of public concern and debate. This book will bring those concerns together to expose a pattern of banking activities that serves the bankers well but ill serves depositors and their communities. It will also demonstrate that bank regulators, by allowing that pattern to continue, have failed to require banks to meet their public responsibilities.

There is no more persuasive evidence of this than the incredible efforts of the banking community to deny the public interest-bearing checking accounts (better known as NOW accounts). We will detail the efforts to extend this benefit to the general public, and the long fight to prevent it. We will also see how even after some NOW accounts have been authorized, they are still not being operated in a manner that best serves the public. Along the same lines, we will discuss how banks and their allies in government have systematically disadvantaged the average saver.

An informed citizenry can change all this. There is growing public demand that banks service their communities. Unless the bankers respond to this demand, the pressure will grow, demanding even more radical changes in bank procedure and governance, and moving much closer to the public allocation of credit bankers rage against. The straws are in the wind.

We will examine the impact of banking practices not only on individuals but on communities as a whole. Bankers helped lead the last generation's "white flight" from the cities, exporting their dollars to the surburbs and making it virtually impossible to obtain a mortgage in many urban communities. When fiscal crises hit major cities and states in the mid-1970s, and the banks' help was most needed, they suddenly ceased being the major buyers of local-government securities. That will be part of our story, as will be the community fight against redlining in several states.

No one claims that the deterioration of urban neighborhoods is solely the result of redlining, but no one doubts that the decline is virtually irreversible if private capital continues to flow out of these communities instead of into them. In places like Boston and Chicago, community groups have fought bank practices, going on the offensive against financial institutions which neglect their responsibilities.

But the banks and thrift institutions have not been alone in dereliction. If bankers make up a close-knit fraternity, the regulators have been members of its auxiliary, and any number of individuals have crossed back and forth from one group to the other. My own experience as a regulator will be part of our story as well.

Finally, we will consider some reforms by which society and individuals can better direct the power of the banks. The first change must come in what we *expect* of them. Bankers' standard line is that their first obligation is to protect their depositors. The key word is "first," and we should note that the federal government, by extending deposit insurance to virtually every financial institution, has largely guaranteed that protection. Now it is time to turn to a second and third obligation: the service of individual depositors and of their communities. It is time for us, as well as the bankers, to consider these obligations. They will never be fulfilled...until we demand it.

—Dr. Carol S. Greenwald,
Cambridge, Massachusetts

# 1
# THE BANKING FRATERNITY

"A few years ago when I charged 14½% interest,
they called it loansharking."

*GRIN AND BEAR IT, by Lichty and Wagner,* © *1979 Field Enterprises, Inc.*
*Courtesy Field Newspaper Syndicate*

# 1.

# The Banking Fraternity

Bankers make up a paper-thin slice of the American community. The banking fraternity is ill-suited to represent or even understand broad community interests. This is not a matter of purely sociological interest: Consider some of the ways their banks function in today's America. Savings institutions were founded out of paternalistic concern for the poor workingman but now fail even to recognize those original principles, often discriminating against minorities in their loan policies and disadvantaging depositors of average means by paying below market rates of interest. The absence of women in key positions, to take another example, helps explain the denial of equal credit for women and the resistance to changes in banking policies toward women.

### A Banker Is Not...

Jewish. Catholic. Female. Black. Italian. Irish. Polish. Hispanic. Asian. Bank *tellers*, on the other hand, have been all of the above, at least since the Civil Rights Act was passed.

Bankers have argued, incredibly enough, that the absence of these groups from banking circles reflects their lack of interest in banking as a career because the pay is too low. Others have argued that change is slow because there are so few openings in banks.

An analysis of the financial industry will not support these conclusions. To begin with, there are more than a quarter-million openings every year in commercial banking alone. If being a teller is the entry to a route into bank management, there are many women starting on the road but very few getting there. As for the claim that minorities lack interest in banking careers, Jews, Catholics, and various ethnic groups *are* more heavily represented in the savings and loan and credit union industries, the lowest-paying of the financial sectors. Moreover, 60 percent of bank employees are women, but are crowded into dead-end, low-paying jobs. It is not lack of interest that keeps these groups out of banking; it is the bankers.

Because of the banking industry's central place in the economy, its discriminatory employment practices have wide repercussions. In fact, discrimination against religious and ethnic minorities in the executive suites of corporate America can be traced to the influence of the Money Trust.

In the latter years of the nineteenth century, as America became an industrial nation, entrepreneurs became dependent on outside capital to finance the expansion of their industrial empires. They borrowed from the bankers of Boston and New York—and in return for their financing, these bankers demanded ownership interest in the business and the right to install their own representatives in the corporate hierarchy.

> *Up to the last decades of the 19th century or the beginning of the 20th, most corporations had been operated by individual founders or their families; responsible positions were more and more often filled by professional managers representing financial institutions. And these professionals, being bank-nominated, naturally were Anglo-Saxon Protestants—the type bankers knew best.*
>
> *It wasn't so much that minorities (not only Jews, but Irish, Italians, Slavs and other recent immigrants) were barred—were discriminated against. Rather, the bankers felt their investments would be best protected by "people like us," who "spoke our language"—"safe" people who had come from the "right" families, had gone to the "right" schools, belonged to the "right" clubs, and attended the "right" churches. Top managerial jobs went to persons who met these criteria; and soon the new managers not only monopolized business leadership but signaled to others that anyone "different" was out of luck.[1]*

Thus, discrimination in banking, aided by the wave of anti-immigrant feeling at the turn of the century, shaped much of the discrimination in corporate America.

General George S. Brown, former chairman of the Joint Chiefs of Staff, could not have been more wrong when he stated that "They own, you know, the banks in the country..." Not only do Jews *not* own the banks, they cannot even work in them, at least not at senior levels. Despite the persistent caricature of the Jew as banker, there was only one Jewish officer on the senior executive level in the nation's twenty-five largest banks outside New York as late as 1974.[2] When all executives at any level in the nation's fifty largest commercial banks are considered, Jewish representation has hovered around 1 percent through the 1970s.[3]

The most blatant discrimination, however, may actually occur in the large New York City banks, where there are perhaps 5 Jews among the 345 senior officers, but not one Jew among the 22 officers who are also directors in the leading New York banks.[4] This is so even though New York has a large and well-educated Jewish population. Nor does the present situation appear to reflect only past prejudices. At some large New York banks, Jews continue to be excluded from management training programs, and Jewish graduates of business schools receive fewer job offers from banks.[5] Those who do work in banks are steered away from national and international lending, the upwardly mobile career paths, because of real or imagined customer preferences. This is the same argument bankers have used to keep women and blacks out of the lending area. Whether this practice affects Jews, blacks, or women, it is illegal.

Religious discrimination is not limited to New York. In Massachusetts, one of the country's busiest banking regions, women, blacks, and Jews are nearly invisible in top management in any bank. Moreover, in Boston, a predominantly Catholic city, there were few Catholics among the senior executives at large commercial banks.

With respect to savings banks, the picture generally is worse for racial, religious, and ethnic minorities than it is with commercial banks. Most savings banks have no Jews or/racial minorities whatsoever on their boards of trustees or among their top officers. There are few women, if any, on boards or in top officer positions at savings banks.

At first glance, banking appears to be a field in which women have achieved more than tokenism. A closer look at the industry, though, shows a dismal record. While more than 60 percent of all bank employees are women, very few advance to management positions, and even fewer to senior management. Stated another way, while men constituted only a third of all bank employees, they represented 80 percent of bank officers and administrators. In the rare circumstance of a woman's reaching the upper echelons of the employment structure, she is likely to remain an assistant to a senior, male officer.

Women are almost totally excluded from the influential commercial lending departments, from which most senior officers come. Women officers are confined to personnel departments or bank branches where major lending decisions are not made. "Branch manager" is the latest job ghetto for women. Giving a woman that title lets her bank classify her as "in management" for official affirmative action forms, while not allowing her to be a real part of management. Since branch manager has become a female preserve, it has ceased to be part of the career ladder toward upper management, in much the same way that tellers' positions ceased to be a training path to management during World War II, when the majority of tellers became female.

Making a woman an officer does not end discrimination, not until that promotion takes place at the same time in a woman's career as it would have in a man's can one conclude that the woman was not discriminated against. Thus, while many women in their fifties are finally receiving recognition and being promoted to officer status at the assistant level, these promotions should occur earlier in women's careers—while they are in their thirties, as is the pattern for men—before it can be concluded that employment opportunities have truly opened for women. This has not happened yet.

Salary comparisons are even more revealing. Women are still paid less than men holding the same positions. At the officer level, a comparison of men and women occupying similar executive positions in the same institution reveals a pattern of lower salaries for women, together with patterns of longer tenure and more advanced age, than for their male counterparts. A study done in 1976 by Kay Bergin, Deputy Commissioner of Banking in Connecticut, noted a commercial bank where the assistant treasurer, a woman of sixty-two years who had been with the bank for twenty-eight years, was being paid the munificent sum of $9,900. In the same commercial bank, a thirty-eight-year-old assistant secretary-treasurer, with the bank seven years, was earning $16,900. In another bank an assistant secretary who was fifty-nine years old and had been with the bank thirty years was paid $11,700. A thirty-eight-year-old assistant trust officer had been there five years and was earning $16,700. Can you guess which one was the woman? Right.

The discrimination reflected by these unequal wages will probably never result in official complaints to the Labor Department. These women have spent their lives in banking, and have only recently received officers' titles, as part of the cosmetic approach to affirmative action. Affirmative action has brought them a title but little monetary benefit. The pitiful wages paid these women should be a source of embarrassment to banking—and would be, if they were not so carefully concealed by all parties to the masquerade. The situation is particularly tragic as older women face retirement, many of them at near poverty levels after so many years of service.

The record for racial minorities is far more dismal. Here we can't even level the charge of tokenism, since there are so few token non-whites found in management positions.

In a variety of employment practices—from recruitment procedures to advancement opportunities to wage and benefit structures—banking is vulnerable to charges of discrimination. How is this possible, sixteen years after the passage of the Civil Rights Act of 1964 which barred discrimination in employment? Banks are, after all, required to adhere to hiring and promotion plans for women and minorities under federal rules that apply to government contractors. Doesn't the federal government enforce its affirmative action laws? If not, why not?

Employment practices in banking have not changed more quickly because the U.S. Treasury, until recently the compliance officer for banks, refused to implement actively Title VII of the Civil Rights Act and subsequent executive orders. State and federal bank regulatory agencies have also encouraged noncompliance, taking the position that the only management practices that they would review were those relating to safety and soundness—that discrimination was not their business.

### Undermining Affirmative Action

The U.S. Treasury was the compliance officer for banks until October 1978. In a highly critical report, assembled at Senator Proxmire's request, the General Accounting Office concluded that Treasury had not only failed to enforce the law, but had undermined the credibility of all affirmative action efforts by its record of nonenforcement.[6]

The lack of enforcement effort did not come about because bankers were doing such a good job that no government prodding was needed. Quite the contrary. The former chairman of the Equal Employment Opportunity Commission, William H. Brown III, characterized the industry as being "one of the three worst industries with regard to employment discrimination (along with construction unions and electric and gas utilities)."[7] The New York-based Council on Economic Priorities, in its 1972 report, *Short-changed: Minorities and Women in Banking*, stated that women "are overwhelmingly concentrated in low-level, poorly paid jobs" and concluded that "no substantial improvement in the proportion of women and minorities in high-level jobs is likely to result if present practices are continued."[8] Even Martin Mayer, in his largely noncritical book, *The Bankers*, noted that "Bank executives have not been recruited from the community at large."[9]

The Treasury did not share this view. Daniel A. Sawyer, director of the Equal Opportunity Program of the Treasury Department, traveled around the country in 1976 giving speeches declaring that the banking industry had made great efforts in providing for equal employment opportunity and should in fact be congratulated for its progress. The Treasury's response to specific charges of discrimination is a more crucial demonstration of its lack of concern. In October of 1971, the Women's Equity Action League (WEAL), a women's rights organization, filed a class-action suit with the Treasury Department charging twenty-seven Dallas banks with violating Executive Order 246. Specifically, WEAL maintained that the banks took longer to promote female employees to the executive level than men; that they paid women less than men for the same work; and that many banks fired women on learning that they were pregnant, while other banks forced women to leave work at a given stage of pregnancy.

In January of the following year, the Treasury sent eight men to conduct compliance reviews in Dallas. Several of the banks reportedly promoted women to vice-president or added them to their boards of directors the day before the Treasury men arrived. The men reviewed twenty banks in four days, then returned to Washington. That was all WEAL ever heard about their charges. The highest-ranking woman in Treasury's compliance section, Deputy Director Inez Lee, when asked about WEAL's charges, responded: "Oh, those ladies. They do upset me." Lee added that a lot of female employees at Dallas banks "think of their jobs as second jobs" and "are not interested in becoming officers because if they were, they might have to travel on the spur of the moment."[10]

Even when seemingly cornered into enforcing compliance because of the filing of discrimination charges by employees, the Treasury had a bureaucratic genius for accomplishing nothing. An example is the way Treasury handled discrimination charges filed against New England Merchants National Bank of Boston by 9 to 5, an organization of women workers. The group formally filed its complaint in August 1976, alleging in part that access to training programs was denied to women, that women were denied promotion and directly discouraged from seeking advancement, that women trained men to be their supervisors, and that women were denied equal pay for work substantially the same as men. Because of the publicity given the charges and the fact that Senator Proxmire personally wrote to the Secretary of the Treasury, Michael Blumenthal, expressing concern over Treasury's commitment to its responsibilities in the New England Merchant's case, Treasury did begin an investigation of the bank's employment practices.

A year later, when the Treasury opened a regional office in New York, the files on the New England Merchants' complaint were transferred there, and lost. After a further delay of several months, the Treasury began the investigation again. In October of 1978, when enforcement authority was transferred from Treasury to the Office of Contract Compliance of the U.S. Department of Labor, the investigation was started again.

By its successful delaying tactics, the Treasury had been able to undercut the credibility of 9 to 5 as an effective organization. Four years later, the investigation was still at its initial stages, for the third time.

Banks used the Treasury's legal responsibility to monitor banks' compliance with affirmative action requirements as a virtual shield from the rare state government official who tried to explore bank employment practices. State inquiries were rebuffed with legal opinions from bank lawyers stating that the banks were regulated in this area by the Treasury. This argument was transparent: It was well known that the likelihood of being audited by the Treasury was almost nil. The Treasury had only 15 compliance officers, compared with over 500 at the Department of Health, Education and Welfare. Until 1976, the Treasury's eastern region extended from Maine to Virginia and was handled out of Washington by three people. In March of 1976, a New York field office was finally opened to handle New York and New England. It was budgeted for a staff of four, but for most of its life it had only a director. The staff could review so few banks that most banks could expect never to be reviewed. Even when a bank was reviewed, the absurd understaffing ensured that no meaningful examination occurred. In 1972, the President issued Executive Order 11246, requiring all government contractors to develop affirmative action plans. These plans had to be available for review by a government agency, but the Department of Labor regulations implementing the Executive Order had a "time-clock" mechanism that required the reviewing agency to reach a conclusion on whether a federal contractor was in compliance within sixty days of receipt of the affirmative action plan. No agency can review the largest banks in New York, each with over forty thousand employees, in sixty days with three people. The understaffing assured lack of enforcement.

Even when it did audit a bank for compliance, Treasury's examiners never insisted on action. If a bank stated that it was trying to comply, regardless of how dismal its actual achievements, then Treasury took no further action. No bank ever actually lost government deposits as a result of a review by Treasury. If a bank routinely filed the forms, and did nothing else, then nothing was done to ensure meaningful action or changes in employment practices. As a result, Treasury "reviews" accomplished nothing.

## Data Collection and Title Inflation

The nonexistent enforcement activity of the Treasury was hardly helped by the meaningless data they collected. Employment data are broken down into nine categories on EEO-1 forms but only four of the categories apply to banks. Employment data are thus so aggregative that it is almost impossible to determine, even if one tried, whether meaningful change is occurring. In fact, banks have been quick to use this reporting form to cover their lack of action by a process known as title inflation. Women are given managerial titles with no change in job responsibilities or salary; the change in title form (for example, "secretary" to "administrative assistant") allows a bank to reclassify that employee into a higher category. By not challenging this process, Treasury implicitly condoned it. The Council on Economic Priorities' 1976 update of its 1972 survey on seventeen of the nation's largest banks found that eleven banks had undergone compliance reviews by the Treasury in 1974 or 1975. The number of female employees reported in these compliance reviews as transferred from clerical to managerial categories had mushroomed by 50 percent from 1971 to 1975. It appears that these changes mainly reflected title inflation: The number of women office and clerical workers decreased by a corresponding amount.

These games make for lots of paper work, but no progress; they are simply means of preserving the status quo, and thus ought to serve as grounds for a finding of noncompliance. In an industry like banking, where 60 percent of bank employees are women, eliminating sex-linked job segregation is crucial to any real affirmative action.

There was no implementation of Labor Department guidelines on religious discrimination. The Labor Department guideline requires that:

> *Employers shall review their employment practices to determine whether members of the various religious and/or ethnic groups are receiving fair consideration for job opportunities. Special attention shall be directed toward executive and middle-management levels, where employment problems relating to religion and national origin are most likely to occur. Based upon the findings of such reviews, employers shall undertake appropriate outreach and positive recruitment activities, ... in order to remedy existing deficiencies.*[11]

After several civil rights groups at public hearings held by the Massachusetts Banking Department in 1976 charged banks with discriminatory religious hiring and recruiting practices, as Commissioner of Banks for the Commonwealth, I contacted the regional compliance office of the Treasury and asked for compliance reviews for Massachusetts banks. The Treasury's regional director in New York assured me that as soon as he got any staff that he would most certainly schedule compliance reviews in Massachusetts; but, he added, he would not check for religious or ethnic discrimination because Treasury was not enforcing that guideline!

When I asked banks to report data on the religious affiliations of senior management, the banks immediately turned to the Treasury, where the Acting Director of the Equal Opportunity Program, Inez Lee, told the inquiring banks that they need not gather such information, since their Compliance Officer, the Treasury, did not require it, nor did existing law. Lee was correct on the first point, but incorrect on the second.

In October 1978, banking was placed directly under the Department of Labor for affirmative action compliance reviews. Of course, the federal bank regulatory agencies—the Federal Reserve Board, the Federal Deposit Insurance Corp., the Comptroller's Office, and the Federal Home Loan Bank Board—could have been the most effective compliance officers for financial institutions if given a clear mandate to use their ample examining staffs to enforce the civil rights laws. The federal regulatory agencies examine banks regularly, and employment compliance reviews could be made a part of these examinations. Financial institutions have close working relationships with their regulators, and they are more apt to be responsive to pressures from them than they are to an outside agency with whom they will not be seeking approval on some other banking matter. Placing affirmative action enforcement in the federal bank regulatory agencies would foster the perception that bank employment practices are a banking concern; now, too often, affirmative action is seen as an extraneous requirement of government, foreign to the real concerns of bank management.

The advantage of placing employment compliance reviews with the Department of Labor, however, is that this is an agency that does not have to be convinced that fair employment practices are important. The Treasury was simply not interested in the issue. In November of 1978, only a month after receiving its new mandate as part of President Carter's government reorganization plan, the Department of Labor announced a settlement with Chase Manhattan Bank. In a landmark suit against Harris Trust Co. of Chicago, the Department of Labor is seeking to make the bank pay for alleged past discriminatory practices against women despite the adequacy of its present affirmative action program. In the opening months of 1980, the Labor Department issued proposed regulations that would allow it to cancel a bank's federal deposit insurance if the bank were found to be willfully in violation of the equal employment opportunity laws. While this proposed regulation is certain not to be adopted, the Department of Labor's actions have finally put the banking industry on notice that equal employment opportunity laws apply to them, too.

### An Atypical Bank Commissioner

I entered the cozy preserve of bankers and bank regulators in March of 1975, when I was appointed Commissioner of Banks for Massachusetts by Governor Michael Dukakis. In the banking community's mind, my Ph.D. in economics and career as an officer of the Federal Reserve Bank of Boston were overshadowed as qualifications for the job by the facts that I am a woman and Jewish. One Massachusetts legislator with close ties to the banking industry immediately held a press conference and denounced the Governor's decision to "keep the banking community and the banking department employees under the matriarchy of a single ethnic group." I was the second women to be appointed bank commissioner in the nation. My predecessor, the first woman ever appointed, had also been Jewish. Two Jewish, female commissioners in the Commonwealth's three hundred years was apparently too much for the banking industry.

By casual observation, I knew that commercial bank officers were white men who were generally Protestants. My own experiences, while slightly out of date, were not such ancient history that they were irrelevant. I had been explicitly discriminated against in employment by the banking industry. While I was a junior at Brown University, a major New York City bank had interviewed Brown economics majors for summer internships in the bank's management training program. I had missed the interviewer because of a scheduling conflict, but the chairman of the economics department told me to contact the bank directly when I went home for spring vacation. I called the bank and spoke to a secretary who gave me all the information and then asked, "Are you requesting this information for your brother?" I said no, it was for myself. Rather annoyed for having had her time wasted, the secretary snapped, "We don't take women in management training programs." The year was 1964. A decade later I knew that that particular bank now admitted women into their training programs, but I was also aware that change had not gone very far.

In fact, only a few months after becoming bank commissioner, I heard a banker relate a story which indicated that women were still discriminated against in bank hiring. I had been having lunch with a group of Massachusetts bankers in a private male-only club when the banker told me the story. He had hired a woman college graduate, but had said he had no management training slots available, so he offered her a position as a receptionist. A few months later, she saw a young man at the bank whom she had known at college. When she asked what he was doing there, he told her that he had just been hired as a management trainee. She was furious. They had been in the same year at college, and she had had better grades. When she complained to the bank's president, he said she could quit if she didn't like it. He concluded the story by saying, "Just shows, you shouldn't hire women college grads." Maybe 1975 and 1964 were not so different, I thought.

I felt that some public discussion of the issues was warranted. A survey of employment practices in the banking industry would be appropriate, to see if my general impressions were wrong.

The bankers argued that this wasn't part of the bank commissioner's job description. Clearly, it had never been done before by a state bank commissioner, but it was equally clear that such a survey was entirely legal. While clear legality is necessary for political action, though, it is not sufficient, by itself. I needed to make clear that there was a public demand for this information to offset the bankers' expected protests and obtain political backing for the survey.

I used the medium of a public hearing to establish that there was a need to collect data on banking employment practices. I had to ensure that the NAACP, the Anti-Defamation League, the Civil Liberties Union, for example, were given an opportunity to be heard. Because of their prestige and long-standing commitments in this area, their endorsement of the survey was crucial. For both the Civil Liberties Union and the Anti-Defamation League, the proposed survey presented problems in the sensitive area of numerical goals and questions about religion. I knew that if I could not win these groups' public backing on these questions, I would not be able to ask them, regardless of the legality of my position.

At a meeting of the Massachusetts Anti-Defamation League, I took the offensive and demanded their public support for the survey. I parried questions about numerical goals' being a cosmetic term for quotas by charging that the banking industry already had a quota system for religious and racial minorities and that the quota was zero. In the end, despite the threat from a major financial contributor and bank director to drop his financial support of ADL if it publicly supported the survey, the Anti-Defamation League agreed to testify in its favor.

With a roster made up of representatives from the NAACP, 9 to 5, the Civil Liberties Union, the Anti-Defamation League, and the Massachusetts Commission Against Discrimination, to offset the testimony of the banking industry, I called for a public hearing on the need for an employment-practices survey.

The hearings were marked by acrimony. My determination to obtain the most detailed information regarding recruitment, hiring, and promotion policies ever sought from the ultra-discreet industry had the bankers furious. They labeled the proposed survey a smear on the industry. Bankers seized upon the request for religious information in their effort to discredit the questionnaire, claiming that consideration of the religion of employees is perhaps illegal or unconstitutional, and certainly un-American. My friendly witnesses pointed out that the requested data would reveal for the first time the true picture of bank personnel practices, about which, as Joan Pinck, Assistant Dean of the Harvard Business School stated, "there is a devastating lack of data available." The banks trooped in women employees, sometimes at embarrassingly low job levels, to testify against the need for affirmative action. Some women from banks testified against the collection of data, arguing that government pressure was creating renewed resentment toward women by men in power.

Unable to persuade me not to hold the hearings, the bankers appealed to Governor Michael Dukakis. The pressure came at a particularly inopportune time for him: With the state near default on its bonds, and capital markets apparently closed to its debt issues, the Governor was in the midst of delicate negotiations with the banking community over their purchases of Massachusetts bonds. At one point, the state's commercial bankers made my removal the price for continuing discussions on the bond sales. But the Governor held firm, and with the help of Salomon Brothers he was able to sell the Commonwealth's bonds out of state. In fact, the only thing Governor Dukakis ever said to me about the bank's pressure on him was to telephone me after the successful bond sale and say, "Next time you hold a public hearing, will you schedule it for a time when I'm not scheduling a major bond sale?" Then he hung up.

Finding that they could not get me removed, the commercial bankers moved to find a compromise. After several meetings and two revised drafts, I accepted a compromise reached with the commercial bankers and cut back the proposed questionnaire from covering all employees to covering only the 5 percent highest-paid.

Massachusetts savings bankers continued to object strenuously to the whole undertaking, which they labeled wasteful duplication and regulatory harassment and overkill.

While compromising with me in private, commercial bankers continued their public protests. The executive director of Massachusetts Bankers Association, Paul Foley, argued that the Commissioner's "priorities" were inappropriate. "Banks," he noted, "have had a lot of bad loans. A lot of bankers would like to see the banking department get involved with the business of banking." I dismissed the argument: In the good years the banks are too busy making loans to talk about equal employment; in the bad years they're too busy writing them off. We just don't have the luxury to pick the year to enforce equal-opportunity laws.

### Massachusetts Employment Survey

Probably one of the most revealing pieces of testimony submitted at the hearings was that of a representative of the Massachusetts Savings Bank Association. Vehemently opposed to any inquiry on the part of the Banking Department, he argued, "State law and the U.S. Treasury regulations all make it difficult or illegal to inquire about religion, nationality, color, or sex as contrasted to making these areas the heart of this questionnaire." Affirmative action was so lacking in the savings bank industry that the president of one of the major Boston savings banks was not even aware of the nature of the information his bank was required to submit annually to the U.S. Treasury.

The data collected by the Massachusetts Banking Department on employment practices in banks clearly indicated how little affirmative action occurred in banks during the eight years that Treasury was the compliance agency for banking.

To avoid the effects of title inflation, the survey defined senior and middle management as the top 5 percent of employees by pay. Women, blacks, and Jews were nearly invisible at all banks at this level, as were Catholics in Boston's large commercial banks. In the 289 institutions surveyed, only 79 banks (27 percent) had any women in senior positions. Women held 4.7 percent of the 2,130 senior positions; if one excludes the smaller banks—where, as chief bookkeepers, many women hold Assistant Treasurer positions—these figures drop drastically. In banks with more than 50 employees, women held only 3 percent of the senior management positions. Racial minorities (black, Spanish-surnamed, and Asian) held only 1.0 percent of the positions, representing a mere 22 persons, who were employed at only 17 of the 289 banks surveyed. Catholics make up more than half of the population of Massachusetts and about three-quarters of the population of Boston. By contrast, in banking statewide, Catholics represented 28 percent of the senior management, and in Boston, only 14 percent of the senior and middle management at the largest commercial banks. Jews were strongly represented in the credit union industry, but elsewhere they held only 1.5 percent of the senior management positions. In the savings bank industry the figure was only 7/10 of 1 percent, representing four individuals, two of whom worked at the same small savings bank.

To demonstrate further how ineffective Treasury's compliance reviews had been, the Massachusetts Banking Department specifically analyzed twenty-five banks which had been audited by the Treasury. All twenty-five audited banks were found to be in compliance by the Treasury, even though only 1.9 percent of their senior and middle management were women (lower than the 3 percent statewide average for large banks) and only 9/10 of 1 percent were black. Despite their poor performance, fourteen of the twenty-five banks did not have on file the required affirmative action data, and fifteen did not recruit at college campuses, twenty did not advertise in community or ethnic publications, and eighteen did not recruit through community groups and human relations agencies.

In its testimony at the Banking Department's hearings, the Anti-Defamation League summed up the situation aptly:

*The progress that has been achieved in changing the patterns of employment in banking during the past fifteen years has been almost imperceptible at the senior executive level. From a national perspective, mutual savings banks—in most cases— continue to be bastions of intransigent exclusion. But far more serious is the situation with respect to commercial banks. Commercial banking, occupying a position of central importance in the American economy, exerts an influence which courses throughout the business world. Their resistance to changes in employment practices are widely known throughout the economy and, therefore, have widespread effects.*

### Senator Proxmire Takes the Offensive

Senator Proxmire, chairman of the Senate Banking, Housing and Urban Affairs Committee, scheduled public hearings in August 1976 to investigate the problems of employment discrimination in financial institutions and Treasury's failure to enforce anti-discrimination requirements. Proxmire pointed out that:

*In its review of Treasury's EEO compliance program for fiscal years 1971–75, GAO found that the Treasury had failed to make any use whatsoever of sanctions available to it, including the power to remove federal deposits from banks. This should be a potent sanction, considering that during the period studied, banks earned upwards of $200 million a year on an average balance of $4.4 billion held in interest-free Treasury tax and loan accounts...*

*By continuing to keep its money in banks which refuse to provide equal job opportunities to minorities and women, the Treasury is, in effect, paying the banks to discriminate. This is outrageous.*[12]

The oversight hearings bore out the findings of the GAO report. The Committee found:

*...strong evidence of continuing discrimination by financial institutions holding government contracts in the employment of women and racial, ethnic and religious minorities...*

*The Committee finds that the Treasury Department's contract compliance program has been ineffective and has not demonstrated a commitment to insuring equal employment opportunity for women and minorities in banks and other financial institutions.*[13]

Drawing directly on the actions of the Massachusetts employment survey, the Committee recommended that:

*...the Treasury collect employment data by salary level as well as by job category. This should help to counteract the problem of category inflation and give a more accurate picture of the progress being made toward providing equal job opportunities.*

*The Committee recommends that the Treasury make a stronger effort to enforce compliance with the guidelines on discrimination because of religion or national origin issued by the Department of Labor in 1973, in view of the evidence of discrimination against Catholics and Jews in financial institutions. In this regard, it would be useful for the agency to obtain better information on the employment of religious and ethnic minorities in financial institutions, at least at the management levels surveyed in the Massachusetts study.*[14]

But Senator Proxmire was railing at a conservative Republican Administration, one whose views were best expressed by Senator Jesse Helms, the North Carolina Republican member of the Committee, who did not concur with the Committee report because the

*...report indulges in post hoc, ergo propter hoc paralogisms by accepting the proposition that because the percentages of*

*those working for or conducting business transactions with bank-*
*ing institutions does not precisely correlate with general popula-*
*tion statistics, this statistical variation must somehow have been*
*preceded by a sinister plan of deliberate racial, religious, or sexual*
*discrimination.*

*I cannot accept such assertions. I may indeed by poor*
*politics not to engage in these fantasies; be that as it may, I do not*
*intend to do so.*[15]

Nor, in its last days, did the Ford Administration intend to "engage
in these fantasies." Fearing that the uproar created by the Massachusetts survey, the GAO study, and the Proxmire hearings might
lead to real enforcement of the law, banks sought protection from a
sympathetic Administration. In one of its final acts, the Director of
the Office for Contract Compliance (OFCC) of the Department of
Labor, Lawrence Z. Lorber, proposed new regulations which would
have exempted most financial institutions from the requirements of
affirmative action. The exemption for banks was hidden within a
proposal to exempt small employers from maintaining formal
affirmative action programs. OFCC's amended regulations, proposed a month after Proxmire's hearings, caught many groups
concerned about affirmative action by surprise. The Labor Department's deliberations on the proposal had been shrouded with
secrecy, and the proposal had been issued without the usual public
hearing. Women and minority groups across the country charged
that the Department of Labor was engaged in a clandestine attack on
the basic civil rights of women and minorities.

Hundreds of letters poured into the Department of Labor
protesting the revised equal employment rules. The letters were
filled with such bitter words as "unconscionable," "shocked" and
"crucial blow." Letters from the American Bankers Association
and from the Treasury's Office of Equal Opportunity applauded the
proposed changes. In response to the furor, the Department agreed
to hold hearings on the proposals in early December. The delay was
critical. The election of November 1976 sounded the death knell
for the revisions. The banks had almost escaped, but not quite.

### Has There Been Any Progress?

I had hoped that the publicity generated by the employment
hearings in Massachusetts would galvanize not only the federal
enforcement authorities but also the bankers, who would no longer

be able to plead that there was no problem. While there was some motion at the federal level (compliance enforcement was transferred from the Treasury Department to Labor) bankers continued to be satisfied with token progress, routinely bringing some women with them to public hearings on branch applications. Each such woman—usually a teller or assistant branch manager earning under $16,000—was pointed to as the one who would be made the new assistant branch manager, or on occasion even the branch manager, if the new branch were approved. One bank actually demoted a token branch manager back to a secretary's job after receiving the branch approval.

To determine what progress in employment practices had in fact occurred during the two and a half years since the tumultuous 1976 hearings, I conducted a follow-up survey on Massachusetts banks in September 1978. This survey, unlike its predecessor, focused not only on numbers of women and minorities, but also on whether women and minorities with equal education or job experience were being paid the same salaries as men with the same title.

This study of Massachusetts banks provides the most current and complete picture of employment practices available on banking. It showed that banks have made only limited progress in affirmative action for women, and that for racial minorities there was no progress at all. In a survey of 306 financial institutions with 2,057 senior management employees, 8.4 percent were women in 1978, compared to 4.7 percent in 1976. Racial minorities remained a constant 1 percent over the period.

The greatest recorded progress for women occurred in the small thrift institutions (those with fewer than fifty employees) and especially in credit unions. In 1978, three-eighths of the small thrifts, up from a quarter in 1976, had women in senior management positions. The percentage of credit unions with at least one woman in senior management went from 31 percent in 1976 to 44 percent in 1978.

Only 28 percent of the commercial banks reported any women in senior management. Over the two years, twenty-one women had been promoted into the top 5 percent of employees by pay in their respective banks, raising the percentage of women in senior management from 1.9 percent in 1976 to 3.8 percent in 1978. The larger thrifts managed to add thirteen women to senior management over the two years, raising their percentage from 6.4 percent to 8.5 percent. It is important to keep in mind that women represent almost 70 percent of the total employees of these institutions.

While numbers are indicative, they are only one measure of change. Banks have often argued that the absence of women in senior management reflects a small pool of experienced women to draw from. This is usually coupled with the promise that as the pipeline is filled with qualified women, progress will be more dramatic.

To evaluate the soundness of this argument, the 1978 survey asked for the work experience and education of all management employees as well as their salary. Analysis of the survey results indicated that even when education and experience levels were similar, sex played a significant role in determining salary levels. At all management levels, women were not paid as much as men holding similar job titles. The survey showed that at large institutions (those with more than fifty employees), male officers' salaries in commercial banks averaged 32 percent more than women's in the same job groups. For non-officer managers and administrators, women managers earned 35 percent less than men doing similar work. For example, male commercial bank vice-presidents on average earned $28,778 while women vice-presidents earned $20,762 (a 39 percent difference). Similarly, male commercial bank supervisors earned $14,585 while women supervisors earned $9,445 a dramatic 54 percent less.

These differences could not be explained away. The survey showed that women who were assistant vice-presidents and assistant treasurers had had at least 20 percent more work experience than men with the same title, although the men were paid 25 percent more.

While publicly professing that their record was beyond criticism, bankers moved to make sure that the public could not check the veracity of their claims. On December 14, 1978, the morning that I was to release the 1978 survey results, the Savings Bank Association of Massachusetts obtained a temporary restraining order preventing the release of the data, charging that it would invade the privacy of bank executives. An executive vice-president of one of the state's largest savings banks explained the bank's suit by saying that, "During this era of kidnap and extortion, we felt the release of such information as salaries would have been extremely dangerous for our people and their families."[16] He added, "We have a very effective affirmative action program and we're proud of it."[17]

The banks were well aware that this information would not

violate anyone's privacy and that it would legally be available
under the Freedom of Information Act. They were engaged in a
delaying tactic. Governor-elect Edward King was to take office in a
few weeks, and he was sure to appoint a bank commissioner more
to the banks' liking, who might withhold the study. I was able,
however, to issue a summary table of the survey that was published
in full by the Boston *Globe*.

The *Globe's* editors expressed concern about the bankers'
action in a December 28, 1978, editorial:

> ...*Labor's abrupt about-face could be ominous if it signals
> a retreat from the commitment to affirmative action Greenwald
> symbolized in Massachusetts.*
>
> *That commitment did not come out of the blue but out of
> an intelligent woman's clear view of a reality.*
>
> *And whether Massachusetts bankers are willing to admit
> it or not, it is that reality which is the problem, not the woman
> who sought to change it.*

### The Three Martini, No Women Lunch

One of the most interesting questions aired by Senator Proxmire
through Senate Banking Committee hearings was whether it
violated equal employment statutes for banks to maintain membership for their employees in private clubs that discriminated against
women and minorities. Banks have long considered membership in
prestigious clubs an important source of contact with the senior
executive of potential corporate customers, and have therefore
reimbursed senior executives for the costs of membership in these
expensive private clubs. Most of these clubs, however, bar not only
women, but also blacks, Jews, and other minority-group members.

Membership in local service clubs—like Kiwanis, Jaycees,
and the Rotary—are also considered to be important sources of
business contacts and good will for managers and lending officers,
and bankers have been permitted to charge dues (and the proverbial
three-martini lunch) as business expenses. Many such clubs, citing
their national boards' policies, exclude women. The Labor Department appears fearful to take on the exclusion of women from these
groups as a discriminatory practice, although it may frown on
religious and racial bias. It is clear that banks are one of the
important mainstays of these civic organizations. If bankers could
not join because of restrictive practices, these practices might

quickly disappear. Silence on this issue condones the practice. But, there is no way to avoid the issue. Banking is perhaps the best leverage the federal government will have in breaking down these discriminatory practices. Businessmen are quite as anxious as the bankers themselves to develop close ties with the banking community through club membership.

The subsidized memberships are rightly the target of bitter criticism by women's and minority groups, which have charged that the practice is discriminatory because women and minorities are being denied the same career-advancement potential as their white male counterparts. The social club, these groups and other analysts of corporate America have argued, often controls admission to the corporate elite. These businessmen's social clubs provide an environment within which friendships and association are formed, and within which business opportunities are opened. The people with whom any of us chooses to do business, of course, are the people with whom we feel comfortable. The exclusion of women and minority-group members from environments where prospective business contacts could feel comfortable with them puts them at a competitive disadvantage.

In April of 1976, the regional office of the Treasury's Office of Equal Opportunity Program in Los Angeles notified banks in nine western states that they could no longer subsidize memberships for officers in clubs which excluded women. The banks questioned the ruling, and Treasury then asked the office of the solicitor of the U.S. Department of Labor, which has jurisdiction over the Office of Federal Contract Compliance Programs, for an opinion. The office of the solicitor, ruling that the practice of paying for memberships in exclusionary clubs had a discriminatory impact on women, stated:

*Membership in these organizations frequently provides the forum for making valuable business contacts which may lead to career enhancement and women excluded from participating in the business contacts may thereby be precluded from advancing their careers to their greatest potential.*[18]

The ruling, banks were assured, did not prohibit bank officers and employees from belonging to clubs which discriminate; it only meant that membership expenses must be paid by the banker himself. Nor did the ruling affect the right of private clubs to discriminate.

The bankers did not take this very limited assault on one of their cherished privileges lying down. They went directly to their friends at Treasury and had the regional office's ruling reversed, even though the Labor Department solicitor had supported it. In early May of 1976, the regional office—under instructions from Washington—sent a second letter to banks, repudiating the edict on membership in exclusionary clubs. Warren F. Brecht, assistant secretary and director of Treasury's equal opportunity program, explained the Treasury's action by saying that the agency had received many calls and letters from bankers during the prior month which "convinced us of the necessity to step back for the moment."[19]

The issue of banks' paying for memberships in clubs which barred women and minorities had also been one of the sore points in the employment practices survey I conducted in Massachusetts. The Massachusetts Banking Department questionnaire had included a question that asked: "Does the bank maintain any memberships at private clubs that regularly restrict their membership on the basis of sex, race, religion, ancestry or national origin?" All of the five largest Boston area banks (which controlled two thirds of the state's commercial bank deposits) did maintain such memberships. But they argued that the practice was not illegal and was acceptable to the Treasury, their compliance officer.

A survey conducted at the request of Senator Proxmire by three of the federal bank regulatory agencies in 1979 found that 58 percent of the banks and 53 percent of Federal savings and loan associations regularly paid membership dues in private clubs or organizations on behalf of their officials. A large number of those financial institutions are knowingly paying for memberships in restrictive clubs and organizations. To condone this use of bank funds is to be entirely insensitive to the subtleties of discrimination. There are many ways to make it clear to individuals that they are not true members of the banking fraternity and never will be. One is simply to make sure they're not members of the club.

An actual story involving a leading Boston bank clearly gets at the subconscious motivations involved in club membership. This bank decided to "reward" several women who had completed the bank's management training program by taking them to dinner at an exclusive private club in Boston at which the bank maintained membership for all senior officers. The club, however, does not let women walk through its front door; they must enter by a side door even if they are guests of members. To the astonishment of the bank executive who had brought these women, they refused to enter by a side door. Rather than being honored by having been taken to this exclusive club, they were angry. The bankers who told me of the incident reported that all these women did was "ruin" it for other women; now the bank doesn't take new women managers there anymore.

### It's 2 P.M. Do You Know Where Your Banker Is?

You might guess that he is hard at work processing mortgage applications, but you would very likely be wrong. He is quite likely to be at a bank convention—sharing half of all expenses with the government. Bankers spend an inordinate amount of time at bank conventions, which always seem to take place at such important and centrally located banking centers as Honolulu, San Francisco, Puerto Rico, and Bermuda. As the invitation makes graphically clear, the main attraction to the convention is not the work to be accomplished.

> *The Officers of The Imperial Bank*
>
> *cordially invite you, your associates, and*
>
> *spouses attending the American*
>
> *Bankers Association Convention in Honolulu to*
>
> *our NEW ENGLAND BREAKFAST*
>
> *on Monday, October 23,*
>
> *or on Tuesday, October 24,*
>
> *8:00 a.m. to 9:15 a.m.*
>
> *Canoe House*
>
> *RSVP card enclosed*

# INDEPENDENT BANKERS ASSOCIATION OF AMERICA

## Index

1        Tentative Convention Program
2        Registration Information
3        Hotel Accommodations
4        Air Travel Information
5        Sample Air Fares and Schedules
6-7      Optional Sightseeing, Tours and Events in Honolulu
8-11     Pre- and Post-Convention Tours in Hawaii
12-13    Foreign Tours . . . The Orient, South Pacific, Around the World
14       General Information
15-16    Official Registration Form
17       Sightseeing, Tours and Special Events — Reservations Form

## Tentative Convention Program

**Saturday, March 13**

9:00 a.m.    Administrative Committee Meeting

             Resolutions Committee Meeting
             Set up exhibits
             Press room open daily through
                March 18

**Sunday, March 14**

8:30 a.m. -
6:00 p.m.    Registration Desk

10:00 a.m.   Agriculture-Rural America Committee
             Bank Study Committee
             Competing Financial Institutions
                Committee
             Federal Legislative Committee
             Government Fiscal Policy Committee
             Resolutions Committee

1:30 p.m.    Executive Council

3:00 p.m.    Hostess Committee

5:00 p.m.    Executive Council and Resolutions
                Committee recess overnight

**Monday, March 15**

8:30 a.m. -
6:00 p.m.    Registration Desk

8:30 a.m. -
11:00 a.m.   Buffet Breakfast

9:00 a.m.    Exhibits open

10:00 a.m.   Executive Council
             Resolutions Committee

6:00 p.m.    Reception

7:00 p.m.    Luau and Hawaiian Show

**Tuesday, March 16**

8:30 a.m. -
4:30 p.m.    Registration Desk

9:00 a.m.    Exhibits open

9:00 a.m. -
12:30 p.m.   First General Session

1:00 p.m.    Men's Luncheon
             Women's Luncheon

5:00 p.m.    Evening free

6:00 p.m.    Reception —
             Past Presidents and Wives

7:00 p.m.    Dinner —
             Past Presidents and Wives

**Wednesday, March 17**

8:30 a.m. -
2:00 p.m.    Registration Desk

9:00 a.m.    Exhibits open

9:00 a.m. -
12:30 p.m.   Final General Session

2:00 p.m.    Exhibits close

6:00 p.m.    Head Table Assembly
             Reception

7:00 p.m.    Convention Banquet and Dance

**Thursday, March 18**

Departure for post-convention neighbor island tours and special tours to the Orient, South Pacific, and Around the World.
   Others may extend their stay in Honolulu or depart for the mainland.

In fact, little time is left for work at a bankers convention. As the convention program for the March 1976, Independent Bankers Association of America's 46th annual convention, in Honolulu, Hawaii, indicates, during the four-day convention only two mornings are devoted to meetings. The importance of those sessions is clear: Nowhere in the seventeen-page convention program brochure does it say what topics will be discussed. Except for two lines on the program on page 1, the remaining seventeen pages are devoted to describing the sightseeing tours and special events. That this is a tax-deductible business expense, half paid for by taxpayers, amply justifies President Carter's labeling the present tax code a national disgrace. But for depositors who are forced to accept lower interest rates on their savings because the bankers insist on cavorting in the sun on other people's money, this national disgrace is particularly infuriating.

### Why Does It Matter?

Even if you're not planning to work at a bank, discriminatory bank employment policies may well affect your economic welfare. Equal credit opportunities for women would have become a reality much sooner if more bankers were women. But the same stereotypes which prevented women from getting management positions in banks kept bank management from viewing women as good credit risks. If bankers won't promote a woman because they "know" that she's not serious about a career and that she's going to quit and have a baby in a year or two, then they won't lend to women either, because they "know" she's only working temporarily and is, therefore, not creditworthy.

Redlining might not have become the overwhelming problem that it has become for older neighborhoods if more bankers were black or Hispanic and lived in cities. In that case, bankers would much less likely be hamstrung by racial stereotypes and fears of the big bad city. The senior officers, directors, and trustees of the major urban banks do not live in the cities where their banks are located. They live in suburban towns outside of the city. The absence of racial minorities in bank management is reflected in the absence of bank lending in areas with high minority populations.

The U.S. Senate Committee on Banking, Housing and Urban Affairs drew the same conclusion: that equal credit laws cannot be meaningfully implemented if banks discriminate in employment opportunities. The Committee report concludes that "if an institution discriminates in the hiring, training and promotion of minorities and women, it is unlikely to have either the will or the staff resources to evaluate and act on all applications for credit in a fair and unbiased manner."[20]

Senator Proxmire has expressed this concern most forcefully. "I don't see," he said, "how there can be any effective enforcement of fair housing law or of the equal credit laws so long as the lending institutions continue to discriminate against hiring women and minorities for responsible positions and Treasury turns a blind eye to these discriminatory practices."[21]

### Discrimination in the Mortgage Market

Few working women understand the extent of discrimination against them in the housing market. Much of that discrimination is based on myths about their capacity to earn money that are like those that surround the ability of minorities to hold stable jobs.

Some of these myths continue to thrive on the assumption that women are unreliable credit risks because they may become pregnant and lose their jobs. This preoccupation of creditors with pregnancy is certainly outmoded, as are any number of other assumptions about housewives and "transitional" workers. Until the passage of the Equal Credit Opportunity Act in 1974, it was the accepted custom of mortgage lenders to discount women's salaries—in whole or part—based on the presumption that women are poor credit risks because of their sex.

When I tried in late 1973 to obtain a mortgage loan based on my own credit, I could not get a mortgage lender to even give me an application. My $25,000-a-year salary as an assistant vice-president of the Federal Reserve Bank of Boston, my Ph.D. in economics, and my seven years of prior work experience were all unimportant. The mortgage officer at the savings and loan association in which I held the funds needed for the down payment suggested that I would have better luck obtaining financing if my husband filled out the application—even though he was unemployed at the time. The officer said, "We assume he won't be unemployed forever. We'll just base it on his last salary." I refused, and finally sought help from the chairman of the board of one of Boston's largest commercial banks, whom I knew through my work at the Federal Reserve. He was amused, and assured me that his bank would grant me the loan.

Another assumption of mortgage lenders that has taken on hypnotic power is the traditional perception of the homeowner as a husband with a wife, or of a household as a combination of man and wife. A white family headed by a male whose income is sufficient by itself to carry the cost of home purchase conforms easily to the traditional criteria of the banking community and is readily approved with a conventional 20 percent down-payment mortgage. But this myth affects minority families, families headed by women, families in which both the wife's and husband's incomes are necessary, and single persons. Their applications fall victim to the traditional view of the homeowner and are frequently handled arbitrarily.[22]

The problems of single women facing these myths are particularly grave. Banks often require a single woman mortgage applicant to present a stronger financial position than a man—that is, her credit and income must be more secure than that of a single man, and her credit history will be more carefully scrutinized.

Divorced women are dismissed as particularly bad risks because their alimony or child support payments are viewed as unreliable. While this particular judgement about income may be correct in some cases, the myth ignores the fact that more and more divorced women support themselves and their children. Well over half of all divorcees are in the labor force. Nor are they likely to leave that work force even if they do remarry: Data show that a divorced woman working at age thirty-five can be expected to work for at least twenty-nine more years.

Real estate brokers reinforce bankers' sex discrimination. The single woman or woman head of household has been shunned by brokers because of the likelihood she would be refused a loan. As an experienced Atlanta real estate broker expressed it, "It was understood that she could not buy, period.... [The result is] very few of us ever make the attempt to get loans."[23]

Brokers screen the woman home purchaser by their perceptions of lenders' criteria. To hedge against discriminatory lending practices, the realtor may tell a woman that the bank requires a higher down payment than the prevailing requirement on a conventional mortgage loan. In refusing to deal with the woman home buyer, brokers themselves point the finger at the bankers as the ones to blame. In March of 1979, HUD again concluded that there is considerable merit in that accusation. The Equal Credit Opportunity Act has made discrimination on the basis of sex in making mortgage loans illegal, but that does not mean that it does not happen.

### But Where Are Our Friendly Bank Regulators?

The Equal Credit Opportunity Act had been passed in 1975 and the Federal Reserve given a year in which to write the implementing regulations. The Nixon-Ford appointees heading these agencies—adopting the bankers' perspective—did not believe that there was significant discrimination or that it was worth the cost to eliminate the discrimination that did exist. As James E. Smith, senior economist in the Mortgage and Consumer Finance Section of the Federal Reserve System, wrote in 1976:

> *The strictly economic competitive aspects of the consumer finance market argue against this sort of discrimination being widespread. If one bank rejects credit applicants for irrational reasons, it is an intelligent and profitable policy for other banks to steal the first bank's customers by granting credit strictly in regard to economic criteria.... The foregoing economic arguments imply that economic benefits from the Act and Regulation B would be small.*[24]

On the other hand, taking data presented by the Consumer Bankers Association and other bank trade groups as gospel, Smith concluded that the costs of Equal Credit Opportunity Act compliance would be very considerable.[25]

Given this perception of the costs and benefits, it is not too surprising that the Federal Reserve issued regulations and then did not enforce them. As late as 1978, the federal bank regulatory agencies were still experimenting with procedures for examining banks for compliance with equal credit laws. An independent study done by Warren Dennis, a former attorney in the U.S. Justice Department's civil rights division, for the Federal Reserve Board in 1978 asserted that the agency failed to provide its examiners with the tools and training necessary to detect violations of civil rights laws. The report stated that the Fed's failure to emphasize the detection of civil rights discrimination resulted in a number of misconceptions by bank examiners. "In some respects," the Dennis report noted, "there was evidence of a mild hostility toward civil rights matters, based partly on a perception that devotion of their time and effort to civil rights matters would not materially advance their progress within the System." In addition, the study found that many bank examiners believed that the enforcement of civil rights might jeopardize "the safety and soundness" of banks being examined.

In 1976, a coalition of civil rights and fair housing organizations, citing eight years of non-enforcement, sued the four federal financial regulatory agencies in order to require these agencies to use their broad enforcement powers to end the discriminatory policies and practices commonly followed by lending institutions and to enforce the Fair Housing Act of 1968. Realizing they would lose the case, all of the agencies other than the Federal Reserve[26] entered into out-of-court-settlement agreements which obligated them to implement a new enforcement program to search out and prevent lending practices that illegally discriminate against minorities and women.

New FDIC Fair Housing Regulations issued in 1978, pursuant to the out-of-court settlement, could portend a brighter future for enforcement efforts. Even these new regulations, however, do not reach the pre-screening procedures which banks use to discourage and prevent those they consider undesirable from filing applications. By limiting enforcement to a comparison of accepted and rejected mortgage applications on file the regulators are winking at the situation, in which a bank loan officer first discusses the loan with an applicant, and encourages the person to fill out the application itself only if it appears likely that the loan will be granted. This kind of pre-screening can be detected only by the use of testers—that is, individuals who pose as applicants.

Instead of assessing penalties or informing affected borrowers so that they could pursue redress, the regulators have acted as management consultants to banks, simply pointing out procedural violations of the law when they find them. A special survey of 400 banks taken by the Federal Reserve in 1977 found 73 percent in violation of regulations issued to enforce the Equal Credit Opportunity Act. Of the 2,859 national banks examined from October 1976 to the end of 1977, the Comptroller of the Currency found 97 percent in violation. As these results indicate, banks will never take equal credit seriously unless violations result in substantial monetary penalties.

### Whose Bank Is It Anyway?

Given the employment and credit practices of banks, one begins to wonder: To whom is the management of a bank responsible? Commercial banks, in theory, at least, are responsible to their stockholders, but mutual savings banks and mutual savings and loan associations have no stockholders. As mutual institutions, they are nonprofit entities legally responsible to a board of trustees or directors, which is supposed to represent the interests of the depositors/shareholders and, more broadly, the community at large.

Savings banks were founded in the nineteenth century as eleemosynary institutions to promote thrift for working people, immigrants, and seamen. Their history is broadcast in their names: The Dime Savings Bank, the Provident, Emigrant Savings, The Seaman's Savings Banks, People's Savings Bank. These were semiphilanthropic institutions, created before Social Security, when the rich knew that the poor needed to save for their old age. Since the commercial banks would not take savings deposits from working people, philanthropic persons in the major northeastern states formed mutual, not-for-profit banks to provide a safe haven for the meager savings of the working classes. In this vein, the net worth of a savings bank is viewed as a community asset.

The idealized characteristics of a trustee are defined by William H. Kniffin in *The Savings Bank and Its Practical Work:*

*No man can buy his way into trusteeship in a mutual savings bank. He can only gain this honor by so conducting his personal and business affairs that his name shall be a synonym for honesty and integrity, and thereby win for himself the right to care for other people's savings...The man who aspires to bank directorship needs only to buy enough stock or control its voting power to elect himself; but in the savings bank, the proposition is rather like this: Become a leading citizen and wait until they elect you!*[27]

The purpose of the savings and loan industry is similarly noble. As one industry member expressed it some years back:

*Let it be known that these associations are not operated for profit; thus the workers, from the leaders of the [U.S.] League to the member in the smallest hamlet, derive sufficient satisfac-*

*tion from the wholesome service in which they are engaged—without monetary consideration...*[28]

Another speaker at the same set of proceedings stated that "Building Associations are maintained as philanthropic institutions...to promote thrift and economy among a class of people hitherto neglected."[29]

The earliest associations were self-help building cooperatives, in which householders desirous of obtaining funds to acquire a house got together with others to save and borrow on a cooperative basis. Loans were extended only to the membership and meetings were held frequently to receive payments and allocate newly available funds. The directors and officers generally served without pay. It was from these modest beginnings that the present savings and loan industry evolved.

In this uplifting environment, to whom is the management of a mutual thrift institution responsible? Certainly not to the depositors, as many depositors assume. In several northeastern state legislatures, including New York, Connecticut and Massachusetts, legislation has been defeated in the 1970s which would have had the trustees of savings banks elected by depositors, rather than being hand-picked by the savings bank president. Legislative banking committees argued that depositors could not be trusted to elect prudent trustees, and expressed fears that savings banks would be taken over by well-organized groups. While many people believe that the issue of participatory democracy was decided in this country two hundred years ago, it's still an open issue to some state legislators.

Election by depositors of at least some savings bank trustees might finally ensure some accountability of management to depositors and to the community. At present, there is no internal check on the policies of savings bank management, or any mechanism to make the bank responsive to the desires of the depositors.

The original idea of noblesse oblige has not worked in the twentieth century. Currently, the president of a savings bank selects the incorporators, who elect the trustees, who elect management. The president, to bring it full circle, selects the incorporators who will be trustees. Thus, the bank president selects those to whom he is to be responsible. This is a situation bound to create abuse, and one which provides little mechanism for ensur-

ing that savings banks are responsive to the needs of their depositors or to the communities they were chartered to serve.

Savings banks and savings and loan associations are now
often run as the personal satrapies of individual thrift institution
presidents. As the president of one large Massachusetts savings
bank so eloquently put it, his diamond-studded fingers flashing in
the sunlight as he stepped into the Mercedes provided by his
savings bank, "There's no ego trip like being a savings bank
president. Who's going to veto what I want to do?"

In the savings and loan industry, the situation is even
worse. In a large number of mutual savings and loan associations,
control is effectively lodged in one or two strategic individuals or
closely knit family groups who occupy one or several of the top
executive positions in the association. Power flows downward from
these individuals. The board of directors is one of their instruments and is recognized by its members to be dependent on them.
The board will often include members of a single family and their
friends and business associates, who will constitute a reliable core,
often a majority, assuring control. Other individuals, who have
some special knowledge or business contacts, may be invited onto
the board, an arrangement with advantages for all parties. These
outsiders typically join the board fully aware of who controls the
association, and with an implicit gentlemen's agreement accepting
the existing structure of control. As Edward S. Herman concluded
in his study of "Conflict of Interest in the Savings and Loan
Industry," for the Federal Home Loan Bank Board in 1969:

> *The vast bulk of the industry is characterized by what
> amounts to personal or family fiefdoms...Personal fiefdoms (or
> patrimonies) are especially common in the mutual sector of the
> industry, where they are made possible by a combination of
> shareholder lack of interest and limited constraints—traditional,
> legal or regulatory—on the accretion and use of management
> power.*[30]

Thrift bankers even refuse to reveal the salaries they pay themselves
to their incorporators or shareholders. In 1976, as Commissioner of
Banks in Massachusetts, I insisted that savings bank presidents
reveal their salary at their annual meeting of incorporators. They
acquiesced only under my threat of publishing their salaries in a
public report to the legislature. The savings bankers ostensibly

objected to revealing their compensation to the banks' incorporators because they feared that if their six-figure salaries became public information, they would become subject to kidnap attempts. They not only argued this point themselves, they also had their wives send me letters repeating it. The absurdity of incorporators not knowing the salaries paid to top management escaped these savings bankers, because the idea of actual responsibility to anyone at the bank other than themselves was so foreign.

There is an obvious contradiction between the ideals of the mutual thrift industry and the refusal of leaders and managers of mutual savings banks and mutual savings and loan associations to provide their depositors with substantial information about their bank or association. Nevertheless, mutual thrift institutions in the United States almost uniformly provide their members with minimal information—far less, in fact, than is required of stock institutions under the authority of the Secruities and Exchange Commission. It is another curiosity of the bank regulatory mindset that the regulators of thrift institutions have not seen fit to provide adequate disclosure to the shareholders and depositors of mutual thrift institutions.

The reason thrift regulators give for supporting virtually no disclosure to mutual shareholders and depositors is that disclosure holds the potential for disturbing the management stability of a thrift institution. The inadequacies in that simplistic view of the world are apparently lost on the regulators.

### Economic Democracy

The imperial bank presidency also leads to arrogance in treating community groups—those groups whose "convenience and needs" banks were originally chartered to serve. There seems to be no compelling reason that thrift institution management should not be responsible to the individuals and communities whose savings they hold. In cases where mutual institutions have converted to stock institutions, the federal and state banking authorities have held that the surplus* of the bank must be distributed to the depositors as owners of mutual savings banks. The time has come to make explicit that mutual savings banks and mutual savings and loan

---

*Surplus in a thrift institution is similar to the capital funds of a stock institution.*

associations are accountable to someone, and their depositors and local communities seem to be the most appropriate groups.

The structure of power, rights, and incentives in the mutual sector involves a vast gap between theory and reality and is in serious need of reform. With depositor election of boards of trustees or public appointments of a significant number of independent trustees to the board, it would be possible for communities to exert direct influence on the policies of their savings institutions. After all, it is your money they're investing, and if you feel you're being discriminated against with your own money, there ought to be something you can do about it.

# 2.

# Unarmed Robbery

*Names of persons and banks have been changed;
all events described, however, actually
happened.*

### It May Not Hurt to Be an Insider—An Introduction to Self-dealing

In the late 1970s home mortgage rates were climbing to new peaks almost monthly. Rates that would have appeared usurious only a few years earlier suddenly looked like good deals. Ordinary people were staggering under the cost burdens of home ownership; young people couldn't afford mortgages at all.

In this situation, the board of the Imperial Savings and Loan Association, ordinarily a sleepy little institution, took decisive action. While others stood around helpless, the Imperial board members helped themselves. The board decided to approve mortgages for board members and their children at interest rates between 6½ and 7¼ percent. They then turned their attention to the other mortgage applications from regular bank customers and approved those at the going market rates, many points higher.

The board did not violate any laws by its actions: Neither federal nor state legislation prohibited preferential rates to insiders. Federal regulations required only that the preferential rate not be lower than the anticipated average dividend rate on savings accounts at the savings and loan. The board members had simply taken advantage of their position as insiders. They had, however, made loans to themselves and their children at rates that deprived the S&L of a fair return on depositors' funds, thereby abusing the trust placed in them by the depositors.

Bank insiders are individuals who are in a position to exert effective influence on the decisions of the bank and may not be subject to normal bank review and control processes. "Self-dealing" is the practice of making loans to insiders, or otherwise having them participate directly in the business of the institution to their personal advantage. Not all self-dealing is improper; there may well be perfectly legitimate insider loans objectively approved on the same terms as loans to any other bank customer. There is nothing wrong with such loans. Indeed, they can be the best credits in the bank. In contrast, a self-dealing loan is an abuse if it could only be granted to an insider because either the terms or the underlying collateral would not normally be acceptable to the bank.

The same is true of self-dealing transactions that don't involve loans: They are abuses if the terms would be different for a noninsider. This phenomenon is most prevalent at smaller banks or others insulated in some way from the rigor of the competitive market. In many cases, transactions with insiders do not involve terms that are disadvantageous to the bank, but they are still disadvantageous to the community because they remove some transactions from the competition of the marketplace. The transaction takes place not because of what you have to offer but because of *who* you are—you're an insider. When competition is removed, a situation that was not originally an abuse can easily become one. It may well be, for example, just a matter of politeness to assume that the bank will give "John Doe" a legal retainer; he's a good lawyer, after all, and a good guy, and an important stockholder of the bank, which is why he's on the bank's board. No one in this situation will question the retainer charged by "John" for his legal services. Nor will any other law firm be likely to get the business. Nor will the bank necessarily get the best deal. Maybe the terms were advantageous when it was first negotiated, but who bothers to check the terms now? Is $80,000 a year too much as a legal fee for a $40 million bank? When there's no competition and no one's checking, it's awfully tempting to make a very good profit.

### Not for Whose Profit?

Mutual thrift institutions, like savings banks and mutual savings and loan associations, are legally described as nonprofit institutions. But as many managing officers and board members could tell you, affiliation with a mutual savings bank or mutual savings and loan association can be very profitable. Conflicts of interest are especially prevalent in the savings and loan industry, where board members are not bound by the same fiduciary principles as are trustees of savings banks. Management interests in activities connected to savings and loan associations can be extensive, leading to situations in which management's interest in their own income does not automatically lead to pursuit of the depositor's interests. The potential divergence of interest between management and board members, on one hand, and depositors on the other, is large, with a considerable burden of reconciliation resting on personal ethics and regulatory control. Self-dealing has traditionally been accepted in the savings and loan industry and has become institutionalized by widespread use. The regulatory authorities have simply adjusted to the prevailing mores of the industry.

The most common insider deal, and one of the most profitable with a thrift, is to become the institution's "conveyancing" attorney, the lawyer who does the title work and presides at the passing of the mortgage. In smaller thrift institutions, if the thrift's president is a lawyer, he'll often reserve this lucrative work for himself. The president's official salary may be quite modest, in line with the rhetoric of thrift institutions as the working people's banks, but his bank-related income may be in six figures. It is not uncommon for a president of a very small savings and loan association to have a $20,000 salary and to earn an additional $60,000 or more in conveyancing fees. At larger savings and loans, the fees are much larger. This bank-related income has not traditionally been revealed to anyone—not even to the other members of the board. But it goes a long way toward explaining why thrifts require mortgage applicants to use the bank's attorney, rather than their own, for mortgage closings.

In 1976, the federal bank regulatory agencies added a new page in their examination report, in which, for the first time, bank income indirectly derived by insiders was listed. At some thrifts, this led the conveyancing attorneys to resign from the bank's board rather than disclose their income to the other members of the board and to the bank examiners. (They didn't stop doing the work, they just resigned from the board.) The examination report required only non-salary income over $20,000 to be reported for banks below $100 million in deposits; $50,000 if the bank was between $100 million and $500 million; $100,000 for banks over that size. Implicitly, the regulators acknowledged that many bank insiders got something, and until the numbers became large, they were not concerned.

It's like the story of the man who propositions a woman and offers her $10,000 to sleep with him. When she accepts, he lowers his offer to $5. Indignantly, the woman snaps, "What do you think I am?" The man retorts, "We've already established that.

Now we're just quibbling over price." The fiduciary standards of a trustee are violated by conflicts of interest regardless of the sums involved. Judge Cardozo's classic description of the duties of a trustee as those of "undivided loyalty" allowed no exceptions. To write a bank regulation that says conflicts of interest are permissible below a certain dollar limit is to quibble over price.

It would appear that requiring a loan applicant to use a specific attorney (who is not on the bank's payroll as its attorney) in order to obtain a mortgage would be considered a tie-in sale and consequently a violation of the antitrust laws. At the very least, it appears to be an unfair trade practice and as such a violation of the Federal Trade Commission Act. Requiring the mortgage applicant to use the bank's attorney adds significant costs to the borrower. Not only may the bank's attorney charge more than other attorneys, since he has a captive market, but the borrower must also incur the additional costs of a second lawyer if he wants his own interests, rather than the bank's, represented at the closing. Banks have so far successfully resisted attempts by a few pro-consumer law enforcement authorities to require them at least to offer mortgage applicants a list of lawyers acceptable to the bank for the conveyancing work. Understandably, it's difficult for bank boards to review this issue dispassionately, since often so much of the income of some board members is involved.

Allowing bank board members or officials to collect a fee for doing the conveyancing work for a bank is also an unsafe banking practice. A board member who must be able to make an objective judgment on whether the bank should make a loan has become biased because he will receive his conveyancing fee only if the mortgage is made. In fact, he may well get a second fee to do the bank's foreclosure work if the loan is made but does not work out. This situation has been known, on occasion, to degenerate into major insider abuses; especially where the bank president is doing the conveyancing and foreclosure practices in order to maximize his legal fees. While it's not a common practice, in some cases the bank requires the borrower to pay the legal costs of the foreclosure work already done before allowing the borrower to bring his loan up to date. Here personal interests clearly have overcome the bank's interests. As a result of this structure of inducements, it is an unsound practice to have attorneys who do business with the thrift institution on its board of directors.

Insurance is second only to law among the leading occupations of directors of savings and loan associations.[1] Directors and officers of savings and loan associations sometimes do virtually all the hazard business (fire, mortgage, life, and such) generated by the thrift institution. This is big business amounting to billions of dollars; nationally, about a quarter to a third of all the hazard insurance sold is handled by affiliates of savings and loan associations.[2] In states where savings and loans' selling of insurance is heavy (like California, Missouri, Florida and Colorado, among others), the ratio is 40–75 percent.[3] This association-generated income from the sale of insurance should accrue to the bank. It should not be appropriated as a tie-in sale by those individuals who are affiliated with the association.

Another not uncommon insider abuse involves realtors, who also derive a major benefit from their association with a thrift institution. Obviously, if a realtor can guarantee his customers that they will get a mortgage at the local bank, his business will be enhanced. This is one reason why some realtors are on the boards of thrift institutions and that some bank presidents' wives become realtors. These insider relationships do not necessarily constitute abuses, although other realtors may be disadvantaged. But, again, the situation can easily lead to abuses. The depositors' interests can easily become replaced by the realtor's. There is a tendency to take less care in evaluating a property and a loan whose application is submitted by a realtor on the board of directors—because of a certain reliance on the realtor's judgment, or because of the constraints of personal relationships of board members, or because of a system of mutual backscratching. In the more dangerous cases, appraisals may be deliberately tailored to permit a sale requiring a low down payment or none at all. If a realtor can obtain more favorable financing—100 percent if need be—he can sell property more readily. Again, the affiliated insider takes all the gains and the thrift institution all the risks.

The story of 2nd Imperial Savings and Loan Association illustrates how this kind of abusive insider dealing operates. In true concern for the bank, the president of the 2nd Imperial Savings and Loan Association takes a modest $12,000 salary. It is a small association, after all. But since the president is a lawyer, he does all the closings for the bank and makes another $56,000. The volume of mortgage activity goes up dramatically, in part because the security committee has learned to trust its judgment in determining the value of property, rather than using market price.

The law allows thrift institutions to grant a conventional mortgage of up to 80 percent of the appraised value of the property, but it allows the bank's board to do the appraising. The law is not stated in terms of market prices, although it is clearly contemplated that market price would normally be the appraised value. And it almost always is, unless the bank is redlining—in which case the bank makes the appraised value considerably less than the market price, thus preventing the bank from making the loan—or unless members of the board, their family, friends, or influential citizens are seeking the loan. In this case the bank may make the appraised value greater than the market price so it can grant mortgages in excess of 100 percent of market price, eliminating the need for a down payment. This means insiders and friendly outsiders are able to supplement their incomes by speculating in real estate without advancing any of their own funds. For a friendly legislator, the bank may be willing to grant a $48,000 mortgage on a property that cost him only $45,000. If questioned, the bank would respond that it was complying with the law, that the purchase price is much below the true value of the building. It's hard to believe, though, that the average person would be able to persuade a mortgage loan officer that 80 percent of the value of the building was really 107 percent of the purchase price. Board members themselves often become rich this way, too, with the bank taking all the risk for any mistakes in judgment.

So while the 2nd Imperial Savings and Loan Association's records show that it is lending at 80 percent of appraised value, it also happens to be lending 100 percent of market price. But that's okay. The association's president's son, also a lawyer and board member, earns legal fees for foreclosure. And inflation insures that most homes foreclosed by the bank can be resold without loss to the bank, most of the time.

Since savings banks have a substantial proportion of their assets in securities (30 percent, on average), brokers and investment managers are often board members. Their advice is clearly appropriate, but their performing the services, and their firm's taking the commissions, involve the same conflicts of interests as those of the realtor and conveyancing attorney.

Businessmen with primary interests in building materials have long had a prominent role in the thrift industry, especially as organizers and directors of savings and loan associations. There is always the possibility that such an insider has an interest in using the leverage of the thrift institution to direct building-material business to a particular supplier. If such leverage is employed, it may damage the thrift institution. If buying from a particular supplier is a criterion for obtaining financing some contractors will refuse this tie-in, and the lending base of the thrift institution will be reduced. Since contractors unwilling to be so coerced are likely to be those who can go elsewhere (that is, those of better credit standing), the quality of the loan portfolio will be reduced.

Further, particular loans may be made based simply on the business likely to be generated for the building-materials supplier. There may be a tendency to make otherwise substandard loans in the interest of the external business.

It would be far better for the thrift institutions and for their customers if board members were paid appropriate amounts for their work on the board. As it is, the bulk of their compensation comes indirectly, under a system where no one can determine whether the bank is being "overcharged" or given the best professional advice or service.

### Easy Loans Are Easy Money

It is in the loan area, of course, that the most lucrative deals can be made. If you're in real estate development, being a bank insider is the easiest way to riches. While loans to insiders at preferential rates are still fairly common, insiders have become much more sophisticated in using the bank's funds for their own advantage.

Take the 3rd Imperial Savings and Loan Association, a small but aggressive urban savings and loan association. The law requires that a thrift institution finance less than 100 percent of the value of a property when it grants a mortgage—that is, the bank can't lend you a down payment. An aggressive bank like 3rd Imperial wouldn't let little technicalities like that keep it from making mortgages on condominium complexes. So the bank creates a subsidiary that offers second mortgages, which are really the down payments. The bank is taking a risk on these loans since the buyers are not putting up any money, but the risk to the bank is worth it to the bank's president since he owns the condominium complexes. It's even more profitable for him when, as in this case, the commercial bank that finances the construction loans for the project does so at highly favorable rates. The savings and loan association, in return, places large certificates of deposit at the commercial bank at interest rates substantially below those set by the market.

Bank examiners frown at such sharp practices, and criticize them in the examination report, but insider abuses such as these won't lead the regulatory authorities to request the president's resignation unless his activities have already brought the bank to the verge of collapse.

Speculating in land is another opportunity insiders find opened up to them. Although savings bank and savings and loan associations are not allowed to make loans for investments in land to officers and directors, "straws" and dummy corporations make it fairly easy to get around this legal barrier. Management interest in land can lead to the familiar process of risk transfer to the thrift institution, with overappraisals permitting investment by affiliated speculators. It is also possible for land speculation to be reciprocally financed by the management of different thrift institutions, thus eluding the prohibition in another way. The 4th Imperial Savings Bank provides one example of how straws can be used to facilitate an officer's looting of the banks assets. The bank president and the bank's lawyer set up a realty trust to buy large tracts of undeveloped land near a proposed highway. With the aid of understanding appraisals from the bank's board, the trust was able to purchase the land with 100 percent mortgages. The lawyer and banker neither had the funds for, nor saw the necessity of, keeping up payments on the loans, or of paying the taxes on the property. Each time the loans became seriously delinquent, the realty trust sold the property to a new realty trust, with the same principals, for an amount which covered back interest, taxes, and profits for the principals. The new bank mortgages covered all these costs. No payments were ever recorded on these successive loans. But in this way, over the decade of the relatively noninflationary 1960s, the bank's appraisal of the underdeveloped land rose from $50,000 to over $1 million.

In one such transaction, the bank president, with the help of the bank's attorney and a member of the bank's Board of Investment, obtained a $650,000 mortgage for a piece of property which the insiders had bought for $40,000 and had tried unsuccessfully to sell for $120,000. The loan clearly violated banking requirements in all respects. As the bank president, board member, and attorney who handled all the paper work for the loan knew, the loan was made to a borrower who did not exist, the property to be mortgaged was improperly valued, and the proceeds of the loan did not go to the borrower, but were used to pay the personal indebtedness of the bank president and his partner, the board member. This loan, like the others, remained in delinquent status from the date the first payment was due.

In the early 1970s, an examination of the bank by the state Banking Department was highly critical of these overdue loans, now totaling over $1.2 million, and the history of repeated refinancing of the same property. An independent appraisal of the property indicated that the bank's appraisal was 800 percent too high. Under questioning by the examiner, the bank president confessed his role. The Commissioner of Banks called a meeting of the bank's board and requested the resignation of the president and the board member, and then forwarded the papers on the case to the attorney general and the district attorney.

However, one of the most outrageous aspects of insider abuses—especially those of a criminal nature, as in this case—is that the respectable people who commit them are rarely prosecuted unless the bank fails. In the event of bank failure, the illegal acts cannot be hushed up; in the case of the 4th Imperial Savings Bank, by contrast, no action was taken against any of the principals, one of whom was by this time a district judge.

## The Highest-earning Savings Bank in the State

A large thrift institution had the mortgages on a number of older hotel properties in a vacation area. But despite the problems that these older hotels had in competing with the newer resorts, this thrift's earnings continued to climb faster than any other thrift institution in the state. The thrift institution proudly advertised its high earnings and its rapid growth. What it did not advertise was that each spring it "sold" a dozen or so of these large hotels out of its foreclosure account with a 100 percent, no-down-payment mortgage, to some sharp businessmen who ran the property for the summer, made no payments on the mortgage (although the bank accrued the income from these payments as though they were made), and then allowed the bank to foreclose in the fall, when vacation season was over. The following spring, it would repeat the process. Each spring the bank's trustees would raise the appraised value of the property on which it was granting a mortgage. Since the new buyers never put up any money and never intended to repay the mortgage, the inflation of price never bothered them. A prestigious independent accounting firm allowed the bank, moreover, to take this "capital gain" as current income! Presto! The highest-earning bank in the state.

By the time the Commissioner of Banks stopped this merry-go-round, the bank's books had become so inflated with overvalued property that writing the assets down to more realistic levels could have endangered the capital adequacy of the bank. There were the usual penalties awarded white-collar abuses. The accounting firm apologized to the Bank Commissioner, saying it wasn't proud of its record in this case, and the partner in charge was allowed to take early retirement. The bank president went to court to fight the Bank Commissioner's demands that he step down; when he lost there, he accepted the bank trustees' offer of early retirement with a $50,000-a-year pension.

### Commercial Banks: The True Bonanza

Opportunities for fast financing practices abound in commercial banking. Since commercial banks have so many more powers than thrifts, the variety of abusive practices is greater. After all, even illegal loans in thrifts are governed by restrictions that they be loans on real estate or real-estate related. Commercial banks have no such restrictions.

Demand deposits (checking accounts) are a bank's most profitable account, since by law banks have been prohibited from paying interest on these accounts, which supply funds for loans and investments. Attracting demand deposits is the surest way of being a profitable bank, but as interest rates have risen on other bank accounts and on Treasury notes and money market funds, it has been increasingly difficult for banks to attract funds into non-interest-bearing demand deposits. Corporate customers have taken to keeping much of their money in certificates of deposit, which pay market interest rates. But another large depositor, government, is still in the demand deposit market, so attracting government deposits can be the surest way to running a profitable bank.

Since wining and dining state, county, and local treasurers can be and is done by almost every bank, a banker has to do more to get the business. The bank can make personal loans to the treasurer and then not press when the loan is not repaid. This is, of course, tantamount to giving a bribe financed by other people's money. These loans can be substantial. For a deposit of $1 million of the county's funds and deposits from other organizations with which the county treasury had influence, the 5th Imperial Bank and Trust Company gave the county treasurer a $400,000 loan which was backed by "cat and dog" stocks as collateral. Even in their heyday, these stocks never came near being worth $400,000. By the time the bank examiners looked at the loan, a few years later, they were valued at $26,000. The bank president readily agreed to charge the loan off, but resisted the idea of suing the treasurer and trying to collect.

The deposit relationship, which continued for years, was just too important to endanger by uselessly trying to collect on a bad loan. In any case, it was likely that the bank president also received a piece of the loan as a kickback.

Some banks are so adept at attracting government business that such deposits constitute a third to a half of the bank's total funds. In these cases, one can well question how the bank got into such a favored position. Such banks are often called political banks. They can be depended upon by state treasurers to make campaign contributions, regardless of any legal limits. The bank's books may be doctored so that bank furnishings are recorded for more than they cost to cover campaign contributions, or other business expenses which can't be documented may be booked. A common slush fund for these purposes comes from bonuses for bank officers. If you've ever wondered why some bankers' bonuses are so large, here is one likely answer. Banks also have been known to establish schemes whereby each officer is advised indirectly as to an appropriate level for his political contribution and is reimbursed through payment of a special bonus calculated to yield the designated contribution after taxes. A policy statement on improper payments by banks issued jointly by the three federal bank regulators in January 1978 took particular note of such "compensatory" bonuses to employees, among other devices—like improperly designated expense-account payments—which would be illegal under federal and state law. The bank regulators warned that "For banking organization to engage in illegal or unethical activities and to attempt to conceal those activities by the use of irregular accounting practices could only serve to undermine public confidence in the banking system."[4]

Another major source of demand deposits for large banks are correspondent balances from smaller banks. The correspondent relationship results from a national policy encouraging many independent banks. The correspondent system enables smaller banks to clear non-local checks and to offer a broader range of services to customers. In earlier days, correspondent banks paid interest on inter-bank deposits. But Congress saw this as a potential hazard to the supply of loanable funds in the smaller communities and, in 1933, prohibited banks from paying interest on these demand deposits. The funds in the respondent's demand account are not only interest-free money for the correspondent, they can be invested by the correspondent or used to meet reserve requirements. As a way of "paying" for these demand balances, the correspondent bank provides the out-of-town bank with services for the balances left at the bank. Pricing correspondent services and identifying their true costs are extremely difficult. The valuation of some services, such as technical advice and loan particiaption for a valued customer, is highly subjective.

While the abuse of compensating balances is most prevalent in commercial banking, it is not unknown in the stock-owned savings and loan industry. Holding companies have been notable for the systematic deployment of the deposit account of controlled savings and loan associations to support their own and other affiliates' credit. According to the Federal Home Loan Bank Board, "virtually every holding company which has a bank loan requires its subsidiary association to maintain a deposit with the bank lender as a compensating balance."[5] Edward Herman cites in "Conflicts of Interest in the Savings and Loan Industry" a savings and loan association in the Cincinnati Home Loan Bank district which kept a $1 million demand deposit account at a large Chicago bank. Herman states that the only reason for maintaining a checking account of that size in a Chicago bank, since the savings and loan association did not do any business in Illinois, would be that the holding company wanted to borrow from this bank and this deposit was one of the requirements for obtaining the loan.[6]

The misuse of correspondent balances and of state and local government deposits is one of the most undesirable side effects of the legal prohibition of paying interest on demand deposits. As long as the returns for placing the deposits must be measured in services, it is very difficult for the public—either as stockholders or taxpayers—to determine whether the best arrangement has been secured. Abuse in the system would be greatly reduced if one could use market rates of interest as a ready price to compare with that accepted for deposits.

As long as some people are able to place a large sum of interest-free money with a bank, those people will have a great deal of leverage in extracting favorable loans. Possibly the most serious abuse associated with the placement of correspondent balances is their use in obtaining bank-stock loans at preferential terms. Thus, an individual can approach a large bank and obtain a loan to buy a smaller bank, pledging as collateral the bank stock he intends to buy; promises of placing the correspondent balances of the acquired bank at the lending bank act as the inducement to make the loan in the first place. By this method, one can purchase a bank with very little of one's own money and postpone indefinitely repaying the loan by simply refinancing the loan at a new bank when it finally comes due, again offering the bank's correspondent balances as the bait for the loan.

The easiest preferential loan is a free one: You overdraw your checking account and nobody does anything. The bank does not bounce your checks, nor does it charge you interest. It acts this way because you are an insider or a good customer. As all of us outsiders are well aware, if we overdraw our checking accounts by $1, our checks bounce (unless we have overdraft privileges, in which case the bank usually charges at least 12 percent for the use of its funds). If you are an insider or a good customer, it's not unheard of to be able to overdraw your account by hundreds of thousands of dollars, using the funds as an interest-free loan. A survey done in 1977 by the federal bank regulatory agencies showed that a third of the banks responding had overdrafts in excess of $500 by their executives and directors, and about 92 percent of the banks with overdrafts had allowed insiders to have these loans interest-free.

The major advantage of being a commercial bank insider is that you are assured of having financing for your other business ventures. This is appropriate, and does the bank no harm, as long as the loans are sound and the lending is done on the same terms any other customer gets. Of course, it's necessary to offer some inducement to get business people to want to serve on bank boards of directors, but the only appropriate inducement should be this greater access to financing. It is not appropriate to provide such access on preferential terms. As Director Le Maistre of the FDIC stated in 1974:

*A bank is necessarily adversely affected when an insider exacts terms not available to members of the public. This is true whether the deal reflects a conscious intent to milk the bank or is merely the result of tainted judgment. In either event, the bank is harmed, since the economic benefit redounding to the insider represents a cost or loss of earnings which is borne by non-benefiting shareholders and/or in some way passes through to the bank's customers.*

*For this reason, any transaction between a bank and an insider or his interests that is significantly more favorable to the*

*insider than a comparable transaction with a noninsider is an
unsound banking practice and should not be tolerated by a bank's
board of directors. Where such conduct is tolerated by a bank's
board, it should be the subject of firm supervisory action. To
follow any other policy is to allow banks to subsidize the non-
banking financial activity of preferred insiders at the ultimate
expense of minority or non-interested shareholders, and, in the
case of bank failure, it is the expense of many creditors and
depositors as well.*[7]

The most glaring abuses of insider dealings often lead to bank
failures, leaving in the wake of these spectacular but infrequent
happenings the impression that this was the unusual case. While
they're not the everyday practice of every bank, abusive insider loans
are not as uncommon as one could wish. If the bank does not fail, if
it simply merges with another bank or has reduced earnings, then
the insider abuses appear only among the bank examiners' comments, not on the front pages of newspapers. 6th Imperial Bank and
Trust Company, a $55 million suburban bank, shows these garden-
variety abuses.

Everyone on the board of 6th B & T has a deal going. In fact,
this is necessary, or some of the deprived, straitlaced, unduly
sensitive directors would have objected to the modus operandi of
the other directors. The bank's earnings are quite low, but for the
time being net sound capital is sufficient to keep the bank
operating and the regulatory authorities at bay. The directors of
this bank and their associates have nearly $3 million of loans to
themselves and their interests that have been classified by bank
examiners as doubtful of repayment. All were written at com-
paratively favorable repayment schedules and interest rates.

For example, Bank Chairman "John Smith", Director "John
Doe II", and six of their associates formed a private company, South
Imperial Merchants Associates, with an original $800,000 capital
investment, of which $700,000 was financed by 6th Imperial B & T
at preferential rates and with no defined repayment program. These
investors didn't get these favorable terms because of their excellent
credit status: five of them already had loans classified as at least
doubtful of repayment, and one's earlier loans were conceded as a
loss by bank management. No matter; it's for the chairman and his
friends.

The new loan was to prevent foreclosure of a shoe manufac-
turing facility in Spain by a foreign bank. The factory tied in nicely
with the business interests of "John Doe II", who was a shoe

importer. The mortgage on the facility was held by a foreign subsidiary of South Imperial Merchants Associates that had lost nearly $200,000 in the previous year. 6th Imperial B & T Bank loaned this foreign shoe company $240,000. No small suburban bank applying consistent and objective credit standards would have approved a loan to another foreign bank; no small suburban bank would have approved loan requests of $700,000 to a customer for the purpose of capitalizing a foreign manufacturing plant, with as favorable a rate and repayment provision as those granted by this bank. The bank was willing to speculate in overseas adventures in this case because the speculators sat on the bank's board.

But this bank is good to many people. A major stockholder in a small bank in which 6th Imperial B & T's president is also a major stockholder has unsecured borrowings of over $300,000 for which no purpose is stated in the bank's credit files. The loans are overdue and the borrower's checking account is periodically overdrawn. Yet late charges are routinely waived, and there is no established plan for repaying the principal. In the past, payout arrangements on his debt have not materialized.

Another director has borrowed $69,000 for "investments." The loan is past due, but to avoid further criticism from the examiners, the loan is rewritten with the $5,000 past-due interest added on to the new loan.

Two directors and the president of the bank borrowed $183,000 from the bank, through a realty trust, to speculate on the purchase, renovation, and resale of a piece of property. The renovations were done by the director's companies. After unsuccessfully attempting to sell the property, the trust deeded it to the bank. An outside appraiser valued the property, as renovated, at $90,000 less than the bank lent for it. The bank, of course, took the loss for this unsuccessful speculation and became the proud owner of the property.

Another director, who happens to be the major stockholder in the holding company that owns 6th Imperial B & T, has $650,000 in outstanding loans in the form of a consolidation of his previous debts due this bank and loans due other commercial banks. Most of this borrowing is unsecured. This insider, like so many of the others, has experienced personal cash-flow problems that have hampered his ability to service his bank debt. The bank understandingly has waived $5,000 in interest and late charges and has foregone establishing a repayment program on his indebtedness.

Another director is a real estate developer with $180,000 in outstanding loans. Some of the loans were used to finance purchases of stock in the bank's present holding company. Bank management indicates that this director's financial condition presently precludes adequate debt service, so they have waived any payments for the time being.

Another director with $150,000 of overdue loans at the bank has renewed them on four different occasions, with interest added on each time. The director knows his rights; he refuses to furnish the bank with current financial statements—it's none of their business. What about the Bank Commissioner? Well, the director's related to a couple of very important political figures.

And finally, the bank's attorney, who is also a director, has a quarter of a million dollars in outstanding loans from the bank— all unsecured, all with overdue interest added to the loan balance at each renewal, none with a repayment schedule. He bills the bank $80,000 a year for his services.

What distinguishes this bank from those which make headlines is that the directors are careful not to become so greedy that the bank actually fails. This is a real bank but not a typical one; the typical case is much smaller in scale and much less interesting. This one, on the other hand, reveals the opportunities for insider abuse that does not call for bank regulators to intervene, since the capital of the bank is still sound and the bank is not yet in danger of failing. As long as the directors are able to attract new wheeler-dealers to invest in the bank by promising them easy loans, then the capital of the bank can be replenished and the regulators kept at bay. Yes, the bank may fail eventually and the directors may lose their investments, but they've more than made them up in loans they have not repaid.

These men are not financial geniuses. They are simply taking liberal advantage of a system which allows insiders to abuse their positions for a long time before the regulator can do anything about it.

### On a Clear Day You Can See ...

Bank holding companies offer great opportunities for insider gain at the expense of the public stockholders. Take the bank holding company which has, besides a bank, a commercial finance company as a subsidiary. Not all stockholders in the bank holding company are stockholders in the finance company, which is very closely held.

The finance company and the bank make loans together, each putting up some of the funds lent to a borrower. Over 40 percent of the subsidiary's loans are lent in conjunction with the bank. The finance company gets 14 percent interest on its share, while the bank gets 10 percent on its. The customer is unaware or uninterested; all he cares about is the total cost to him. In addition, the finance company gets a management fee from the bank for finding the customer, and on occasion, it has large overdrafts on its account. The bank's earnings are depressed, but not those of the principals in the finance company.

The holding company also gets a $1 million annual management fee, prepaid 12 months in advance. Every quarter, a check is issued for $250,000 to re-institute the 12 month prepaid status. The result is that the prepaid management fees never go below $750,000 and bear a striking resemblance to an extension of credit rather than a fee.

More abusive is the practice of selling substandard loans from the closely held subsidiaries to the more widely held bank, where, if the loan is in a nonearning position for a period of time or must be written off as a loss, the loss is mainly borne by public shareholders. In some cases, the substandard loans were loans to insiders at the holding company. For example, several members of the board of the holding company borrowed money from a nonsubsidiary for a land-development company in Arizona. The loan soon went into default and eventually was re-written as a loan at the bank with accrued interest added to principal. The nonbank holding company subsidiary was thus made whole. This new bank loan was also soon in default. The debt was allowed to remain steady for five years with no collection of income, a preferential treatment that would not be extended to the ordinary borrower.

On the other hand, when the bank finds a particularly attractive credit, loan participations are sold to insiders at the holding company. The sale of a loan participation to individual investors is considered unorthodox banking at best. That they are sold to insiders puts the insiders in the untenable position of serving two masters, with the best interests of the bank competing with their own best interests.

In addition, the principals in the holding company borrowed $10 million from a large New York bank to buy the stock of this bank. Despite the fact that the New York bank performs few services for the bank, the loan to the holding company requires the subsidiary bank to maintain a compensating balance at the New York bank equivalent to 20 percent of the current principal outstanding on the debt.

In theory, the holding company is supposed to be the source of strength to the total organization. On occasion, as in the example described, the reverse is true: The entire strength lies in the bank. The earnings of the bank roughly represent the total earnings of the holding company, despite the existence of several other closely held affiliates. The bank's earnings have been used to dress up the balance sheet and earnings statement of the subsidiaries. To a certain point there is nothing wrong with this, but in conjunction with the rate differentials on loans in which the finance company participates and other techniques, the entire operation shows evidence of over-reliance on the bank that subtly suggests abuse. The heavy volume of participated loans with a lower rate to the bank smacks of a profit transfer technique; the substantial service fee charged the bank for accounting work and managing loans, covering almost all the back-office costs of the subsidiary, again appears to have some characteristics of a profit-transfer technique. In addition, the dual lending status of officers in the subsidiary and the bank involves an inherent element of conflict of interest, although the practice is not unusual. When executives of a closely held finance company simultaneously have lending powers in affiliated banks, it does not take much imagination to see which affiliate is going to be the loser.

The Federal Reserve has become increasingly concerned about the problem of weak non-banking affiliates' draining the vitality of bank holding companies. This concern was created by the failure of two large banks in the 1970s, the $279.9 million Palmer Bank of Sarasota, Florida, and the $1.1 billion Hamilton National Bank of Chattanooga, Tennessee, due to too many sales to banking affiliates of loans generated by mortgage companies within the bank holding companies. The Fed circulated a letter to bank holding companies stating its concern about such companies dumping bad loans to their bank affiliates and reminded banks that this could involve criminal prosecution. There have been no such prosecutions.

Another area of insider abuse was addressed by Comptroller of the Currency John Heimann who formally warned national banks in September of 1978 not to divert income to major stockholders and insider-related organizations through the payment of excessive fees. The formal warning came, Heimann explained, because of the observed increase in the number of instances where banks were paying fees in excess of the value of goods and services received. Heimann said such practices included paying excessive fees to directors, to holding companies to subsidize unprofitable operations, and to shareholders or insider-related organizations solely to meet a need for funds. In addition, the Comptroller's office said it had uncovered excessive salaries and bonuses and prepayment of fees for services not yet received. Past national bank regulators had also ruled these and similar practices as unsafe and unsound banking activities because the payments were believed to dissipate the bank's profits and capital and were adverse to the bank and the financial interests of minority stockholders. When such activities had been found in the past, bank boards had been told to stop their unsound practices; they were criticized but not financially penalized. The significant change initiated by the September 1978 Comptroller's letter was to warn bank boards of directors that the examiners would now demand restitution to the bank when these kinds of income diversion were found. There still was no penalty imposed, just requiring the return of ill-gotten funds. We have progressed from slaps on the wrist to restitution. The logical next step is stiff fines for abusive behavior.

One of the most intriguing aspects of bank insider abuse is how often it is found in newly chartered banks. For those who believe that open entry and increased competition is in the public interest, this is particularly distressing. This abuse appears to be a function of the chartering process, not simply an accident. For more than thirty years after the Great Depression, virtually no banks were chartered, as bank regulators sought to minimize competition and to maintain stability in banking. Then, in the early 1960s, James Saxon, then Comptroller of the Currency, started giving bank charters again, and he was followed by state bank commissioners. Charters were not freely given, however. One had to pass a "convenience and needs" test. The statutory language referred to the needs of the public; in practice, too often, the needs of the bank commissioner, state treasurer, local or national politicians took precedence. Often only those with political influence found that they could get a bank charter. The situation was reminiscent of the early nineteenth century when one needed to bribe much of the state legislature to buy a bank charter. Public repugnance at that spectacle had led to the free chartering of banks.

The restrictions on entry into banking created after the Depression finally led in the late 1950s and early 1960s to a similar type of corruption of the chartering process itself.

## Insider Deals—Who Cares?

Why should anyone care if there are insider abuses, even if it leads to the bank's failure?

First, let's be clear that abuses do lead to bank failures. The FDIC has found that abusive self-dealing has been a significant contributing factor in more than half of all the bank failures since 1960. It is also a significant factor in leading to regulator-arranged bank mergers. Still, you may ask, do I care? I'm paid the maximum rate allowed by law on my deposits. Even if the bank earned more, under the present system, I as a depositor wouldn't get any benefit. If the bank fails because of too many abusive insider deals, I'm still not particularly harmed. There are plenty of other banks I can use, and my money is insured by the federal government. So if there's insider abuse in banks, it doesn't really affect me, does it?

Clearly, federal deposit insurance has removed much of the terror from bank failures, especially for individuals. But not all. Business and government deposits usually greatly exceed the deposit insurance limits. A bank failure may well wipe out the working capital and payroll funds for many local businesses. You may be out of a job, if you worked for a business that kept its funds at this bank.

Towns and cities may also find the salaries for city employees and teachers gone, as well as pension funds and other tax receipts. A failure doesn't have to involve a large bank to have serious effects on a town's financial stability. When Citizens State Bank of Carrizzo Springs, Texas, failed, in 1976, it had only $14.7 million in deposits, but at least five area governments found themselves without operating funds as a result of the closing. The local school district had had $1 million in deposits at the bank to be used for teachers' pay, and the county had about $700,000 in the bank. Virtually all of this money was lost when the bank was closed, and it clearly would have to be made up by increased taxes. In this $14.7 million bank, $2,350,000 was not covered by deposit insurance.

While we need have no sympathy for the stockholders of a failed bank who were the insiders creating the abuses, most stockholders are innocent of any wrongdoing. Stockholders usually lose all their investment when a bank fails.

And while major cities and some suburbs have an abundance of banks, not every community nor every neighborhood in a large city, enjoys this luxury. A bank failure may mean that the only bank in town is gone, or that the number of banking alternatives has been significantly reduced. If you need to borrow, the absence of local competition may well make a big difference in the terms you can get, or your ability to borrow at all.

The failure of a bank, or its lessened ability to serve its community, will have a negative impact on the financial strength of the community as a whole. Banks are catalysts for economic development. Without their proper functioning, the cards are stacked against local businesses and the economic life of the neighborhood or community.

The average citizen's concern is not only that abusive self-dealing leads to bank failures, but that it misdirects the focus of the bank away from serving the needs of the community. If insiders' business ventures get funding on preferential terms, then the rest of us must borrow on more onerous ones. If the bank is making risky loans for the bank's insiders, it must be more cautious in the loans it makes to other borrowers, if the bank is not to fail.

The lines that divide smart businessmen, fast financiers, self-dealing insiders, and white-collar criminals are not all that clear. What is clear is that what is unfair may not be illegal. It is possible to bring significant financial benefits to yourself, your friends, and family without breaking laws, simply by abusing trust. It is, of course, possible, if not easy, to change the laws to make what is unfair also illegal.

If you rob a bank with a gun and you are caught, you definitely go to prison. If you embezzle the bank's funds, you may go to prison. But if you sit on the bank's board as a director and make "loans" to yourself and don't repay them, you remain a respected businessman in the community even after the regulators punish you by making you resign from the board. Heads you win; tails you don't lose much.

The failure of law enforcement authorities to prosecute bank presidents for their part or acquiescence in this criminal behavior is in part responsible both for the amount of self-dealing and for the public suspicion that it's who you know that determines your ability to borrow. As Martin Mayer has observed in his book *The Bankers:*

*The number of prosecutions for this sort of criminal behavior, however, seems to be almost invisibly small. No doubt many loan officers who are dismissed under this cloud are men who have seen the error of their ways, for whom an injunction to go and sin no more is defensible charity... But much of the force of any law derives from the belief of those subject to it that if they break it they will suffer a public punishment...*[8]

Because of the rarity of punishment for bankers guilty of self-dealing that does not lead to bank failure, a banker who is prosecuted feels singularly mistreated by the system. In an unusual 1979 prosecution of a banker for self-dealing, the banker tried the "everybody did it" defense. This banker was a prominent man who had been faulted for overdrawing his checking account by thousands of dollars, of making loans to his relatives, and getting personal loans from banks where he had deposited his own bank's funds. He complained that the government was persecuting him and that other bankers have done the same things with impunity. Perhaps the banker had a point: In early 1980 his conviction was reversed by the United States Court of Appeals, just two weeks before Bert Lance was acquitted in federal court of similar charges brought against him.

People concerned with current practices have tried to redraw the lines. They were ridiculed and defeated. For several years a good many members of Congress led by Representative St. Germain and Senator Proxmire unsuccessfully tried to pass laws prohibiting some of the most abusive self-dealing practices. Even the Bert Lance affair, which focused national attention on bank self-dealing, proved inadequate to overcome the powerful opposition of the bank lobbyists.

### "The Bert Lance Memorial Act of 1978"

However singular Bert Lance's banking deals were or weren't, the most striking thing about the story was the inaction of federal regulators in response to acts which, if not criminal, at least raised eyebrows and resulted in long and expensive legal proceedings. Bert Lance, the President's trusted friend and budget director, was accused of and later indicted for misusing his position as president at two Georgia banks. (He was later acquitted after a trial in 1980.) The revelations of his wheeling and dealing forced him to resign his position as budget director in September of 1977 and led to public demands for banking reform legislation.

The *National Journal* described Lance as "a friendly bear of a guy with the charm of an old song-and-dance man and the irrepressible guile of a safecracker." One of Lance's questionable practices was his free use of bank overdrafts, in amounts ranging from $26,000 in 1972 to a high of $821,000 in 1974 when Lance was running for governor. To some, it appeared that he was financing his political campaign with the money. Since the Calhoun Bank neither bounced Lance's checks nor charged him interest for the use of the bank's funds, these overdrafts were literally interest-free loans. According to charges in his indictment, the use of overdrafts by Lance and his friends and family cost the banks of which he was president, the National Bank of Georgia and the Calhoun First National Bank, more than $500,000 in lost interest income.

The public was also highly critical of the no-down-payment loans which Lance had used to purchase the banks in the first place. Lance became president of the National Bank of Georgia by becoming its major stockholder, and he became its major stockholder by borrowing $3.5 million from an out of state bank. The loan was based on the value of the bank stock he was going to buy with the money. In other words, he advanced none of his own money to buy the bank. Lance was also advanced an additional $80,000 he needed to pay the interest on the loan. In return, the out of state bank became the National Bank of Georgia's correspondent bank and kept millions of dollars of the Georgia bank's deposits in interest-free accounts. In effect, the other Georgia bank stockholders were paying the interest on Lance's stock loans through reduced bank earnings.

The Lance disclosures led to congressional demands for a national bank survey to determine how widespread this sort of behavior was. The federal bank regulatory agencies which conducted the survey looked at the results and pronounced that all was well. With banking, innocence, like beauty, appears to be in the eye of the beholder.

The national survey of commercial banks covered bank loans of more than $25,000 secured by bank stock, insider loans, loans to officers and directors of other banks, and overdrafts exceeding $500. The survey results showed that bank stock loans totaled about $1.4 billion as of September 30, 1977. About 86 percent of the loans were made to insiders of the banks or bank holding companies whose stock was pledged. Not surprisingly, it appeared that the quid pro quo for these loans involved using the acquired banks' deposits. The survey found nearly two-thirds of the money lent by banks to executives and directors of other banks involved a correspondent relationship with the lending institutions. Borrowers whose banks maintained such relationships were able to get loans at lower rates than those who didn't. The lower interest rate, however, is not the ultimate arbiter of whether preferential treatment occurred. The collateral for the loans may have been substandard, that is, the borrower might never have qualified for the loan in the first place, much less at the preferential rate.

Banks responding to the survey held 99,602 loans to their own insiders—executive officers, major stockholders, and directors. The loan data showed that during the tight-money years of 1970, 1973, and 1974, bank insiders were able to get loans below the average prime rate for those years. The survey found that nearly one-third of the banks responding reported overdrafts in excess of $500 by their executives and directors, and about 92 percent of those banks allowing the overdrafts charged no interest.

These results hardly justified the conclusion of the regulators and the banking industry that Bert Lance introduced new practices to banking! In Bert Lance's case, the federal bank regulatory agencies were only forced into some action by media publicity and public indignation. The major action engaged in by the federal bank regulators was to take surveys of bank insiders' practices, which were used to calm the public's demands for stronger regulations by showing that Lance was quite singular. This was a whitewash, as both the examples already cited and the survey results themselves indicate.

Congressional reaction to the Lance uproar was to write the Safe Banking Act, introduced in September 1977. The author, House Committee Chairman St. Germain, was ridiculed and his bill initially defeated in committee.

The original 175-page bill included provisions to clamp tighter restrictions on the personal borrowing practices of officers, directors, employees, and their families in all financial institutions, not banks alone. It would apply also to all companies affiliated with such insiders and to their political or campaign committees if they should be in politics. The St. Germain bill prohibited loans to insiders from a bank holding a correspondent balance from the applicant's bank. It barred checking account overdrafts to insiders.

The bill would have made all bank stock loans subject to margin requirements. The federal regulatory authorities would be required to approve or deny in advance any change in control of an insured bank. Loans to any one insider would be limited to 5 percent of capital accounts. All extensions of loans to insiders would have to be listed in public reports of condition, along with aggregate dollar amounts of loans classified as substandard, doubtful, and loss by the regulators. Interlocking directorships would be banned among banks, savings and loans, mutual savings banks, credit unions, insurance companies, title companies, companies which appraise real property, and companies which close real estate transactions. Management officials would be prohibited from providing legal services for the financial institution or in any transactions involving a customer of a financial institution. Civil monetary penalties would be provided for violations of banking laws (such as insider loans and loans to affiliates). Additional power would be granted to remove officers for breach of fiduciary duty, rather than actual personal dishonesty. The authority of federal regulators to issue cease and desist orders would be broadened to include actions against officers, directors, or any person participating in the affairs of a financial institution. (Under then current law, such actions had to be taken against the institution.) And finally, the bill would require the Federal Reserve Board to set regulations that a "reasonable number of persons" on the board of directors and executive committees of bank holding companies and bank subsidiaries be outside directors.

This was real and meaningful regulatory reform. It attacked many of the known outstanding abusive practices in the banking and thrift industries. It therefore stood little chance of passage. Only the public uproar over the Bert Lance revelations made it impossible for the House Banking Committee—some of whose members were the recipients of generous campaign contributions from the banking and thrift lobbies—to ignore the whole issue.

The various provisions of the bill were attacked and ridiculed. The loan limits to insiders were decried as preventing banks from "attracting talented directors,"[9] which would in the end, it was declared, be a "disservice to the public."[10] The loan restrictions, it was argued, would "make it difficult, if not impossible to lend to worthy customers who also happened to be associated with the bank."[11] The prohibition on interlocks between financial institutions and insurance companies, title companies, or companies engaged in real estate operations was rejected as "unnecessary."[12] Furthermore, it was argued that these interlocks are often needed because banks require a "particular expertise."[13] Even the proposed requirement that acquisitions of bank stock be subject to prevailing margin requirements was attacked as causing "undue problems in effecting ownership transfers at smaller finan-cial institutions in rural areas."[14] Limitations on insiders' obtain-ing loans from banks at which their financial institution kept its correspondent account was described as hamstringing the corre-spondent banking system. "Banks," it was argued, "would be limited in establishing correspondent banking relationships and bank officers and directors would find themselves handicapped in finding sources of credit ... furthermore, it would make it signifi-cantly more difficult to secure financing to help broaden the base of bank ownership, particularly in smaller communities, and could be viewed as leading to ownership of banks primarily by wealthy individuals or bank holding companies."[15] Public disclosure of loans to insiders and of classified bank loans was rejected as "misleading or meaningless to the average depositor and share-holder and could result in unfairly damaging a bank, as well as an unwarranted invasion of privacy on the part of shareholders."[16]

The requirement that financial institutions select some outside directors was angrily denounced as

*an unjustifiable pre-emption of the rights of shareholders under state law; there has been no demonstrated need for this proposed action ... [The bill] would place the federal government in the position of determining management and members of policy bodies for holding companies and bank subsidiaries therein. Such a move would be repugnant to a relatively free society. Such a step toward widespread determination of manage-ment plus already existing techniques of the federal government plus those being proposed would constitute a most serious threat to the freedom of this Nation. Such would be perilously close to basic concepts embodied in the Russian Gosbank.[17]*

While the banking lobbies and bankers expressed these and more objections to the proposed new statute to curb conflict of interest abuses in banking, these particular quotes all come from the position espoused by the Conference of State Bank Supervisors, an organization representing the state bank commissioners. As these objections to the provisions of the Safe Banking Act make clear, there is usually no better lobbyist for the banking establishment than their friendly state regulator.

Rep. St. Germain described the bill as "an affirmative step by the Congress to meet the public's demand for the firmer and more vigorous federal regulation of financial institutions—in place of the present timid hesitant supervision which serves neither the interests of the public nor the banks."[18] The bill eventually was watered down greatly, and finally passed eighteen months later, just before the October 1978 congressional elections, so that legislators could tell home town constituents that they had done something to curb bank insiders' abuses.

The Financial Institutions Regulation Act of 1978 (dubbed the Safe Banking Act by one of its sponsors, Rep. St. Germain, and the "Bert Lance Memorial Act" by the banking industry) was labeled an omnibus bank reform bill, the first major reform legislation to pass in the 1970s. The passage of the bill culminated several years of intense work by the Senate and House Banking committees and extensive debate within the banking community.

The statute did give the bank regulatory authorities some new supervisory and enforcement powers. Rather than prohibiting abusive practices outright, the regulatory agencies were given the authority to issue court-enforceable cease and desist orders directly against individuals—directors, officers, employees, agents, or other persons participating in the conduct of the affairs of the institution. While the possibility of taking this sort of action was expanded, the procedures involved in a cease and desist action are cumbersome and formal. Most self-dealing transactions usually have marginal damaging effects that slowly chip away at a bank or thrift institution's solvency. They are not properly handled by the administrative machinery of a cease and desist order.

The regulators were also given the authority to impose monetary penalties on individuals and institutions alike for violations of various provisions of the banking laws. The regulators' authority to remove officers and directors of financial institutions was expanded, as was the power to require divestiture by a bank holding company of a non-bank subsidiary if that subsidiary was deemed to present a serious risk to the safety of the bank.

In addition, a glaring loophole was closed. Previously, the federal bank regulatory authorities could remove an officer or director only if the individual were indicted or convicted of a felony, or had done something that had caused or probably would cause substantial financial loss and was guilty of personal dishonesty in his action. This extreme standard, involving both substantial damage and personal dishonesty, had rendered this regulatory power virtually useless. The new statute eliminated the need to prove personal dishonesty; the regulator had only to show that the actions would result in substantial damage to the bank.

Furthermore, bank regulators were given the authority to disapprove a change in bank ownership. While persons seeking to charter a new bank have had to undergo intense financial scrutiny by regulators, persons acquiring control of an established bank by purchasing its stock have been outside the regulatory purview.

The statute also dealt, albeit weakly, with the issue of insider lending, by providing that loans to executive officers or significant bank shareholders must be aggregated with loans to companies and campaign committees controlled by them, unless they are outside directors. This total insider lending was also limited to 10 percent of the bank's capital (twice the percentage amount originally proposed in the St. Germain bill). It did restrict a prior practice: Previously, an insider or major stockholder could borrow up to the 10 percent limit personally while loans to controlled companies and personal campaign committees were considered separately. Another provision required that any lending in excess of $25,000 to insiders or their controlled companies or campaign committees had to be approved in advance by the board of directors.

Finally, the law made explicit the fiduciary principle that loans to bank insiders may not be made on preferential terms, but must have substantially the same terms as those prevailing at the time for comparable transactions with other customers. (This provision did not apply to thrift institutions.) It completely prohibited free overdrafts for the accounts of executive officers or directors. Attacking the issue of insider borrowing between correspondent banks, the measure stated that such deals should not be on preferential terms. Monitoring was left to public disclosure. Banks must aggregate the amount of insider loans, and this total is to be public information.

The law, however, sidestepped a major loophole in all these restrictions about lending to insiders: the practice of reciprocity. If bank and savings and loan officers cannot borrow from their own bank or association, they borrow reciprocally from another. The threat of reciprocal lending rests primarily on the possible and even probable breakdown of lending standards implicit in such arrangements. Reciprocals often involve an exchange of privileged loans, which are often expressed in mutual interest rate subsidies, but which more importantly relate to the granting of excessive or unduly risky loans. Although reciprocal lending is recognized to be a collusive method of evading the prohibition and restrictions of direct loans to officers and directors, there are no laws or regulations seriously interfering with this practice. The Safe Banking Act of 1978 also avoided the issue.

The law does prohibit management interlocks between depository institutions or bank holding companies where one of the institutions has total assets of more than $1 billion and the other has total assets of more than $500 million. In addition, most management interlocks between financial institutions with offices in the same metropolitan area are prohibited, but to take the sting out, present interlocks are "grandfathered" for another ten years. Moreover, the act timidly ignored the prevalent pattern of interlocks between more ordinary-sized financial institutions. Local banks and savings and loan associations are, or ought to be, competitors for savings accounts and mortgage loans. Interlocks reduce competition. The rapid growth of savings and loan associations has been a concern to commercial bankers. This concern may be reflected in policy recommendations of association officers or directors on such items as advertising expenditures, rates charged on loans and paid on deposits, branching decisions, and on the size of and rates paid on the compensatory balance of the savings and loan association held at the commercial bank.

The Safe Banking Act did not address nepotism in the mutual thrift industry. Nepotism is regarded by many knowledgeable observers as a real problem in the savings and loan industry. A survey in the late 1960s indicated that one-third of savings and loan associations had at least one nepotistic relationship and over half of the large mutual savings and loan associations had at least one nepotistic interlock.[19] Management performance can be expected to be lower where nepotism is a major basis for the selection of managers. Moreover, managerial performance will also be adversely affected by the inability to hold and attract quality managers and strong independent directors when there is lack of opportunity at the top and the reward system is geared to loyalty to a controlling family.

Nepotism also leads to excessively high salaries, partly because its very purpose is to provide sinecures for family members and also because there is more likely to be a complete absence of independent board members. The Safe Banking Act did not address this problem. The solution is simple and straightforward: The bill need only have specified that a mutual thrift institution have no more than two family members as officers or directors of the same institution.

Bankers have objected heatedly to the new banking rules,

limited as they are. They don't like having to reveal to other board members the amount of money they're borrowing from the bank. Although the public disclosure lumps together any individual's own borrowing with all the other borrowing by bank officers, board members and major stock-holders, bankers fume that "It's like standing nude out in the main intersection of town."[20]

The legislation became effective March 10, 1979. Bankers and their regulators have categorized the act as regulatory overkill and have charged that, "in small communities [the new law is] going to make it tough to get good directors."[21]

The Conference of State Bank Supervisors echoed their bankers' concerns. The Safe Banking Act of 1977 was criticized as "an unfortunate, over-reaching effort to correct isolated banking practices."[22] The law and regulations, the Conference insisted were leading directors to relinquish their board seats. Is this bad? Now there will be empty board seats for women and minorities and outside directors who can ensure that bank lending is community oriented rather than so heavily tied to the business interests of a few insiders.

Bankers in states where branch banking is not allowed, bankers argue, are the ones which will be most affected by the law's restrictions on insider loans and bank stock loans. "This is really going to dry up the source for the small unit banks," the chairman of the American Bankers Association, Community Bankers Division, stated.[23] In unit banking states, many banks are sold to one-bank holding companies which are financed through insider loans.

Several of the bankers commenting on the law and the proposed regulations argued that they saw nothing wrong with allowing preferential interest rates on loans to insiders, likening them to the discounts department stores offer their employees. Some bankers have been giving out gifts in lieu of paying market interest rates on deposit accounts for so long that they no longer know the difference between a bank and a department store. They've lost sight of the fact that they have a fiduciary responsibility because, as Justice Louis Brandeis pointed out long ago, they are using "other peoples' money."

While bankers are openly resentful of the insider rules, actually, the law had been watered down almost to the point of non-recognition and lobbyists had used the corpse as a vehicle for attaching their pet projects, like a federal charter for mutual savings banks. In exchange for this long-sought prize, Congress did not address the widely known abusive practices at thrift institutions. Not a word about nepotism. Not a word about letting mortgage applicants choose their own lawyers for mortgage closings. Not a word prohibiting a thrift institution from making mortgages on commercial property owned by a bank officer. Not a word about stricter supervision of commercial sales out of a bank's foreclosure account that are made with 100 percent mortgages. Not a word about seizures of corporate opportunities, like increased income from the sale of mortgage insurance. Not a word about breaking down the traditional patterns of extensive interlocking relationships with outside business interests. Not a word about limiting the business activities of management, or, better yet, complete elimination of any transactions between a management person's own business and his financial institution. Not a word about reinvigorating corporate democracy in the mutual thrift industry.

In 1978, the Federal Home Loan Bank Board responded to the pressures of the times and issued new conflict of interest regulations which addressed many of the abuses cited in this chapter. Rather than prohibiting many current practices in the S&L industry, they simply required disclosure. For example, board members may still do all the title work for the S&L, but the board member must disclose in the S&L's annual report the income derived from this activity. The new regulations do not allow the S&L to finance the business activities of directors and officers, and tie-ins are now prohibited. But the regulations may be so easily circumvented that their net effect on practices in the S&L industry has been almost nil.

# 3.
# Where Have All the Bond Buyers Gone?

In the mid-1970s, for the first time since the financial debacle of the 1930s, several large American cities, and even states, faced debt crises and possible defaults. In these financial crises, the roles played by the banks and bond underwriters, the Federal Reserve System, and the municipal and state pension funds were critical. The legacy of these crises is important not only for Massachusetts, New York City, and Cleveland, where they occurred, but for state and local governments everywhere, all of whom are dependent on a handful of banks and underwriters for access to the capital markets. These crises highlight how extremely limited that access is for state and local governments.

### Nixon Takes Aim

During the years 1974 and 1975, the United States suffered through the worst worldwide recession since the Great Depression of the 1930s. Ten million Americans were unemployed. Tax revenues for state and local governments plummeted, while expenditures for welfare and unemployment compensation soared. Inflation hit 12 percent, and interest rates in bond markets rose to the highest levels since the Civil War, vastly increasing governments' costs for borrowing.

While OPEC had the world economy on the rack, President Nixon took aim at the cities. In 1973, Nixon impounded all federal housing subsidy funds, and in one blow, jeopardized the economic viability of state public housing projects and the state agencies responsible for them. (The Housing and Urban Development Act of

1968 contained direct subsidies—Section 236 money—that reduced the interest charges on approved projects to only 1 percent. These subsidies made viable many housing projects that would otherwise have been unrentable.) Nixon's budget cuts, purported to be anti-inflation measures, were in fact targeted at programs that were meant to benefit cities. Revenue sharing formulas were changed significantly, reducing funds to Northern cities while increasing the funds going to the suburbs and the Sunbelt. Through the budget, Nixon punished all those constituencies who had not supported his re-election. And at the head of the list were the urban poor and the Northern cities where they lived.

The financial debacle of New York City has been extensively analyzed elsewhere. Reviewing the major events will serve, however, as a prologue to telling the story of some less well-known financial crises that occurred at the same time. The critical role of banks in magnifying the underlying financial problems of the time will clearly emerge.

### The New York Crisis

How could it happen? The nation's largest city suddenly teeters on the brink of bankruptcy. The state legislature clamps a moratorium on repayment of $2.4 billion in city notes. If New York City defaults, the economy of the Western world may collapse, says investment banker Felix Rohatyn and others.

Part of New York City's crisis can be traced to New York politicians as seemingly different as John V. Lindsay and Abraham Beame, both of whom used a glittering array of fiscal gimmicks to hide the simple fact that expenditures were exceeding receipts: budget notes, inaccurate revenue figures, capitalized expenses, siphoning off "excess" pension-fund earnings. The tricks multiplied, and so did the hidden deficits—to a staggering $6 to $8 billion. New York, with the blessing of its banks, created money by borrowing it.

While the banks had been active and profitable participants in this fiscal legerdemain, collecting handsome fees for underwriting the ever larger borrowing needs, they got cold feet in the summer of 1974 as they realized what impact soaring interest rates and the Nixon budget would have on New York's finances.

The *coup de grâce* came in February of 1975, when the Urban Development Corporation (the New York State housing authority) defaulted on its notes, in large measure because of the

Nixon administration's impounding of Section 236 monies. The UDC default was the first by a major state authority since the Depression. The bond market went into shock. Within days, the bond markets were closed to New York City, and other Northern city and state securities were being eyed warily.

In June of 1975, Representative Benjamin Rosenthal of New York held hearings on the New York crisis. George Mitchell, Vice-Chairman of the Board of Governors of the Federal Reserve, admitted that the Federal Reserve System had the legal authority to make loans to New York, but he denied that the city met its criteria that the bankruptcy "would have a significant detrimental economic and financial impact on the surrounding area, the region or the nation."

In his testimony before Rosenthal's committee, Secretary Simon explained that the President and his advisors were opposed to aid to New York City because a New York default would not severely impact securities markets or the municipal bond markets, and because default could easily be weathered by the major banks. Nor were they concerned that a default would seriously affect public confidence nationally. Although New York City "would suffer severe harm," the administration felt that default for New York City was the best solution to get New York and other cities back on the track of fiscal responsibility. The administration, Federal Reserve Chairman Arthur Burns, and Treasury Secretary William Simon asserted that a New York City bankruptcy would be good for the moral fiber of the country. They assured the nation that default by New York would have little effect on the rest of the nation.

As Paul Dubrul and Jack Newfield concluded in their book, *The Abuse of Power:*

> *The city, in the minds of Arthur Burns and William Simon, had to be punished. Burns and Simon saw New York City as a guinea pig, whose death in an ideological test tube would prove, scientifically, that liberalism is a failure.*[1]

In October of 1975, President Ford vowed, "I can tell you—and tell you now—that I am prepared to veto any bill that has as its purpose a federal bailout of New York City to prevent default." The New York *Daily News* succinctly summarized the Administration's position in a classic banner headline: FORD TO CITY: DROP DEAD.

On October 17 New York almost defaulted, until Albert Shanker, president of the United Federation of Teachers, bailed it out late in the afternoon by buying bonds with his union's pension fund. In New York, the municipal unions' pension funds, not the banks, became the major source of emergency financing. (By the end of 1976, the union pension funds held $3.8 billion of city debt, almost 40 percent of their total assets.) A federal law had to be passed to allow the unions to violate federal pension reform legislation that prohibited pension funds from investing more than 10 percent of their assets in the securities of any one issuer.

Early in November of 1975, Governor Hugh Carey called a special session of the legislature to increase taxes, increase employees' contribution to pensions, and declare a moratorium on $1.6 billion of New York City's outstanding notes. Noteholders would be paid interest, but not principal, on their investments. They could exchange the notes for long-term, higher-interest Municipal Assistance Corporation bonds or hope that they could cash in the original short term notes at the end of the city's three year recovery period, in 1978.

New York had defaulted, although it was agreed that it would not be called a default, so that the banks would not have to write off their holdings of New York securities as losses, an action which would have depleted the capital of a number of banks. In return for the state's actions, President Ford agreed that the federal government would make seasonal loans of $2.3 billion to the city to finance its day-to-day needs. An interest rate one percent higher than the rate paid by the federal government for these funds would be charged.

Although they had neither rushed to the city's aid when it was most in need nor provided prudent fiscal advice in prior years, the banks received rewards after the debacle in New York City in the form of increased leverage to legislate their social priorities. As Jack Newfield and Paul Dubrul wrote in their book about the New York City default, *The Abuse of Power:*

*The tragedy was that Beame's abdication was the justification for the bankers taking over. The bankers did not exactly seize power; there was a vacuum, and they rushed to fill it. Wriston, Rockefeller and Rohatyn used New York City's fiscal crisis as a cover to do what the bankers wanted—kill free tuition, freeze wages, raise the subway fare...But it was difficult for reasonable people to oppose the creation of MAC, and later EFCB*

*[Emergency Financial Control Board], because Beame was not functioning. His personal default of leadership allowed the permanent government to arrange a coup that looked like salvation.*[2]

What is most surprising in this whole affair is that no one was indicted for perpetrating an enormous swindle on the investing public. The Securities and Exchange Commission's *Report on Transactions in Securities of The City of New York* assesses culpability on every player. The report concludes that:

> *The City employed budgetary, accounting and financing practices which it knew distorted its true financial picture...*
> *For example, on October 1, 1974, a consultant to City Comptroller Golden prepared an internal memorandum, stating in part:*
> *To balance the expense budget, the city employs a series of unusual budgeting and accounting practices including carrying forward bogus receivables, levying taxes on City-owned property...[and] overestimation of revenues...*
> *In sum, the Mayor and the Comptroller misled public investors in the offer, sale and distribution of billions of dollars of the City's municipal securities from October, 1974, through at least March, 1975.*[3]

In classic understatement, the SEC report documents that the financial institutions which regularly served as underwriters for the city—Chase Manhattan, Citibank, Morgan Guaranty, Manufacturers Hanover, Bankers Trust, Merrill Lynch, and Chemical Bank—failed to fulfill their responsibilities to the investing public. These giants of the financial system, between October of 1974 and April of 1975, sold $4 billion of

> *...city notes to the public as safe and secure investments without disclosure of significant risks.* At the same time, certain of the underwriters were in the process of reducing or eliminating their holdings of the notes...
> *Whatever reasons led the underwriters to market the City's securities without adequate disclosure, their conduct cannot be justified under the federal securities laws.*[4]

Federal laws prohibit underwriters from selling securities out of their own portfolio at the same time that they are marketing an issue. The SEC staff report surmises that the refusal of the New York banks to buy any more city securities for their own accounts played a role in the saturation of the market. Thus the report concludes:

> *During the October 1974 to February 1975 period, the underwriters' concern over the saturation of the marketplace increased significantly. This concern was based on the rapid escalation in the amount of City note issuances,* combined with the narrowing of the market for City securities, resulting, in part, from the inability or unwillingness of financial institutions, including the underwriters, to absorb additional City paper.[5]

The SEC report also concluded that the rating agencies had been derelict:

> *Based upon the record of this investigation, it appears that both Moody's and S&P failed, in a number of respects, to make either diligent inquiry into data which called for further investigation, or to adjust their ratings of the City's securities based on known data in a manner consistent with standards upon which prior ratings had been based.*[6]

What distinguishes this group from others who have violated the securities laws and gone to prison for it? They were dealing with municipal securities, not corporate issues; therefore they were operating in an area in which the Securities and Exchange Commission does not have jurisdiction, in which none of the federal disclosure requirements enacted after the financial disaster of the 1930s apply.

This obvious gap in the securities laws has not been closed. Successive congressional attempts to bring municipal securities under the same standards of public disclosure that apply to corporate securities have been defeated. Local officials have argued that it would be too burdensome for them to disclose all.

And while the debate over these standards goes on, other cities and states have learned the lessons of depending on banks for their access to capital. Consider the cases of the city of Boston, the Commonwealth of Massachusetts, and the city of Cleveland.

### Boston Tried to Dip Into the Pension Funds

Boston's mayor, Kevin White, was up for re-election in November of 1975, and the last thing he wanted to do was raise taxes before the election. Instead, he covered the city's budget deficit by issuing "tax anticipation" notes. As the name suggests, these notes are issued in anticipation of projected tax receipts. They are a legitimate fiscal device for evening out the cycle between discrete tax-due dates and continuous expenditures. In 1975, however, White was not smoothing out Boston's fiscal cycle; he was issuing these notes to cover a budget deficit and to forestall raising taxes until after his re-election. The banks became nervous about buying these notes as it became clearer that there were insufficient tax receipts to cover them. But the banks—which held more than $40 million of notes—felt cornered. If they didn't buy the new issue, who would?

One alternative was to sell the city's notes to the municipal pension funds. The trustees of the municipal pension funds were hardly eager to go along. Since pension funds are tax-exempt, their trustees' purchase of lower-yield tax-exempt securities rather than higher-yielding taxable corporate issues could raise conflict of interest charges that might send them to jail.

The trustees for the Boston Municipal Pension Funds asked the Retirement Law Commission to issue a ruling on the legality of such a purchase. The Commission decided to ask the Insurance Commissioner, James Stone for an opinion. As insurance commissioner, Stone was the auditor for the Commonwealth's state and municipal pension funds; in this capacity, he wrote back that such purchases would be illegal because they violated the purposes for which the pension fund was created. Stone reasoned that if the city's pledge to pay had been sufficient guarantee for city employees, then there would have been no need to actually have a pension fund. Since funding was mandated by law, that implied that security beyond the city's pledge to pay was warranted. Funding the city's pension fund with other city pledges to pay— that is, investing in municipal debt issues—clearly violated the point of requiring that moneys be set aside for pension liabilities.

As one of the three trustees of the state pension fund, I soon found myself lunching at a major Boston bank. For two hours, a senior bank officer patiently advised me why it was appropriate for the state pension funds to bail out Boston. There were no threats, just counsel. Lunch was interrupted by a phone call for me from Dan Taylor, the governor's legal counsel, who told me that that bank's president had left the governor's office at noon. He had told Governor Dukakis that if the state pension funds did not buy any Boston paper that Thursday, his bank would not roll over its note holdings on Friday, and the city of Boston would be forced into default. He had pointed out that the state's credit was tied to the city's, and a city default would force the state into default. The governor wanted to talk to me that afternoon.

I returned to the luncheon angry. The atmosphere at the table changed abruptly. The banker said that Taylor's account was accurate. "You've got forty million dollars to lose," I pointed out. He rose, stiffly answered that he planned "to cut his losses," and strode out of the room.

Secretary of Administration and Finance, John Buckley, Insurance Commissioner, James Stone, and Jim Bailey, the governor's special advisor on debt management, were waiting for me at the State House. They wanted to know what I intended to do. In a rather constrained manner, I explained my objections to using the state's pension funds to bail out the city. I believed that using the pension funds in this manner was opening a Pandora's box—it would be just that more difficult to achieve fiscal integrity if the pension funds could always be dipped into to stave off the unpopular step of raising taxes. I also argued that using the pension funds would tie Massachusetts closer to New York and would scare away out-of-state investors, who would know that independent judgment wasn't being used. No fiduciary of a tax exempt fund would buy a tax exempt security. If the state did so, it would signal to the market that prudent and decent standards were being violated.

The room remained quiet. When Dukakis called from Vermont, where he was attending a governors' conference, he simply said, "Carol, do whatever you think is right." Then he hung up.

Buckley shrugged his shoulders and walked out. Taylor said, "There's a four o'clock meeting with the other two trustees of the state pension fund. You'd better tell them your decision."

At 4:00 P.M., I walked into the wood-paneled office of State Treasurer Crane, another trustee, and without sitting down announced that I would not vote to authorize the pension funds to buy either the city's or the state's notes or bonds. The public trustee, Alan Fulkerson, said he wanted to be helpful, but that he would vote with me.

Crane asked me if I would repeat publicly what I had just said. I said, "Sure," and Crane responded that he would call a meeting of leaders of the financial community for the next morning to hear the trustees' decision. Then, looking pointedly at me, Crane said, "You're voting first. And I'm voting any way you do." And, he did.

I announced our decision the next morning, getting an

angry response from the Mayor; the discussion was turned over to the bankers, all of whom advised that the use of the pension funds was the only way to save the city and the state and that they could not buy any more as fiduciaries themselves unless the pension funds did. As the meeting drew to an unresolved close, Joe Lombard, a partner in Salomon Brothers, was the only one to speak in my favor. He agreed that if the city and state pension funds bought Boston's paper, Massachusetts would be closed out of the markets; it would be a signal that things were very bad indeed.

On the following days, the Boston banks rolled over their holdings of Boston's paper and the city's savings banks emerged from a breakfast meeting with the Mayor having pledged to take a substantial chunk of new note offerings. When I asked how White had been able to get such an agreement, one banker told me that banks owned a lot of property in Boston and that everyone knew the tax assessor had great leeway.

Mayor White was re-elected. Soon after, Boston's tax rate was hiked 25 percent. The sewage and water department was spun off into a separate commission outside the city's budget, which then levied charges to cover its $25 million deficit.

### Massachusetts Near the Brink

When Michael Dukakis was elected governor of Massachusetts in November of 1974, he inherited a state budget that had almost as many gimmicks as John Lindsay's. Dukakis had promised during his campaign, that he would levy no new taxes, and he resolutely tried to keep that pledge through the spring of 1975.

David Bartley, then the Democratic Speaker of the Massachusetts House, offered in December of 1974 to call a special session of the legislature to pass an emergency tax package, to balance the budget while making sure the new taxes would be clearly identified with the outgoing Republican Governor, Frank Sargent. Bartley was offerring a precious gift to Dukakis—to pass the tax increase before Dukakis assumed office—but Dukakis turned him down. He did not realize the magnitude of the budget problem, and he wanted to study it. Like everyone else, he thought that if there was a deficit, it was in the range of $100–$150 million, and that it could easily be taken care of by a bright, thrifty manager like himself.

No one knew at that time what fiscal chaos the previous

administration had created. The Welfare Department had been piling up payables in shoe boxes, including bills that went back six years. There was no accounting system in place that let anyone know the magnitude of the situation. The state had simply not recorded $90 million of bills to vendors and local governments. It could only estimate that it employed between 60,000 and 90,000 people; it could not come closer because personnel files were neither centralized nor computerized.

During Governor Sargent's tenure (1969–1974) the state's expenditures skyrocketed from $1.4 billion to $3.3 billion. Much of the jump was due to the state's assumption, in 1968, of local government's share of welfare, and the passage of Medicaid legislation. Edward Moscovitch, Deputy Commissioner for Fiscal Affairs during the Sargent administration, described agency heads as spending what they wanted despite the appropriations in the budget. Financial accountability was an all but alien idea.

Tax receipts were also falling much faster than anyone could have predicted in the fall of 1974. The economy was heading into the worst downturn since the Depression; the Arabs were embargoing oil. Massive layoffs cut incomes and purchasing power, reducing projected income-tax revenues and sales-tax receipts. State-funded unemployment-compensation payments rose with the state's unemployment rate, which finally reached 14 percent.

Early in the spring of 1975, just a few months after being inaugurated as governor, Dukakis was confronted with a pending budget deficit of as much as half a billion dollars for fiscal 1975, and of $650 million for 1976—rather astounding amounts for a state budget of only $3 billion.

The Governor's fiscal crisis soon translated into a debt-funding crisis. While Massachusetts securities are nationally traded, and the state is not confined to a local investor market, the state must obtain offers from a handful of underwriting syndicates, generally comprising New York commercial banks and investment houses, to issue new notes and bonds. The state belatedly discovered its dependence on the First National Bank of Boston. If the First refused to participate in underwriting a state debt issue, the New York banks would not do so either. In that case the state would find itself without access to any market for capital, and have no alternative but to use its own cash to avoid default. Without access to the market for debt financing, the state hovered on the brink of bankruptcy.

### The Fiscal Crisis, 1975

When the size of the fiscal 1975 budget deficit became known, the First National Bank of Boston, the state's largest bank and long-standing spokesman for the business community in matters of state tax policy, recommended that the state's sales tax be doubled and social service expenditures slashed as the first prerequisite for financing the needed debt issues.[7]

At this point, Dukakis was faced with a fiscal crisis which arose from a shortfall between expenditures and revenues as the economy sank into the steepest recession in forty years. The groundwork for the debt crisis was laid as the end of the fiscal year approached, and the governor was forced to resort to selling bonds to cover the estimated budget deficit of $450 million. As a condition of this issue, new excise taxes of $90 million a year were passed and earmarked for repayment of this debt. This funding of a current account deficit with five year notes was accepted because it was seen as tying up all the old bad practices and letting the state start with a clean slate and a balanced budget.

Though placed out for competitive bid, in June 1975, the $450 million was too large to have more than one syndicate bid on it. So actually there was no competitive bidding; there was only one bid, and that one was not negotiated. The state was faced with a take-it-or-leave-it offer from the First.

The prospectus for the note issue to fund the fiscal 1975 budget deficit had clearly implied that future state budgets would be balanced. The financial community was understandably angered when two weeks after the $450 million note issue, Administration and Finance Secretary Buckley issued the fiscal 1976 budget, which was more heavily in deficit than the last one had been.

For the next five months, there followed a heated debate between the governor and the legislative leadership over how taxes should be raised and expenditures slashed in order to balance the budget for the coming fiscal year. While the debate raged, the state ran on monthly budgets based on previous year's appropriations, and the deficit grew. The denouement of the fiscal crisis was a budget which enacted the tax-expenditure program initially outlined by the First National Bank, and a debt crisis.

### The Housing Authority Debt Crisis

Two months after the state's deficit note issue, one of its independent authorities, the Massachusetts Housing Finance Agency

(MHFA) encountered serious difficulty in marketing its short-term notes. In August of 1975, MHFA withdrew an issue when the Executive Director learned how high the bid rates were to be; the hope was that the market would improve by September. Because of the UDC-New York crises, the market deteriorated further, and emergency legislation had to be enacted giving the state's guarantee to $500 million of MHFA debt. MHFA notes were then privately placed through a syndicate led by the First.

The legislature did not understand why the state had to guarantee the MHFA debt. The Housing Authority was after all, an independent agency. Yes, it was backed by the state's "moral obligation," but when the members had been sold on MHFA, in the 1960s, it had been on the clear understanding that the debt was to be self-liquidating, paid off from the income of its housing projects, and that the credit of MHFA would not be tied to the credit of the state. Were the members of the legislature now being tricked?

The bankers, Frank Morris, the President of the Federal Reserve Bank of Boston, and I spent endless frantic hours explaining to legislators and the House and Senate leadership that if the MHFA went bankrupt the state's rating would be undermined; that to the markets, there was no difference between a moral obligation and a general obligation when the chips were down. Our message was that to save the state's rating, the legislature had to guarantee the MHFA notes. The legislature complied, but not gladly. Immediately thereafter, with this additional indebtedness tied to the state's current obligations and the projected deficit in the fiscal 1976 budget, Moody's dropped its rating of Massachusetts from Aa to A. The legislature was angry and baffled.

The crisis atmosphere continued in October, with the state's general obligation note issues for local public housing authorities. On the advice of advisory committees composed of Boston bankers, the Massachusetts Housing Finance Authority and the local authorities had for years been paying for housing projects with nine-month notes. During the debt funding crisis, when the Governor's office basically took over the functioning of the Treasurer's office and hired a financial whiz kid, Jim Bailey, the issue was finally raised: Can we afford to finance forty-year loans to housing authorities on a year-to-year basis?

In mid-October of 1975, the Financial Advisory Board advised the state Treasurer that the scheduled $131 million sale of local housing authority notes could only be marketed through a negotiated sale to a syndicate composed of all the normally competing underwriting groups. The Advisory Board, led by the

First, insisted that the market had so deteriorated that the usual competitive bid and public sale of these notes could not be accomplished.

With a $110 million issue to finance the annual operating deficit of the Massachusetts Bay Transportation Authority (MBTA) pending, state officials' concern mounted. Ultimately one of the investment houses consulted by the Governor's office, Kidder Peabody, agreed to assume underwriting responsibility for the MBTA issue. Much to the dismay of state officials, Kidder was able to sell only $25 million in notes, and the state had to repurchase the remaining $85 million through the State Treasurer. To boot, the state had to pay Kidder a brokerage commission on the sales to itself!

The inability of the state to go into the market during this period stemmed not only from deteriorating investor confidence in municipals generally, as a result of New York's debt crisis, but from the deadlock between the Governor and the legislature in enacting the budget for fiscal year 1976, which was now four months overdue.

### Tender Loving Clutches

In the panic atmosphere gripping the municipal bond markets, the First assumed a role of crucial importance to the state: The bank had to be part of an underwriting syndicate if any investor outside of Massachusetts was to buy the state's securities. The first question to be asked by the municipal bond desk at Bank of America, or at any New York bank or insurance company would be, "How much is the First taking?" And if the answer to that question was none, then the issue was unsaleable. If the First wasn't in, the assumption was, something must be wrong.

The state found itself in the position faced by every small-town businessman who is truly a captive of his local banker. If this small businessman were to seek financing at an out-of-area bank, the first question would be, "Why isn't your local bank making the loan?" and the first phone call would be to the local bank. Similarly, the first phone call the high-paid analysts would make would be to the First.

State Senator Chester G. Atkins, a member of the governor's task force on debt management, wrote in a January 1976 piece in *The Boston Globe* ("Banks Gain Critical Power Over State Bonds"):

*There used to be three co-equal branches of government. Now there are four.*

*Once, when a new proposal was aired, three questions were asked. First, is it legal? Will the courts uphold its constitutionality?*

*Second, is it politically feasible? Can the idea make it through the state Legislature?*

*Third, will the Governor approve?*

*Now there appears to be an additional branch of government, one that is anonymous, unelected, and unaccountable—the multinational commercial banks. We must now also ask if those financial institutions will provide the government access to funds, through the bond markets, to finance the proposal.*

To Dukakis' great credit, the banks and insurance companies, who kept trying to use the debt crisis as a means of getting other things that they wanted which were not related to the state's financial picture, were largely unsuccessful. The banks wanted the bank commissioner fired; the insurance companies wanted the insurance commissioner fired. They wanted the state pension funds used to buy the state's bonds. They wanted tax concessions.

During January of 1976, those on the governor's staff assigned to work with the Advisory Committee on debt management directed most of their efforts to dealing with the $500 million in local housing authority notes which needed to be rolled over in the coming year. The timing of these note issues was seen as critical. In April, New York was scheduled to issue almost $4 billion in notes, $800 million of which was essential to prevent New York City from defaulting. Some debt underwriters and investors were concerned that the bottom might fall out of the market altogether.

The situation had worsened since the MHFA and MBTA note issues, when the State Treasurer and some state agencies had purchased the unsold portions of publicly marketed debt. Now none of these sources had sufficient surplus funds. Thus, it would be necessary to sell this full new amount in the private sector.

The Boston banks maintained that the fiscal uncertainty of the state made its debt unmarketable, but at least two New York investment houses, Salomon Brothers and Goldman Sachs, each contended that a Massachusetts bond issue could be successfully sold to private investors. In January, Salomon Brothers proposed that while only $137 million of these notes had to be rolled over in

March, the full $543 million should be financed with a long-term bond issue. Salomon Brothers and the governor's staff set about developing a plan for refinancing the maturing short-term debt of the Commonwealth and its agencies. On January 24, this plan was forwarded to the governor for his review as "the best, and perhaps the only chance of avoiding default."[8]

In mid-February, Governor Dukakis submitted the legislation needed to offer the restructured debt issue. The Emergency Debt Restructuring Act was enacted several weeks later, just days before $137 million in public housing notes came due and the administration had to issue 25-year bonds for all of the $543 million outstanding housing authority debt, which could only be done under this new legislation.

The week that ensued was utter chaos. With less than a week to go, little of the $543 million issue had been sold. At a special meeting of the partners at Salomon Brothers, the firm committed $100 million of its $164 million in capital to swallow the remainder of the issue if necessary.

Salomon Brothers and Merrill Lynch sold the issue in small packages to non-institutional investors through a retail network. Dan Taylor later recalled, "I don't know how they did it, but within twenty-four hours the whole issue was sold and even I was getting calls from brokers asking for a bigger piece and crying on my shoulder, 'They won't give me any more.'" Dan asked them, "Where were you a month ago?" and got the response, "I didn't understand the package then." The issue was so hot that Salomon was able to cut the usual ½ point commission to brokers to ¼ point and kept the difference for itself.

The picture went from probable failure to being oversold in a matter of hours. As soon as it became clear that John Hancock and the Prudential and some other big buyers were taking a piece and that the first $135 million had been sold (the amount needed to avoid immediate default), it became a hot issue. It became clear it was going to go, and it became the hottest issue around. But earlier in the week, at the underwriters meeting, when Salomon Brothers went around the room assigning shares—"You said you would take fifty"—the brokers would say, "Oh, I can't do that. Give me five."

After the bond sale, much criticism was directed at the extraordinary interest rate of 9.04 percent paid by the state on this issue, subsequently named the "Mass 9's." Despite a drop in interest rates and the improved market for Massachusetts debt soon after, the state could not recall the bonds for eleven years, and even then could do so only by paying a 4% premium.[9] The price was very high but after two unsuccessful note issues, the MBTA in December and the MHFA in January, the state could not afford another failure. Salomon Brothers was the first to approach the state with a "can do" proposal. Moreover, Salomon Brothers, unlike the underwriters on the two previous issues, was able to get the First National Bank of Boston to serve as a joint managing underwriter on the issue, thus bringing the bank into openly sanctioning the issue as a sound investment. As one observer of the crisis wrote, "In a market where institutional clout and word of mouth are paramount, this maneuver was seen as key, if not essential, to the viability of that issue."[10]

What is most striking about the Massachusetts story is just how dependent on a single commercial bank a government can be. For states like Massachusetts, which generally have access to capital markets, this dependency is largely limited to crisis situations, but for many cities and towns whose debt issues are not recognized and traded nationally, it is now the normal state of affairs. This sort of "normality" cannot be tolerated; it offers banks far too much influence over governmental policy. The story of Cleveland's default indicates how far banks will go to maintain that influence.

### Cleveland and the Power Brokers

On December 15, 1978, Cleveland was forced to default on $15.5 million in city notes when the city's six leading banks refused to renew them. A congressional staff report on "The Role of Commercial Banks in the Finances of the City of Cleveland" concluded:

> *The interlocking relationship of Cleveland Trust Company and some of the other banks with much of the corporate community, and the deep animosities and political cross-currents in which some bank officers became involved suggest the strong possibility that factors, other than pure hard-nosed credit judgments, entered the picture. At a minimum, it is impossible to conclude that key bankers donned green eye shades, locked themselves in their board rooms, and made dispassionate decisions based solely on computer runs.*[11]

Cleveland is unique only in that the conflict of corporate power versus elected government became so open; usually these diffi-

culties get worked out in private. The open warfare between a
populist mayor and a conservative corporate class over how the
city's resources were to be used throws into stark relief the power
that the banks exercise in every American city.

"Cleveland's powerful corporate community has been accustomed to getting what it wants from City Hall," wrote one
Cleveland observer.[12] Despite the perilously shrinking tax base and
the critical fiscal problems this was creating for Cleveland, corporate interests continued to insist on receiving millions of dollars in
tax abatements for new buildings. National City Bank, one of the
nation's most profitable, and one which would refuse to refinance
its $4 million holdings of city notes in December of 1978, de-
manded and obtained in 1977 a $14 million tax abatement—almost
enough money for the city to have paid off all of the $15.5 million
outstanding in city notes.[13] Mayor Kucinich's refusal to issue any
new tax abatements for banks or corporate giants angered the city's
business establishment.

A major test of power between the mayor and his blue-
collar constituency on one side and the banking community on the
other was over the sale of the city's municipal electric system to a
private power company, Cleveland Electric Illuminating Company
(CEI). The sale of the municipal electric system was supported by
the banks as a means of cutting the drain on the city's funds to
cover the utility's deficits. The municipal electric system has had,
however, considerable value as a symbol of opposition to corporate
power among Cleveland's working class voters. It was an earlier
mayor of Cleveland—populist Tom L. Johnson, who served from
1901 to 1909—who gave this opposition its most ringing statement:
"I believe in municipal ownership of all public-service monopolies
... because if you do not own them, they will in time own you.
They will rule your politics, corrupt your institutions and finally
destroy your liberties."

The animosity felt by the bankers toward the Mayor may
also have played a role in their support for the sale of the utility.
Defeating Kucinich in a fight involving one of his major political
stands—a promise not to sell the municipal electric system—
would at the least make him look foolish, and it might even
alienate his working-class power base.

Corporate leaders were openly bitter about Kucinich's
challenge to their authority. They had bankrolled an unsuccessful
attempt to recall the mayor. That failed narrowly. Financing the
city's debt was the perfect handle to embarrass the mayor and to

destroy him politically. As Brock Weir, President of Cleveland Trust, told the *Cleveland Plain Dealer*, "We had been kicked in the teeth for six months. On December 15, we decided to kick back."[14]

The city's reliance on Cleveland's banks to buy its debt issues gave the banks the leverage they needed. According to Mayor Kucinich, Cleveland Trust Company made the bank's refinancing of the city's notes contingent on the sale of the municipal power company to CEI. The bank has vigorously denied the mayor's charges.

For six months prior to the default, Cleveland Trust refused to roll over a series of city notes, forcing the city to refinance them by dipping into other city funds. Cleveland Trust appeared to be betting that the mayor would have to give in at the last second and sell the city power system to avert a politically crushing default. If he didn't, the banks would have accomplished their political goals—to get rid of Kucinich.

Bankers have this kind of political power in large part because of city and state governments' almost total dependence on their local banks for access to the capital markets. Reform of the municipal debt markets is critical to lessening the banks' political power. It's time we began that reform.

### The Breakdown of the Market

The market for state and municipal bonds is made up of banks and of certain corporations and wealthy individuals seeking to shelter their incomes from taxes. Constitutionally, different levels of government cannot tax one another's financial instruments, and this escape from some portion of taxation is the major attraction of these instruments. The attraction should not be underestimated: For someone in the 50 percent bracket, for example, a tax-free bond paying 8 percent is the investment equivalent of a 16 percent taxable corporate bond.

Until recently, the largest purchasers of "municipals," as the bonds are called, have been commercial banks and, to a lesser degree, the casualty-insurance companies. Wealthy individuals are the third major participants in the market. Between the late 1940s and the 1970s, as state and local governments required more and more funds, banks played a growing role in their financial arrangements.

Quite aside from the purchase of municipals, banks have found tax shelters in foreign operations and in equipment leasing.

In recent years, more than half the profits of the largest banks have come from operations in foreign countries, and taxes paid in those countries can be deducted dollar-for-dollar from U.S. tax liabilities. Moreover, the banks have learned to use their holding companies to take advantage of depreciation and investment tax credits allowed by Congress to encourage capital spending: They lease high-cost machinery, especially computers, to other businesses. It is this sort of change that has produced the decline in effective tax rates paid by the bank over the last two decades. And with that decline has come a decrease in the advantage to be gained from investment in state and local debt.

### Broadening the Market

Part of the reason there are so few non-institutional buyers for these notes is that they come with minimum denominations like $25,000 or $10,000 or (occasionally) $5,000. Banks and securities dealers have opposed lowering these minimums because, they say, administrative costs would be vastly increased if more smaller purchasers had to be accommodated. In fact, such higher costs might well be offset if, as seems likely, interest rates could be lowered without making the notes less attractive to this broader market. Of course, banks have a more direct motive for opposing the lower minimums: Any opportunity for moderate- and middle-income investors to earn municipal-bond rates would threaten the banks' vast holdings of these investors' funds, in the form of the savings accounts for which the friendly bank regulators set conveniently low interest rates. These smaller investors were given one break in the Tax Reform Act of 1976, which allowed mutual funds to invest in municipals for the first time.

For generations, on the other hand, tax reformers have in fact been campaigning for an end to all tax exemptions on municipals. The visible tax inequity involved in wealthy individuals' paying little or no taxes on incomes derived from "clipping coupons" from tax-exempt bonds has long enraged wage-earners. In fact, though, there may be much more to the idea than equity. Fully taxable municipals underwritten by federal interest subsidies could expand the market for debt issues, bringing in much-needed new capital, while, taking account of the financial needs of state and local governments.

Such taxable bonds would, of course, have to carry higher interest rates in order to attract buyers. But they might not actually raise issuing governments' costs, if the higher rates were subsidized by the federal government. In turn, the cost of this subsidy could be offset by the additional tax receipts: It is estimated that the Treasury currently loses $1.40 for every $1 saved by municipalities. A direct subsidy might actually save money at both levels of government.

While taxable bonds would have to pay higher yields, this increase would be modified if they opened up a market for municipals among tax-free institutions, whose fiduciaries now have no motive for purchasing tax-free bonds. Specifically, taxable, high-yield bonds would end the isolation of the municipals from the largest and fastest-growing sector of the bond-buying market, the pension funds. No longer would pension-fund trustees reject municipal bonds out of hand. Moreover, the very existence of the taxable-bond option would reduce the number of tax-exempts on the market, therefore making the remaining ones more attractive.

Opposition to these proposals comes primarily from municipalities who fear dependency on a federal subsidy that might be withdrawn by some future Congress. They also fear federal intervention in the use of funds raised if in fact the bonds bore a direct federal subsidy. Investment bankers are also opposed because a simpler market might put them out of business.

If state and local governments are to be able to obtain their fair share of capital flows without giving up crucial political clout to bankers, they must be able to issue securities that will appeal to all sectors of the bond-buying public—and, in particular, to the pension funds. With the option of moving into the broader taxable market, state and local governments would find themselves much less dependent on commercial banks.

Along with making state and local debt offerings taxable, the market should be broadened by lowering the minimum purchase so that average investors can purchase municipals. If state and local debt were sold in $1,000 denominations, as corporate bonds are, many more people could invest in them. State and local bonds, as well as U.S. Treasury securities, could be issued at terms—rates, denominations, and maturities—which would make them attractive to the average citizen. If commercial banks have found it economical to offer so-called minibonds in maturities as short as two years and denominations as small as $100, it is difficult to believe that state and local government issues could not also be so marketed. In fact, Massachusetts in 1979 experimented with such sales which were bought out in a matter of hours. As underwriters of state and local securities, the banks have opposed these ideas for broadening the demand for municipal securities, because this would undermine the crucial political and economic leverage they hold over state and local governments.

### Where Was the Lender of Last Resort?

The final reform which would ensure the viability of the state and local bond markets, freeing state and local governments from dependence on the local banker, would be for the Federal Reserve System to include state and local issues among the vast amount of securities that the Fed regularly buys and sells as part of the conduct of monetary policy.

The Federal Reserve affects interest rates and the supply of money in the economy by purchasing (or selling) daily U.S. Treasury securities. To raise interest rates and slow money growth, the Fed enters the market and sells Treasury securities. Buyers of these securities pay with money. The Fed, unlike a private seller, does not place this money in a bank and thus back into the system; it takes the money out of circulation, and—presto—the money supply is reduced. To increase the money supply, the Fed performs the opposite operation: it buys Treasury bills and places newly created money in the hands of the public. To increase or decrease the money supply, of course, the Fed could buy or sell anything— chickens, wheat, stocks, or state and local bonds. The advantage of Treasury notes over the first two is that they don't spoil or die. There is always a market for them and a plentiful supply. A major side benefit is that the U.S. Treasury never has to worry, as New York and Massachusetts do, that their debt issues will find no buyers. The Fed is the lender of last resort.

The Fed could play the same role for state and local governments if it chose to do so. There is no law which bars the Fed from purchasing state and local debt issues. It has been the Fed's choice to limit its activities to buying and selling only short-term U.S. Government securities—and not state and local issues. If one is a believer in perfect capital markets, as the Governors of the Federal Reserve are, these policy distinctions make little sense: If the market really is perfect, then any change in the interest rate on one type of security will be quickly translated into changes in other rates. As free market believers, the Federal Reserve itself argues that it does not matter which debt instruments it buys; the important point is how much money it pumps into the economy.

This would be true if capital markets were perfect, but as the crisis in the state and local bond markets of 1975–1976 showed, this is not true. The Federal Reserve's argument should be stood on its head: If it does not matter what the Fed buys, let the Fed buy only state debt issues and let the free market filter the funds throughout the market to federal issues, rather than vice versa. Or we could compromise, and the Fed could buy all kinds of government issues.

This point was raised by Representative Rosenthal of New York when his Congressional Committee held hearings on the New York crisis. George Mitchell, vice-chairman of the Board of Governors, admitted that the Federal Reserve system had the power to make loans to the city. But as we've seen, he denied that the city met the emergency lending criteria (that is, that its bankruptcy "would have a significant detrimental economic and financial impact on the surrounding area, the region or the nation.")

Governor Dukakis and I raised a similar point during a luncheon discussion with Arthur Burns, then chairman of the Federal Reserve Board, in August of 1975. We tried to persuade him that the Fed should purchase a portion of states' debt issues in time of economic crisis. The Fed refused to budge from its position of "neutrality."

# II
# YOUR MONEY, THEIR POWER

"Sure we have mortgage money. It's just that you can't have any."

# 4.

# Banks Are Dangerous To Your Wealth

"We pay the highest interest rate allowed by law."

This message has been brought to you over the years by virtually every bank and thrift institution in America. Understandably, no bank ad man in the land can refrain from assuring potential customers the highest legal interest rate. The phrase not only seems to promise the customer that no one can do any better, it also suggests, however subtly, that the bank being trumpeted is on the front lines, battling bravely against the government, the "law," to provide its depositors with every possible advantage. Neither implication could be further from the truth.

To begin with, people of above average means who have savings of $10,000 and who can afford to leave the money in the bank for periods of six months or longer *are* doing better. They, of course, don't put their money into passbook savings accounts. Why should they? Right now, the "highest interest rate allowed by law" in a regular savings account at a thrift institution is 5½ percent. Inflation, in 1980, was running at an annual rate of 18 percent. Who would invest his money at 5½ percent? Only those whose savings were too limited to allow them to take advantage of the more lucrative options the law has provided for the well-heeled. The "little guy" has been stuck with a system that year in and year out robs him of purchasing power. If the ads came right out and promised to return $90 for every $100 you left on deposit, keeping your money in a savings account would appear much less attractive.

### "Q" Is Not Just the 17th Letter of the Alphabet

The ordinary passbook savings account has been the major repository for savings of low- and middle-income individuals since the

**93**

turn of the century. Yet in the current decade of high and rising interest rates, it has become one of the least lucrative investments available. Rather than fighting for the little guy they were purport-edly established to aid, rather than waging a vigorous battle to get him a fair return on his savings, thrift institutions and those who regulate them have for years carried on a rear-guard action against virtually every effort to raise or eliminate the interest-rate ceiling on passbook savings accounts. Predictably, they have fought these regressive fights wrapped in the flag of the same little guy who is, in fact, being cheated.

They have adopted two arguments for continuing the battle. First, they maintain, bank interest rates must be regulated to prevent ruinous competition that would jeopardize the savings of the household of average means. Perhaps if banking were totally unregulated, if there were no restraints on investment policies, if there were no federal insurance to protect savers, this argument would make sense. But that is not the world of banking today. In constructing a system that protects the little guy's savings from the hazards of bank competition, the nation has made it one that systematically depletes them. From time to time, the prophets of free enterprise, of old-fashioned entrepreneurial capitalism, are heard to bemoan the lack of savings in the land, the shortage of investment capital and the resulting decline in productivity. But where is the incentive to save for a rainy day in a system that virtually guarantees that when the storm comes the financial umbrella will be smaller?

The argument that interest ceilings are necessary to pro-tect the institutions themselves turns the world on its head. When thrift institutions were established in the nineteenth century, their birth occasioned reams of rhetoric about how they would serve the little guy and give him a place to secure his money and to earn interest at the same time. Thus, many thrifts have prosaic names such as the Emigrants Savings Association, or the Working-men's Savings Bank, or they take their names from local neighbor-hoods. Legally, most of the savings and loan associations are owned by their depositors. To argue now that their depositors should effectively have their purchasing power stolen to protect the institutions is ludicrous. In the current economic climate, in which the inflation rate is far higher than the permitted interest rate on passbook savings, depositors would be better served by withdrawing their funds and spending them today rather than keeping them in the bank and earning interest for tomorrow. In the short range, at least, thrift institutions could best serve the people they were established to serve by encouraging them to make a run on the bank.

The second battle cry of the bankers is that low-interest rates on savings accounts are necessary to keep down the interest rates charged by savings banks on home mortgages. Raise the passbook rates, it is argued, and mortgage rates will explode, shattering the American dream of home ownership. It's an argument that for years has sailed smoothly through congressional hearings and meetings of bank regulators. After all, it is noted, thrift institutions provide most of the nation's home mortgages; raise the rates the banks must pay to attract depositors and, of course, they will have to raise the interest they charge on mortgages. Those on the other side of the battle have noticed that, despite the artificial ceiling on the return paid depositors, interest rates on mortgages have reached nightmare heights anyway. They might be inclined to believe that mortgage interest rates are not determined by deposit rates.

And, in fact, they are not. Deposit rate limits simply lower the cost of money to banks and raise their profits; they do not determine the rate at which they lend. Mortgage rates are largely determined by bond rates, which in turn are set by market forces. Commercial banks, savings banks, and insurance companies are free to invest their funds wherever the yield is highest. Their investment choices between high-grade bonds and mortgages keep interest rates on these investment alternatives extremely close. When bond rates rise, because of inflation or increasing demand for funds by corporate and government borrowers, all interest rates are pulled higher, including mortgage rates.

Thrifts could not push mortgage rates out of line with bond rates even if they wanted to, even if they were inclined to set "ruinous" deposit rates. If thrifts raise rates on deposits and successfully attract funds, the supply of mortgage money available for mortgage investment is increased, thus exerting a downward pressure on mortgage rates. The idea that thrifts could raise mortgage rates out of line with bond rates assumes that banks are pure monopolies. Few communities are unfortunate enough to be such captives. Instead, higher rates paid on deposits would largely come out of bank profits.

Home buyers will have noticed that in the last decade, despite the controls on interest paid on deposits, the interest rates on mortgages have fluctuated considerably—and mostly upward.

Rather than facilitating home purchases, the effect has been to make them ever more difficult. The paltry return on savings accounts encourages buyers to put their money into real estate—a home—as a hedge against inflation. That, in turn, increases the demand for housing and forces its value to rise even faster than inflation. And, of course, it puts housing even further out of the reach of the little guy saving in a passbook account to buy a house. John Tuccillo, a Georgetown University economist, explained it all nicely to the House Subcommittee on Commerce, Consumer and Monetary Affairs:

> *When you have a household that is attempting to save to buy a house, where the downpayment on the house is rising at 10 percent a year, and attempting to do so by having a savings account which is returning, say, 6 percent a year, you have a modern middle class treadmill.... Ceilings, rather than making the problem go away, are, in fact, intensifying it.*

Even from their unique perspective, one thing ought to be clear to the banking fraternity. Even if artificially low interest rates on savings could be given the credit for keeping home mortgage interest rates down, the folks who are paying the price, who are seeing the purchasing power of their savings diminished day by day, are not reaping the purported advantage. By and large, they cannot afford the housing which the "cheap" mortgages that their savings subsidize are allegedly designed to provide.

Deposit rate ceilings are no more effective in ensuring a flow of funds into housing finance than they are in containing mortgage interest rates. In fact, deposit rate controls have had the perverse effect of increasing the instability of the housing cycle by causing mortgage funds to dry up every time market interest rates rise sharply. When market interest rates rise above deposit rate ceilings, sophisticated savers take their money *out* of the banks and invest them in U.S. Treasury securities or money market funds in order to receive the higher market rates. Only the less affluent, who don't have the $10,000, or the special knowledge necessary to use these more esoteric alternatives, are left with their savings in the bank. While there is no obvious equity in the argument that savers should subsidize borrowers or bankers, the perverseness of the situation is accentuated because mortgage borrowers have, on average, substantially higher income than do depositors. Thus, the ceilings, especially those on passbook accounts, represent a regressive tax on lower-income families who tend to hold all their wealth in thrift institutions—the institutions created to help the working person.

In any event, with deposit outflows exceeding deposit inflows, thrifts must either curtail or entirely cease their mortgage lending. The deposit-rate controls have simply failed to ensure a supply of funds for home purchases. The limitation of interest paid on savings accounts was originally promoted as a protection for common citizens. It is governed by something known as Regulation Q, promulgated by the Federal Reserve Board in the 1930s. Initially, the interest-rate ceiling was set at 2.5 percent, rather adequate for the times; in the last forty-plus years, though, it has risen to an insubstantial 5¼ percent for traditional savings accounts in commercial banks. (Thrift institutions have been allowed since 1966 to pay an extra quarter point, on the theory that they can thereby attract money to be loaned out for home mortgages.)

Bankers in the 1930s argued that competition for deposits in the previous decade had led to the banking collapse and the Great Depression. So Congress set out to save the bastions of competitive capitalism from competition. It outlawed the payment of interest on checking accounts, and set its 2.5 percent ceiling on savings account interest. The Fed has carried the ball ever since. As we now know, neither Congress nor most economists understood in 1933 what had caused the Great Depression. Later scholars have clearly shown that the interest rate paid by banks for deposits had nothing to do with causing the catastrophe.

It has been suggested that the prohibition against checking account interest had less to do with concerns that the payment of interest had caused the Depression than it did with a political deal to finance the newly created Federal Deposit Insurance Corporation. In return for the banks' agreement to pay an insurance premium on deposits, the Congress legally removed the necessity to pay interest on checking accounts. To make the change politically palatable, it was presented to the public as a means of saving the people from ruinous bank competition rather than as a means of shifting the cost of insurance from banks to depositors. When more scholarly studies, especially those by Milton Friedman and Anna Schwartz, analyzed the Great Depression and began to focus on the policy mistakes of the Federal Reserve Board, whose actions had deepened and drawn out the Depression, it became convenient for the bank regulators to focus attention on the bogus issue of interest rate competition. The bankers and regulators' interests converged to create the myth of the saving grace of interest rate controls.

### Protection From the Tentacles of the Money Trust

Embracing that mythology, many congressmen support deposit-rate controls now as a way of saving small banks and thrift institutions from ruinous competition with big banks. They argue that if big banks could pay higher interest rates America would be at the mercy of a bank monopoly; only deposit interest rate controls will save us from the Money Trust. The only thing missing from their arguments is evidence. Every study of banking has shown that there are virtually no economies of scale in retail banking. A bank is not necessarily more profitable because it is larger: large banks cannot offer services at lower cost, or deposits with higher interest rates, than smaller banks. Small and medium-size banks should be able to meet any price competition from larger banks, even if rate controls are lifted.

It is true, of course, that larger banks can make multi-million-dollar loans and offer international services and provide more sophisticated trust services, but none of these are of interest to the average depositor. If a customer needs these kinds of services, he already uses one of the large wholesale banks in our large cities. Large banks offer nothing more than tellers' smiles to the average depositor. There's rarely a service offered by a large bank to the average depositor which every other bank in the city doesn't offer.

Rhode Island's Rep. Ferdinand St. Germain, (D-R.I.) chairman of the House Subcommittee on Financial Institutions, once explained it all rather bluntly:

> Let me tell you something. In the financial industry competition is a lot of hogwash.
> For example, a big bank in one market area comes up and says, "We are going to give you free checking accounts." All of a sudden all the banks follow suit. Then the big bank finds it is losing a little money on it. So they make it a $500 minimum. Next thing you know, all the others go to a $500 minimum. They do not compete. They do the same.

Rather than helping small banks, interest rate controls are actually increasing the dominance of the largest banks at the expense of smaller commercial banks and thrifts. With rates on accounts for small savers (defined as those with under $100,000) held below market rates, entrepreneurs have seized the opportunity to make a fortune by creating money market mutual funds and using pooled funds to obtain the higher rates paid by banks on large accounts. Money market funds sprang up in the 1970's as a means of getting around interest rate controls: By pooling individuals' savings, the money market funds were able to buy $100,000 bank certificates of deposit on which banks were paying market rates. These rates were often double the passbook rate.

In order to sell shares in these money market funds, the funds had to persuade the public of their total safety. The easiest way to do this was to show that the money was being placed in certificates of deposit in nationally known banks—that is, the nation's largest banks. By 1980 the money-market mutual funds had assets of $60 billion, much of it money that had been siphoned out of smaller banks and thrift institutions and, via the money market funds, deposited in the giant ones. Deposit-rate ceilings, rather than protecting the small banks from competition, had in fact increased the drawing power of the very largest banks. The giants were delighted to have the small bankers defending the present system in Congress. They stayed home, studied the mythology, and counted the money.

It is perhaps not surprising that the big bankers were able to hoodwink their smaller competitors. Nor is it surprising that bankers are, in general, rather enamored of a regulatory scheme that limits the interest they have to pay without limiting the interest they can receive, that functions to transfer wealth from low- and moderate-income families to wealthier households and bankers. What is shocking is that federal regulators, who after all are supposed to be regulating in the public interest, would countenance such a sweetheart system. What is shocking is that they would sit back and watch the interest rates available to sophisticated and moneyed savers move steadily to 8, 9, 10 percent and beyond, while keeping the earnings available to the not so affluent below six percent.

### Big Brother Says: Savings Bonds Are Good for You

U.S. savings bonds have been touted for years as an investment ideally suited to the small saver, although the Series E bond rate was a mere 4¼ percent for years, until it was raised to 5 percent in 1969. In contrast, yields over 9 percent have been available to wealthy investors who buy other types of Treasury securities in larger denominations with comparable seven-year maturities. The buyer of a savings bond has obviously been getting a very bad deal; he has in fact been losing money in the current inflationary period. Public Advocates, in a suit filed against the Treasury charging that savings bond promotions are unfair and deceptive, has put the loss to savings bond holders at $2.4 billion a year. Yet sales go on, supported by "public service" advertising featuring appeals to patriotism, and by commitments to savings bond purchases through payroll savings and "bond-a-month" plans. Even the Internal Revenue Service used to offer taxpayers the choice of taking income tax refunds in the form of savings bonds rather than cash, a sort of "pay me now *and* pay me later" scheme (now it merely uses space on the 1040 form to advertise them). In spite of inertia and the continuing promotion, many people are beginning to wake up to the fact that they can get a better return for their money elsewhere.

The Treasury Department's sensitivity about its savings bond marketing program was revealed in a notable episode in California in 1970. In an advertisement entitled "An Open Letter to Holders of U.S. Savings Bonds," the president of a small bank gave some good and straightforward advice to the local populace, suggesting the small saver might be hurt by investments in savings bonds.[1]

Because the advertisement "clearly violated" a Treasury ruling that all advertising dealing with savings bonds must be cleared by the Treasury before it appears, the bank's authorization to sell or redeem savings bonds was revoked. A Treasury spokesman described the action as "just routine" (presumably it would have taken exactly the same action if the bank had failed to get clearance for a more typical statement in praise of savings bonds). In a subsequent letter to its customers, the bank explained that "since we have been repeatedly urged by the government to sell the bonds, we felt an obligation to advise people of their comparative worth as an investment."[2] It went on to apologize to customers who wanted to cancel their bonds and offered to direct them to "less vocal" financial institutions that could still redeem them.

### Ma Bell to the Rescue

Ironically, the small saver almost got a hand from a most unexpected source: American Telephone and Telegraph, the largest private borrower in the U.S. This was a possibility that clearly would have had major repercussions; the mere prospect rocked financial markets.

Rumors began circulating in early October 1970 that AT&T was seriously considering offering "savings bonds" at the retail level as part of a program to finance approximately $7 billion in capital spending in 1971. Knowledgeable sources described the plan as involving Ma Bell "savings bonds" paying at least 6½%, available in $100 denominations, to be sold through the company's 2,000 offices nationwide (after convenient advertising in monthly bills to millions of customers.) Thus, Ma Bell, in tight financial straits, would provide the small saver with a savings alternative more desirable than anything the federal government had ever contemplated. Sidney Homer, a leading investment banker, called the plan "quite a brilliant idea," and he voiced the reasonable prediction that Ma Bell savings bonds could cause "quite a drain of capital from the bond market," particularly since individuals were (and are now) entering the bond market in unprecedented numbers.

The Treasury Department, with about $50 billion in savings bonds outstanding, took a predictably dim view of the prospect. The Department was already having trouble peddling its savings bonds and could have been hurt further by competition. Also predictably, spokesmen for the thrift institutions raised an outcry. After all, Ma Bell might start a trend. Many other corporate borrowers could try to tap the funds of small savers by offering their own savings bonds. Sears, Roebuck, large utility companies, and gas companies with stations all over the country were in particularly good positions to market competitive corporate savings bonds. There was even speculation that General Motors was considering the idea.

But Ma Bell, under pressure, shelved its plan, which could have saved it money and was perfectly within all laws and regulations. Announcing that the savings bonds plan had been dropped, a Ma Bell spokesman said:

> ...We believe that such an offer would represent a welcome opportunity for small investors and we expect to give it further consideration in our future financing. However, we have concluded that the [conventional] issue just announced is the best financing vehicle at this time...[3]

Have patience, small saver; perhaps another day.

When, in the late 1970s, Congress moved to throw a small bone to buyers of savings bonds, and approved legislation providing for bonds priced to yield 6.5 percent at maturity, it was over the objections of the Treasury. The Treasury had opposed all proposals to raise the rate paid to small investors, voicing concern about withdrawals from thrift institutions and the resultant harm to the homebuilding industry. The compromise allowed the beleaguered savings bond holder to glean a half-percent "bonus" by holding bonds to maturity (five years, ten months). Since thrift institutions are allowed to pay 6½ percent on deposits held for only two years, the "bonus" plan was clearly non-competitive. Being harmless, it moved swiftly through Congress.

As market interest rates rose rapidly in the late 1970s, more and more people realized that savings bonds were bad investments. In 1978, Americans cashed in more than they bought. It's hard to be patriotic when savers had finally figured out that their government was no Robin Hood.

Or, at least, they had begun to figure it out. The word is out on savings bonds, but less widely understood is the pattern of activity of the government's bank regulators, activity that never seems to benefit the small saver.

### Commercial Bank "Mini-bonds"—A Collectors' Item

In early 1970, a handful of aggressive commercial banks discovered and offered to the small saver a way to get around the interest rate constraints of Regulation Q: They floated capital notes and debentures in small denominations and sold them directly to customers, with no brokerage fee. When issued in small denominations, these notes and debentures—which became known in the trade as "mini-bonds" —were quite suitable, from the consumer's point of view, as substitutes for savings account deposits; moreover, since they were not legally treated as deposits, Regulation Q ceilings did not apply. At the time, federal regulations required a two-year investment in these notes but did not set any minimum denominations for them, so the little guy could play. Two banks floated subordinated notes in $100 denominations, paying 7¼ percent, with thirty-month maturities. Others offered mini-bonds at higher rates, in larger denominations and with longer maturities. Mini-bonds appeared to be on the road to success, with the small saver at last in the driver's seat. Experts on bank capital predicted that the market for the new capital instrument would grow to several billion dollars.

Once again, rumblings were soon heard from the Treasury

Department. A spokesman there said he was "concerned." It quickly appeared that the federal bank regulatory agencies were indeed worried about mini-bonds. A trade weekly, *Washington Financial Reports*, reasoned that if the agencies decided to tighten the rules on capital notes and debentures, the tightening could be accomplished either by lengthening the minimum maturity or by establishing a relatively large minimum denomination. In a very short time, the Federal Reserve announced that it would do *both*: It raised minimum maturities to five years and established a minimum denomination of $20,000. The small saver was once again forced off the road to a decent return.

### Big Banks to the Rescue, Again

In July 1974, the cause of the small saver was championed by some corporate biggies, none other than the parent holding companies of two of the nation's largest banks, Citicorp (the holding company of New York's Citibank) and Chase Manhattan Corporation. Between them, these two firms proposed to raise more than $1 billion by issuing consumer-oriented "mini-bonds," with variable rates. Several other large-bank holding companies, including that of Bank of America, were rumored to be preparing several billion dollars' worth of similar issues. These variable-rate notes provided the first large scale opportunity for small investors to put their money where only the wealthiest individuals and the institutions had gone before—corporate IOUs with floating interest rates. By no accident, the issues would give corporations which were hard-pressed to raise capital a means of tapping a vast new source of funds. It also appeared to signal a new trend toward offering small savers indexed debt securities to counter the uncertainties of inflation.

Above an initial order of $5,000, these mini-bonds were to be written in denominations of $1000. The bonds were to have nominal maturities between fifteen and twenty-five years. But they were also to have been redeemable at face value at semiannual interest dates, given thirty days' notice. Most important, the rate on these instruments would be tied by a formula to average interest rates on U.S. Treasury bills and would pay 1 percent above the Treasury bill rate. At issue, the bonds would be set at 9.7 percent, far above the 7.25 percent rate ceiling on the most attractive bank deposits. With double-digit inflation roaring and short-term interest rates rising to record highs, the issues immediately attracted the attention of the investing public.

They also attracted substantial political opposition from

thrift institutions, small banks, and sympathetic Congressmen. Critics viewed mini-bonds as an ill-conceived attempt to circumvent Regulation Q. Because the holding companies themselves are not banks, however, the Federal Reserve lacked the clear legal authority to regulate their debt issues. The National Association of Mutual Savings Banks, angered by the Fed's inaction, sued the Board, arguing that it did have the power to stop these offerings.

The resulting political conflict cast the players in unusual roles. Walter Wriston, Citicorp chairman, took up the banner of the little guy. "It is difficult to believe," he charged, "that in today's value system, with Congress constantly concerned about the treatment of consumers, that responsible people would seriously advance the thesis that large investors are somehow entitled to a higher return on their money than the consumer."[4]

AFL-CIO President George Meany inveighed against the idea. This champion of the working man clearly felt that the building trades belonged on the side of the thrifts; he charged that the government's "failure to use its authority" to stop the issues was "another in a number of government actions and failures that are clubbing residential construction into a depression.... [Moreover,] if these two major New York City banks can get away with it, other banks are expected to follow and several more billions of such notes will be issued in the next few months."[5]

In response to these pressures, the SEC did delay the Citicorp issue long enough to enable Federal Reserve Chairman Arthur Burns to pressure Wriston into making the proposed mini-bonds less competitive with ordinary savings accounts. Their compromise made it much more costly for people to cash their bonds to meet unforeseen needs. To prevent future outbreaks of innovation, Congress rushed through legislation putting note offerings by bank holding companies under the control of the ever-vigilant Federal Reserve.

### Treasury Securities for the Little Guy?

Small savers with sophisticated knowledge may consider marketable Treasury securities as an attractive alternative to savings bonds. There are several catches, however. First, there's the sophistication itself: These securities (which are, in effect, loans to the government) have never been advertised to the ordinary consumer. Anyone fortunate enough to live near a Federal Reserve Bank can purchase them directly, by placing a non-competitive bid in person on specified days at the Bank. Otherwise, it is necessary to buy through a commercial bank agent and incur a ticket fee (typically fifteen to twenty dollars per transaction).

The major catch, from the point of view of the average saver, is that the securities are not available in denominations smaller than $10,000, and therefore not available at all. Before 1970, U.S. Treasury notes had been sold in $1,000 denominations and Federal National Mortgage Association debentures in multiples of $5,000. But small savers began purchasing them in unprecedented numbers during the period of sharply rising rates in the late 1960s. So the government, consistently solicitous of the thrift institutions, moved to protect them. In February 1970 the Treasury boosted the minimum denomination of Treasury bills and FNMA debentures to $10,000, putting them nicely out of reach of even the most sophisticated small saver.

### Pooling Small Investors' Funds to Get Higher Yields

Since 1970, certificates of deposit issued in amounts of $100,000 or more have been exempt from interest rate ceilings. At times, rates on large CDs have been as much as seven percentage points above those on passbook savings. This exemption did nothing for small savers, with the exception of those clever enough to pool their savings into funds of $100,000 or more.

In 1974, a small group of entrepreneurs tried to devise a way for the little investor to take advantage of the high interest rates available in the wholesale money market and still be protected by federal deposit insurance. These plans, devised by placement services, aggregated funds in custody accounts and assigned shares to each participant, so that each continued to be covered by the then maximum $20,000 coverage of the FDIC. The placement concerns, mindful of the lessons of recent history, did not advertise their services, for fear of attracting regulatory attention. As one person in the business said. "Whenever something like this gets in the newspaper, the little saver always gets the short end of the stick."[6]

Such fears were, of course, fully justified. The Federal Reserve Board had issued an official opinion stating that "a bank that pays a higher rate on a deposit that it knows or has reason to know results from pooling of funds principally for the purpose of obtaining a higher rate of interest would be acting contrary to the spirit of interest rate-regulations."[7] Violations of the spirit of a regulation is not, of course, legally the same thing as actual violation of the regulation. As the knowledge of the benefits of pooling grew, more and more small investors wanted to get in on the action. As might have been expected, the federal bank regulators moved quickly to close off this latest escape for the captive small saver, to bring the letter of the law into line with its anticonsumer spirit.

In March 1976, the Federal Reserve Board and the Federal Deposit Insurance Corporation proposed almost simultaneously a regulation that would prevent banks from paying above-ceiling interest rates in cases where the institution "knows or has reason to know that the time deposit consists of or represents funds obtained or solicited...for the purpose of pooling such funds primarily to achieve the exemption from interest rate ceilings."

Professor Edward J. Kane described how the proposed regulation would operate in practice in a parable entitled: "Get Your Dirty Money Out of My Bank":

*Let's look in at the CD desk of a typical bank as it opens for business the first morning after the new rule becomes effective.*

*Three men are waiting to talk to the bank officer in charge of selling $100,000 CDs. The first man in the line is much better dressed than the others, who appear downright scruffy. When the bank officer calls him over, the first customer approaches the desk confidently. He draws $100,000 in cash from his jacket pocket and lays it on the banker's desk.*

*FIRST CUSTOMER: I would like to put this money to work at the preferential high interest rate that your bank pays on $100,000 CDs.*

*BANKER: Before we can contract with you at the preferential high interest rate, we have to determine how you accumulated this money. You had better tell the truth. We will check your answer carefully, using information from a number of different sources. We have access to all sorts of confidential records. If you lie to us, we will void your certificate and pay you no interest at all. However, any true statement will be treated as privileged information*

*FIRST CUSTOMER: (pales noticeably and finally stammers in embarrassment):...Oh, what's the use! You'll probably* *find out anyway. I'm a former congressman. I saved this $100,000 from bribes and kickbacks I took in during my time in office. (Turning to go) I guess I can't expect to earn the special preferential high interest on money like that. I'm sorry to have wasted your time.*

BANKER: *(stopping him):* No, no...Don't go away. Your *money qualifies for the high interest rate...Just sign this form.*

*As the first customer leaves smiling with relief and shaking his head in puzzlement, the second customer approaches the desk to offer the banker his $100,000.*

SECOND CUSTOMER: *(obviously uncomfortable):* I *heard what you asked the first customer. I suspect that I would be wiser to keep my mouth shut and put my money in Treasury bills. You'll never give me the special high interest rate for money earned through peddling vice. I have done it all: bookmaking, pimping, pushing dope...*

BANKER: *Say no more. Don't be ashamed.* Your *money easily qualifies for the high interest rate. Just sign this form.*

*As the customer strolls off happily, the third customer proudly approaches the desk and spreads his $100,000 before the banker.*

THIRD CUSTOMER: *I couldn't help overhearing your conversations with those other fellows. If their dirty money qualifies for the high interest rate, I'm sure my funds do. You see, I live in a low-income neighborhood, which was the scene of a disastrous factory fire last month. You probably read about it. Ten workers, all neighbors, perished in the fire. Most of them carried less than $10,000 in life insurance. It occurred to me that by pooling the insurance checks paid out to the bereaved families and combining the proceeds with my own savings, these funds would qualify for the preferential high interest rate on large CDs. Since these widows and orphans are living on the edge of starvation, the extra income they would receive from the preferential interest rate should benefit society at large. It will keep some of these families off the welfare rolls and teach their children self-reliance.*

BANKER: *(standing up and pointing at the door angrily):* You dirty cheat! How dare you ask for the preferential high interest *rate on money like that. We don't pay the preferential high interest rate to small savers. Either accept the low rate on small CDs or take your money out of here.*

*Flustered and annoyed, the third customer gathers his money and literally runs out the door. Two minutes later, the second customer reappears.*

SECOND CUSTOMER: *I have another $100,000 to deposit at that preferential high interest rate.*

BANKER: *As before, we need to know how you accumulated these funds.*

SECOND CUSTOMER: *Yes, sir. I understand. But what I say is privileged information?*

BANKER: *That's right.*

SECOND CUSTOMER: *Well, I just mugged a sad-looking guy in the alley behind the bank.*

BANKER: *As long as you didn't sell him the high yield CD I sold you earlier. Now if you'll sign this form...*[8]

Adverse publicity, and opposition from the new mutual fund industry, forced the federal agencies to back down from their overt actions. Ever ingenious, however, the Board of Governors of the Federal Reserve System announced in April 1977 that it would not adopt its regulatory proposal to prohibit member banks from paying interest on the pooled time deposits because in February the Federal Deposit Insurance had limited its insurance coverage for pooled deposits to $40,000. Having effectively denied deposit insurance to the small savers, the Federal Reserve magnanimously acquiesced in allowing them to pool their money in uninsured accounts.

### The Bizarre Case of the Massachusetts Morris Plan Banks

The federal bank regulators were as alert as ever in their efforts to protect their sacrosanct interest ceiling regulations. No institution was too small to escape the scrutiny of these diligent public officials. And regulatory authority could be stretched when necessary. One of the most bizarre vendettas occurred in the winter of 1977 and involved two small and obscure Morris Plan banks (similar to stock-owned and for-profit credit unions) in Massachusetts.

These two tiny banks had presented perpetual headaches to the Massachusetts Banking Department. Although they were small, their deposits were uninsured. Prior attempts by the Massachusetts Banking Department to obtain FDIC insurance for them had been rebuffed by the FDIC, which asserted that Morris Plan banks did not come under its authority. Finally, the day came when the parent holding company of the banks filed for bankruptcy, leaving the state banking department with two insolvent and uninsured institutions on its hands.

Depositors in Morris Plan banks are generally people of very modest means who are attracted by the borrowing opportunities that a deposit relationship with such a bank offers. In this case, the two banks were in the very poor urban areas of New Bedford and Chelsea. The impending closing, with the resulting loss of depositor funds, would have been a financial tragedy for most of these depositors.

When the banking department was presented with an alternative, it seized the chance to make the depositors whole and to innovate in the area of deposit accounts for the small saver. A large Rhode Island bank holding company, Old Stone Corporation, offered to buy the banks, to recapitalize them, and to make good all the depositors' money, if the banking department would look favorably on future branching requests and would authorize new competitive deposit accounts. It was a clear opportunity to show how attractive bank acounts could be made.

The Morris Plan banks were authorized to offer two new types of savings accounts. The first reduced from $1,000 to $100 the minimum balance needed to receive the higher interest rates available on longer-term deposits, and reduced from six to four years the term eligible for the highest (7¾ percent) deposit rate.

The other new account authorized by the department worked much the way U.S. Government Series E bonds do. The savings deposit had a six-year term, with interest rates varying from 5½ percent in the first year to 7¾ percent in the final two. This account was also to be available for depositors with as little as $100 to deposit. Unlike other time deposits available either then or now, there would be no penalty for early withdrawal at any time. It was possible to authorize these accounts, which offered greater benefits to the public than those allowed under federal regulations, because Morris Plan banks as uninsured banks were not covered by federal interest rate controls. This freedom was not to be long tolerated.

The FDIC lumbered forth, proposed that Morris Plan banks should be regarded as "akin to savings banks," and asserted that they were therefore subject to Regulation Q. In fact, Regulation Q had never been applied to these companies at all, not in Massachusetts nor in any other state with industrial or Morris Plan banks.

After a meeting of the heads of all the federal bank

regulatory agencies in Washington, the interagency committee instructed the FDIC to tell the Massachusetts Banking Department that as long ago as 1973, the FDIC had informed four noninsured commercial banks in Massachusetts, including the offending Morris Plan banks, that they were under Regulation Q controls for commercial banks. The Massachusetts Banking Department in turn politely pointed out to the FDIC that in fact the said banks were four very large and very prestigious banks: Boston Safe Deposit and Trust Company, the Fiduciary Trust Company, Brown Brothers Harriman & Co., and Barclay Bank. The FDIC had misrepresented its files, replacing the last two banks with the Morris Plan banks. Tongue in cheek, the Massachusetts Banking Department inquired how the FDIC had chosen to assert jurisdiction over these two Morris Plan Banking companies and not Brown Brothers and Barclays.

If history could not be written, regulations could. Less than two week later, the FDIC issued "proposed amendments pertaining to certain 'noninsured banks' in Massachusetts."[9] The proposed amendment gave the FDIC the authority to regulate deposit interest rates on banking companies only in Massachusetts. Posing as a friend of the consumer, the FDIC proposed to treat Massachusetts Morris Plan banks as thrift institutions rather than commercial banks, thus allowing the Morris Plan banks to enjoy the ¼ point differential. The FDIC proposal explained:

> *Banking companies operate on a limited scale. The bulk of their loans are consumer loans. They are prohibited from making commercial loans and are subject to strict limitations on real estate loans. Banking companies accept and pay interest on deposits. The existing banking companies operating in Massachusetts are few in number, small in size, and generally located in low to moderate income neighborhoods.*
>
> *Banking companies are more akin to mutual savings banks than to commercial banks and because of the similarity they are viewed as competitors of mutual savings banks. Part 329 of the Corporation's regulations is currently worded so that banking companies are treated as commercial banks and, therefore, they are limited to the payment of a lower maximum rate of interest on time and saving deposits. To eliminate this unfair competitive disadvantage and to permit banking companies to effectively compete with mutual savings banks, the Board of Directors of the FDIC proposes...to afford such banking com-*

*panies the same .25 percent rate differential advantage over commercial banks as that afforded mutual savings banks.*[10]

There was not a hint that in fact the proposed amendment would *lower*, not raise, the rate paid to depositors at these banks. Even without the new deposit accounts authorized by the Massachusetts Commissioner of Banks, the Morris Plan banks had been paying 5½ percent on passbook certificates for many years, a quarter-point more than the FDIC's new largesse would allow.

In response, the Massachusetts Banking Department attacked the FDIC's actions as supported by neither logic nor precedent. In a letter to the chairman of the FDIC, Robert Barnett, the department pointed out that even a cursory knowledge of Massachusetts banking institutions would immediately reveal that banking companies in Massachusetts do not even remotely resemble commercial banks or mutual savings banks, and that if they have any resemblance to any depository institution, it is to credit unions. In fact, the department charged, the proposed amendment was specifically and solely intended to prohibit the pro-consumer deposit accounts for small savers authorized by the Massachusetts Banking Department.

But the board of Old Stone Bank decided not to oppose the FDIC and signed an agreement that the two new acquisitions were in fact "akin" to a mutual savings bank. Thus, the unseemly and undignified proceedings terminated, with the small saver again the loser.

### Subsidizing the Banks

And the small saver will continue to lose—to lose billions of dollars a year—until "the highest interest rate allowed by law" is the interest rate set by the marketplace, until the government-imposed ceilings are lifted, until Regulation Q is wiped from the books.

At a congressional hearing in March of 1978, Robert Gnaizda, a San Francisco public interest lawyer representing the Gray Panthers, an activist organization for the elderly, charged that federal interest rate controls were "the largest government-led consumer fraud in American history." This is an age of inflated rhetoric, but when annual losses attributable to interest rate ceilings approach $20 billion, it's hard to fault Gnaizda's verdict. The Gray Panthers and allies have filed a class action petition with the whole panoply of federal bank regulating agencies accusing them of violating their discretionary authority by permitting institutions to offer lucrative money market certificates that only the rich can afford. The Gray Panthers urged that the minimum denomination of the certificates be lowered from $10,000 to $500 so that small savers could invest. If that notion were rejected, the petitioners suggested an alternative: Every savings passbook, every advertisement for a savings account, every bank door should carry the printed warning that "Savings May Be Hazardous to Your Wealth."

As we have seen, there are two justifications repeatedly offered on behalf of the artificial limit on interest rates: that they are necessary to prevent the savings banks from engaging in suicidal competition that will endanger the small savers' deposits and the institutions themselves, and that they serve to keep the interest rates on home mortgages down. Even if a compelling argument could be made on behalf of both assertions—and in our view both lack any substantial factual base—they would still not justify a system that relies on a massive subsidy from the least affluent savers to keep itself afloat.

Yet that is the plain truth about the way thrift institutions have functioned. In the past decade, they have time and again used their alliances with government to have small savers' alternatives shut off, to ensure that the little guy won't be able to move his money somewhere that pays a fair return. Each time, they have complained about the "unfair competition" such alternatives represent. Yet each time they have avoided *competing* with the competition—they have stuck with the system that forbids them to pay competitive rates of return.

It is so remarkable to hear a representative of a thrift institution actually advocate a fair return for small savers that when one actually did so during a congressional appearance, Rep. Benjamin S. Rosenthal asked with mock incredulity: "Are you sure you are in the banking business?"

### Shackling the Invisible Hand

The first year of the decade, 1970, set the pattern for all that was to follow. In January, Regulation Q was revised: Savings rates were increased to 4½ percent at commercial banks and 5 percent at savings banks and savings and loan associations. In addition, three categories of time deposits were established. (Time deposits are accounts that pay better returns if the borrower does not withdraw funds before a pre-established maturity date.) The best of these paid 5¾ percent for deposits left in the bank two years or longer. Were the banking regulators responding to the plight of small savers? No. They were responding to the plight of the banks. A surge in market interest rates was attracting those savers with enough money to get into the market and passbook savings accounts were, as a result, shrinking. The explicit goal of the Regulation Q revision was to aid the banks, to make them a tiny bit more competitive, not to aid savers. After all, the new rates did not really approach market rates.

If any small saver harbored even the slightest doubt whom the government was trying to protect, he had to wait but a month until February 1970. In that month, Treasury bills, which had long been available in denominations of $1,000, were altered. The minimum denomination was set at $10,000. The reason—the only reason—for the change was to make Treasury bills with their attractive interest rates unavailable to small savers, to force them to keep their money in savings accounts.

The pattern for the decade has been established. Almost invariably deliberate efforts to alter it would be rebuffed; unintentional deviations would be quickly corrected. The objective was always the protection of the institutions, never the protection of their depositors. And when it proved essential to benefit depositors in order to protect the institutions, it was invariably only the big depositor who gained.

### Topless "4's"

In 1973, when market interest rates again rose sharply and deposit growth at the savings institutions was stunted, Regulation Q was once more revised. Again the interest rate on regular savings accounts was nudged upward and time deposit accounts were polished up. But that was not all. In its exuberance, in its haste to aid the savings institutions, the Fed went too far. It created two new categories of accounts that actually promised savers—albeit only savers with enough financial security to salt their money away for a time—returns near and even at market rates. Depositors who committed their funds to the banks for between two and a half and four years were given an opportunity to earn 6½ percent, and time accounts of four years or longer had no interest ceiling at all. These deposits were widely dubbed "wild-card" deposits and "topless 4's." Sensing something incredible, a fair shake, depositors quickly poured billions of their savings into these new instruments. Within five months, however, the banking interests had regrouped, organized its frontline troops in Congress and crushed this move toward economic justice. *Barron's*, in a biting editorial, commented on the massacre:

> *During that brief but glorious moment in history, the thrifty caught a glimpse of a whole new financial world, bulging with such goodies as Equibonds, which fetch a minimum of 7% or more depending on what happens to one year Treasury bills; the National Bank of North America's "Supreme Interest," 7.9% compounded hourly; the First Pennsylvania Banking and Trust Company's "Inflation Fighter," the yield on which rises with the cost of living up to a top of 10% per year.*
>
> *But no longer—by courtesy of Congress, the wild cards (effective November 1) have been dealt right out of the money game. In so doing, the lawmakers professedly sought to bolster the competitive position of the thrift institutions and the home mortgage market, both of which were falling behind in the escalation of rates. Willy-nilly, however, they have achieved something else. They have succeeded in focusing attention on the remarkable and rather frightening clout wielded by the banking fraternity in a deliberative body which boasts a high concentration of members with similar interests. By sheer disregard of legislative procedure—no committee hearings, no expert witnesses, curtailed debate on the floor and voice vote—they have given good government, at a particularly sensitive and anguished time in the nation's history, another black eye. When every dollar counts, they have shown a striking contempt for the financial well-being of their constituents, many of whom, in the savings realm, once again are relegated to the status of second-class citizen. In the land of equal opportunity, some are more equal than others.*[11]

Before the "topless" deposits were voted back under a deposit rate ceiling, they were made the scapegoat for all the funding problems experienced by the thrift and housing industries during the summer of 1973's rapid run-up in interest rates. A passage from the 1975–1976 *Hearings* on financial reform makes clear the outlines of the wild card mythology. A representative of the U.S. League of Savings Associations testified:

> *We need only go back to mid-1973, when the Federal Reserve Board lifted ceiling rates on consumer certificates of deposit, for an example of near-disastrous competition—the "wild*

*card" fiasco familiar to many of you. Heavily advertised commercial bank CD rates of 8 percent and 9 percent were common, and the drain on savings association funds was heavy until Congress wisely stepped in and instructed the banking agencies to put a lid on all consumer-sized deposits.*[12]

The mythology carefully constructed by the savings and loan industry held that wild card interest rates of 8 and 9 percent were common at commercial banks and that because of these high rates, commercial banks were able to gain $4 billion in deposits at the expense of the S&Ls. The S&Ls conclusion was that the outflow of deposits experienced during the summer of 1973 was caused by this relaxing of deposit-rate controls.

Analysis of the rates actually offered by commercial banks, though, simply doesn't support this picture. In their efforts to attract deposits with wild card rates, banks never offered interest rates even as high as those available on open-market rates of similar maturities. Bankers never lost their heads, despite the newfound freedom. They left themselves a respectable margin to cover their costs. The average interest rate on wild cards was 7.2 percent at commercial banks and 7.34 percent at thrifts. Less than 1 percent of the commercial banks ever offered rates over 8 percent.[13] The loss in S&Ls' deposits is more easily explained by the rapid run-up in Treasury bill rates at this time and the bulge in noncompetitive bids for Treasuries. The major shift in consumer accounts was into open market instruments. In fact, the wild card rates, by allowing thrifts and banks to compete with these open-market rates, probably saved them from even more severe outflows. However, any freedom from the deposit-rate ceilings was a precedent too threatening to the thrifts. They seized this opportunity to solidify their differential ceiling and to reinforce deposit controls. This scapegoating left small savers' chances for fair treatment more bleak than ever. In November of 1973, ceiling rates of 7¼ percent at banks and 7½ percent at thrift institutions were placed on the "topless 4's." A year later, in December 1974, yet another deposit category was established, with a maturity of six years or more and a ceiling rate of 7½ percent at banks and 7¾ percent at thrifts. The inequities of the system are continually compounded.

### The Northeast Experiment

In 1975, when a couple of attempts were made at fundamental reform, the thrift industry used its congressional muscle to rebuff them. Rep. St. Germain sought in that year to win enactment of the

Financial Institutions Act, legislation that would expand the powers of the thrifts, enabling them to earn a better return and thereby to pay more equitable interest to all their savers. The legislation would have granted thrifts expanded powers to offer checking accounts and to make personal loans. In return, they were to lose the right, under Regulation Q, to pay an extra quarter percent on deposits. The idea was to initiate a gradual move toward competition between all banking institutions as a first step toward weaning the thrifts from Regulation Q. The savings and loan industry, surveying the options, chose the present system, in which the industry could demand government protection because it lacked the powers to compete. The thrifts killed the legislation in the House.

With its defeat, state banking regulators in the Northeast, led by John Heimann, the bank commissioner of New York, and me as the bank commissioner of Massachusetts, proposed an even more ambitious move—the lifting of Regulation Q in the Northeast on an experimental basis. It was the ideal place and the ideal time for such an experiment. Interest rates were at a cyclical low; the lifting of Q would not have caused radical changes in the money market. In addition, savings banks in the Northeast already had many of the expanded asset and liability powers that would have been granted nationwide by the St. Germain legislation. The Northeast would provide a good laboratory to observe how the banking industry would perform without Regulation Q, because parity of powers between thrifts and commercial banks was more advanced here than anywhere else in the nation. To ease whatever minor pain might have been inflicted on the thrifts as they ventured into the untested waters of the free market, I proposed that the ceilings be lifted gradually—at the rate of a half-point every six months—until they became meaningless.

The Savings Bank Association of New York attacked the proposal as "ill conceived" and "destructive." The proposed experiment was attacked as "so naive, so simplistic as to defy credulity" and the commissioners as misinformed for believing that Regulation Q was established to prevent deposit outflows from thrifts, and that it had failed to do so. The Association argued that Regulation Q was instituted in the early 1930s to prevent ruinous rate wars between financial institutions and that it had generally succeeded in doing that. Without deposit ceilings, the Association warned that the average family would be faced with mortgage rates starting at 13 percent!

Nonetheless, it seemed, at least briefly, that the lifeguards for the industry—the key members of Congress and the regulators—thought the Northeast's thrifts might just be able to paddle in the free market if forced to do so. Under the leadership of Senator Thomas McIntyre of New Hampshire, several Northeastern senators signed letters supporting the experiment. Rep. St. Germain expressed interest. Members of the Federal Reserve Board left John Heimann and me with the distinct impression they would go along. Nevertheless, Fed chairman Arthur Burns, a champion of the free market, did not approve. He threw the thrifts a lifeline, a letter to Sen. Proxmire, chairman of the Senate Banking Committee, opposing the experiment. It died in committee.

### Revising Q One More Time

If, however, the thrifts thought they were now going to rest in peace, they were sadly mistaken. Continuing and near-chronic inflation and its impact on market interest rates assured that. Once again, as funds started to leach from the savings institutions, Regulation Q was modified. Still another time deposit category was established, with an eight year maturity date and interest ceilings of 7¾ percent for commercial banks and 8 percent for thrifts. But the more dramatic change was the authorization of six month "money market certificates," whose interest rate was to be keyed to the latest weeks rate for six-month Treasury notes. Banks were allowed to offer this market rate on their money market certificates (MMCs); thrifts were given their customary quarter-point differential.

Yet, the concern of the regulators continued to be the institutions, not their depositors. The minimum denomination of these new MMCs was set at $10,000. The small saver was again forced out of the game. One can get at least a taste of the impact of the $10,000 ante by reviewing a 1975 analysis by the United States League of Savings Associations. While inflation has certainly changed the details, the pattern it reveals is depressingly instructive. At that time, 85 percent of all accounts in the association's member institutions were smaller than $10,000 and about 70 percent were smaller than $5,000. For households with incomes between $10,000 and $14,999, the median account balance was $1,870 (that is, half the households had less); more than 80 percent had savings accounts below $7,500.

The authorization of the $10,000 MMCs was so bad that

it's good. It was the accommodation to the irrationalities of Reg Q that finally forced its collapse. Desperate to retain and expand their deposits, banks and thrifts advertised widely the availablity of the new certificates. And in the first seven months they sold $115 billion worth of them. By the fall of 1979, they accounted for 20 percent of thrifts' deposits.

But that same advertising brought home to small savers— such as those represented by the Gray Panthers—the blatant economic discrimination resulting from the $10,000 minimum denomination. Depositors without $10,000 in their savings account were forced to receive a negative return on their savings. As the accompanying Table I shows, $1,000 left in a passbook savings account at the 5¼ percent Regulation Q interest rate ceilings, after taxes and inflation, was worth only $900 at the end of a year.

---

*Table I/What $1,000 Is Worth in a Savings Account After Inflation and Taxes*

*(After one year in a savings account at 5.25%, reduced by inflation and U.S. income taxes)*

| Depositors' Total Taxable Income | $1,000 Deposit for a Single Person | $1,000 Deposit for a Family of Four |
|---|---|---|
| $10,000 | $906.55 | $908.93 |
| $20,000 | $900.37 | $906.55 |
| $30,000 | $895.62 | $901.33 |
| $40,000 | $893.25 | $896.10 |
| $50,000 | $890.39 | $893.25 |

*Reprinted by permission from* Time, *The Weekly Newsmagazine; September 10, 1979, p. 73; © Time Inc. 1979.*

---

"I'm one of those small savers who is being robbed by the federal government," said seventy-five-year-old Hilda Cloud.[14] She was sporting a yellow button that proclaimed: "Savings may be HAZ-ARDOUS to your Wealth." Labeling the government a "reverse Robin Hood," a thief that steals from the poor to give to the rich, she descended on Washington, D.C., with representatives of the Consumers Union, the National Organization of Women, and labor unions to challenge the low-interest-rate ceilings on savings available to small savers. The banking and thrift industry lobbyists had finally met their match in this gray-haired lady, the president of the Gray Panthers' San Francisco chapter. Here was finally an important constituency vocally opposed to interest ceilings—the elderly.

Depositors are beginning both to demand regulatory changes and to look in the nooks and crannies of the money market for places where they too can receive a fair return on their savings. As had happened almost a decade earlier, large retailers and utilities proposed in 1979 to tap the consumer savings market by offering small-denomination notes. Sears announced that in 1980 it planned to sell at its stores $500 million of unsecured $1,000 notes to its customers at money market rates. Many thrifts and banks shuddered at the invasion of their turf. Citicorp, the parent holding company of Citibank, was less concerned. It announced that it would consider drawing on its own growing base of consumer finance outlets and six million credit card holders as a source of capital funds if the Sears offering was successful.

Even some banks found a way around Regulation Q. This time the instrument was a so-called "retail repurchase agreement." First Pennslyvania Bank was one of the first to offer these to the public, in the spring of 1979. Maggie Kuhn, founder of the Gray Panthers, purchased the first certificate. For a $1,000 investment, she received a contract specifying that she had purchased a U.S. Treasury security held in First Pennslyvania's portfolio. The contract also specified that First Pennslyvania agreed to buy back the security in one year with a 9 percent return to the customer. While repurchase agreements are not new to banking, they had mainly been used to allow corporations to earn interest on short-term deposits. (Regulations of the Federal Home Loan Bank Board ban the sale of consumer-type repurchase agreements for savings and loan associations.) The First Pennsylvania action was quickly followed by a similar plan at State National Bank of Rockville, Maryland.

In January of 1979, Massachusetts became the first state to offer tax-exempt bonds in denominations low enough ($100) to make them accessible to the small saver. The first $1 million issue was snapped up in three hours. It didn't take much longer for the thrift industry to start complaining. "This calls into serious question the whole tax-exempt concept," Saul B. Klaman, president of the National Association of Mutual Savings Banks asserted. "It could have a devastating effect on the savings bank industry. Where would housing funds come from? I'm all for competition, but I think this takes the tax-exempt concept to an extreme."[15]

What had really been called into question, of course, were the traditional practices of the industry. Klaman virtually admitted as much in a subsequent hearing before a House subcommittee.

There, the subject turned to money market mutual funds, which were established in reaction to the high interest rates of 1973–1974 and the government-imposed restraints on small savers. By 1979, there were over fifty of them. They pooled small savers' resources, sometimes in denominations as low as $1,000, for investment in short-term securities such as Treasury bills and commercial paper. By the spring of 1980, the assets had soared to $60 billion, compared to less than $5 billion two years earlier.

With their free check-writing privileges and no penalty for withdrawal, the money market funds offered the saver a better deal than anything the banks were willing to offer. Even Klaman seemed to agree they were a wise investment for the small saver, as this dialogue with Rep. Rosenthal during the House hearings in June 1980 over lifting Rate Q and the $10,000 minimum for money market certificates illustrates:

*ROSENTHAL: I am asking you how we explain it to this little old lady [a Gray Panther]. She is subsidizing the big depositors and the borrowers, and she can hardly pay the rent.*

*KLAMAN: For want of an explanation, are you going to suggest that the nation's savings industry be put up against the wall because they cannot pay it, because you cannot explain it?*

*ROSENTHAL: That is a thought. I do not know. I cannot justify what we are doing to these people. You justify it by saying the industry cannot afford it.*

*KLAMAN: I would have to reluctantly say that, since we cannot afford to pay, there are other institutions which can. For example, the money market funds are offering one-thousand-dollar certificates.*

*ROSENTHAL: They are not insured. She cannot take any risks.*

*KLAMAN: Yes, but what they invest in is pretty safe.*

*ROSENTHAL: I know. But what you are saying publicly is that what you want me to tell the twenty-five million senior citizens is to take all their money out of savings and go to a brokerage house and buy money market certificates.*

Well, it has finally come to this. Even bankers acknowledge that equity demands that small savers stage a run on their banks. The time for the abolition of Regulation Q is at hand. Faced with the strains imposed and the inequities revealed by the money market certificates, the thrifts have, predictably, sought to shore up their defenses.

The MMCs were an unwanted marketing success. Thrifts didn't want to compete with the market. They liked protection. They had not asked for this change in rate Q; it had been thrust upon them. They had offered them to the public only as a defensive strategy, to keep a share of the market. The thrifts and small bankers quickly went to Washington to get rid of them. They wanted to continue what the *Wall Street Journal* so aptly called "the inflation-era robbery committed against small savers by federal ceilings on bank deposits.[16]

The spectacle of financial executives begging for government regulations to prevent them from paying market rates for funds in this antiregulatory era is one of the great ironies on the banking scene. It is in fact downright silly, since no one forced bankers to offer these rates. The new regulations simply gave them a choice that they did not have before: Offer competing rates or lose funds. In the past, the only choice was losing funds. But swallowing their usual complaints about over-regulation, they have demanded more protective regulations.

This time, the bankers' demands for protection achieved only partial success. The returns on the certificates were shaved slightly in March 1979, and allowable interest rates on passbook savings have again been minimally increased incrementally.

In April 1979, Senator Proxmire held hearings on the rate ceilings and their impact on small savers. The bank regulators rejected the Senator's proposals to give the $1,000 depositor the same interest rate as the $10,000 depositor on the grounds that it would be too costly! Robert McKinney, chairman of the Federal Home Loan Bank, countered these Senate proposals by pointing out that nearly half of the money poured into MMCs was "new" money, whereas most of the funds for $1,000 MMCs would be "old" money from persons upgrading their savings accounts. In essence, he was arguing that these people were already bank captives, so why give them a fair deal?

Rather than eliminating the ceilings, the bank regulators proclaimed a new set of inequities. Their proposals chipped away at the problem but didn't solve it. They were designed to stifle consumer outcries while still protecting banks from market prices. The bank regulators grandly announced that the ceiling on passbook savings rates would be raised a whole quarter-point, to 5¼ percent for commercial banks and 5½ percent for thrifts. They also announced a new variable rate four year or lower savings certificate with a ceiling set at only 1 to 1¼ percent *below* the yield on four year government securities! The sole advantage was that they had no government-mandated denomination. The regulators in fact proposed eliminating all government-required minimum denominations for consumer-type time deposits, except for the $10,000 minimum required for MMCs. Thus, the only deposit with a rate and maturity structure actually approximating free-market rates was still denied to the average saver. And as if to drive home that all this was a special privilege, the regulators sharply increased early withdrawal penalties, although they did ask for public comments on whether the penalties should be relaxed if the depositor died.

### Possibilities for Reform

What is most wrong with these proposals is their continuation of the unjust policy of considering the banking and housing-subsidy package as one that must be paid for by small savers. It won't work any longer. In 1979, President Carter finally called for a phaseout of the ceilings. In his message to Congress, President Carter said it was "particularly unconscionable" during times of high inflation for the federal government to prohibit small savers from receiving a return on deposits that is available to holders of large accounts.

In March 1980, Congress passed the Depository Institutions Deregulation and Monetary Control Act of 1980 which finally heralded the eventual end of interest rate ceilings on savings deposits. Deposit rate ceilings are to be phased out over the next six years. The act specifies that deposit rate ceilings in the first eighteen months after the act's passage must be raised at least ¼ percentage point! The bill thus offers no relief to savers now. The captives of the banking system, those persons with less than $10,000 in savings, must continue to subsidize the banks and thrift institutions to keep them afloat. While the bill offers no help today to the average guy whose savings are being depleted, the principle has finally been established that "all depositors, and particularly those with modest savings, are entitled to receive a market rate of return on their savings..."[17]

The abolition of Regulation Q should attract more money to the thrifts and thereby provide more money for mortgages at lower rates. If sensible social policy suggests that the nation should provide further subsidies of mortgages and homeownership, fine. But that subsidy should not be paid by small savers.

A major cost of Regulation Q is that by hiding both the cost to savers and the fragility of the thrift institutions, it has hampered the task of restructuring our capital markets to ensure a reliable flow of funds into housing and of putting our thrift institutions on a sounder basis, so that they don't need to be protected from the market. Thrifts need more asset powers, like interest-bearing checking accounts and consumer loans, to increase their revenues and thereby their ability to pay the higher market rates on all deposits.

Only when it became certain that rate controls would have to be lifted did thrifts mount the necessary lobbying effort to gain the additional loan and deposit powers that they needed to survive in a free market environment. In the past, rather than concentrating their efforts on gaining expanded powers, thrifts used their political muscle to force federal protection.

*Thrifts lobbying strategy is very interesting. It is based on what Transactional Analysis terms a psychological game! S & L's portray themselves as Victims and force Congress to see itself as both persecutor and rescuer. They play a mean game of YOU GOT ME INTO THIS, a game with the implicit command, AND YOU'D BETTER GET ME OUT OF IT. Thrifts wrap themselves up in the mantle of Congress' avowed housing goals and, standing in coalition with the labor and building lobbies, effectively dare Congressmen and Senators NOT to rescue them.*[18]

But inflation and money-market funds finally made deposit-rate ceilings untenable. The funds provide such a convenient deposit-like alternative that commercial banks and thrifts may have a difficult time regaining deposits in any form other than one which is responsive to market interest rates. Money-market funds are designed to appeal to bank depositors: They offer small savers the convenience of checking and other services, as well as market-level yields. The only major shortcoming is that balances are not insured by the federal government.

Until now, investors' knowledge and understanding of money-market funds has been limited. Advertising is certain to change that. Furthermore, the money-market certificate, by increasing depositors' sensitivity to interest rates, has set the stage for depositor acceptance of money-market funds as an alternative to traditional deposit accounts. Once consumers switch their deposits to a money-market fund account, it seems unlikely they will switch back.

Removing deposit-rate ceilings is essential to maintaining the long-term health of the thrift industry, but it is not a sufficient step toward providing adequate housing finance. There are several alternatives, not necessarily mutually exclusive. We could continue to subsidize institutions which provide mortgage funds as we have done with thrifts, or we could subsidize individuals directly. Or we could do both.

The point is that expanded long-term sources of funds must be found to supply a stable base for housing finance. It's like playing Russian roulette to create financial intermediaries, like thrifts, that lend long and borrow short. Housing finance should be based on long-term savings flows. Here the pension funds and life insurance companies quickly come to mind. Pension funds, because of the funding requirements of the Employees Retirement Insurance Safety Act (ERISA), will soon control 30 percent of the outstanding value of the stock market; the amount of money now held in them exceeded the deposits at thrift institutions in 1978. Legislation requiring pension funds to invest 10 percent of their funds in residential mortgages in order to keep their preferred tax treatment would be one option. Of course, this requirement would have to be phased in over a number of years so as not to swamp the market. Pension funds now hold only about one percent of their assets in residential mortgages, about half of what they held ten years ago. Clearly, this proposal would channel a large and growing pool of funds into mortgages.

This proposal need not imply a subsidy approach to housing finance; that is, mortgages need not be made at rates below those of the market. Pension funds could insist on receiving a rate on purchased mortgages equal to that available on high-grade bonds, their normal investment vehicle. The pension funds would buy only seasoned mortgages and the original mortgage lender would both guarantee the mortgage and service it. The pension funds would not be subsidizing the mortgage borrower at retirees' expense; the pension funds would simply increase the pool of available mortgage financing. Traditional mortgage lenders, like thrift institutions, should support the proposal, because it would provide them with a source of liquidity in tight money periods, allowing them to stay in the market longer, just as FNMA and GNMA now do. This is simply a proposal to provide funds through pension funds to do what federal agencies are now doing. It is a proposal to get the capital market back into private financing.

Until now, it has been the federal government's direct lending to the mortgage market that has kept the housing market from completely collapsing. The big increase in funds for mortgage loans has come not from thrift institutions, whose relative contribution for housing finance has been steadily diminishing, but from direct lending by federal agencies like FNMA, GNMA, and the FHLB. In 1965, these programs held three percent of residential mortgage debt; by 1978, they held 15 percent, or $160 billion, in mortgages, $70 billion more than all mutual savings banks. The federal agencies provided by far the largest relative increase in funds available to housing. This is yet more proof that it is not deposit rate controls that are channeling money into housing; it is direct federal lending.

Life insurance companies are the other major contract thrift institution, and like pension funds they should repay the public for their favorable tax treatment. Life insurance companies view themselves as in two businesses: insurance and savings. As savings institutions, they receive funds from individuals, hold them for an uncertain number of years, and then return them with interest. The money they earn on the funds left with them is added to reserves to be paid back to savers, in part. The insurance companies have been able to persuade the Congress that these earnings are not income, and therefore should not be taxed as such. Of course, if individuals held these same earnings in a bank, the earnings on them would be taxed as income as the earnings accrued. In essence, life insurance companies have convinced the Congress that they are more of a savings bank than any savings bank.

The law could easily be changed so that these tax-free transfers to reserves would be dependent on maintaining a certain percentage of assets in residential mortgages, as is the case with deposit thrift institutions. Again this change would have to be phased in over time. While contract thrifts—life insurance companies and pension funds—would not replace depository thrifts, with these proposed tax changes they would supplement the depository thrifts' role in maintaining a significant place for private capital in mortgage markets.

The movement to eliminate Regulation Q has unnecessarily led to throwing overboard many consumer safeguards. The Federal Home Loan Bank Board has agreed that without Regulation Q, thrifts must abandon fixed rate mortgages in favor of variable rate mortgages or move to five-year mortgages instead of the present twenty-year mortgage. Both of these changes shift the burden of interest rate risks from the financial institution to the bank's customer. Incredibly, the Federal Home Loan Bank Board has also seized on the elimination of Regulation Q as an excuse to pursue the coversion of mutual S&Ls to stock institutions. None of these changes are required by Regulation Q's demise. This is just a further example of a regulatory agency playing the role of a trade association.

The time is long overdue for the recognition that deposit-rate controls are not only unfair, but unworkable as well. It is time to get on with the job of redeveloping the private capital mortgage market and establishing thrift institutions on a solid footing for the future. Elimination of Regulation Q will not end the housing cycle. When monetary policy is tight, housing will continue to suffer. The question of the 1980s will be how to solve the housing cycle without putting all the burden on savers in thrift institutions.

# 5.
# Redlining:
# So You Want to Buy
# A House in the City

*Deposit a few bucks in most any savings bank in
town and you'll walk out with a toaster, a TV, or
some other promotional come-on. Ask that same
bank for a mortgage and it's as though you
mouthed an obscenity. Sure the banks are
ripping us off. They're not killing the city all by
themselves, but they are the gravediggers.*[1]

In Baltimore, bankers had a policy of not lending on homes less than
eighteen feet wide. They just happened to pick that figure, eighteen
feet: It had nothing to do, they maintained, with the fact that the
bulk of the homes in Baltimore's older neighborhoods are narrow
row houses. By this simple rule of thumb, the banks found that they
"couldn't" lend in much of Baltimore.

In Boston, where triple-deckers, or three-family homes, are
the predominant urban form of housing, one of the largest Boston
banks used as a rule of thumb that there had to be a separate
furnace in the basement for each unit—that is, they wanted three
furnaces in each triple-decker. The energy-inefficiency of requiring
three small separate furnaces rather than one larger one, energy
crisis notwithstanding, meant nothing to this bank, especially
since such a rule of thumb easily allowed the bank to turn down
many urban mortgages. Other large Boston banks had other handy
rules, like not lending on homes with asphalt siding, or limiting
mortgages to single-family homes. Only the bankers failed to see
the absurdity of these masks for redlining.

"Redlining" is shorthand for describing the urban disinvestment practiced by banks and insurance companies. Mortgage

officers and insurance executives once drew red lines around a section on a map and refused to make loans or insure property in the proscribed neighborhood. No loan officer would now be crass enough to commit his bias to paper; this is, after all, the age of the "equal-opportunity lender." But disinvestment, as we will see, has survived the red line itself, and the original name has survived with it.

No one claims that the plight of deteriorating urban neighborhoods is solely the result of redlining; but no one believes that this deterioration can be reversed without a steady flow of capital into them. The thrift institutions are the mechansim society relies upon to insure that flow. They have failed to meet that responsibility. The result has been a crisis of confidence in the lenders. The once arcane term "redlining" is slowly entering the average city resident's vocabulary. "And," as Jack Newfield and Paul Dubrul have stated, "with it comes the growing sense of outrage and victimization that must befall someone who has just been robbed with his own gun."[2]

Over the past decade, savings and loan associations, the financial institutions chartered to provide home mortgages, have refused to lend in many urban neighborhoods despite their obligation to do so. The purpose for which federal S&Ls were given their charters is clearly stated in Section 5(a) of the Home Owners' Loan Act of 1933, the legislation which created them. It states that the objective for organizing federal savings associations shall be "In order to provide local mutual thrift institutions in which people may invest their funds and in order to provide for the financing of their homes. ..." The language of the act clearly ties the mortgage lending of the institution to the deposits in that institution—it is depositors' money, to be lent for their homes. More and more, though, depositors' money is going elsewhere.

Bankers claim that any decline in their mortgage activity in the cities results from a lack of applications from credit worthy borrowers. In Boston, Chicago, Milwaukee, Minneapolis-St. Paul, Providence, San Francisco, and elsewhere across the nation, urban residents rejoin that banks are redlining, writing off their neighborhoods as being too risky to bank on and categorically refusing to make any conventional mortgage loans. The issue is disinvestment. The question is, whose? Are the lenders designating neighborhoods potential slums, thereby dooming them to deterioration and abandonment? Or have prospective homebuyers largely abandoned the cities for the suburbs, leaving urban homeowners with no credit worthy buyers?

Regardless of the cause of disinvestment, the results have been devastating: city block after block of rundown or abandoned homes, vast wastelands which have been created in the very years of concern about a national housing shortage and soaring costs of new construction.

*The working families in urban neighborhoods whose homes represent their entire equity, and who watch their communities slowly decay because local financial institutions have decided not to make home improvement or mortgage loans in those same neighborhoods—even though their savings deposits are from those neighborhoods—are the people most affected by these problems, referred to as redlining, the self-fulfilling prophecy of a deteriorating area.[3]*

In the past, the federal government has addressed urban housing problems almost exclusively by developing special programs or by spending federal money in a limited number of neighborhoods. These federal programs have not affected the majority of urban neighborhoods. As new funds for even these limited projects have not materialized, community groups have increasingly argued that government must mobilize the financial resources generated by urban residents through their savings dollars in banks, and adopt strong bank regulatory policies which ensure that sufficient funds are made available through the banking system to credit worthy homebuyers in the cities. The key point in their argument is the charge that financial institutions discriminate against mortgage applicants on the basis of the property's location, regardless of the financial ability of the applicant, the condition of the property, or the bank's actual loss experience in the area.

City residents tell their own stories best. The Council on Urban Life, working in the West Side of Milwaukee, has been carefully compiling individual reports like this one:

*My husband and I were mortgage shopping last July, before the money situation got really tight. We were attempting to buy a house on 34th between Walnut and Lisbon. The first savings and loan we approached is the one that has currently held our mortgage for the past nine years to the tune of $188 a month.... Their comment was very plainly that its current board seldom lent money "in that area."... We finally did get a mortgage from another savings and loan institution. The rate is 9 percent, 10 years, for a full 42 percent down. Not one savings and loan asked* *the condition of the house or the credit that we have until we had already been told that the loan had gone through...It bothers me that they are less concerned about the character of the people buying homes or their credit than they are about the area. It bothers me even more that none of the institutions that we talked to would consider terms of [more] than 10 years. They were very plainly saying to me that in 10 years our neighborhood would be worthless. If they continue on this trend, they will fulfill their prediction.[4]*

Members of the Banking Committee of the Jamaica Plain Community Council in Boston relate similar stories:

*I have owned my house in Jamaica Plain for 11 years. Several months ago, I decided to make some major improvements and went to the bank that held my first mortgage. The mortgage officer declined to even give me an application for the loan, saying, "Why don't you think about moving out of that area? We'd be glad to give you a new mortgage somewhere else." I think he saw my request for a couple of thousand dollars as an opportunity to get me to sell off so that they could call in the mortgage they'd made on my house in the first place....Jamaica Plain isn't being abandoned by us. It's being strangled by our would-be banks. The red line goes right down Center Street, and we're on the wrong side.[5]*

Similar stories are told by Chicago residents:

*Two years ago, the banks were rejecting new mortgage applications outright, and even advising us as customers to move out. Their reasons were really outright racist. As we got sophisticated and began to record their remarks, planning to get them on violations of the 1968 Civil Rights Act, they became less explicit. The code words we're faced with now are "the effective age of structure," that is, our 60-year-old houses are too old. But the ones built at the same time several suburbs over don't seem to have any geriatric problems, according to the mortgage practices of the same banks.[6]*

Such disinvestment by banks is a dangerous, self-fulfilling prophecy. If banks designate a neighborhood a potential slum, they doom it.

The bankers have angrily denied all such charges. "These groups just don't understand that you don't concentrate all your mortgages in one area," says one Chicago executive of a savings and loan association. "The critics are entering an area demanding a highly sophisticated approach to investing money that they'll never understand."[7]

Banks are "convinced nothing's going to be good if its black, brown or poor,"[8] charged Gale Cincotta, a feisty Chicago housewife-turned-community activist who heads a nationwide coalition of neighborhood groups called the National People's Action on Housing.

Many other people, like Cincotta, are charging that the banks are discriminating on the basis of fear rather than reality. As a result of these allegations, community groups demanded public disclosure of where banks write mortgages and where they get their deposits. The public is coming to believe that banks should serve the community from which it draws its funds.

## Why Would Banks Redline a Neighborhood?

Part of the answer, as indicated by Cincotta and others, is racial change. The banks, appraisers, and real-estate brokers make an a priori judgment that a particular neighborhood is likely to undergo racial change and therefore decline in the near future. This leads the appraisers to reduce, by some arbitrary percentage, the sales value of the houses there. It leads real-estate brokers to counsel prospective white buyers to look elsewhere, and leads the banks to say that they can't take the risk of lending there. The actions of all these groups make the original prophecy a reality, justifying in their minds their original judgements; and another urban neighborhood does decline markedly.

Bankers are more fearful of minority-group members, and less informed about them, than the average American; they have less exposure to such people. As conservative men, they tend to be distrustful of alternative life-styles. Myths may not be true, but to the degree that they influence perceptions, they influence behavior. When I was Massachusetts Commissioner of Banks, I went to lunch with a group of western Massachusetts bankers at a private club with membership open only to white Protestant men. The bankers explained to me that they did not redline: they made sound loans to anyone. But no one could expect them to "lend to those Puerto Rican welfare cheats who fly home to Puerto Rico every weekend...What those people have done to the apartments they rented was criminal," thundered one banker. "They keep chickens in the pantries and eat dinner in the bathtub. We can't lend to people who live like that," he explained. "They destroy property values."

Nor is the proof of redlining strictly a matter of anecdotes; there is ample documentation that conventional mortgage lending by financial institutions is part of the white flight from the cities. A series of studies by the Committee of the Judiciary, the U.S. Senate, the U.S. Civil Rights Commission, and the National Committee Against Discrimination in Housing have revealed the decreasing commitment by financial institutions to make single-family residential mortgages in areas undergoing racial transition, areas that would soon be in transition, or in areas already dominated by minority groups. Other studies through the 1970s have supported these earlier conclusions of a racial bias in mortgage lending. If justice is blind, bankers are not.

A 1971 study by the National Urban League concluded that in Chicago and Cleveland, black homebuyers were unable to secure conventional mortgage financing. The study also found that in St. Louis, mortgage lenders freely admitted to shutting off housing funds to large areas of the city populated by minorities. Another study prepared for the Urban League found that as the number of minorities increased in various neighborhoods of the Bronx, the number and dollar value of conventional mortgages decreased.

Still later studies have continued to confirm a racial bias in mortgage lending. A 1977 report prepared by the Massachusetts Banking Department for Governor Michael Dukakis concluded that the "racial composition of the neighborhood was found to be a significant factor in determining bank investment patterns even after statistically controlling for economic and risk-related investment determinants."[9] A 1978 study of mortgage lending in New York State conducted by Robert Schafer of Harvard-MIT's Joint Center for Urban Studies similarly found that "black applicants have a much greater chance of being turned down than do white applicants, even though the socioeconomic, property, and neighborhood conditions are otherwise equivalent."[10]

Appraisals and underwriting are central elements of banks' residential lending. The appraiser estimates the value of a home, judging the effect of neighborhood conditions on the house as well as the condition of the house itself. If the appraiser estimates, for whatever reason, that the neighborhood is declining, the value of the house may be adjusted downward from the agreed-upon sale price. The appraiser often also guesses the number of years that current neighborhood conditions or trends will continue. The proverbial criteria appraisers use in estimating property value are three: location, location, and location.

The banker as loan underwriter then estimates the risks involved in making a loan, which means answering two basic questions. First, what is the probability that the borrower will repay the loan? In considering this question, the loan underwriter looks at the applicant's past credit record, his current debts and income, and his future income prospects. Second, the banks asks, if the borrower does fail to repay the loan, will the lending institution be able to sell the house for a price equal to the amount of the unpaid loan? In answering this question, the underwriter judges the long-range effects of neighborhood trends on the future value of the property. A property's location becomes a major factor in a lender's decision.

Some appraisal concepts are patently discriminatory and lead directly to redlining. For example, traditional appraisal techniques equate racial transition with deterioration, despite the publication of statistical data disproving this assumption. According to the textbooks written by the American Institute of Real Estate Appraisers, "The principle of conformity holds that maximum value is realized when a reasonable degree of sociological and economic homogeneity is present."[11] Similarly, another appraisal manual admonishes that "When the residents are of varied economic, social and cultural backgrounds, the appraiser must determine whether this lack of homogeneity reduces the neighborhood's desirability to present and prospective occupants."[12] Entire neighborhoods are considered higher lending risks because the current or prospective residents have different income levels, ethnic and racial heritages, and life-styles. Potential borrowers, both white and black, are unable to obtain mortgage money at reasonable terms for either purchases or home improvements.

This decision not to invest in integrated neighborhoods is an extension of a larger conceptual model in appraising called "filtering." This model is based on the assumption that as housing ages, it filters down through the social structure, into the hands of poorer and poorer people, until it reaches a point where it is abandoned and demolished. According to this model, age indicates the level of deterioration and abandonment is the inevitable result.[13] It is not surprising that loans for the purchase or rehabilitation of older urban homes are difficult to obtain.

The Federal National Mortgage Association (F.N.M.A., known as Fannie Mae) had also accepted this life-cycle analysis of housing. As a result, Fannie Mae would not purchase a mortgage from a bank if the age of the house plus the term of the mortgage exceeded sixty years. Thus, mortgages to older homes were denied access to the government's secondary-mortgage market, where financial institutions sell mortgages in their portfolio to Fannie Mae for cash in order to replenish their capital available for lending. Fannie Mae's rule meant that banks making loans on older homes had a less liquid asset. Moreover, the government agency's rule of thumb gave legitimacy to refusing to lend on older properties. This rule of sixty was not ended until the late 1970s.

Racial bias has also haunted the regulations of the Federal Home Loan Bank, the regulator for the nation's primary mortgage lenders, federal savings and loan associations. In 1940, the FHLBB's Division of Research and Statistics published articles on how neighborhoods should be rated. Integrated or minority-group-occupied areas were to be given low ratings, while all white neighborhoods were to be given higher ratings.[14] As late as 1961, the FHLBB and other federal regulatory agencies that supervise the nation's mortgage lending institutions still held the view that the entrance of minority groups into a neighborhood could be the cause of a decline in property values.[15]

While the FHLBB no longer publicly views mortgage lending in integrated neighborhoods with a jaundiced eye, some of the FHLBB's administrative actions have clearly been meant to discourage mortgage lending in older, integrated neighborhoods. Through the mid-1970s, applicants for a charter from the FHLBB for a new savings and loan were required to furnish the FHLBB with information on the minority population in the proposed institution's service area and the extent of racial segregation by census tract. Information on racial segregation was to have a bearing on calculating the savings potential of the prospective savings and loan.[16]

Even more convincing evidence that the FHLBB contributed directly to redlining surfaced in testimony given before an Illinois commission examining mortgage practices in 1974. Nelson Brown, assistant counsel to Illinois Federal Savings and Loan of Chicago, testified that FHLBB examiners continually discouraged the directors of his savings and loan from granting conventional mortgage loans in neighborhoods on Chicago's south side. This discouragement took the form of the FHLBB examiners' requiring Illinois Federal to post higher than average reserves for mortgage loans made in certain areas of Chicago.[17] The posting of higher reserves for inner-city mortgages, even those showing no signs of default or delinquency, not only reduced Illinois Federal's earnings, it appeared to make the FHLBB an accomplice in both bank and appraisal redlining.

Nor is it surprising, given the guesses that pass for appraisal science, that banks have vigorously fought efforts to make them disclose to loan applicants the bank's appraisal reports or to disclose the bank's underwriting criteria. Only in Connecticut and Seattle, Washington, have public groups been able to make banks reveal these important reports. In 1977, the Connecticut consumer protection commissioner issued regulations requiring Connecticut's financial institutions to disclose the results of real-estate appraisal reports to prospective borrowers who had paid for them. The regulations were issued as the result of the commissioner's investigation of charges by a Hartford consumer group that some banks might be redlining by turning down mortgage loans based on arbitrary, negative, or inaccurate real-estate appraisal reports. Not giving copies of appraisal reports to prospective borrowers who pay for them is "an unhealthy business practice at the very least," the commissioner commented.[18]

In an out-of-court settlement with the Justice Department, the American Institute of Real Estate Appraisers agreed in late 1977 to forbear alleged discriminatory practices such as using the age, ethnic, or social composition of a neighborhood in their appraisers' handbooks. In approving the settlement, the court held that real estate appraisers must comply with the fair housing laws; Judge George N. Leighton ruled that appraisal standards which scale down the value of homes because of race and national origin of area residents are in violation of the Fair Housing Act of 1968.

### How Do Banks Redline?

The most blatant form of redlining is for a bank simply to tell a mortgage applicant that "we don't lend in that area." While some loan officers might still be this candid, more subtle forms of redlining have grown up to mask the practice as disinvestment has come under fire. Underappraising a property is a common ploy. For example, a person may agree to pay $22,000 for a home and seek a mortgage for $17,600. The bank, rather than turning the applicant down outright, may value the home at only $13,000. Since the bank will lend only 80 percent of its appraised value of the home, it cannot offer a mortgage of more than $10,400. The purchaser would have to come up with such a large down payment—in this case $11,600, compared with $4,400—that the underappraisal would effectively redline the buyer out of the market.

Banks may also employ loan restrictions which make homes harder to buy in the city. Sometimes the restrictions are patently anti-urban, like the Baltimore bankers' restrictions on the width of homes, or Boston bankers' requirement for separate furnaces for each unit in a triple-decker. A more subtle form of discrimination is a practice like requiring a higher down payment on any home other than a single-family. "We ask for that 30 percent on all multi-family homes everywhere," explained one Boston banker, "regardless of whether a house is in the city or the suburbs. It's a uniform, nondiscriminatory policy." Since there are far more multifamily homes in Boston, however, the higher-down-payment policy makes it more difficult to buy homes in the city. It's fine to say that you'll require 30 percent down on all the two-family homes in Pride's Crossing, an upper class suburb of large estates, but how many are there?

Another form of redlining is bank refusal to grant conventional mortgages in an area. In many urban areas, potential homebuyers can obtain a mortgage only if its insured through the Federal Housing Administration (FHA). An applicant need put down merely 10 percent of the purchase price to get an FHA loan, which makes home ownership affordable for many. But FHA loans may actually be more expensive than conventional mortgages. When a lending institution grants an FHA mortgage, it often charges "points." Each point represents 1 percent of the purchase price. For example, a seller may have to pay four points, the buyer one. Thus, if one were to buy a $60,000 house with a mortgage at $50,000 in the city, the seller may have to pay $2,000 to the bank to get it to agree to make the mortgage to the buyer. The buyer may have to pay the bank an additional $500 to get the loan—$500 which will not count toward amortizing the mortgage or increasing the owner's equity, as a down payment does. The buyer often effectively ends up paying the points charged the seller in the form of a higher selling price. The use of points is, of course, essentially a market adjustment to FHA rate ceilings, which are often set below conventional mortgage rate levels. The ceilings allow the

FHA to take credit for lowering the cost of home ownership while in fact it does no such thing.

### Aren't There Legitimate Concerns?

Bankers argue that there is a conflict between their fiduciary obligations and their responsibility to serve the "public convenience and advantage." They insist that neighborhoods allegedly redlined receive fewer mortgages or mortgages on less favorable terms because the risk of loss is higher in these areas. Studies have not supported these allegations. The most extensive one, by Robert Schafer, scrutinized the mortgage delinquency experience in five metropolitan areas in New York State, including New York City. Schafer found that

> *after accounting for the characteristics of the borrower, the loan and the property, risk of loss is not consistently associated with the age of the property, the age of the housing stock in the neighborhood or the location of the property in an area alleged to be redlined.... Some of the neighborhoods that are alleged to be redlined have higher-than-average default rates; others have lower-than-average default rates.... Based on the survey of mortgages held by the mutual savings banks, changes in borrower characteristics (mainly financial difficulties and marital problems) are the most frequently cited reasons for serious delinquencies leading to foreclosure proceedings.*[19]

A 1973 study by the Boston Redevelopment Authority (BRA) on residential property values in Boston belied the bankers' claim that urban homes were not good security for a mortgage because property values were declining in the city. The BRA study had paired identical home sales in Boston over the period 1946–1972. Dividing the data into series covering Boston's fourteen neighborhoods, the study showed that there was no neighborhood in Boston in which homes, on the average, sold for less in later years than in earlier periods. All Boston real estate values had reflected the inflation of the prior decades, regardless of whether the area was still predominantly white, in transition, or almost totally black. With 1946 values set at 1.0, homes in the predominantly black sections of Roxbury, Dorchester and Mattapan sold for 2.1, 2.8 and 2.4, respectively, in 1972, compared to a citywide value of 2.8. While prices in the suburbs and in other sections of Boston had risen faster, these increases in home sale prices provided more than adequate security for bank mortgages, since, in fact, the bank had only lent 80 percent of the original purchase price. As long as prices did not fall, the bank's position was protected.

The data fly in the face of widely held beliefs shared by bankers, that home sales prices fall when minorities move into an area. This belief has been fostered by urban residents who have sold their homes—usually for considerably more than they paid for them, but for less than the standard price for homes in the suburbs. The discrepancy between home prices in the city and suburbs has created the erroneous belief that prices have fallen in the city, or have not kept up with inflation. That is not true. It is more accurate to say that in some urban neighborhoods, prices have not risen as fast as new construction costs in the suburbs. But that has little to do with the value of the urban property as security for the bank's loan. (The belief has also been fostered by episodes of "blockbusting," which may bring temporary drops in home prices.)

### Shortchanging the Cities

New York City, with three-quarters of the state's savings bank deposits, is the nation's largest single capital exporter, at a time when its housing stock is crumbling for lack of capital. While New York's savings bankers argued in the mid-1970s that it was the state's usury ceiling of 8.5 percent which prevented them from making in-state mortgages, in fact New York City savings bankers never lobbied strenuously to have the usury ceiling removed, because it gave them a reasonable excuse for redlining New York.

Brooklyn provides a case study of the murder of a city. "God himself could not get a mortgage in Brooklyn," one bank loan officer told a loan applicant.[20] The data provide the outlines of the bank abandonment process. While Brooklyn based savings banks had $16.8 billion in deposits in 1976, mortgages on Brooklyn homes were worth only $841 million, or 5.1 percent of these banks' deposits.[21] Although they lent hardly any of their funds in Brooklyn, the Brooklyn banks were even more selective to whom they lent, and where, in Brooklyn. Almost 85 percent of the residential mortgages held by Brooklyn savings banks were in census tracts with almost all-white populations. Savings banks had only a handful of mortgages in the extensive belt of non-white communities that stretch across north central Brooklyn. Only one percent of their mortgages were in tracts that were heavily non-white, although these areas made up 45 percent of Brooklyn's population.

The Schafer study clearly tells most of the redlining story:

> *Redlining in New York City means that most upper-middle-class communities, particularly those farthest from minority areas, receive as much as 90% of their mortgages from conventional sources; whereas conventional bank mortgage lending is very low in neighborhoods experiencing racial change. There is virtually no conventional lending in low-income minority communities, and very little in high-income minority areas. In racially changing neighborhoods, which up until recently many academic urban affairs housing experts said experience declining home values, mortgage companies met a great demand for housing in these neighborhoods. In addition, sellers were found to finance from a fifth to a third of the sales in several types of neighborhoods, indicating strong demand not being serviced by either conventional or government-insured mortgage originators.*[22]

Similar bank disinvestment was strangling urban neighborhoods throughout the nation. Almost half the home sales in Boston in 1975 were taking place without bank financing; in predominantly black neighborhoods, Boston area banks provided financing for less than a quarter of sales.[23] Clearly these lending practices were racially discriminatory, with real estate brokers playing an important supporting role in steering applicants in minority areas away from banks and to mortgage companies.

While the First National Bank of Boston has forty branches throughout the city of Boston, it makes very few home mortgages in the city itself. An advertisement run widely by the $8 billion First graphically showed the bankers' perception of a bankable loan. The full-page ad showed pictures of thirty-five styles of single-family homes, under the heading "Whichever house is yours, we like your style. Here's extra cash help of up to $10,000 because you're a homeowner." Missing from any of the photos were pictures of Boston's predominant working-class and middle-income housing—the detached, three-story, three-family frame buildings known as triple-deckers. Not one in the lot. When a local columnist complained about the obvious, the First re-ran the ad, depicting thirty-four expensive-looking landscaped suburban homes—and one triple-decker.

### Streetfighters for Better Neighborhoods

The fight to save urban neighborhoods was a grassroots, populist movement, faced with numerous government-imposed hurdles. Individuals banded together to force banks to stop taking their deposits and reinvesting them elsewhere. Access to credit was not a privilege to be conferred at the whim of the bank president, they argued; it was a right that could be denied only for financially sound reasons.

To get their message across to bankers, community groups started "greenlining" programs—they asked customers to sign pledge cards to withdraw their deposits unless the local bank agreed to reinvest in the surrounding neighborhoods. "No mortgages, no deposits" was the chant.

Community groups in major cities across the nation demanded that the banks disclose where they made mortgage loans and from which neighborhoods they derived their funds. The cry was that mortgage money should be reinvested in the neighborhoods that supplied the deposits. Community groups in Chicago and Washington, D.C., by studying deeds, were able to produce studies showing that most mortgage loans made by major savings institutions in their cities were to suburban borrowers.

The community-group antiredlining movement began in Chicago, led by the formidable Gale Cincotta. In 1972 she was organizing neighborhood meetings, explaining that the banks were killing neighborhoods by their refusal to lend there. Cincotta mobilized Chicago residents and organized the National People's Action on Housing as an umbrella organization for community groups across the nation. One of NPAH's early achievements was obtaining, through a federal savings and loan administrator, a rudimentary survey of mortgage-lending and deposit patterns in metropolitan Chicago. The survey revealed that for every dollar deposited in the inner-city zip-code areas, as little as one cent (and no more than sixteen cents) was reinvested in that area. For suburban Chicago, the statistics showed that thirty cents or more were reinvested by the savings and loan associations in zip-code areas where they were located.[24] These initial data were the beginning, the first documentation of bank disinvestment.

Meanwhile, another Chicago community organization, the Southwest Community Congress, attempted to take over Chicago's Republic Federal Savings, which they alleged was redlining their neighborhoods. Because of the practice of having depositors automatically sign away their voting rights when they open accounts, giving management the right to vote the proxies, the community group had to solicit proxies from the association's depositors for a proxy fight. But management of this Chicago S & L refused to give this particular group of depositors the names of other shareholders.

Unable to communicate with shareholders in the traditional manner, SCC took its message to a series of block-club meetings in advance of the anticipated showdown. Each saver, it was explained, had one vote per $100 on deposit, up to a maximum of 50; mortgagors could cast one vote each. Either group could take back their proxies and vote directly. If a customer wanted to revoke his proxy but not vote it himself, all he had to do was assign it to an SCC third party, it was explained. The showdown finally arrived at Republic Federal's annual meeting in March 1974.

Some 300 concerned shareholders showed up for what is ordinarily an event attended only by the association's directors. Vocal and bitter, the SCC's members stormed out of the meeting after their demands—for geographic disclosure of mortgages and deposits, for the election of two community directors residing within a mile of Republic's office, and for the development of a marketing program to increase mortgage lending in the local community—went down to defeat one by one. The 11,000 or so votes under their control were swamped by the more than 300,000 proxies left in the hands of the association's proxy committee.

"Republic Federal, however, is not bent on gloating over its victory," Republic's president told *Savings and Loan News*. In fact, as a conciliatory gesture, the association is considering adding one or two community residents to its board of directors. "However," stated President Martinek, "this won't be done under duress; any persons selected must be of 'our choice.'"[25]

Having gotten nowhere in trying to deal with bankers directly, community groups turned to the political process. Activist politics led to the Chicago city council's passage, in August 1974, of the very first antiredlining ordinance. City funds could no longer be deposited in banks which did not sign an agreement with the city that they would lend in all Chicago neighborhoods. A year later, in the fall of 1975, Pittsburgh and Boston required banks to sign statements pledging not to redline in order to qualify as depositories for city funds.

### The Numbers Game

In the mid-1970s, redlining charges were a major political issue in most major northern cities. The immediate public demand was that the banks should reveal in which neighborhoods they made loans.

This kind of disclosure did not seem unreasonable to some local and state officials in Chicago, Massachusetts, California, and New York. It certainly did not endanger the safety or soundness of the banks. Banks are chartered to serve "public need and convenience," and at their chartering and for every application to open a new branch, they must satisfy the bank regulatory authority that they will meet a public need.

Banks across the nation continued to refuse to disclose the data, but to an increasingly skeptical public. As the *Boston Globe* editorialized:

> *The irksome opposition of banks and other lending institutions to public disclosure of mortgage information is an example of a witness incriminating himself by refusing to take the stand. Banks for years have denied charges that they discriminated capriciously in withholding mortgages on houses located in certain districts—a practice known as "redlining."*
>
> *It thus figures that banks would leap at the opportunity to produce the data to prove their case. The opposite has occurred...*
>
> *In their fear of revealing mortgage information, the banks are arousing speculation. They appear as though they have more to fear than fear itself.*[26]

State and federal bank regulators refused to antagonize the banks by demanding disclosure. The bankers protested that they couldn't provide mortgage data by census tract breakdowns because they did not keep their records that way, and that to go through all their mortgages and look up the street address on a census-tract map would be prohibitively expensive. Some bankers even charged that disclosure could bankrupt their banks.

Banks continued to denounce disclosure as a "$1 million extravagance,"[27] even though the actual costs were readily ascertainable. In California, savings and loan associations had been supplying the state with such data, by zip code and census tract, monthly for over a decade (although the data were not made available to the public). According to the California Department of Savings and Loan, the computer costs for an association of moderate size ($100 million in assets) to produce the monthly report would be less than $600 annually. For a billion-dollar association, the computer costs were roughly $1,200 per year.

Most bank regulators agreed with the banks that making this information public was the first step toward credit allocation and thus would send us down the road to socialism, and that detailed disclosure would be excessively burdensome. In 1974, when Freyda Koplow, then state banking commissioner of Massachusetts, was presented with figures on the mortgage drought facing home buyers in Boston, she said, "Community renewal is not part of my job,"[28] describing her responsibilities in terms of protecting depositors' investments. An irate homeowner and long-time civic-association leader in one of Boston's neighborhoods replied, "But Commissioner, we are depositors, and the banks are destroying our greatest investment, our homes, by channeling our savings into mortgages made on homes in suburban and vacation areas."[29]

In 1974, in answer to demands by the National People's Action for geographic disclosure of mortgage lending, the Federal Home Loan Bank Board announced at NAPH's annual convention that a disclosure requirement

> ...is not contemplated at this time or in the foreseeable future. It is the agency's opinion that such an effort on a national basis at this time would not lead to reasonable conclusions or solutions.
>
> In addition, the cost of such an effort would be prohibitive; and it would be passed on to home buyers who are already severely burdened by high costs.

The 600 delegates from all over the nation booed and shouted in vain.

"Disclosure is a must," contended the director of Oak Park's Citizens Action Program, saying the public could not be expected to believe denials of redlining. "Associations won't be believed until they produce the records. The burden of proof is on them."[30]

In New York, in 1974, the Housing and Development Administration hired Professor Emmanuel Tobier of New York University to gauge the extent of the mortgage financing problem in New York City. Although Tobier was working under official auspices, many of the city's largest banks refused to give him the data he requested. "They treated us like we were from San Salvador," said Tobier,[31] who then unsuccessfully turned to the New York State Banking Department for help. "The department doesn't collect the information," Tobier said, "probably on the theory that what they don't know can't hurt them. Like most regulatory agencies, the banking department is more interested in protecting the industry it regulates than in protecting the public. The department acts like the lap dog of the banks. Not the watchdog, the lap dog."[32]

While redlining had become a major political issue in many state legislatures by the middle of the decade, only three states—Illinois, Ohio, and New Jersey—enacted significant legislation in 1975. Regulatory agencies in four other states—Wisconsin, Massachusetts, New York, and California—issued regulations which incorporated a variety of antiredling techniques.

In May of 1975 the Massachusetts Banking Department—under its new commissioner, myself—issued a directive requiring banks in the Boston area to make available to the public, at their branches, a breakdown of their mortgage holdings and deposits by census tract for the city of Boston and by zip code for the remainder of the metropolitan area. The directive was the first of its kind in the nation. In June, a score of Massachusetts savings and cooperative banks—including the state's two largest, the Boston Five Cents Savings Bank and the Provident Institution for Savings—took me to court, charging that I had exceeded my authority. The banks sought both a preliminary and a permanent injunction. According to the complaint,

> *On May 20, 1975, in a speech delivered to the Massachusetts Bankers Association, the Commissioner publicly stated that she expects to accomplish two things from her program of disclosure. First, mortgage funds may be somewhat more available in certain areas simply from the political leverage created by disclosure. Second, if there is a redlining problem, we will have some basis for determining its extent and for devising appropriate legislation.*
>
> *Thus, plaintiffs charge the Commissioner personally advocates as a solution to the problem of financing properties in (certain high-risk or depressed) areas, that certain banking institutions which come within her supervision be compelled to grant mortgage loans in the areas concerned.*

Critics of mortgage disclosure charged that it was part of a benighted effort to confine thrifts to their own backyards. These efforts would obstruct the flow of capital from areas of surplus to those of shortage and would inevitably lead to credit rationing. A *Barron's* editorial applauded the Massachusetts bankers' stand:

*Whatever form it takes, credit rationing will inevitably undermine management's authority to make decisions, and pressure fiduciaries into violating their obligations. And while casting about for scapegoats in the private sector, the powers-that-be pointedly ignore the destructive public policies—rent control for one—that have done so much to turn the inner cities into slums. "No more Mr. Nice Guy," so the Massachusetts bankers in effect have proclaimed, and we are moved to applaud. In dealing with the government, nice guys finish last.*

*Right now the pressure is on from coast to coast and the box score looks pretty grim....Only in Massachusetts, apparently, have the embattled bankers opted to stand their ground.*

*Yet this is far too significant an issue to go by default. And for all the sound and fury, foes of "redlining" have produced remarkably little hard evidence....*

*The abuses, in short, are largely illusory (although mounting concern and caution by mortgage lenders about some inner cities would strike us as wholly justified). Contrariwise, the hazards of the proposed "reform" are very real....*

*On either the state or federal level, moreover, a disclosure law is an open invitation to community coercion....*

*In the final analysis, thrift institutions are responsible to their depositors. As the Massachusetts savings banks charge in their complaint: "Under Massachusetts law, boards of investment have responsibility for investing the funds of depositors of the bank in a prudent manner, consistent with the duties and obligations of trustees of an ordinary trust. Other trustees of the bank are likewise held to the same duties and obligations....The Disclosure Directives have as their object an attempt by the Commissioner to compel the investment of the funds of depositors in a manner other than that which the plaintiffs, their boards of investment, trustees, and officers may in the exercise of their legally imposed fiduciary duties deem prudent, sound and safe." That, it seems to us, is not only contrary to law, but also akin to tyranny.*[33]

The savings bankers' lawyer explained in court that the directive was unneeded because the data were available from the Registry of Deeds as well as from a private computing company. The judge was incredulous that the bankers wanted him to rule that they did not have to give to the Commissioners of Banks data that they sold to a private company. The case was dismissed without comment.

While it was now clear that state-chartered banks would have to comply with the Banking Department's disclosure requirement, there was considerable question about the national banks and federally chartered savings and loan associations. A state banking commissioner has regulatory authority only over state-chartered institutions. To counter the objections of state-chartered banks that they were being competitively disadvantaged by disclosure, I asked the national banks and federal savings and loan associations to provide the state with the data voluntarily. The four largest Boston national banks turned to their federal regulator at the Boston regional office of the Comptroller of the Currency to protect them. The regional administrator obligingly wrote a letter to all national banks in Massachusetts telling them that providing data to the public on where their banks made mortgages was "not in the best interest of the public." That's regulatorese for "don't do it."

The regional administrator had unwittingly given me the public-relations opportunity I needed. I immediately wrote to members of the Massachusetts congressional delegation asking for their help, pointing out that the regional administrator's letter was a deliberate attempt to undermine the sincere effort of the Commonwealth of Massachusetts to address itself to a most serious problem. I then requested them to ask the Comptroller immediately to write to national banks in the Boston area and to tell them that they are certainly free to do as they wish and that nothing in the letter from the regional office was meant to preclude them from giving data to the Commissioner of Banks if they so desired.

I then called a press conference to denounce Comptroller Smith for subverting the good working relationship between a state official and the state's banks. One public official attacking another is news: *The New York Times* picked up the story from the Associated Press. The next day, the Comptroller apologized to me, a few minutes before my scheduled televised newscast. He further promised to send a letter to national banks in Massachusetts explaining that he had never meant that the banks should not send the requested data.

Some banks decided to take the offensive by trying to mobilize their depositors as an offsetting political weight to the influence of community groups. The $1 billion Boston Five Cents Savings Bank took the lead in Boston. After losing the court suit over mortgage disclosure, the bank, in late 1975, began an effort to "motivate" its depositors to write to state legislators to halt antiredlining moves. The bank tested a letter on a sample of depositors, solicitously asking them to answer a few questions; by "so doing," the Boston Five wrote, "you may learn about a situation that could have adverse effects upon you and The Boston Five." Among the eight questions asked of depositors were the following:

> *4) It is quite true that in certain urban localities we make few mortgage loans because we receive few mortgage applications from these areas....This is particularly true in areas of urban blight where there is higher unemployment, lower income, and rising vandalism, robbery and violent crime. Many residents would move out of these areas if they could—few people want to buy homes there.*
>
> *Would you say that the lack of demand for mortgage loans in these areas is caused:*
>
> *( ) By the unwillingness of banks to lend there? Or, ( ) By the existing condition in such areas? ( ) Don't know*
>
> *5) As you know, the funds controlled by savings banks like the Boston Five, are the deposits of its customers...typically individuals of moderate income who depend on the bank as a safe place for their savings, while earning reasonable interest. And savings banks are charged by law to invest funds of their depositors as carefully and prudently as they would invest funds of their own.*
>
> *What do you believe the primary responsibility of the savings banks should be in making mortgage loans in distressed inner-city areas?*
>
> *( ) To apply normal lending standards...thus providing maximum protection of depositors' funds....( ) To assist disadvantaged groups and inner-city areas by lowering lending standards and with special lending programs—even though loss to the bank—and ultimately to the depositors—appears inevitable.*
>
> *6) Recent attempts have been made to pass legislation and impose regulations which could interfere with banks' responsibility to their depositors. Such legislation, for example, could lead to a quota system that would allot loans by district or neighborhood. In other words, not the banks, but a regulatory agency would direct the investment of depositors' funds.*
>
> *Banks foresee two destructive effects from such legislation. First, that forcing the banks to make loans in deteriorating neighborhoods would increase the probability of foreclosures—with resulting financial loss to both borrowers and depositors.*

*Second, that such legislation would force banks to set aside funds for mortgages in areas where there was little call for them—and curtail mortgage loans in areas where they were in demand.*

*Would you agree that The Boston Five and other banks have good reason to fight such legislation and regulation?* ( ) *Yes* ( ) *No*

The survey questionnaire contained grossly misleading distortions. There was not a hint that the depositors' funds were not only insured by the Federal Deposit Insurance Corporation up to $40,000, but that under Massachusetts law, the deposits were insured in full by the Mutual Savings Central Fund.

I wrote to The Boston Five that as Commissioner of Banks I was concerned that its letter in its present form would unduly frighten depositors and cautioned against implementing the bank's plan to send it to all its depositors. I also questioned the racist overtones in the letter and the inflammatory impact it might have on a city already torn by stife over forced busing. I also mentioned that I intended to discuss these concerns with the Consumer Protection and Civil Rights divisions of the Attorney Generals Office and wondered aloud whether the half truths in the letter did not violate the state's consumer protection law about "unfair and deceptive trade practices."

The Boston Five went to Washington, D.C., to seek help from Republican Senator Edward Brooke of Massachusetts. The only black member of the Senate was quite sensitive to the redlining issue, however, and did not offer his aid. The bank scotched its plans for further mailings.

Massachusetts' success in getting the banks to reveal their lending policies was followed by similar actions in New York, California, and Illinois. In June of 1975, the state of California held public hearings on redlining, under the auspices of the state's Secretary of Business and Transportation Donald Burns. "There's absolutely no question 100 reasonable men out of 100 would agree that loans are not being made in certain geographic areas and those areas correspond to areas where people's skin is darker than that of the Caucasian majority and whose language is other than English," Burns said in announcing the hearings.[34] An aide to Secretary Burns, Llewellyn Werner, said that the hearings would "put to rest within the first few minutes" the question of whether redlining exists by the presentation by state officials of statistical evidence which would prove it a reality.[35]

The California hearings documented extensive redlining in

Los Angeles, Sacramento, San Francisco, and Pasadena. Never before had such practices been so thoroughly documented in California. The furor created by publicizing that "almost one out of every 10 persons in the Sacremento area lives in a redlined neighborhood...[and] an estimated one million people live in redlined areas of Los Angeles where conventional loans are almost never made"[36] led to widespread demands for state action. The banking community's response, as expressed by the President of the Federal Home Loan Bank of San Francisco was that

> ...*the decision to grant or not grant a mortgage loan is ultimately a judgment matter—based on such simple factors as risk, profitability, return and community responsibility and service....[It is extremely difficult to] regulate, legislate or otherwise dictate matters of judgment without creating more and greater problems.*[37]

The President of the American Savings and Loan Association added "Housing is not the only problem in these areas. Unemployment, crime and other factors have created a very grave situation."[38] Notwithstanding, the hearing had legitimized the community activists' charges. *The Los Angeles Times* intoned in its lead editorial:

> *Redlining is a loaded word. It evokes an image of powerful people in paneled offices who can blight entire neighborhoods permanently with the stroke of a pen on a map. It smacks of a capricious disregard for the welfare of troubled communities.*
> *Redlining describes only part of a larger picture. But it is enough of the picture to be a problem.*[39]

The stage had been set for state action. In August of 1975, the Department of Business and Transportation (which supervises the State Department of Savings and Loan Associations and the State Department of Banking) issued proposed antiredlining regulations which required extensive monthly reporting of loan data by census tract and prohibited the consideration of neighborhood or geographic factors in making loans. The California regulations also called for boards to be set up in Los Angeles and San Francisco to review rejected applications. Each three-person board would consist of a representative of the savings and loan industry, a member of the State Savings and Loan Department, and a public member appointed by the state. The boards would review rejected applications at the request of the applicants.

Massachusetts, California, and New York attacked redlining through administrative regulations because the state legislative banking committees essentially represented banking interests. It was in Illinois that the nation's first legislation was passed. In August 1975, Governor Dan Walker signed a bill meant to outlaw the "evil practice called redlining" as well as one to require public disclosure of mortgages by geographic area. "These are the neighborhoods," Governor Walker said, "where people work hard, pay their taxes, observe and respect the law. They are entitled to our protection."[40]

Activist groups in Chicago, which had helped write the legislation, were jubilant. "Having these bills under our belt," said Gale Cincotta, "will carry considerable weight in Washington."[41] Having the data collected at the state level undercut opponent's argument that disclosure was technically unfeasible or prohibitively expensive.

With state actions in California, Illinois, Massachusetts, and New York as a precedent, Congress passed Senator Proxmire's Home Mortgage Disclosure Act of 1975, in which all federal depositories were directed to disclose to the public their patterns of mortgage lending by census tract and zip code. The banks were able to defeat at the national level any disclosure of the geographic distribution of their deposits. This was Congress's first direct attack on redlining. The act offers no solution to the redlining problem other than disclosure; the Senate Banking Committee expressed the belief that "once depositors are aware of the lending practices of institutions located in their communities, marketplace competition will lead lenders to become more community-minded, and mortgage credit will become more plentiful in older neighborhoods."[42]

The passage of the Home Mortgage Disclosure Act was a triumph of democratic politics. In 1970, few people had even heard of the term "redlining." Five years later, community groups had made it part of the nation's vocabulary and had gotten a major piece of national legislation passed to deal with the problem, despite the strenuous opposition of the well-financed banking lobbies.

### The Federal Regulatory Agencies and Disclosure

The federal bank-regulatory agencies steadfastly refused to be drawn into the position of criticizing "their" banks, or of providing data so that others could do so. After Congress passed the Home Mortgage Disclosure Act, Senator Proxmire, chairman of the Senate Banking Committee, asked the Federal Home Loan Bank Board staff to analyze the data for thirty major cities to determine how widespread urban disinvestment by thrift institutions was. The FHLB, with a large research staff and a huge budget, answered that it could not do such a study because it lacked the resources.

The federal law that required banks to compile their mortgage-loan data left implementing regulations to the Federal Reserve Board. The Board decided not to have banks send the information to Washington because the Fed was determined not to have its enormous staff of more than 200 economists analyze it. Instead, the Board's regulation provided that computer printouts be kept where interested community groups could look at them. There would be no federal study of lending practices in urban areas.

While the federal regulatory agencies steadfastly undermined the intent of the Home Mortgage Disclosure Act by refusing to analyze the data, state officials and community groups with minimal resources undertook the task. In Massachusetts, the Banking Department historically had no research department and no computer facilities. A research director was appointed to an examiner's position, and a research staff recruited from college students who worked as volunteers. The computer analysis for the study was done by one of these researchers as part of her work for an undergraduate computer course.

What did the data demonstrate? The information for Boston showed that for every dollar residents deposit in their savings banks, on average only thirteen cents is reinvested in mortgages in their neighborhoods. Boston's outer suburbs are on the other side of the money flow: there, banks invested at least $1.12 for each dollar deposited, and in some suburban communities, investment exceeded three dollars for every dollar deposited by town residents.[43] The city rather than being the "deposit desert" that bankers tried to depict, was clearly the well that was watering suburban growth.

Getting the data only proved that banks redlined; it didn't necessarily mean the practice would stop. It didn't even make redlining illegal. If the banks had been less politically sophisticated, they could have continued thumbing their noses at the community groups. But in several cities, some bankers realized that they had to answer the public's perceptions that their policies were unfair, even if they were not illegal. Voluntary action plans were initiated, often after long and acrimonious public debate about the role of banks in the city. In Philadelphia, there was the Philadelphia Mortgage Plan, a voluntary agreement by banks to revise their underwriting standards so they could make sound loans in previously redlined neighborhoods. Seattle had a similar plan. In Los Angeles, San Francisco, Pittsburgh, and Boston, there were mortgage review boards, voluntary groups of savings bankers and community leaders which met and reviewed rejected mortgage loans if the denied applicants alleged redlining. New York, Denver, and St. Louis bankers set up mortgage pools to provide loans in inner-city areas.

### The Philadelphia Mortgage Plan

The Philadelphia Mortgage Plan got its start in early 1975, when activists challenged the city's banks to consider the whole problem of urban disinvestment. Three bank presidents took up the challenge: M. Todd Cooke of the Philadelphia Saving Fund Society, Frederick Heldring of Philadelphia National Bank, and James F. Bodine of First Pennsylvania Corp. These executives entered discussions with community leaders under the aegis of the Philadelphia Partnership, a non-profit consortium of civic and business leaders. Philadelphia's forty city-based savings and loan associations, which make 60 percent of Philadelphia's mortgages, held aloof from the discussion and never joined the city's four mutual savings and commercial banks in implementing the Plan.

Fundamentally, the Philadelphia Mortgage Plan is a set of underwriting guidelines that redefine "neighborhood." A neighborhood is usually understood to be an area measured in square miles; inevitably, an area of that size in any major urban center will include blighted sections, causing lenders to write off the whole sector. Under the Philadelphia Mortgage Plan, mortgage officers agreed to limit considerations of neighborhood to the particular block on which the house was located. If that block had less than 10 percent abandonment, the Plan called for assessing the neighborhood as bankable, regardless of whether the next street happened to be burnt out. Participating banks pledged to base decisions only on the structural soundness of the house itself and the creditworthiness of the individual applicant. The banks have covered their own exposure by requiring private mortgage insurance for all loans in excess of 75 percent of the appraisals. As a result, they have been willing to make loans with down payments as low as 5 percent.

"The plan is not a cure-all," said William Gray, a Baptist minister who helped draw it up. "But it is a very powerful step in the right direction."[44] And banker Cooke explains: "What we're trying to do is make it just as easy for a creditworthy moderate- or lower-income family to buy in some of these older areas as it is for those who want to buy in Levittown."[45]

The participating banks agreed to meet whatever market demand developed for inner-city loans rather than establish specific lending goals. By early 1979, they had made more than 4,700 low- to moderate-income mortgages to 7,000 applicants, primarily in those sections of the city that bankers had previously avoided.[46] There have been only twelve foreclosures and an extremely low delinquency rate.[47] Before any loan request is rejected, the applicant is reviewed by all participating bank lending officers at regular weekly meetings. Every other month, bankers and a community review committee meet to iron out difficulties.

The Philadelphia Mortgage Plan, while it does not entirely meet the city's mortgage needs, has been widely praised, and even copied in Seattle and Detroit. Robert Kuttner, a staffer for the U.S. Senate Banking Committee at the time, expressed the widely held view: "We think very highly of the plan because it shows what the private sector can do and dispels some of the mythology surrounding urban lending."

### The Mortgage Review Boards: A Panacea or a Placebo?

Disclosure, of course, is not a solution. One approach tried in Boston was the Mortgage Review Board, a court of appeals of sorts. During the fall of 1975, the Massachusetts Department of Banks negotiated with savings banks and community leaders to find a mechanism by which individuals who believed they had been redlined could get speedy redress.

The formation of the Boston Mortgage Review Board occurred only after a long public controversy with the savings banks after I had been appointed Commissioner of Banks. As commissioner, I had originally proposed an assigned-risk pool for mortgages in redlined areas, as was done, for example, in Massachusetts "FAIR" plan for insurance in certain districts. Membership in a Massachusetts mortgage agency would have been mandatory for all financial institutions. These would have been assessed up to 2.5 percent of their capital and surplus accounts to support the agency. But the proposed plan for mortgages would have required legislation. Savings bankers confidently told me they could defeat any such measure introduced in the legislature. I agreed that no bill would pass if introduced that year, 1975; new concepts very rarely win passage the first time they are broached. But I challenged the bankers to bet on the odds of passage by the fourth year the legislation was introduced.

The bankers were not willing to gamble. In return for the savings bankers' agreement to create a Mortgage Review Board with community participation, I committed the Dukakis administration not to submit legislation during the next four years for a legislatively mandated mortgage pool for inner-city lending.

Despite the agreement, the savings bankers dragged their feet. Nonetheless, at the last minute, after the public announcement of the Board in September of 1975, the savings bankers said they couldn't join without prior approval from the U.S. Justice Department—assurance that the Review Board would not violate the antitrust laws. I duly obtained the requisite letter from Justice.

The banks continued to delay, and in fact agreed to the Review Board only after seeing the results of a Becker Research Corporation survey in late 1975 indicating that most people throughout the state felt that banks should be involved in community programs. The overwhelming number of persons who favored bank involvement, the survey found, did so because they believed that banks have an obligation to put community money (that is, depositors' money) back into the community. Eighty percent of those contacted responded that it was at least "fairly important" for banks to be involved in lending programs of all types to improve the local community. A majority of residents, moreover, believed that banks had no obligation to finance home ownership in areas of declining property values. A small but significant group favored the financing of home ownership in declining areas even if it meant that banks would lose money, or would pay lower interest rates on savings accounts. This group tended to be younger, better educated, and more affluent than most depositors; since such people are likely to make up a very vocal minority, the survey concluded that banks could anticipate major criticism if they failed to get involved in this type of financing. As a result of this survey, the bankers knew that stonewalling on the redlining issue was no longer politically possible, and while they continued to insist that the banking commissioner was legislating only her social priorities, they decided to change tactics. They agreed to stop putting up obstacles to the formation of a Mortgage Review Board.

In January of 1976, the Mortgage Review Board was established as a voluntary agency, with no legal powers under any statute. It comprised three community leaders and three banks representing most of the savings banks of Boston. Neither group trusted the other enough to allow there to be a possible majority on either side. When a mortgage application was rejected by a participating bank, on a one- to four-family, owner-occupied home in Boston, the bank automatically attached a form letter to the rejection stating that its decision could be reviewed by the Mortgage Review Board if the applicant desired. To obtain a review, the applicant need only sign the form, and put it in the attached envelope, addressed to the Banking Department. The Review Board met every two weeks, in the commissioner's office. If a majority of the Board agreed that the loan was bankable under the Board's rules (mortgage payments could not exceed 25 percent of income; all debt payments could not exceed a third of gross income; and the property must be in reasonable condition, according to an appraisal report from the bank), then the Board would ask the original bank to reconsider making the loan. If that bank declined, the Board would find another bank to make the loan. Individual banks' management thus maintained their control over loans.

After their initial intransigence, savings bankers have come to welcome Mortgage Review Boards as a way of defusing the redlining issue. "Voluntary boards are the best way to deal with the issue," Elliot Carr, executive vice-president of the Massachusetts Savings Bank Association, told the *Boston Globe*. "Much more can be accomplished informally than by outlawing something."

In looking at the limited numbers of mortgage appeals reviewed by mortgage review boards, one senses that they are only marginally effective. Part of their problem derives from the fact that the burden of appeal is on the applicant, who may not perceive that his application was rejected because of redlining rather than for the apparent reason stated on the loan rejection. Moreover, review boards can deal only with cases in which someone has been denied a mortgage in writing and has the time and sophistication to appeal. Many people may be discouraged verbally or steered by mortgage brokers to non-bank means of financing, like mortgage companies.

The Mortgage Review Board and constant public pressure from community groups, the *Boston Globe*, and the Banking Commissioner did affect Boston bank's lending patterns. Banks significantly increased their support of the mortgage market in

Boston. The percentage of home sales in Boston financed with bank mortgages rose from 55 percent to 64 percent over a two-year period, with the most impressive gains in areas with heavy minority populations. In heavily black neighborhoods, like Roxbury and North Dorchester, the ratio of home sales financed with bank mortgages rose from 20 percent to 42 percent.

Local efforts to combat discriminatory lending practices can be successful while there is community vigilance and cooperation from state officials, but it places a large burden on community groups to place continuing pressure on institutions and to monitor developments. Whatever success the Mortgage Review Board has had in Boston has come not so much from the applications reviewed but from its very existence: every mortgage officer in the city is aware that his actions may be challenged and his bank publicly embarrassed. For the long haul, however, cities cannot rely on unpaid volunteers to give their time to monitor lending practices; this is clearly the job of regulatory agencies. It has fallen to community groups because the bank regulators and the Department of Housing and Urban Development (HUD) have failed to carry out their Congressional mandates.

While disclosure requirements had documented the existence of widespread disinvestment in America's cities, it had been very nearly impossible to get either federal or state laws to declare geographic discrimination illegal. For a brief while in late 1977, it appeared that Massachusetts might pass a strong antiredlining bill. The political support for the bill emerged from a rare combination of forces: an activist bank commissioner, community ferment, and controversy over a legislative junket paid for by the banking lobby, the exposure of which had embarrassed legislators who might otherwise have anchored the opposition.

While the banking commissioner and community groups had been leading the battle for antiredlining legislation, the legislation would have had little chance of passage were it not for an act of misjudgment by the Savings Bank Association. In September of 1976, the association held its annual three-day convention in Bermuda. The Massachusetts House and Senate banking committee chairmen flew down, with their wives, for three days with all expenses paid by the savings bankers.

At first, the legislators' trip seemed to have been a solid, low-risk investment for the bankers. The legislators had even assured the bankers that they need not worry about antiredlining legislation. In March, however, a reporter for a tiny biweekly periodical called *Beacon Hill Update* (funded with federal money to keep community organizations informed of State House goings-on) got wind of the junket. The reporter found that full details of the trip had been published in a bankers' magazine. The *Update* printed the story; more significantly, the *Boston Globe* picked it up three days later. Coming at the height of a controversy over legislative corruption and conflict of interest, the trip became a made-to-order example of questionable ethics.

The legislature rushed through the weakest bill it could draft and hoped that the public wouldn't notice the bill's non-contents. But Governor Dukakis refused to be part of the charade and vetoed the bill.

Legal support for community activists' charges that redlining was not only unfair but illegal came in February of 1976, with a landmark decision in Cincinnati. A federal court ruled for the first time that the practice of refusing to lend mortgage money to potential home buyers in racially integrated neighborhoods was illegal under the Fair Housing Act of 1968. The decision was given by Federal District Judge David S. Porter in a suit brought by a white couple against a Cincinnati financial institution on charges of refusing a mortgage loan in a racially integrated neighborhood.

In June of that year, the Senate Committee on Banking, Housing and Urban Affairs issued a report sharply criticizing the efforts of four federal regulatory agencies to enforce the Fair Housing Act of 1968. The committee found a "generally unsatisfactory history of enforcement activities by all four agencies" and recommended that they "adopt an immediate program for enforcing the fair-housing-lending provisions of the 1968 Civil Rights Act."[48] The committee was particularly disturbed by its finding that, almost eight years after passage of the Act, only one of the four agencies had published fair-lending regulations. All four agencies had required the banks they regulated to display posters and include in their ads that they are "equal-housing lenders," but only the Federal Home Loan Bank had moved beyond poster requirements and issued specific antidiscrimination regulations.

What is to be done? "One alternative," says economics Professor Emmanuel Tobier of New York University, "is to do nothing and watch the city go down the drain. Another is to *force* the savings banks to invest..."[49]

# 6.

# The Bank Branch as Hostage

*The Act can best be described as a
Congressional rebuke to the banking agencies for
their shamefully long neglect of a paramount
national problem, the destabilization and
decline of urban neighborhoods and to a lesser
extent rural communities.*[1]
—*Ralph Nader*

As 1975 faded into 1976 and 1977, it became clearer that disclosure of and publicity about banks' disinvestment in neighborhoods were not enough to promote reinvestment. A better lever was needed. Holding new bank branches as "hostage" for bank commitments to serve the credit needs of their present communities, requiring reinvestment as the quid pro quo for permission to branch, seemed to offer just the leverage required. This was a dramatic departure, however, from the bank regulatory agencies' traditional approach to evaluating branch applications: The agencies, like the applicants, had always defined the "convenience and needs" stipulated in statutes as referring only to deposit facilities in the *new* area rather than to credit needs of older or existing service areas. And in the redefining lies a tale.

Banks want to branch, of course, because they compete in the convenience provided by their multiple locations rather than by offering higher interest rates on deposits or lower rates on loans. And urban banks are eager to establish themselves in the (presumably more lucrative) suburbs. In the decade since the late 1960s, bank branching laws have been liberalized in many states, contributing to the great suburban rush. Urban community groups opposed allowing banks to branch out of the city because they feared that this would only exacerbate banks' anti-urban/pro-suburban lending policies.

And so community groups began to argue that banks should not be allowed to branch out of their present service areas unless they offered commitments to maintain or improve their services provided there. As early as April of 1975, for example, Boston's Jamaica Plain Community Banking and Mortgage Committee, in its first meeting with the newly appointed Massachusetts Bank Commissioner, challenged my position in favor of unlimited, statewide branching. The group argued that branching is often a ploy to allow a bank in an older neighborhood to stop servicing that neighborhood. They wanted, as a quid pro quo for any relaxation of state branching restrictions, guarantees that the neighborhoods would be protected from losing their banks' lending services.

The National Urban League was among the first groups to proprose the idea that a bank's record in serving the credit needs of its present depositors should be criterion for evaluating its branching applications. In 1973, the League had pointed out: "It appears that strict regulations of the branching process might be able to stem the pace of central-city disinvestment."[2]

Some four years later, Richard W. Golden of the New York Public Interest Research Group, Inc. (NYPIRG) would make similar demands of the New York State Banking Department:

*Thrift institutions loudly and often allude to their responsibility as custodian of depositors' savings. Their responsibility to satisfy the credit needs of people living in their service areas is at least as important, although unfortunately not as often acknowledged.*

*Withdrawal of credit from their neighborhoods injures depositors just as gravely as if their savings were thrown into the sea....*

*The obligations of banks to supply credit for the benefit of their depositors is so fundamental that the responsible governmental agencies should take any opportunity to enforce it....*

*The Board should not grant any branch application to a bank which disinvests its existing service area....*

*A bank's record in its existing service areas is of crucial importance in determining whether to grant a branch application. The Department's regulations should be amended so as to require applicants to demonstrate that they are satisfying demand for credit in their existing service areas. Failure to meet this requirement should be grounds for denial of the application.*[3]

The gauntlet had been thrown down. The bank branch was to be hostage to urban reinvestment goals.

While federal bank regulators, and most state regulators, were openly sympathetic to the banks' flight from the cities, some state regulators did reflect concern about urban neighborhoods in their branching decisions. To reconcile community groups to branching, banking departments in several states devised ways to extract from applicant banks commitments to serve the credit needs of their original communities. This represented something of a revolution in state regulation: State bank commissioners have traditionally shown themselves to be even more pro-bank than their federal counterparts. But in the mid-1970s, seven states appointed actively consumerist bank regulators. In New York under Superintendent John Heimann, in Connecticut under Commissioner Lawrence Connell, in Michigan under Commissioner Richard Francis, in Massachusetts under Commissioner Carol Greenwald, in California under Secretary Donald Burns and Commissioner Carl Schmidt, in Maine under Ralph Gelder, and in New Jersey under Virginia Long, the public had a chance to see the difference pro-consumer regulators could make.

The bankers were horrified. They had been so used to having bank commissioners who were their lobbyists in government that they could not adjust to the notion that a public official represents the public interest. As one disgruntled banker asked me, "Are you *our* Commissioner or the public's Commissioner?"

What were the terrible things these "public commissioners" were trying to do? They believed that bankers redlined and they wanted it stopped. They were trying to make the state-chartered banks respond to the needs of their users.

In return, bankers charged that bank regulators were becoming "social engineers" without legislative authorization in their efforts to make inner-city mortgage lending a precondition for branching. Ira O. Scott, Jr., executive vice-president of the Savings Bank Association of New York, led the counterattack:

> *It is not, I think, overstating the case to say that the savings banks of New York State are today in a state of siege. The industry is under attack....Serious, and sometimes successful attempts are being made to coerce individual savings banks into taking actions that may tend to take the power to make investment decisions out of the hands of savings bank trustees, where it clearly and legally belongs....*

It appears that the regulatory authorities are considering making the mortgage lending record of a savings bank one of the criteria for determining whether or not an application for a new branch office or a merger is to be approved. [author's emphasis] *The concern seems to be whether the savings bank has adequately serviced the areas in which it presently has offices with mortgage loans....*

*The legitimacy of injecting such a criterion into the procedure of acting upon an application for a branch office or a merger proposal is doubtful, to say the least. It must be challenged....*

*Will the supervisories try to accomplish what the legislature has refused to authorize? Will they assume the role of social engineers? Is it their function to rebuild the inner city? To declare that the right to a mortgage is a human right?"*[4]

### The Activist Bank Commissioners and the Quid Pro Quo

As Bank Commissioner for Connecticut, Lawrence Connell, Jr., used the powers of his office almost immediately after taking office, in 1975, to insist that banks participate in the food stamp program. When he could not get voluntary agreement, he simply announced that he would approve no new branches in the state until the state-chartered banks found a way to sell food stamps. The branching freeze lasted only six acrimonious weeks before the banks gave in. At that point, Connell raised the ante by including student loan programs, extended banking hours, and mortgage availability in low- and moderate-income neighborhoods as essential criteria in his determination that the convenience and needs of the community would be served by a new branch.

In Massachusetts, after creating a Mortgage Review Board, I asked Steven Weiss, the Deputy Commissioner of Banks, to come up with an affidavit of community service that urban banks would be required to sign before they could receive approval for suburban branches. The affidavit he designed was patterned on one being considered by the New York Banking Department. The Massachusetts version differed in that it required a bank to justify its refusal to make certain kinds of housing-related loans in particular areas, or its practice of making such loans available only on less advantageous terms, by citing its own loss experience with such loans. As in the New York affidavit, banks applying for branches had to agree to make mortgage loan applications available at all their offices; to announce the availability of loan applications to any member of the public who inquired about a loan; and to consider on their merits all applications for loans on residential properties.

The affidavits of community service also required that banks hold meetings with interested community groups and engage in "affirmative marketing." To make known their willingness to lend in the neighborhoods where they had branches, banks had to advertise in community newspapers and expand contacts with local realtors. Mutual thrift institutions were further required to make concerted efforts to assure that their boards of directors or trustees were truly representative of the population in the communities where their branches were located.

The affidavits did force banks to change their underwriting policies. For example, in order to receive regulatory approval to relocate a branch office sixty feet, one of Boston's largest savings banks had to change a major loan policy and agree to consider on the merits requests for mortgages and home improvement loans on structures with more than five units that were not owner-occupied. Another large western Massachusetts banker, complaining that "Your affidavit of Community Service puts us between a rock and a hard place," agreed to hand out mortgage applications at all its branches, and to stop quoting mortgage rates of ¾ percent to 1 percent higher for older properties than for new ones, in order to receive regulatory approval to move into the bank's newly constructed main office.

In California, the Business and Transportation Agency, which has overall regulatory authority for state chartered savings and loan associations, issued tough antiredlining regulations in 1976. In addition to requiring public disclosure (monthly, by census tract) of deposits and mortgage loans and setting up two regional mortgage-review boards, the department announced public hearings on applications for new branches from state-chartered savings and loan associations and written statements from them indicating how their planned operations in the new branch would affect mortgage-deficient areas. The new regulations also created new requirements for branching, chartering and merging of associations, including the filing of a neighborhood impact statement and an affirmative marketing plan. They further required written notice to a mortgage applicant within twenty-one days of a loan rejection explaining why the loan application was rejected and how the applicant might appeal the decision. Donald Burns, head of the

California Business and Transportation Agency, added, "We're asking for a commitment of dollars, not glittering press releases. We won't exactly require a certified check but we will be asking the S&Ls to share the risk in funding necessary loans to mortgage-starved communities."[5]

The California department also was the first bank regulatory agency to try to make nondiscriminatory lending practices part of the normal bank examination process. While the principal focus of the bank examination continued to be upon safety and soundness, the California Department of Savings and Loan issued "Fair Lending" regulations which involved having bank examiners view lending policies from a new perspective. In a fundamental change in the examiners' orientation, the regulations called for the examiner not only to criticize loans that should not have been made, the examiners' traditional function, but also to criticize loans that should have been made but were not. The examiner was to review the results of the financial institution's practices and underwriting criteria to determine if they had a disproportionate impact on certain groups. (The "effects test," which grew out of civil rights cases, was now being applied to lending practices. The key principle in the test is that if a practice has the effect of discrimination, even if it's unintentional, the burden is on the institution to show that such a practice is necessary to achieve an overriding legitimate business purpose.) The examiner was also to evaluate the adequacy of the affirmative-marketing programs adopted by the savings and loan associations. The use of bank examiners to enforce antidiscrimination regulations as part of the regular examination process was an almost revolutionary attack on redlining practices. If the examiners hadn't been so well schooled in the old philosophy of bank examination, and so sympathetic to the bankers' views, these regulations and procedures would have represented the toughest and most comprehensive attack on redlining practices ever undertaken in the nation. The problem in practice arose from trying to get new regulations enforced by agents whose hearts were still with the old ways.

In New York, neighborhood groups, led by the New York Public Interest Research Group (PIRG), were demanding change. Early in 1977, New York PIRG and several such groups petitioned the banking department to issue regulations requiring that consideration be given to whether a savings bank or savings and loan association applying for a new branch was satisfying the need for mortgage and home-improvement loans in the service area of its existing offices. The NY PIRG proposed as a standard that "If the applicant has not reinvested 'a stated proportion' of its deposits in the neighborhoods served by its existing office, the application will be denied unless the applicant can show that there was no demand for mortgage or home improvement loans despite public awareness that these services were available."[6]

The New York Banking Department, like other state and federal banking agencies and the Congress, shied away from criteria that required banks to invest a certain percentage of their funds in local area mortgages because such proposals would, in effect, mandate investment or allocate credit. "Credit allocation" is one of those pejorative terms that immediately rallies all right-thinking people; as with other buzz words, it affects even those it is used against. In every attempt to encourage banks to consider inner-city lending more sympathetically, almost every advocate has observed the prevailing ideology and explained that his proposal was *not* credit allocation. The New York PIRG's recommendation of explicit rules violated the required subtlety.

In late 1977, the New York Banking Department proposed new procedures which went part way toward meeting the recommended standard. Banks wanting branches would have to prove that they were meeting the newly defined public need in areas where they already had offices. A bank's branching application was required to state that application forms are available at each office, that prospective applicants are not discouraged from applying, that a written record of all inquiries (including telephone requests) is maintained, and that advertising is placed in local media stating mortgage loans are available. The proposed application also required banks to agree to try to induce landlords of buildings on which mortgages are held to follow sanitary and building-code stipulations and to meet with community groups. The department stopped short of requiring any dollar commitment to the existing service area.

The department did, however, take an increasingly active role as an intermediary in the heated controversy over redlining between savings banks and community groups. The department hosted meetings between neighborhood groups and savings banks applying for new suburban branches to work out affirmative-marketing agreements. An application by the $1.4 billion Greater New York Savings Bank of Brooklyn to branch into the suburbs was approved only after the bank, in Superintendent Siebert's office, had worked out with a community organization called

"Bank on Brooklyn" a program of increased mortgage lending in that borough. The agreement with the Greater New York Savings Bank involved an annual mortgage investment target of $25 million, the inclusion of community representatives on a lending advisory committee, and the assignment of additional bank personnel at selected branches to take part in activities to stimulate business and housing in their areas. The advisory committee would meet each quarter to review the number of mortgages granted or refused by the bank and to consider the merits of the current terms and conditions for mortgage credit.

Although the commitment to mortgage lending in Brooklyn satisfied the New York Banking Department, it did not satisfy the Federal Deposit Insurance Corporation. In a closely watched test case of how a newly passed federal statute, the Community Reinvestment Act, would be enforced by the federal regulators, the application to branch was denied in April of 1979 by the FDIC. The agency gave as its reason that the percentage of the bank's funds committed to mortgages in the Brooklyn area, although increasing, remained at a fairly low level. It was the first action of its kind by a federal agency—but hardly the first chapter in the story of the CRA.

## The Community Reinvestment Act of 1977

In his opening statement on the hearings for the Community Reinvestment Act, Senator Proxmire stated:

*This bill would provide that a bank charter carries with it an obligation to serve the credit needs of the area the bank is chartered to service, consistent with prudent lending practices. Furthermore, it would provide regulatory machinery to carry out this policy.*

*The bill is based on two widely shared assumptions.*

*First: Government through tax revenues and public debt cannot and should not provide more than a limited part of the capital required for local housing and economic development needs. Financial institutions in our free economic system must play the leading role.*

*Second: A public charter for a bank or savings institution conveys numerous benefits and it is fair for the public to ask something in return.*

*In theory, and in law, banks and savings institutions are*

*charged to serve local convenience and needs. In practice, the regulatory agencies look only to the capital adequacy of the applicant, his character and reputation, and whether the proposed service area contains sufficient deposit potential to support another new bank or branch. The Community Reinvestment Act would provide that "the convenience and needs" of communities includes the need for credit service, and further, that regulated financial institutions have a continuing and affirmative obligation to help meet the credit needs of the local communities in which they are chartered.*

*Under the bill, the regulatory agencies would review the lender's record of community service and consider it when an existing bank applied for a new facility. Groups applying for new charters would also be required to assess local credit needs and indicate plans for meeting them.*[7]

Anticipating criticism of the proposal, Senator Proxmire concluded that the bill

*...does not provide for credit allocation. The worst thing we could do, in my opinion, would be to empower Dr. Burns or anyone else to allocate so much credit to this sector or so much credit to that one. The Fed does too much of that informally already. To criticize reinvestment incentive as a form of credit allocation is disingenuous. We already have credit allocation, as one commentator has observed, and it is credit allocation for the Fortune 500.*[8]

Senator Proxmire pointed out that, when it chartered a bank or approved a branch application, the government was conferring "substantial economic benefits on private institutions without extracting any meaningful quid pro quo for the public."[9] Among the economic benefits conferred is a semi-exclusive franchise to do business in a particular area, since the government limits the entry of competitors. The government also helps ensure the profitability of banks by restricting the rate of interest payable on savings deposits (usually to below market rates) and by prohibiting any payment of interest on checking accounts. Furthermore, the government provides deposit insurance for banks, allowing them to operate with lower capital ratios that would otherwise be required: Banks are able to operate with 16:1 leveraging rather than a 10:1 or lower ratio that would be required by prudent depositors without federal insurance. The government also provides banks with ready access to low-cost loans in times of need through the Federal Reserve Banks or Federal Home Loan Banks. In return for all these economic benefits, Senator Proxmire insisted, banks should be obliged to meet the credit needs of their communities.

Bankers strongly opposed the Act, calling it credit allocation, as did the Nixon-Ford appointees heading the federal bank regulatory agencies. The American Bankers Association testified against the bill. Bankers' opposition surprised no one: After all, they had opposed the Federal Reserve Act in 1914, the Federal Deposit Insurance Corporation Act in 1934, the Truth-in-Lending Act in 1967, the Equal Credit Opportunity Act in 1969, the Home Mortgage Disclosure Act in 1975, and so forth.

The commercial bankers and the bank regulators decried the bill's "narrow focus" upon retail markets, which they claimed ignored the important role of banks as suppliers of credit to business. Opponents maintained that the bill would block the flow of funds from capital surplus to capital deficit areas by forcing banks to give special preference to the credit needs of their local communities, to the detriment of distant ones. The historic mission of banks to be financial intermediaries, they argued, would be undermined. Moreover, they contended, the effects of the bill might even be perverse: Banks and savings and loan associations would refrain from applying for branches in inner city neighborhoods, or even close down their present branch offices there, because of the examination of their lending policies that these offices would bring.

Not one federal agency—not the banking regulators, not even the Department of Housing and Urban Development—went on the record in favor of this bill. They lauded its fine intentions, but said that in practice they were against it. Only community groups, labor officials, and the few consumerist state bank commissioners were supporters.

The free flow of credit lauded by bankers and regulators alike was described as "this destructive pattern" of neighborhood disinvestment by Ralph Nader in his testimony.[10] The "myth of lack of demand" was attacked by Gale Cincotta:

> *I would like to point out to the committee that the industry, while talking lack of demand out of one side of their mouth, are talking about coinsurance out of the other side. They admit to demand when the topic comes around to the Federal*

*Government subsidizing their private institutions, but they
scream "there's no demand" when the topic under discussion is
lack of their services to the depositors, the public and the
community.*[11]

Henry Schechter, director of urban affairs for the AFL-CIO, likened
the crisis of neighborhoods in the 1970s caused by the lack of bank
credit to the economic collapse of the 1930s, in which the
contraction of overall bank credit played a devastating role. In short,
labor, community, and public interest groups saw the free flow of
credit as contrary to their interests. Allowing credit to go to the
highest private bidder, they argued, equated social returns with
private returns. Yet the two were not always the same. Letting urban
neighborhoods die had high social and economic costs which
private lenders acting individually could not adequately take into
account in making their decisions. That was why legislation was
needed.

Some legislators were unconvinced. Senator John Tower of
Texas, for example, a Republican member of the Senate Banking
Committee, charged that the act

> ... *would require the federal financial-institutions-regula-
> tory agencies to pressure commercial banks as well as savings and
> loan associations to use their consumer deposits for loans to
> borrowers physically located in the same geographic areas in
> which the deposit-accepting institutions are located. Such imped-
> iments to the free functions of financial markets necessarily
> hampers the economic efficiency with which those markets
> allocate credit....*
>
> *From the standpoint of the welfare of the nation as a
> whole, economic efficiency is maximized if credit is given to those
> productive borrowers willing to pay the highest interest rates after
> allowance for risks. Now this is because those borrowers will use
> the available credit for the most productive purposes. This is what
> enables them to pay the highest interest rates. If Government
> sponsored credit allocation is used to channel credit to other
> borrowers, it necessarily will use the credit for less productive
> purposes and economic well-being of the Nation as a whole will
> suffer.*[12]

These are principles espoused in economics courses. The assumptions underlying the conclusion that the market left to itself will

allocate resources perfectly include that the distribution of income is just and that there is in fact perfect competition in markets. If either of these two assumptions were violated, economics professors will admit that market determined allocations may not be socially optimal.

Moreover, there is something disingenuous in a savings and loan association's arguing against credit allocation. The savings and loan industry is itself a beneficiary of credit allocation, being created expressly to channel funds into housing and being sustained by interest rate controls on competitors. The irony is compounded because the original concept of the savings and loans was that they were to be controlled by depositors/shareholders and that local control was to ensure that they would serve their local communities. To further ensure that local needs were the sole focus of savings and loans, they were initially prohibited from making mortgages more than fifty miles from their main office.

Part of the Act under which the Federal Home Loan Bank Board was originally chartered makes clear the role to be played by the federal agency and the savings and loan industry. It is also a striking statement of how far they have moved from this congressionally mandated purpose. It is described in part as:

> *an act to provide emergency relief with respect to home mortgage indebtedness, to refinance home mortgages, to extend relief to the owners of homes occupied by them and who are unable to amortize their debt elsewhere....*[13]

At one time, it was clear that the savings and loan industry was meant to help people who couldn't get credit elsewhere to buy homes.

Despite the bankers' insistence at the congressional hearings that their showing more concern for local credit needs would not be in the nation's best interest, bankers have been at great pains to advertise that this is exactly what they do with depositors' money. The American Bankers Association itself has sponsored such community-oriented reinvestment television advertising. The Community Reinvestment Act was one manifestation of the public's determination to turn the myth of bank service to its community into a reality.

Not every senator was as concerned with the problems of urban disinvestment as was Senator Proximire. Nor did all senators see banks as the villain of the piece. Many, in fact, had the same reaction to the CRA that Republican Senator Jake Garn of Utah, a Banking Committee member, did. After listening to some testimony in favor of the Act, Senator Garn exploded:

> ...*I would like you to know there are some members of this committee who feel that it is the banking industry and savings and loan industry in this country who have been responsible for building this country, and not government. Damn it to hell, we have had 200 years of the private sector building the greatest country. There are problems and I know a lot about them firsthand, having spent 7 years in local government. The answer isn't more rules and regulations. Piecemeal, we are heading for credit allocation and Government bureaucrats sitting back here interfering with the private sector. I'm sick and tired of the anti-business attitude of this committee. I think the record speaks for itself. It is constant.*
>
> *You come in here; you are insulted day after day, treated rudely, but the Kathleen O'Reillys, the Ralph Naders have their asses kissed every day and told how wonderful their testimony is over and over again, while we are building up a regulatory burden that is going to destroy the housing industry in this country.*
>
> *I get so sick and tired of it. Talk about negativism. This committee is negative. You have a staff that is so overwhelmingly anti-business that—and they don't have a practical bit of experience in their brains—every answer is: "Pass another law." I deliberately stayed away from these hearings most of this week, so I wouldn't have an outburst like this. I couldn't stand to come and hear Ralph Nader over and over again representing himself as representing millions of people....*
>
> *I suggest maybe his Golden Fleece Award [Senator Proxmire's] go to this committee for the costs it has imposed on the American consumer and not on the financial institutions, because they have to be passed on to the consumer and when we are going to get reason and balance in these decisions, I don't know.*[14]

Given the relative strengths of the proponents and opponents of CRA, it is indeed surprising that the bill was enacted. In favor of the bill was an assortment of public-interest types like Ralph Nader and Gale Cincotta, and some activist state bank commissioners like Connell and myself. Opposed to the bill was every federal bank regulatory agency, as well as HUD and the combined lobbying power of all the banking groups. The bill shouldn't have stood a chance of passage. There's a rule of thumb in Congress that unless at least one banking group is in favor of a piece of banking legislation, the legislation can't pass.

The bankers believe that rule, too, which may have been their undoing. They were so sure the bill couldn't pass that they didn't lobby very hard against it in the Senate. Commercial bankers were more worried about what the thrifts were up to, and thrift executives were keeping their eyes on the ABA's proposals—who was worried about proposals backed by Gale Cincotta?

### *Implementing the Community Reinvestment Act of 1977*

The Community Reinvestment Act, like the Home Mortgage Disclosure Act of 1976 and the annual extension of deposit interest-rate controls (Regulation Q), represents a congressional effort to realize the national policy goal of providing sufficient housing. Deposit interest-rate controls are supposed to guarantee an adequate supply of funds for housing loans by attracting deposits for thrift institutions, which will then relend them in the mortgage market. CRA is designed to ensure that the flow of funds through thrift institutions meets the specific needs of low and moderate income neighborhoods for mortgages. CRA is also meant to encourage financial institutions to help meet the other credit needs of the communities in which they are chartered, since stable, livable neighborhoods require credit for activities other than housing purchases.

The Act directs bank regulatory agencies to use both their examination and regulatory functions to enforce it. CRA requires the federal bank regulatory agencies to make an affirmative finding that banks are serving the credit needs of their communities before the regulators can approve a new branch, merger, or bank holding company acquisition. It also requires that examiners, in performing their regular safety and soundness examination, determine whether a bank is meeting community credit needs. The radical departure started in California, Massachusetts, and New York has thus become a national program.

As a controversial bill, CRA was watered down in committee as the price of passage. Instead of embodying a series of standards that regulators and public groups could use to challenge both financial institutions and the regulators' decisions, it contained less specific requirements that regulators "assess the institution's record" and "take such record into account" when awarding new deposit facilities. "It's what's called a gutting amendment," one Senate staff member observed. But heavy pressure from bankers and thrift executives on members of the Banking Committee probably would have ensured the bill's defeat without the changes.

In this case, most of the regulators were clearly contemptuous of the new law at the outset. By 1978, though, President Carter had appointed two bank regulators—John Heimann, Comptroller of the Currency, and Robert McKinney, Chairman of the Federal Home Loan Bank Board—who were concerned with urban problems and the role banks could play in their solution. At their urging, the bank regulators held a series of public hearings around the country which at least allowed community groups as well as bankers to comment on how to implement CRA. Bankers and most state bank regulators called for CRA's repeal, denouncing the act as a public nuisance if not a disgrace. Most bankers' testimony echoed the position of the New York State Bankers Association that since "most regulated banks are doing an excellent job of serving the credit needs of their communities, we believe that CRA does not impose new obligations on regulated financial institutions...."[15]

The testimony of some banks and savings and loan associations expressed anger and frustration.

*This whole act is just another example of socialism developing in this country with all types of lending institutions. ....All it looks like to me is another excuse to hire more bureaucrats and spend the taxpayers money.*

*In effect this means that some agency person or persons with perhaps no experience in lending money, and in all probability residing in an area far remote and with no commonality with the area or conditions in the subject institution's community, will pass judgment on the action of a very experienced loan officer totally familiar with his institution's financial resources and totally knowledgeable about his local area.*[16]

The most constructive proposal the bankers made was to recommend letting the banks themselves define the boundaries of their communities and document how the banks met their communities' credit needs. The state bank regulators, with only a few familiar exceptions, echoed the bankers' disgust with CRA.

Community groups, of course, viewed CRA very differently. They saw its implementation as a chance to make credit available to urban residents as well as local small businesses. New York PIRG recommended that banks not be considered in compliance with the act unless they reinvested approximately half of their local deposits in their communities. PIRG also suggested that although regulatory agencies would be authorized to deny a branching application if it found that a bank was not meeting local credit needs, they should consider less drastic action, such as requiring an affirmative-action plan from the bank, in some cases. (Failure to implement an approved affirmative-action program could then be punished by revocation of the approval, or by denial of future applications.)

Community-group leaders, like James Carras and Hugh McCormack of the Boston Mortgage Review Board and Jamaica Plain Banking and Mortgage Committee, argued that it was absolutely essential that bank examiners' comments about a bank's reinvestment performance be made available to the public. Traditionally, all bank examination reports are kept confidential by the banking agencies, for bank safety reasons and to protect individual privacy. These traditional concerns were not relevant to CRA examinations. As these community leaders stated:

> *The task of assessing bank lending records will require a dialogue between the bank regulators, community organizations and local and state officials. If these other parties do not have access to the reinvestment examination reports such a dialogue will be impossible and the Act will become a failure, and most likely a dangerous failure since the bank regulators will not be publicly accountable for their actions.*[17]

Richard Golden, testifying for New York PIRG, concluded:

> *More important than the specific proposal made during these hearings, however, is the recognition I hope you all have of the importance of this Act. Had there been a Community Reinvestment Act twenty years ago, the leaders of our financial communities would have had to confront the causes of urban decay while there was still time to save many areas which are now beyond help by conventional means. It is still not too late in many areas where credit loss has just begun. When drafting the regulations implementing this Act, please keep in mind the vast consequences for all of us if you do the job poorly.*[18]

When regulations were finally issued, a year later, such pleas were ignored. The regulations echoed the bankers' proposals; CRA had been turned into a paper tiger.

Possibly the regulatory agencies feared that strong measures would so anger an already aroused banking community that bankers would mount an all-out campaign to get CRA repealed. Certainly, it was hard for bankers to object to regulations that simply said that a bank should define its community and explain how it met its community's credit needs. The innocuousness of the initial regulations may have been the law's salvation. It also provided the bankers with possibly their last chance to avoid credit allocation: The law remained as a clear rebuke to their past performance, while its regulations gave them time to prove that they could respond to their communities' credit needs without having government spell out for them what those needs were and how they were to be met.

The bankers immediately recognized that the law had been defanged. The new regulations were hailed in the financial press as providing "flexibility" and "no high-risk obligation."[19] The CRA regulations, which went into effect on November 6, 1978, required each federally insured financial institution to adopt a CRA statement and to have it available at each branch. A bank's CRA statement was to include, for each local community, a map delineating that community, a list of the types of credit the bank was prepared to extend in that community, and a copy of the CRA notice. Banks were quick to make a mockery of the spirit of the law by defining their local community as an entire metropolitan area, writing CRA statements that were brief repetitions of the required wording in the Act, and listing in about four words the types of loans they made. The exhibit shows a typical CRA statement. Bankers clearly understood that these regulations had no teeth; they seemed slower to understand that this was their last chance to maintain control of the credit process. As Senator Proxmire had stated during the Senate debate over passage of CRA, "I would say to those who fear increased bureaucracy: If the private sector fails to do the job of re-investing capital in older communities and the government has to pick up the pieces, then you will really see red tape."[20]

The Community Reinvestment Act has clearly had some positive impact on bank regulatory examination and application procedures. The agencies have developed CRA assessment procedures that place special emphasis on evaluating a bank's record

## IMPERIAL BANK AND TRUST COMPANY

### *Community Reinvestment Act Statement*

Imperial Bank and Trust Company makes this statement pursuant to the Community Reinvestment Act of 1977 and the regulations of the Board of Governors of the Federal Reserve System promulgated thereunder.

The stated purpose of the Community Reinvestment Act regulations is:

"to encourage regulated financial institutions to fulfill their continuing and affirmative obligations to help meet the credit needs of their communities, including low- and moderate-income neighborhoods, consistent with safe and sound operation of such institutions."

Attached to this statement is a map showing the local community we serve.

Within this local community, we make the following types of loans:

Home improvement loans, government subsidized housing loans, consumer loans and loans to businesses.

We endeavor to make loans to our customers in our local community with regard to their ability to repay the loans and without regard to race, color, national origin, marital status, religion, age or sex.

The following is the public notice which we are required to make part of this statement:

The Federal Community Reinvestment Act (CRA) requires the Federal Reserve Board to evaluate our performance in helping to meet the credit needs of this community, and to take this evaluation into account when the Board decides on certain applications submitted by us. Your involvement is encouraged.

You should know that:

* You may obtain our current CRA statement for this community in this office.
* You may send signed, written comments about our CRA statement or our performance in helping to meet community credit needs to the Senior Vice President, Imperial Bank and Trust Company, Boston, Massachusetts, and to Community Reinvestment Officer, Federal Reserve Bank of Boston, 600 Atlantic Avenue, Boston, Massachusetts. Your letter, together with any response by us, may be made public.
* You may look at a file of all signed, written comments received by us within the past two years, any responses we have made to the comments, and all CRA statements in effect during the past two years at our office located in Boston, Massachusetts.

*(continued)*

*You may ask to look at any comments received by the Federal Reserve Bank of Boston.

*You also may request from the Federal Reserve Bank of Boston an announcement of applications covered by the CRA filed with the Federal Reserve System.

*We are a subsidiary of Imperial Corporation, a bank holding company. Applications filed by bank holding companies that are covered by the CRA are included in the Federal Reserve announcement of applications referred to in the previous paragraph.

*Local Community Served*

BOSTON

in providing mortgages, small business and community development loans in low and moderate income neighborhoods. But central to a meaninfgul assessment of bank lending records is the need to reeducate bank examiners. Honest CRA assessments will not be made unless bank examiners share the commitment to community reinvestment. The effectiveness of CRA examinations has been further weakened by not providing any profile of community credit needs. The regulations provide no way to determine if a bank is meeting the needs of its community, especially in low- and moderate-income neighborhoods. As Jonathan Brown of the Public Interest Research Group in Washington, D. C., said, "The net effect of the regulations is that a bank can argue that any credit extended in a community is serving the community and therefore is a satisfactory record."[21] Community groups bitterly charged that the regulations had obscured the foremost purpose of CRA, which was to promote reinvestment in disinvested urban neighborhoods.

To further assure bankers that CRA would not mean credit allocation directed from Washington, the banking agencies quickly let it be known that they were more likely to negotiate changes in lending activities rather than reject protested applications and to suggest, rather than demand, improvements when they encountered banks which had unsatisfactory lending records under CRA.

The regulators also ignored community groups' pleas that the CRA examination reports be public documents. To be evenhanded, the regulators determined that not even the bank would be told where it fell on a rating scale of one to five that examiners would use to rate a bank's performance under CRA.

Passage of the Community Reinvestment Act and issuance of weak regulations a year later did not still the debate. If anything, bankers were so enraged by their legislative defeat that they became even more vigorous in their own defense. In October 1978, the President of the Federal Savings League charged at the New England Saving and Loan's annual convention that the layers of regulation and repeated criticism of the banking industry were simply an attempt to distract attention from "the true issue of urban decay." Calling on League members to abandon their traditional "defensive" attitude in the face of "false charges from obscure sources that claim to be pro-consumer," he expressed the outrage of his members. Thus, he insisted, "We did not create urban decay and financial intermediaries cannot be looked upon as the sole source for solution. Urban blight and neighborhood decay will not be solved by compulsory lending," nor will "horrendously administered government programs," accusations of redlining and non-discrimination regulations provide housing for all Americans.

The bankers' charge that CRA would force them to make risky loans, endangering the safety of the banking system was also a gross distortion. No one has yet read about a financial institution that has failed because it made too many conventional mortgage loans to owner-occupants in an urban neighborhood. Safety and soundness risks have been caused by speculation in REITs, Eurodollar trading, tanker loans, and big condominium projects in the Sunbelt.

Rather than mount a direct frontal assault on CRA by working for its repeal, though, the bankers decided on a more oblique course which would leave CRA in place but make verification of any changes in reinvestment patterns impossible. Banking groups went after the Home Mortgage Disclosure Act (HMDA) which was due to expire after five years, in 1980. Labeled "Project Unravel" by the American Bankers Association, the non-extension of HMDA was seen as an essential means of undercutting CRA. Without HMDA data to show the amounts invested in specific geographic areas in previous years, bank statements for CRA alleging greater investment would be unchallengeable. Community groups would be back where they were before 1975, arguing about whether disinvestment was occurring or not. Repeal of HMDA, bankers reason, would gut CRA while leaving it in place as an obstacle to other legislation addressing the same problem. The fight over reinvestment has hardly begun.

### Ransoming the Branch

Meanwhile, despite lax federal regulations, state regulators in Massachusetts, New York, and California were implementing the Community Reinvestment Act with conditional approvals of branch applications. Community groups in Washington, D.C., were forcing such agreements on thrift institutions as the price for withdrawing their protests of the bank's branch application.

In the first case of its kind, the Federal Home Loan Bank Board in August of 1977 approved a branch in Washington, D.C., for the $783 million-deposit Perpetual Federal Savings and Loan Association only after that institution had signed a ten-page agreement with community groups which spelled out the liberalized mortgage lending policies the S&L would follow. Community groups had protested the branch application to the Federal Home Loan Bank Board in 1976, stating that Perpetual's conservative mortgage lending policies would accelerate displacement of low- and moderate-income and minority residents from Washington, D.C. More than five months of negotiations between the Savings and Loan and the community groups, who were ably assisted by the city's Public Interest Research Group, preceded the agreement. The Federal Home Loan Board's action marked the first time that a federal regulator had included an agreement between a community group and a bank in the branch application itself.

The community groups had unsuccessfully challenged the branch at the regional level, had then charged that the hearing officer at the (regional) Atlanta Federal Home Loan Bank had been biased, and successfully demanded a review in Washington of the

Atlanta bank's decision. In its original protest, the community group charged that the areas' "minority and moderate- and lower-income members who seek to purchase or improve homes in Adams Morgan, a section of Washington, D. C., are being adversely affected by Perpetual's lending policies." The group further argued:

> *Perpetual refuses to recognize the impact that its lending policies have on home ownership opportunities. According to Perpetual, the renovation of the housing stock in Adams Morgan and Mt. Pleasant for purchase by affluent persons and the attendant displacement of moderate and lower income persons is a matter over which Perpetual has no influence.*
>
> *Contrary to Perpetual's disclaimers, adjustments in lending policies can have a significant impact on home opportunities. The following lending policies, if adopted by Perpetual, would substantially broaden home ownership opportunities and minimize the displacement of moderate and lower income persons: 1) lower down payment requirements; 2) extension of 5% loans under the FHA 235 program; 3) wrap around mortgage loans, second mortgage loans and home improvement loans for moderate rehabilitation with low cash investment requirements; 4) mortgage loans to non-profit corporations for cooperative housing.*[22]

Agreeing to these loan policies was the price the community groups asked for dropping their objections to the branch application. The community's demands were accorded little credence by either the S & L or the hearing officer at the Federal Home Loan Bank of Atlanta. Only when the new chairman of the Federal Home Loan Bank Board, Robert H. McKinney, surprisingly agreed to review the Atlanta decision did Perpetual move to reach accommodation with the community group. McKinney was eager to prove to the consumer, labor, and civil rights groups which had opposed his nomination that he would be sensitive to their concerns.

While the Perpetual agreement was precedent-setting, it was at the state level that regulators first began negotiating community agreements directly with banks. In mid-1977, the Superintendent of Banks for the State of California, Carl J. Schmidt, became involved in requiring specific banking policies before approving branch and merger applications. In the case of an application from the County Bank of Santa Cruz to open a branch in a Spanish-speaking section of the city of Watsonville, approval was conditioned on the bank providing the Banking Department with a comprehensive marketing plan of how the bank intended to service the special needs of that community.

A second such decision was triggered by the challenge of Public Advocates to the Sumitomo Bank purchase of nineteen branches of Bank of California. Public Advocates asked that the Banking Department assure the affected employees and communities that acquisition by a foreign bank would not diminish the bank's commitment to the communities they serve and that the employees in the branches would be guaranteed that opportunities for advancement, including affirmative action, would not be diminished.

After an initial reaction of consternation, the Department decided that the challenge was reasonable. The Department then set to work to draw up standards for the bank in terms of explicit numerical goals for American citizens as a proportion of bank officers and the inclusion of four community representatives on the bank's board of directors. The acquisition was approved only after the Department received a letter from the Sumitomo Bank committing itself to these actions.

As Commissioner of Banks in Massachusetts, I was the first public official to predicate a bank branch approval on an agreement between the Banking Department and the applicant bank for a specific lending goal in a given geographic area. In a very controversial decision, in May of 1978, I approved the $53 million Eliot Savings Bank request for a branch in the largely white section of Boston known as West Roxbury in return for an agreement to a series of relatively modest ($700,000) lending goals in several largely black neighborhoods of Boston. I reserved the option of revoking the branch permit and forcing the bank to divest itself of the facility if the goals were not met.

The Eliot had not been chosen at random as a test case. The Eliot Savings Bank had originally been headquartered in Roxbury, now the Boston neighborhood with the highest minority concentration. In 1973, the bank had sought to move its main office to downtown Boston, and in its application had made repeated assurances that it did not intend to abandon its commitment to Roxbury. Then, in 1975, it applied to close its Roxbury branch.

In this new application, the bank argued that the branch was unprofitable and that the magnitude of its losses endangered the solvency of the bank. For a savings bank with the highest surplus position in the state, this was patent nonsense. Moreover, the unspectacular performance of the branch was attributable to bank policies.

The branch's hours were just 9:30 to 2:00, Monday through Friday, the shortest in the neighborhood and shorter than the downtown office's hours. Current bank advertising did not even mention the Roxbury location. Eliot's recent record of service to the Roxbury community was also anything but exemplary. The bank's mortgage holdings as a percent of assets were among the lowest of any savings bank in the state, and loans in the Roxbury area were minuscule. Although the request to close the branch had been denied in 1975, Eliot Savings Bank had done little to increase its lending in Boston. As shown in its own 1977 annual report, the bank had less than half its portfolio in mortgages, had only $16,500 in outstanding home improvement loans, and, in a city with a large student population, did not make student loans.

Nonetheless, bankers were quick to attack the agreement as a dangerous precedent. *Banker and Tradesman*, a Boston-based banking and real-estate weekly, editorialized:

> *At issue is whether bank branch applications can be held hostage to the advancement of the Commissioner's social goals— whether, in fact, banking decisions are going to be made by bank executives based on their assessment of what is best for their financial institutions, or by government regulators, based on their desire to right social wrongs. The two interests do not always coincide. In weighing their decision, the Eliot Savings Bank must decide if what is gained by the new branch outweighs what will be lost by the continued erosion of whatever independent management authority bank executives have left.*[23]

Executives at the Eliot Savings Bank had not found it easy to sign the agreement. In a tense and angry confrontation with the commissioner, the bank's president had demanded, "Show me the law that says I have to make mortgages!" I responded just as hotly, "Show me the law that says I have to approve this branch." The bank's final recognition that an accommodation would have to be reached came in a counter proposal with a scaled down sum (half to be exact) to be invested. I accepted the offer, thinking the principle well worth the price.

The Savings Bank Association of Massachusetts was not beguiled by the modest sums involved. The Association announced that it would oppose in the future such agreements "as strongly as possible," by which it meant that it would hurry off to its friendly legislative banking committee and get legislation passed prohibiting me from asking questions about a bank's planned lending policies. "If this [Community Service Agreement] can be used without state legislation," Elliot Carr, executive director of the Savings Bank Association of Massachusetts warned, "the state can use that device to control investments in every savings bank .... The first step is the gigantic one here."[24]

The conservative Boston daily, the *Herald American*, called for the Governor to rebuke his commissioner publicly. Instead, Governor Dukakis called me and said that the Eliot agreement was a great thing for Boston.

### The Counterattack

The savings bankers in Massachusetts had had enough progressive regulation. They joined with other savings bankers from other northeastern states in a massive lobbying effort to obtain the power to seek federal charters for savings banks, as an escape from the activism of their states' regulators.

Commercial bankers can have as their primary regulator either a state or federal official, depending on how the bank is chartered. (A federal presence is felt in either case, however, because commercial banks, even when state-chartered, are federally insured.) Savings and loan associations also have the option of choosing a federal or state charter. Only savings banks have not had this option. This is due to their age: Most were established in the nineteenth century, before the federal government got into the chartering business. For the past twenty years, savings banks' efforts to get federal charters had been vetoed by savings and loan lobbyists who didn't want competition from newly chartered mutual thrift institutions. The federal charter had also lacked appeal to savings bankers, since savings banks have far more powers than savings and loan associations. They can offer checking accounts and personal loans, for example, and are much freer to invest in bonds and stocks than savings and loans. S&Ls have always insisted that any federally chartered savings bank should be limited to the powers of a federal savings and loan association.

Savings bankers insisted that, in the name of equity, they should be free to choose between state and federal regulation. But while federal charters had never struck them as a life-and-death matter, now they needed a cudgel to keep state regulators in line, and they got it. The savings banks successfully lobbied to slip a new section onto page 164 of Rep. St. Germain's "Safe Banking Act," a bill to end these abuses. The new title XII was shamelessly narrow in its focus: It gave existing savings banks the option of converting to a federal charter and of then being regulated by the Federal Home Loan Bank Board. To open the option to savings bankers but not make it a threat to savings and loans, federally chartered savings banks would be allowed to keep all the powers they had when they converted, but the Federal Home Loan Bank could charter no new federal savings banks, only converted ones.

The state bank commissioners from the Northeast argued that no public need would be served by a federal charter for savings banks and that much would be lost. Specifically, the people and state legislatures of the Northeast would lose their ability to influence the investment policies and practices of the major thrift institutions in their states.

Although a friendly member of the House Rules Committee tied the Safe Banking Act up in his committee for three weeks to give me time to build enough political pressure to get the federal charter out of the bill, the bill passed in the wee hours of the closing session. The only victory I achieved was to get language into the bill that a conversion could take place only if allowed by state law. Massachusetts was the only state at the time which required approval of the state officials before a thrift institution could change to a federal charter.

Some of what the federal government had given with one hand with the passage of the Community Reinvestment Act may have been taken away with the other, with the passage of the federal charter for savings banks. The negative impact would be most felt in the Northeast, where savings banks and pro-consumer bank commissioners alike are most concentrated, but the impact would be nationwide. Within days of the passage of the Act, the Superintendent of Banks in New York, Muriel Siebert postponed further action on tough state antiredlining rules and announced that the state would instead monitor enforcement using the weaker federal regulations issued under the Community Reinvestment Act. Faced with the prospect that savings banks would now be able to escape state regulation by converting to a federal charter, Superintendent Siebert explained her actions by saying, "There is no reason that we should lead the savings banks to the door."[25]

### Shock Waves

The main contribution of CRA to date has been that it has given standing to community groups and their concerns about reinvestment. A bank's investment performance in its current market was once dismissed by both regulators and bankers as beside the point. Now it has to be taken seriously.

The Federal Deposit Insurance Corporation made that clear when it rejected the application of the Greater New York Savings Bank for a branch in April of 1979. This was the first application contested under CRA, and the rejection sent shock waves through the banking community. Community groups were jubilant. Both sides probably overreacted.

But the decision did send a message, to which the industry has apparently responded. At the very least, dialogues have been started across the country between bankers and their communities.

CRA has also given community groups leverage. According to community group leaders, bankers have apparently increased lending in low- and moderate-income neighborhoods as a result of their fears about CRA. Even in cases where a CRA protest failed and the bank received regulatory approval, community groups report that the bank has increased its urban lending. Thus, in St. Louis, despite the Federal Reserve's approval of a holding company acquisition for Commerce Bankshares, community groups believe that the bank has increased its lending.

The Greater New York Savings Bank decision apparently has had a ripple effect on bank lending practices across the nation. However, to sustain the momentum, the regulatory agencies have to continue to issue denials. After their running start, they've stopped in their tracks. While contested applications are piling up at the federal level, no other bank had been denied a branch or merger in the six months since the Greater New York Savings Bank decision. If CRA is not to fade away, the language of the Act must be implemented with regulatory actions.

Almost immediately after the CRA regulations went into effect, the federal bank regulators found themselves struggling with the idea of conditional approvals as a middle ground between approving and denying CRA protested applications. Several of the regulators, notably the Federal Reserve and the FDIC, were wary that conditional approvals in CRA cases might be construed as a type of credit allocation. One of the three FDIC board members, William M. Isaac, expressed this view. "We must be decisive," he said, "in casting unconditional votes for or against applications with CRA implications; approvals conditioned on specific requirements will surely lead us along the path to credit allocation."[26]

Comptroller of the Currency John Heimann and the Board of the Federal Home Loan Bank were less troubled by such concerns. In his first dissent on a CRA contested application, John Heimann wrote that the Greater New York Savings Bank's application for a branch should have been approved "with the understanding that considerable additional and continuing progress would be expected of this applicant and that this progress would be the subject of careful evaluation during future examinations and action on future applications."[27]

Community groups would strongly prefer outright denials to conditional approvals. Allan Fishbein of the Washington-based Center for Community Change argues that if the regulatory agencies do not issue denials, the bank regulatory agencies effectively undercut community groups' ability to get negotiated agreements with banks themselves. Instead of talking with community leaders, the bankers will be dickering with the bank regulatory staff, which is likely to be more sympathetic to the bankers' concerns and less knowledgeable about the specific credit needs of a particular community.

The bank regulatory agencies are the crucial enforcement arm of CRA, but they have left it to community groups to prove disinvestment. Confrontation is the regulator's job, too: It should not, as Gale Cincotta insists, "always be the community groups' bag." The most effective enforcement tool of the agencies is to issue a denial.

CRA depends on signals from the bank regulators. We like to think of laws as making the crucial difference and the composition of the regulatory agencies as irrelevant. This view of the world is rarely true, and nowhere is it less true than for CRA. This was a law which left it to the regulators to define and implement its meaning. It is thus peculiarly a regulation caught in crosscurrents of politics and changing social values.

# 7.

# The Great
# Checking Account
# Robbery

There is no more glaring example of the antipublic behavior of the banking community than its efforts to deny the public interest-bearing checking accounts. A bank charter has on occasion been characterized as a "license to steal" exactly because banks have been able to take people's money and to invest it without paying for the use of it. Bankers, meanwhile, have tried to excuse the theft by arguing that paying interest to checking account depositors would be bad for the public!

### David and Goliath

For forty years, bankers got away with this robbery. They were finally undone by a competitive innovation introduced by a Massachusetts savings banker and quickly adopted by other savings bankers in the area despite the strenuous efforts of state officials, the Federal Reserve, Congress, and the banking lobbies to stop them.

In June of 1972, Ron Hazelton, president of the Consumers' Savings Bank of Worcester, Mass., then a $200 million bank, offered his depositors a new service: They could write checks against their savings accounts. Called the NOW account (for "negotiable orders of withdrawal"), this simple innovation represented a revolution in banking—the functional equivalent of an interest-bearing checking account.

Commercial bankers were quick to realize the implications of this new consumer service. Their access to free funds was endangered. In wrath, they arose to battle the upstart with all the powers of the state. The first line of defense was the state bank commissioner whose office immediately informed the savings bank that it legally could not offer check-writing privileges with savings accounts. Hazelton, risking regulatory displeasure, challenged the Banking Department's legal interpretation in the state courts and won.

The Commissioner then drafted legislation to accomplish the purpose, arguing that the public interest would be served by legislation of this kind. The commissioner's actions were consistent with the conservative bent of bank regulation, which has tried to maintain stability in the industry by preventing competition. The commissioner may have feared that the entry of savings banks into the checking account business would be potentially disastrous for commercial banks. When the Massachusetts legislature rejected the proposed emergency legislation to prevent savings banks from offering checking account privileges, the commissioner did not approve, during the final two years in office, any savings bank applications for branches.

The commercial bankers, meanwhile, fled to the protection of their federal regulators. In an October 1972 petition addressed to all the federal banking regulators, Massachusetts and New Hampshire commercial banks pleaded to be saved from this "new and dangerous type of banking." Their proposed resolutions for this "aberration" were:

*FIRST. The clear first choice of the undersigned is that a complete moratorium on use of third party withdrawal orders by Massachusetts savings banks be declared forthwith. By moratorium is meant the complete cessation of the use of third party withdrawal orders in savings accounts on which interest is paid.*

*SECOND. The second choice of the undersigned is that if Massachusetts mutual savings banks are permitted to continue to make available third party withdrawal orders on savings accounts, then the savings banks should be prohibited from paying any interest on this type of account.*

*THIRD. A third possible alternative is that if Massachusetts mutual savings banks are still permitted to offer and utilize third party withdrawal orders in a special kind of savings account and pay interest on these accounts, then each of the undersigned types of banking institutions should be accorded the same privilege, but that the maximum interest to be payable on all special accounts of this kind would be not in excess of 1% or 2% per annum.*

*FOURTH. A fourth possible alternative would be that if Massachusetts mutual savings banks are permitted to continue to offer and utilize third party withdrawal orders on savings accounts and pay interest on these accounts at the rate of 5¼% per annum, then exactly the same powers and privileges should be conferred upon each of the undersigned types of organizations."*[1]

Lest the regulators be confused into thinking that commercial bankers wanted this new freedom, or wanted competitive equity, the petition reiterated that the four alternatives had been listed "in descending order of wisdom and desirability."[2] Furthermore, they demanded that the Federal Reserve refuse to allow its check clearing facilities to be used to clear these checks and that the Fed join with commercial bankers in obtaining congressional action to stop the phenomenon before it spread any further.

To their surprise, the president of the Federal Reserve Bank of Boston, Frank Morris, thought that NOW accounts were a good banking service, and he refused to be a party to trying to prohibit them. Instead, he offered to play the role of a mediator between commercial bankers and savings bankers to see if some accommodation could be reached.

The Banking Acts of 1933 and 1935 had prohibited the payment of interest on checking accounts (demand deposits). While the federal banking legislation did not expressly prohibit negotiable orders of withdrawal or checks written on savings accounts in commercial banks, Federal Reserve Board regulations did effectively preclude their use.

The Federal Reserve Board was less supportive of NOWs than was the Boston Fed. But Morris and Robert Eisenmenger and Steven Weiss of the Boston Fed's research department convinced the Governors of the Fed not to throw their considerable weight behind the bankers' lobbying efforts in Congress. The Boston Fed's position was that "NOW accounts provide a unique and valuable financial service for consumers; we believe that regulations should not substantially curtail their usefulness."[3]

By March 1973, the considerable agitation by commercial bankers for curtailment of NOW accounts had led to congressional hearings. The bankers demanded that Massachusetts savings banks be placed under federal deposit interest rate controls, even though their deposits were not federally insured. (No other non-insured institution must observe the controls.) The state bank commissioner warned the Massachusetts legislature that if it did not immediately outlaw NOW accounts, Congress would do so and would in addition impose federal interest rate ceilings on Massachusetts savings banks, which had been paying ¾ of a percentage point more than the rate allowed commercial banks (that is, a 5¼ percent passbook savings rate *vs.* a 4½ percent ceiling on commercial banks). This, the commissioner argued, would cost Massachusetts consumers far more than giving up NOW accounts.

The congressional banking committees were divided over the issue. But it was soon recognized that it was politically impossible to take the new service away from the depositors of Massachusetts and New Hampshire. Several thousand letters to Massachusetts congressmen made this quite clear. Not surprisingly, people liked receiving interest on their checking accounts. So Congress agreed to limit the plague by allowing banks and savings and loan associations in those two states to offer the accounts, but prohibiting them elsewhere. This political compromise was named "the NOW account experiment."

### The Plague Spreads

In 1974, savings banks were running ads in local newspapers and on television and radio asking, "Didn't you always wish your checking account paid interest?" Advertising spread the word of NOW accounts into adjacent states, frustrating congressional intentions to localize the disease. Soon the residents of Rhode Island and Connecticut were demanding to know why they too could not receive interest on accounts they could write checks against.

In 1975, Congress reluctantly acceded to their requests, over their bankers' vociferous objections, and permitted NOW accounts to be offered in all six New England states starting the following year. Presto, we had the "New England experiment."

While an attempt by Senator McIntyre to extend the authority for NOW accounts nationwide failed in the summer of 1977, the bankers' and congressmen's tactics of isolating the insurrection were again undone by modern technology. Despite Federal Reserve regulations prohibiting NOW account advertising in states that did not already offer NOWs, mass communication and modern transportation again spread the word. Commuters from Connecticut told their New York friends, and soon New Yorkers were demanding banking benefits accorded their Yankee neighbors. But if New York banks could offer NOW accounts to their customers, bank advertising in papers like *The New York*

*Times* and *The Wall Street Journal* would spread knowledge nationwide. Moreover, New York's banks are so large and so central to the nation's banking system that if they began paying interest on "checking" accounts, it would be hard to call this an experiment; this would be the end of the game. To the banking industry's shock, and over the objection of New York savings bankers and commercial bankers, in November 1978, at 4 A.M. on the last day of the legislative session, Congress authorized New York banks to offer NOW accounts.

But to maintain the remnants of the old system and the treasured privileges of commercial banks, Congress reaffirmed that these checkable balances were savings accounts, not demand deposits, although functionally the two were identical. The legal distinction had to be observed to maintain two important pillars of the status quo: that thrift institutions cannot by law offer demand deposit checking accounts and that no financial institution can pay interest on demand deposits. In every meaningful sense, however, thrifts had gained checking account powers in the form of NOW accounts, and were paying interest on what for all intents and purposes were demand deposits.

There was little doubt that the NOW "experiment" was irreversible. By August 1978, there were more than 2 million NOW accounts, with $3.4 billion in them, in New England institutions.[4] As we've seen, New York banks received authority to offer NOWs only in November 1978; by early in the following year, New York banks had well over a quarter of a million accounts, representing balances of over $1 billion.[5]

NOW accounts have deeply penetrated the market for household transactions balances throughout New England. As of March 31, 1979, there were more than 82.2 NOW accounts per 100 households in Massachusetts and 79.8 in New Hampshire.[6] More than two-thirds of the nearly 1,000 eligible institutions in New England had entered the NOW market by the end of 1976.

The New England experience indicated that the consumer can expect substantial benefits from NOW accounts. In 1976, New England consumers received almost $68 million in interest payments on NOW balances. Because service charges were only $2 million, consumers in the six New England states received net benefits worth $66 million from their NOW accounts.

This rate of public acceptance of a new banking service is unprecedented and certainly indicates the public's preference. The question was no longer whether NOWs could be stamped out, but how much their spread could be slowed. Bank lobbyists have prevented the rest of the nation from enjoying this service for almost a decade. Yet despite the bankers' claims that the notion of paying interest on demand deposits threatens their continued existence, there is no evidence that commercial banks were seriously hurt by NOW accounts.

### Consumer Benefits

To argue the benefits to the public from payment of interest on demand deposits is to recite the obvious. NOW accounts provide consumers with the convenience of a checking account while providing them with a return on their money. The public should have the convenience of "one-stop banking" at thrift institutions as well as at commercial banks. Moreover, the average person has the right to be paid for the use of his money.

Low-income households have particularly benefited. Poorer people are far less likely to have checking accounts at commercial banks, and more likely to keep all their money in thrift institutions. NOW accounts have allowed these people to enjoy the convenience of a checking account without losing interest income.

NOW accounts give savings account depositors a new flexibility to make withdrawals at times and places of their own choosing. The first customers to use NOW accounts were savings depositors who may not have had checking accounts and instead came to their savings bank to make a withdrawal, buying several counter checks to pay bills. In 1972, Massachusetts savings banks sold more than nine million counter checks.[7]

As Ron Hazelton, the father of NOWs, put it:

> *Until the NOW account offered these breakthroughs to consumers, banking had been like an industry which offered only Cadillacs or Volkswagens to the public. You could either write checks or be paid interest, but you could not obtain a combination of the two.*[8]

Finally, NOW accounts provide other consumer benefits by increasing competition among depository institutions. By permitting consumers to select among different types of depository institutions in making third-party transfers, they would end the monopoly of commercial banks in this area. This is bound to increase competition, particularly in areas currently served by one or a limited number of commercial banks.

The federal prohibition of paying interest on checking accounts had not actually stopped the practice, it had merely changed the form. Instead of paying interest directly, banks compete for checking account deposits through implicit interest payments in the form of goods and services. Typical ads take the form of "free" gifts to new customers now so ubiquitous in newspapers. They also often include more attractive loan rates for depositors, miscellaneous nondeposit services, and the offering of checking account services at charges below cost. This subsidization of checking account services is in effect an interest payment, if an indirect one.[9]

Thus, the real question is not whether interest should be paid on checking accounts but whether it should be paid in goods and services, as at present, or in money as explicit interest. The latter is clearly preferable. Explicit payment for deposits, combined with explicit charges for services, give the consumer the greater freedom to choose between income and services according to his own needs. Whereas, the payment of implicit interest, through the offering of free or below-cost checking, encourages overutilization of the service and adds unnecessary expense to its operation. Explicit payment of interest equalizes return to unsophisticated individuals of moderate means and to sophisticated large depositors and businesses.

Furthermore, the payment of interest to consumers provides them with additional income they can spend in any manner they desire. At present, the consumer can only effectively "spend" his "interest" on whatever free gifts or services are offered by the depository institution. As Comptroller of the Currency John Heimann pointed out, "Governmental policy that forces a young family—which is seeking to accumulate sufficient savings for a down payment on a house—to choose between a color television set or an outboard motor, simply because federal regulations prohibit their bank from paying a realistic rate of return on savings deposits, should be questioned."[10]

### Supposed Disadvantages to Consumers

Bankers have argued that NOW accounts were bad for the public. The "no free lunch" argument ran that any benefits to NOW depositors must ultimately be paid for by other consumers, particularly small depositors or borrowers. First, they argued, borrowers would have to pay higher loan rates to cover the increased cost of obtaining loanable funds. But banks should pay depositors the true worth of their deposits to the banks and charge borrowers the true costs of loans. In fact, though, banks may not be able to recoup the costs of NOW accounts by raising loan rates, since they must compete with other lenders. They can offset the costs by raising service charges on checking accounts, by pricing existing free services, or by suffering a decline in profits.

Banks also argued that since NOW accounts are a high-cost source of funds, thrifts will be forced to seek higher-yielding loans and investments, thereby reducing the supply of funds for residential mortgages. There is no evidence to support this. Rather, by making thrifts more competitive with commercial banks, it is more likely that NOWs will increase the deposit base of thrifts and, therefore, the supply of funds available for mortgages.

NOW accounts, bankers charged, would result in higher service charges to checking account users that would more than offset their 5 percent interest income on their checking balances. Those with lower incomes would be especially hurt and misled by NOWs, they charged.

This was a major argument of bank lobbyists, who relish assuming the cloak of the people's protector. It would be an extraordinary feat of lobbying indeed if they could persuade the American people and their elected representatives that receiving interest on their checking account balances is bad for them.

Of course, the banks could price NOW accounts in noncompetitive banking markets in such a way that a NOW account would be a bad buy. But it is an insult to people's intelligence to argue that people would not recognize this. After all, no one would be forcing a depositor to open a NOW account instead of a free checking account that did not pay interest. From the consumers' viewpoint, the NOW account would then at worst merely have served to increase the number of options available. Banks have not ceased offering personal checking to depositors, however small, on at least as attractive a basis as in pre-NOW-account days, and it seems unlikely that this situation will change.

Even if NOW accounts did raise service charges on checking accounts, this effect may not actually be detrimental. From the point of view of economic equity, depositors should pay the full cost plus some fair return to capital for transactions services, while banks should pay interest for the use of deposited funds. Some studies indicate that less than half of the direct demand deposit operating costs in commercial banks were covered explicitly through service charges.[11] When banks are not allowed to pay interest, or the rate is held below the true market rate by regulation, discrimination results: Concessions can be granted to informed and skillful depositors and borrowers, at the expense of less knowledgeable depositors who have little choice but to maintain their deposits for transactions and precautionary needs.

### Effect on Commercial Banks

Bankers' final argument against NOWs has been to raise the specter of the banking collapse of the 1930s, contending that NOW accounts would promote excessive interest rate competition and would threaten the stability of the entire financial system. Indeed, Congress did originally ban interest payments on demand deposits in the Banking Acts of 1933 and 1935, after banks had been paying interest on them for 130 years, because of two staunchly held, though fallacious, beliefs: that competition between banks for deposits led to bank failures and was one of the causes of the Depression, and that demand deposit interest sucked funds out of small communities. More important, as we have seen, eliminating the expense of paying interest on checking accounts was part of a political deal under which the banks accepted the costs of federal deposit insurance.

But the discredited argument that the banks will fail if they pay interest on their deposits has survived to become part of the battle against NOWs. Despite the actual experience of New England banks over the past six years (not one failed or got on a bank regulator's problem list because of paying interest on deposits), the statement that NOW accounts are inimical to the safety and soundness of the banking system has been chanted at every bank meeting around the country and in the hearing rooms and halls of Congress.

There is no evidence that instability occurs when interest rate restrictions are removed. No restrictions exist on competition in lending funds, and this has not led to instability—bankers have not argued for floors on their loan rates. Competition among financial institutions for borrowers is frequently vigorous but prices tend to recover costs and guarantee normal profit without instability. Similarly, vigorous competition for deposits need not lead to instability and may promote increased efficiency.

Considerations of transitional profitability, however, "should not be confused with the more fundamental considerations of safety and soundness,"[12] pointed out the Report of the Senate Committee on Banking, Housing and Urban Affairs when the issue of nationwide NOWs was examined in 1977. Testimony before the committee had indicated that there was no bank on the FDIC's "problem list" at the time because it offered NOW accounts. The report went on to conclude that "The extension of [interest-bearing transaction] accounts nationwide represents a logical, wholly safe and sound, and desirable step in the direction of increasing the overall efficiency of the banking system."[13]

Nonetheless, the prospect of paying for deposits that were previously free has been a cause of dismay for the banking industry. As Wilson Brunel, chairman of the Board of the Massachusetts Bankers Association, told a Senate Subcommittee in September 1975:

> *In conclusion, we believe that the current NOW account situation threatens both the profitability and the ultimate viability of commercial banking in Massachusetts.*[14]

Commercial bankers are principally concerned about the effect of interest rate competition on earnings. They foresee large transfers from checking to NOW accounts and a sharp deterioration in earnings. They argue that the additional cost of NOWs to them is higher than it is to thrifts, who already pay 5½ percent on their passbook accounts. The additional cost to thrifts is simply the servicing of these accounts; thrifts, the bankers argue, will therefore be able to offer lower charges and higher rates, thus costing banks their household checking account base.

In response, critics of the status quo point out that banks inevitably compete for funds in one way or another. If price competition is eliminated, then "non-price" competition emerges: free services, guaranteed lines of credit, heavy investment in convenience branches, long banking hours, and promotional giveaways, for example. While agreeing in principle, bankers are quick to point out that the cost of non-price competition will not quickly disappear, and that NOW accounts do not usually attract new accounts to the bank; they simply make money cost the banks 5 percent more.

This conviction holds firm despite the fact that commercial banks are probably going to keep their market share by attracting NOW deposits. Despite offering them later, not promoting them as aggressively and offering somewhat less favorable terms on them, Massachusetts commercial banks took only three years to amass twice the volume in NOW accounts attracted by the thrifts. Since the NOW experiment spread to all of New England, in March 1976, commercial banks have retained three-quarters of all deposits shifting to NOWs in the six states. Thus, NOW accounts have not significantly altered the competitive balance between savings banks and commercial banks.

In practice, of course, only consumers are forced to provide their transactions free. To an increasing extent, corporate depositors sell their deposits to banks in the form of certificates of deposit. NOW accounts simply extend this practice of paying for deposits from corporations to the average person. Even when a corporation does have a demand deposit, its money is not just sitting there. The demand deposit is usually a compensating balance for a loan; in addition, the corporation also receives services for its deposits. Banks have argued that NOW accounts are expensive, but they are certainly less expensive than CDs. The servicing costs of a personal checking account are between 2 and 3 percent of the balance. Thus 5 percent NOW accounts cost banks on average between 7 and 8 percent—far below current market rates for any other funds.

A 1976 study of the effects of NOW accounts on bank profitability by a Federal Reserve Board economist found that after-tax earnings dropped only slightly in the first two years of the NOW experiment, while the banks' share of the market fell only 1 percent. The study concluded that "the NOW experiment has been an almost unqualified success to date."[15]

The evidence suggests that the principal concern expressed over the NOW impact on commercial bank earnings may be exaggerated. According to studies done by the Federal Deposit Insurance Corporation,

> *the earnings of commercial banks do not seem to be especially impaired by NOWs overall; the banks have evidenced an ability to adjust to both the payment of explicit interest on certain demand deposit accounts and the new competition from thrifts entering the payments service market heretofore legally reserved for commercial banks. This is true in Massachusetts, a state in which competition between thrifts and commercial banks is more intense than is generally the case nationwide. In*

*Maine, Connecticut and New Hampshire, NOWs do not appear to have had an impact on commercial bank earnings.*[16]

Comparison of bank earnings before and after the introduction of NOW accounts indicates that only for the very smallest banks may there have been a negative impact on net operating earnings. This might well result from the higher proportion of personal checking accounts in the total deposit base of small versus large banks. The data, however, does not unambiguously indicate that NOW accounts were the cause of the deterioration in earnings at banks with under $10 million in deposits, but even if this were the case, there is no reason for consumers to subsidize the operation of small inefficient banks. Regulators and government have for too long worried about the effects of policies on banks rather than on bank customers.

It is interesting to see in NOW account evaluations how overwhelmingly dominant is their impact on the financial institutions involved. If banks' operating expenses are increased and net revenues fall, NOW accounts are thereby shown to be bad. The fact that competition is supposed to bring benefits to consumers via price concessions imposed by market forces—as well as by cost savings forced on firms scrambling to offset the effects of competition on expenses and net income—seems to have escaped the notice of many commentators on NOW accounts.

As Edward S. Herman, Professor of Finance at the University of Pennsylvania's Wharton School, commented:

> *The anti-competitive spirit reflected here, which pushes the consumer into the distant background, was well captured in a 1934 letter from I.G. Farbenindustrie to fellow cartel member Winthrop Chemical, which noted that price-cutting "is of benefit only to the consumer, and the maintaining of a certain price level would be to the advantage of all competitive [sic] companies."*
>
> *NOW accounts are only of benefit to consumers; the preservation by law and agreement of zero rates of interest on checking accounts is to the advantage of all competitive [sic] banks.*[17]

### Government Price Fixing—Again

The American economic system is supposed to be based on a market economy, in which the forces of the market determine pricing and the allocation of resources. It would certainly be appropriate for banks, the bastions of capitalism, to join the market economy. Instead, they have been protected from competition by government, at the request of bankers. Government has outlawed price competition by prohibiting the payment of interest on checking accounts and by setting below-market interest rate ceilings on savings accounts. Government has also restricted competition by apportioning markets, both by limiting entry with restrictive branching laws and by segmenting deposit and asset authorities so that thrifts and commercial banks are limited in competing for each other's customers. (Thus, by law, thrifts cannot compete with commercial banks by offering checking accounts.) Even when NOW accounts were authorized in a few states, the federal regulatory authorities were quick to limit these accounts to individuals and non-profit organizations, thus leaving small business and local governments firmly in their commercial banks' embrace.

It is difficult to imagine that the public has benefited from these restrictions on competition. Authorizing interest-bearing checking accounts for all thrifts as well as for commercial banks could be an important pro-consumer step, both because of the idea's immediate consumerist effect and because it would help determine whether our banking system needs its artificial barriers.

Bankers' basic lobbying position towards NOW accounts was to find a way to stop them. Failing that, they aimed to slow it down by various legislative tactics. The American Bankers Association (ABA) used the controversy over the interest differential allowed thrifts—the quarter-point-higher interest thrifts are permitted to pay—as the basis for one such tactic. The ABA stated that it would accept the power to offer NOW accounts for individuals only if the differential were to be eliminated. Since the proposed NOW accounts would not have any such differential (the same 5 percent ceiling would apply at all types of financial institutions), the issue was not really germane.

The ABA is strongly opposed, however, to taking the next step after NOWs and accepting the power to pay interest on checking accounts without a government imposed ceiling. They insist on government protection from having that competitive weapon in their arsenal.

### Caveat Depositor

Savings bankers in Massachusetts originally offered free NOW accounts paying 5 percent interest as a competitive and attractive bank service. As the accounts have grown more available, and have been used by more people, banks have moved to make them less attractive. Even in Massachusetts, which has probably the most competitive banking climate in the country, most banks have raised minimum balance requirements and imposed service charges. Minimum balances to get free NOW accounts in Massachusetts are, on the average, between $200 and $500.

In New York where neither the commercial banks nor the thrifts wanted the authority to offer NOW accounts, minimum balances are much higher. The largest commercial banks there require minimum balances of $2,000 to $3,000. The trend toward higher minimum balances is likely to continue for a while when NOW accounts are offered nationwide. At a Bank Marketing Association Convention in New Orleans in September of 1979, delegates from banks all over the country planning for NOW accounts were warned not to offer them for free.[18] The implicit collusion in price setting can be expected to be broken eventually, probably by a smaller bank or a new bank in an area that will be seeking to expand its deposit base. It's difficult to keep a cartel with over 20,000 members all in line. Or so we can hope.

But having lost one battle over NOW accounts, banks are trying to win the second one by means of confusing and deceptive advertising. A General Accounting Office (GAO) study in 1979 concluded that "Although it is advisable for most people to shop around for the best plans, this may be a difficult task for many consumers."[19] The way banks advertise service charge arrangements is designed to confuse and hide real costs rather than to allow ease of comparison. Banks misuse the word "free." This problem has been addressed seriously in a code of ethics in bank advertising that has been widely promoted (perhaps in an effort to hold the Federal Trade Commission at bay). The word "free" should mean just that, *free*—with no financial conditions such as a minimum balance or charges for checks. It rarely has that meaning in bank advertising.

Many depositors have concluded that the time and trouble involved in figuring out which type of account at which institution will give them the best deal won't be worth the effort. So why bother? Many Americans don't. Which is exactly what the bankers wanted to accomplish in the first place.

### We Don't Want Them

Unlike the New England savings banks, the savings and loan industry has insisted that is does not want the authority to offer

NOW accounts, or even non-interest-bearing checking accounts. The S&Ls have seen NOW accounts as a double-edged sword. On the one hand, the accounts would make them stronger competitors for funds against commercial banks; on the other, their newly gained strength could be used as a weapon against them by commercial banks, who would then argue that thrifts no longer needed the quarter point differential on savings accounts. As Norman Strunk, Executive Vice President of the U.S. League, the trade association of the savings and loan industry, has told the congressional banking committees, if it comes down to a choice between NOW accounts and the differential, "There is no question which we prefer—we have to keep the differential over NOW accounts."[20]

In an attempt to thwart the expansion of NOWs, the savings and loan industry has been joined by the smaller commercial banks, represented by the Independent Bankers Association. The U.S. League, embracing the self-serving argument of the smaller commercial banks argued against lifting the prohibition of interest on demand deposits by stating:

*We think the Congress ought to move cautiously before substantially increasing the money costs of our commercial banks....We fear it could lead to the disappearance of many smaller commercial banks and accentuate the already considerable concentration of the banking assets of this country into the hands of a few super-sized banks.*[21]

Instead of endorsing NOWs, the U.S. League in May 1979 called for a ten-year extension of interest-rate ceilings (including the zero rate on checking accounts) with the quarter-point differential guaranteed for at least five years.

In exasperation, Rep. St Germain, an ardent supporter of NOW accounts, threatened that if the savings and loan industry did not want NOW account authority, he would exempt them from the bill while approving NOW accounts for all other financial institutions!

### The Fed and NOW Accounts

The Fed's attitude toward NOW accounts has varied, with the accounts viewed sometime as a valuable service to be encouraged, sometime as a threat to bank profitability to be controlled, and sometime as a tool for shoring up the Fed's own bureaucratic empire.

Frank Morris, the President of the Boston Fed, and Robert Eisenmenger, his Director of Research, were early champions of NOW accounts in the Federal Reserve System. They fought to prevent the Fed from becoming the commercial bank's weapon against NOWs. But even they were concerned about "equity" among financial institutions and preservation of market shares. The Fed's concern took the form of issuing regulations limiting NOW accounts to households and nonprofit institutions. The Fed and FDIC also rolled back the interest rate Massachusetts savings banks could pay on NOW accounts from 5½ to 5 percent, the maximum rate commercial banks could pay on savings accounts. The Fed also toyed with the idea of pricing NOW accounts for banks so that the NOW account competition would be restrained. Rather than allowing the free, no-minimum-balance NOWs being offered in Massachusetts and New Hampshire, the Fed proposed that NOW account users be charged fifteen cents per draft after the first five monthly checks and that NOW accounts be limited to 150 checks per year. Although most of the government price-fixing was eliminated, the Fed did retain for ten months a restriction that no more than 150 drafts could be drawn on a NOW account in any twelve-month period.

Federal Reserve bureaucrats nearly decided that NOW account drafts could not be cleared in Fed check clearing facilities in the same manner as checks, and triumphantly announced, "We've got them now!" The Fed could thus clear checks for nonmember commercial banks but not NOW account drafts for thrifts. Then the Fed discovered that the big commercial banks were clearing the NOW account drafts for their correspondent thrift banks at a profit—at the same time that they were insisting that the Fed not process them.

Later, when legislation was being considered to allow NOWs nationwide, the Fed asked for the authority to set interest ceilings for them, and Chairman Arthur Burns let it be known that the ceiling would be 2 to 3 percent rather than the 5 percent prevailing in the New England states. The Fed was clearly more concerned about appearing to befriend its banks than it was about being fair to the users of bank services.

Finally, the Fed saw NOW accounts as a way of solving its membership problem. Memberhips in the Federal Reserve System is voluntary for commercial banks, and entails both costs and benefits. Benefits include access to a lender of last resort in times of need and access to the Fed's check-clearing facilities; the only cost is the requirement to keep idle reserve balances at the Fed, earning no interest on them. As years of economic stability have made concerns about bank failures fade, commercial banks have come to chafe at the cost of Fed membership. For all but the largest banks with large correspondent bank networks, the costs appeared to outweigh the benefits in the 1970s, as interest rates rose. As a result, an increasing number of banks simply dropped their membership in the Fed so they could invest those reserves. Between 1970 and 1979, more than 500 banks, with combined deposits of $10 billion, left the system. This attrition is referred to as the "membership problem."

(While this decline in membership in the system does not thrill the officials and staffs of the Federal Reserve, by the way, it creates no regulatory concerns. The withdrawing banks transfer to the jurisdiction of the FDIC for federal supervisory purposes; their withdrawal from the Fed does not leave them unregulated.)

The major reason for the decline in the membership is clearly the high reserve requirements imposed on member banks. To anyone outside of the Federal Reserve System, the membership problems would appear to have no connection with payment of interest on household checking accounts. But the Fed has linked the two by arguing that Congress should only approve nationwide NOWs if it resolves the Fed's membership problem. Pointing to the accelerated rate of bank withdrawals from the Federal Reserve System after the introduction of NOW accounts, the Federal Reserve Board insisted that it could support nationwide NOW accounts only if Congress would require all banks to be members of the Fed and allow the Fed to set reserve requirements for all checklike accounts at any type of financial institution. The Fed has contended that the cost of NOWs will accelerate banks' withdrawals from the Federal Reserve as they seek to save money, but that a high level of bank membership in the system is essential for the conduct of monetary policy. And membership could be made more attractive, the Fed has argued, if the Fed could pay interest on reserves. Thus, the Fed seized on the NOW account issue as a heaven-sent opportunity to pass its top legislative concern: a universal membership requirement.

The pillars of the Fed's arguments are very weak. It is not true that paying interest on reserves held at the Fed would offset the cost of NOWs for the majority of banks in the country, because most banks are not now members of the Fed and would not be eligible to receive this interest income. At the beginning of 1977, there were 5,759 members and 8,735 nonmember commercial banks. For nonmembers, it makes little sense for the Fed to set reserve requirements for NOW accounts when it does not for checking accounts. (If the states set reserve requirements for state-chartered banks on non-interest-bearing checking accounts, it is not clear why they should not set them for interest-bearing accounts; the only rationale for this proposal is as a precedent for the Fed to set reserve requirements for all depository institutions on all types of accounts.) Nonmembers do not want to maintain reserves at the Fed, even if paid the stipulated 2 percent on these reserves, because it is much more costly than their present reserve arrangements. Since nonmembers already make a return on their reserves by holding them in the form of earning assets under state banking laws, the fact that they might continue to receive a return on reserves as Fed members could not be understood to help them absorb a new interest expense.

Even for members, 2 percent interest paid on reserves held at the Fed will do little to offset the earnings impact of NOWs on banks which have large numbers of household accounts and which will be in direct competition with thrifts for NOW accounts. The largest commercial banks will receive a windfall from payment of interest on reserves because they have large required reserve balances and a small proportion of household accounts in their deposit base. Thus payment of interest on reserves does little to ease the cost burden of NOW accounts, but may have anticompetitive implications for banking structure by increasing the earnings of large banks versus small ones. This windfall for the larger member commercial banks would, of course, come out of the pocketbook of the taxpayer. As Jonathan Brown, staff attorney for the Public Interest Research Group, stated in his opposition to a Senate bill linking NOWs to the payment of interest on reserves, "...the NOW account bill...[pays] tribute to the manipulative skills of the Federal Reserve Board and the bank lobbyists.... Title II, which authorizes the Federal Reserve to pay interest on required reserves and to reduce reserve requirements, represents a $300 million federal subsidy designed to strengthen the political power base of the Federal Reserve."[22]

The Fed has tried to portray its membership problem as a national issue by insisting that overwhelming membership in the Federal Reserve is essential to the Fed's ability to conduct monetary policy. On this issue, the weight of scholarly opinion is heavily against the Fed.

When the Federal Reserve purchases, for example, $1 billion of securities, by that action it injects $1 billion of funds into the system. Similarly, when the Fed sells those securities it withdraws $1 billion of funds. Nonmember banks do not escape the effects of these actions because they are not members of the Fed. When money is tight, for example, savings and loan associations and nonmember banks are not awash with funds while Federal Reserve member banks have nothing to lend. And when monetary policy is easy, it is not just member banks that advertise for borrowers. As Professors Ross M. Robertson and Almarin Phillips have put it:

*Like the rain from Heaven which falls on all of us regardless of our merits, open market operations [by the Federal Reserve] affect member and nonmember banks alike. There is not one shred of evidence to the contrary.*[23]

The public benefits of allowing banks to offer interest-bearing checking accounts is clear. Congress should not allow the Fed to hold NOW accounts hostage to its political ambitions. Paying interest on demand deposits and paying interest on reserves held at the Federal Reserve are two separate issues. Each should have to stand or fall on its own merits.

### The Politics of a NOW-Reserve Bill

In 1977, Senator McIntyre tried to gain backing for a nationwide extension of NOW accounts by drafting legislation that would offer something to every banking lobby. But in the words of one lobbyist, "It just created new foes without making new friends."[24] The bill authorized nationwide NOW accounts and special low reserve requirements for small banks to reduce the costs of Fed membership. It also allowed mutual savings banks to switch from state to federal charters.

The political outlook for the bill was bleak because the legislation lacked support among the financial lobbies, the primary requirement for passage. The larger commercial banks, which generally like NOWs, were displeased with the section granting smaller banks a favorable reserve rate, which they considered discriminatory. The smaller banks liked this part, but were so dead set against interest-paying checking accounts that they opposed the bill. Mutual savings banks loved the federal charter provision but they already had NOWs (except in New York, where the mutuals did not want them). And the savings and loans did not want NOWs, which they saw as a threat to the continuation of the differential. The bill made this threat real by proposing a phase-out of the differential over a two-year period. More importantly, consumers of financial services, among the primary beneficiaries of the bill, were ignoring it.

One of the problems was that the NOW accounts and Fed membership are highly charged emotional issues to bankers. The strategy was that the one was supposed to carry the other. But S&Ls were not wild about NOWs anyway, and would fight to the end to maintain the savings rate differential, whose elimination was made a condition of ABA support of a NOW package.

Finding itself stuck between the banking and S&L lobbies over elimination of the differential, Congress chose to walk away from the battle and pass no legislation. As James E. Smith, former Comptroller of the Currency, remarked, "A shoot-out at the OK Corral between banks and S&Ls would be viewed by lawmakers 'as a no-win deal' since they would have to offend one industry group or the other—and possibly in an election year."[25] The bill disappeared in the Senate halls.

## WOW: NOW, POW & NINOW...ATS

While legislative approval for nationwide NOW accounts languished, innovation continued to spread. Credit unions, benefiting from an independent regulatory ruling, began offering "share draft accounts," again the functional equivalent of an interest-bearing checking account.

In Pennsylvania, meanwhile, consumers were caught in a crossfire by savings banks and commercial banks, as commercial bankers challenged the thrifts' right to offer non-interest-paying checking accounts, or NINOWs. Again, having lost in the Bank Commissioner's office and in the courts, the commercial bankers were working for a legislative rollback.

In Washington, with his NOW legislation defeated, Senator McIntyre tried another tack. He convinced Arthur Burns, chairman of the Federal Reserve Board, to offer a regulatory ruling that would afford bank customers many of the benefits of an interest-bearing checking account. On May 1, 1978, the Federal Reserve made effective a plan to permit automatic transfers from savings accounts to checking accounts to cover checks or to maintain a minimum checking account balance, if the customer had voluntarily entered an agreement with the bank. Such agreements were not previously permissible under Regulation Q. Like NOWs, the automatic transfer service (ATS) was to be available only to individuals, not to businesses or governments. Implementation of the plan was delayed until November 1, 1978.

Under ATS, an individual keeps both a savings and checking account, but puts all his money into the interest-paying savings account. As checks are written, the bank automatically transfers the money from the savings account to the checking account to cover the drafts. ATS helps depositors by allowing them to earn interest on their transactions funds, and relieves them of concerns about bouncing a check.

Within a few months after the service became available, more than a third of the nation's commercial banks were offering ATS. Virtually all large banks offered the service, along with many medium-sized institutions.

The savings and loan industry objected to allowing bank customers to make these automatic transfers because it would impose "murderous competition"[26] on the thrift industry and would violate the spirit of the banking laws prohibiting interest on demand deposits. ATS is not quite the functional equivalent of the NOW account, as the depositor still must maintain two accounts and will still not be able to earn interest on a portion of his or her funds. Nevertheless, it was a step in that direction and was another crack in the wall prohibiting interest on demand deposits.

In order to maintain the competitive standing of savings and loan associations, the Federal Home Loan Bank Board on November 6, 1978, authorized payments to third parties through a new category of account—the "payment order of withdrawal" account (POW).

But trouble was brewing. The 1976 ruling by the National Credit Union Administration authorizing credit unions to offer share drafts accounts was successfully challenged by the American Bankers Association in the U.S. courts. After initially losing, ABA won in the Court of Appeals for the District of Columbia, in April 1979. But the victory was Pyrrhic.

The judge went too far. He ruled that these market innovations and regulatory approvals—credit union share drafts, automatic transfers from savings to checking accounts at banks, and remote service units at savings and loan associations—contravened the legal prohibition against the offering of checking accounts by savings and loans and credit unions. Recognizing the disruptive impact of his ruling, the judge made his decision effective only on January 1, 1980. If it were to become effective, it would adversely affect more than 750,000 bank customers, one million credit union members, and many depositors at about 200 savings and loan associations. The judge implicitly acknowledged this undesirable effect, and gave Congress time to make the existing hodgepodge of financial services legal.

The ABA suit had an effect the bankers never intended: It had created a major impetus for allowing NOWs nationwide. In June 1979, Congress again took up legislation to authorize all depository institutions to offer interest-bearing transaction accounts. With NOWs and POWs and NINOWs and share drafts threatened, there was finally a constituency clamoring for the legislation. Even the administration said that a bill should not be held up pending resolution of the Fed's "membership problem."

### The 1980 Time Bomb

Support for the removal of the prohibition of interest payment on checking accounts was unqualifiedly endorsed by only one federal bank regulator as late as the July 1979 congressional hearings. The Federal Reserve tied its support to resolution of its membership problem. The chairman of the FDIC, Irvine Sprague, endorsed NOW accounts only for individuals. Comptroller of the Currency John Heimann was the only bank regulator to endorse legislation simply to end the forty-five-year prohibition against paying interest on demand deposits and to extend the authority to offer checking accounts to all federally insured financial institutions. Lawrence Connell, Jr., National Credit Union Administrator, and the U.S. Treasury also strongly endorsed immediate passage of legislation allowing all depository institutions to offer interest-paying checking accounts, although the Treasury chose to have these initially limited to households.

The Credit Union National Association and National Association of Federal Credit Unions both pleaded for prompt action by Congress, arguing that for them, the judge's ruling that share drafts were illegal was potentially "disastrous."[27] The credit union associations testified:

*Mr. Chairman, it is not the check-like interest-earning share draft that will challenge the safety and soundness of credit unions, but rather the lack of it....*

*At worst, NCUA estimates the outflow of funds from FCU share draft and share accounts if the program is shut down could total as much as $2.1 billion. The most conservative consequence from shutdown is estimated by NCUA at between $500 and $800 million. The liquidity problems at credit unions that would result from such outflows would severely curtail lending and dividend rates and could well outstrip the ability of the fledgling Central Liquidity Facility to deal with the problem.[28]*

But the Independent Bankers Association continued to be dead set against the extension of NOWs nationwide and to the granting of checking account powers to thrifts. They once again raised the specious allusion to the Depression:

*The country's experience with interest-bearing accounts prior to their prohibition more than 40 years ago was disastrous and a major contributing factor in bank failures. Also unsatisfactory has been the current experience with NOW accounts in New England....Such accounts mean only one thing—increased costs to consumers.[29]*

The two largest banking associations, the American Bankers Association and the U.S. League, demanded mutually exclusive preconditions for accepting the interest-paying checking accounts. The U.S. League demanded new protections of its quarter-percent interest rate differential as its price for supporting the bill. ABA demanded the end of the differential as its price for accepting nationwide NOWs. Their in-fighting threatened to kill the bill.

One did not have to be a seer to conclude that commercial banks would be paying interest on checking accounts again soon, as they did for 130 years before Congress was misled into prohibiting it. In fact, in March 1980, Congress passed an omnibus banking reform bill which authorizes nationwide NOW accounts as of December 31, 1980. The Fed was successful in tying the extension of NOW accounts to realizing its political ambitions of setting reserve requirements on all transaction accounts—both checking accounts and NOW accounts for member banks as well as non-member depository institutions.

Again, deregulation will take place over the opposition of the exponents of the free enterprise system. The nation's financial system has been undergoing dramatic change, with regulatory change drifting along behind. The regulators administer a system born in the banking crises of the 1930s. As former Secretary of the Treasury Michael Blumenthal stated,

> *The marketplace has not waited upon governmental action. It is changing all around us, while those who believe the Congress should not act now continue to defend a status quo that no longer exists.*[30]

Where individuals exercise any discretion, they are likely to choose to receive interest on their deposits. Only where banks control the funds entirely are substantial deposits likely to be left in interest-free checking accounts. The story of the great checking account robbery may soon be down to its epilogue: the story of funds left in the trust departments of banks.

### Trust Funds

Receiving interest on your checking account balance must be bad for your wealth: After all, the money managers in the trust departments of commercial banks do not use them, even when their own banks offer NOW accounts for other customers. This decision of bank trust departments is, curiously enough, not shared by private trustees, like the Yankee law firms which hold billions in trust funds.

The failure of bank trust departments to place their uninvested cash in available NOW accounts may well constitute a violation of their fiduciary obligations to their clients. Soon after NOW accounts began, the largest savings bank in Massachusetts, the Provident Institution for Savings, made this point by advertising that trustees had a fiduciary responsibility to keep their uninvested cash in NOW accounts. Mysteriously, this ad was quickly discontinued.

There appears to be a serious conflict of interest here for bank trust departments—the interests of the shareholders are being placed over those of the trust department's customers. The FDIC's annual report on bank trust operations showed that trust departments hold billions in uninvested cash. By not holding this money in NOW accounts, the trust beneficiaries lost millions. The reasoning that led trust department officers, acting solely in the best interest of their trust department clients, to choose non-interest-bearing checking accounts over interest-bearing NOW accounts, escapes the disinterested observer. For that matter, it is no excuse for a Philadelphia or New York trust officer to reply that his bank does not offer NOW accounts. The trust officer is under no fiduciary obligation to keep uninvested cash in his own bank.

Bank trust officers have countered that they keep only small balances in non-interest-bearing checking accounts. As a vice president for trust legal matters at Morgan Guaranty Trust of New York stated, "I don't think you're ever going to get every last dollar of trust cash invested."[31] At the end of 1976, Morgan's trust division had $44 million of trust funds in non-interest-bearing checking accounts, an amount that hardly seems to deserve the title "last dollar."[32]

A trust officer at a large Massachusetts bank explained that some trust customers want instant access to their money in case of untoward eventualities. He cited the case of one elderly woman who feared not having funds available to place her in a nursing home if she needed to go to one. To ease her mind, the bank kept the entire $1 million in her trust fund in a personal checking account for her. When I pointed out to this trust officer that his client would have the same immediate access to funds in a NOW account, he exploded that "That would mean a transfer of fifty thousand dollars from the bank's pocket to hers!"[33]

While the use of NOW accounts might well result in an increase in trust department service charges, it would at least make it possible for trust customers to compare the service charges offered by competing banks. Such charges are now hidden by the placing of trust funds in a checking account in the bank. That foregone interest income is a hidden service charge.

If the uninvested cash of a trust department is not in a NOW account or other interest-paying account, the trust beneficiaries should be asking whether the interests of the bank's shareholders are being placed over those of the trust customers. Moreover, trust officers should be seriously questioning whether they have violated their fiduciary obligations. As Benjamin Cardozo, then Chief Judge of the New York Court of Appeals, set forth in his now classic description of the obligation of the fiduciary:

> *A trustee is held to something stricter than the morals of the marketplace. Not honesty alone, but the punctilio of an honor the most sensitive, is then the standard of behavior....*[34]

It does not appear that a commercial bank trust officer who ignores NOW accounts in favor of a checking account at his own bank which does not pay interest has met the required standards of "undivided loyalty."

# III
# POLICING
# THE BANKS

*"Now as through this world I ramble,*
*I see lots of funny men.*
*Some will rob you with a six-gun,*
*And some with a fountain pen."*

—Lyrics from *"Pretty Boy Floyd,"*
by Woody Guthrie.

# 8.
# Who's Regulating The Regulators?

Regulation of commercial banking is fractured under the present system—divided not only between the states and the federal level but also, within the federal government, among three autonomous regulatory agencies—the Federal Reserve System, the Comptroller of the Currency, and the Federal Deposit Insurance Corporation. Though state control is older, bank regulation by the federal government does date back to 1864, which makes it older than railroad regulation, frequently cited as the oldest form of economic regulation in this country.

Bank regulation needs to be completely revamped if the regulatory agencies are to serve the public needs of the 1980s. Banking may be the most regulated private industry, but much of that regulation ill serves both the public and the economy's need for an efficient and responsive banking system. It is not that banking needs more regulation; it doesn't. It needs different regulations—regulation that is more consistently pro-consumer and less designed to protect banking from competition. These changes will require a fundamental restructuring of both banking regulation and the bank regulatory agencies.

### Changing the Regulator's Constituency

Even before this structured reform, though, we need to pursue a more political reform, one aimed at correcting what one former Comptroller of the Currency called "mistakes of geniality."[1] The regulators must learn whom they work for.

While the federal bank regulatory agencies have improved significantly in recent years because of the high quality of most of the Carter administration's appointments in this area, the agencies still suffer from their failure to focus on the correct constituency. A bank regulator's primary job is to represent the public interest, to ensure that banks adhere to publicly established rules of equity and that they deal with the social and economic implications of their actions. Simply put, the bank regulator's constituency is the public. Too often, a regulatory agency acts as if its constituency was a particular kind of financial institution.

By concentrating on the public issues in bank regulation, of course, regulators open themselves up to the charge that they are "politicizing" their offices. But bank regulators have always been involved in the political-legislative process. It's just that their traditional role has been to represent the banking community's interests in public forums. They have seen their role as mediating differences between banking groups—large banks versus small ones, or thrifts versus commercial banks—and then presenting a united front against the opposition: consumers, savers, borrowers—that is, the public. This is not, of course, considered politicizing the office, from a banker's perspective. Nor does it seem like a corruption of the regulatory process, from that perspective, that there is a revolving door between banks and the agencies that oversee them. Most often bank regulators have been bankers or bank lobbyists; if they weren't before they became regulators, they become bankers or their lawyers or their consultants afterward. President Carter's choice for Chairman of the Federal Home Loan Bank Board, Robert McKinney, was the chairman of an Indiana savings and loan association. President Nixon's Comptroller of the Currency, James E. Smith, was a former lobbyist for the American Bankers Association. If a president appointed the lobbyist for the Atomic Industrial Forum to head the Nuclear Regulatory Commission, he would be run out of town. But in banking, this is somehow totally acceptable. The revolving door also includes congressmen and their staffs. The last four former staff directors of the Senate Banking Committee have returned to the congressional scene as active bank lobbyists. It partly explains the timidity of bank regulation, not only on social issues but also on safety and soundness. "What there should be," Rep. Rosenthal of New York, chairman of the House Subcommittee on Commerce, Consumer and Monetary Affairs, has stated, "is an adversary relationship, not a warm, cozy relationship, with the regulators running in and out of the industry at will."[2]

It is far easier for a bank regulator to see the users of banks as his constituency if he is an outsider to the banking industry and can confidently believe that he will never need to find employment in the industry. This "outsider's" perspective is not an easy qualification, but it would help if bank regulators were prohibited from working for banks or bank holding companies for several years after leaving the agency. Only someone from outside the industry is likely to be able to judge the issues independently and from a public-interest viewpoint.

Clearly, bankers should not be appointed to head the federal bank regulatory agencies; if they are, they should at least bear a heavy burden of proof that they can represent the public interest. Names of nominees should not (as they do now) circulate among bank trade associations for their veto or approval. It should not be an important qualification that the proposed regulator can get along with the industry. The criterion in selection should be that this regulator will understand the issues and will see them through the eyes of the bank consumer.

Even with good intentions, though, it is difficult not to develop the banker's point of view since the regulator spends so much of his time with bankers and their lobbyists. What public-interest group has so many informal meetings over a friendly drink in a sunny, luxurious resort to explain his side of the issue? A glance at the travel schedule of any former regulator clearly indicates that these regulators were captives of the bank convention circuit. For example, in 1975, Comptroller of the Currency James Smith spent 154 days attending bank conferences at luxury resorts.[3] It is very difficult to give talks which consistently may antagonize your audience, or to intermingle with a hostile audience every day of the week. The audience *becomes* the constituency.

Perhaps regulators should be limited to only a few bank conventions a year, so they would be forced to find broader forums for giving their addresses. There must be a way to make sure that regulators discuss banking with a wider spectrum of the community. In all of his travels, Comptroller Smith only once addressed nonbanking groups, and then only as a favor to a friend.[4] When bank regulators address regional meetings of public interest and small business groups more often than they address bank conventions, we will be on the way to ensuring that bank regulators know their true constituency.

It's not as though the regulator's current constituency can't assert itself. In fact, the banking lobby may well be the most powerful among all regulated industries. Jonathan Brown, a bank specialist in Nader's Public Interest Research Group, has asserted that "the banks are without question the strongest lobby in Washington."[5] The strength of the banks and thrift institutions means that, to an unusual degree, banking sets the terms of its own regulation and stays clear of effective independent view.

A lobbyist for one of the nation's largest banks, long regarded as the dean of the fraternity, made much the same point. "The bank lobby," he said, "can almost certainly stop anything it does not want in Congress."[6] The power of the banks rests on an intricate political and financial structure: political contributions, the power to make loans, a highly sophisticated lobbying effort, and a close similarity of interests with such powerful groups as the Chamber of Commerce.

The banking lobby in Washington employs scores of lawyers, economists, public relations advisers and other specialists, costing millions of dollars each year and growing in sophistication and size.

The ABA has had for years a system of "contact bankers" who could be called to get a message across to Senate or House members with whom they had developed personal ties. The political action committees of the nation's banks, savings and loan associations, and associated trade groups are a large and increasing source of political financing. Unlike any other industry, the banks can magnify the impact of their campaign contributions by making timely loans to finance expensive fund drives in the crucial early weeks of primary or general elections. Not surprisingly, seventeen of the twenty-five congressmen receiving contributions from at least four of five bank political action committees were on the House Banking Committee.[7] Among them were six Democratic members of the subcommittee which was unable to muster a majority to approve legislation aimed at tightening Federal bank regulation. Moreover, the campaign committees of twelve current members of the House Banking Committee had loans from banks, and six of the committee members had not repaid these loans at the time the Banking Committee was considering reform legislation strongly opposed by almost all banks.[8]

Once regulators do see the public as their constituency, it should become clear that banking regulations should not be limited to ensuring that banks are operated in a safe and sound manner. Given this new constituency, bank regulators would insist that regulations stimulate banking performance in local markets, so that the spur of competition would lead banks to provide a variety of services at reasonable prices. Regulators would then insist that bank policies adhere to publicly established rules of fairness.

An emphasis on competition and equity is new to bank regulatory agencies, which for forty years suffered from a Depression-induced obsession with preventing bank failures. Until the early 1960s, this meant chartering few new banks and restricting branching for fear of the effects of increased competition. Then federal regulations rediscovered competition and its benefits. Since the late 1960s, Congress has increasingly made clear to bank regulatory agencies that the scope of their concerns must be broader than safety and soundness. Congress has passed a number of consumer protection laws, including the Truth-in-Lending Act, the Equal Credit Opportunity Act, the Fair Credit Billing Act, the Home Mortgage Disclosure Act, and the Community Reinvestment Act, all of which indicate that the focus of regulation is for the users of banks. Clearly, Congress views the role of bank regulation as more than preventing bank failures. But most bankers and bank regulators, particularly state bank regulators, still do not.

### The Struggle for Pro-Consumer Bank Regulation

While anticompetitive restraints on banking abound in financial regulation, regulatory agencies have been much more reluctant to issue consumer protection regulations. Even when these have been legislated by the Congress, as in the case of Truth-in-Lending (1968) and the Equal Credit Opportunity Act (1974), the regulatory agencies dragged their feet. The traditional relationship between the regulatory agencies and the banks has weighed against strong consumer protection regulation and has led to less than whole-hearted enthusiasm for the new effort to protect consumers.

The Federal Reserve, for example, has issued voluminous regulations on the subjects—Reg Z (truth-in-lending) and Reg B (Equal Credit), as they are called. While these regulations are infamous for their intricacies, the details are smokescreens for regulatory inaction. The Fed wrote the regulations; then the agencies ignored them. They never insisted that banks observe them, and the banks didn't. For years, the Federal Reserve Board blithely filed annual reports to Congress stating that the banks were in "substantial compliance" with the Truth-in-Lending Act. As subsequent studies were to show, that conclusion was based on non-examinations.

A survey done by the Comptroller of the Currency's office in 1977, after John Heimann became Comptroller, found that 88 percent of all national banks were violating the regulations. And the violations were not all technical in nature, as bankers would like the public to believe. The Comptroller found the most frequent violations to be failure to calculate annual loan interest rates correctly and failure to make full and complete disclosure of loan terms.[9] There were also numerous violations of the Equal Credit Opportunity Act, such as requiring a spouse's signature and using old forms which violated present legal requirements. The Comptroller estimated that the overcharges uncovered could range from $30 million to $100 million.[10]

These injustices simply cannot be eliminated by individual consumer action. In terms of continuing oversight, the federal bank regulatory agencies are the only effective enforcement vehicles. Individual private lawsuits for damages or civil penalties can add to the deterrent effect, but they do not permit a systematic review of bank practices and do not assure future compliance. As the 1976 Senate Report on Consumer Protection Enforcement Activities concluded:

> With the present limited utility of class actions as private enforcement devices, the importance of active, thorough and imaginative enforcement efforts by these agencies cannot be overstated.[11]

Let us see just how thorough and imaginative their efforts have been.

### Truth-in-Lending: Confusion in Regulation

The Truth-in-Lending Act is intended to provide consumers with meaningful information about credit costs and is unquestionably one of the most important consumer protection statutes. The Act requires lenders to set forth in a uniform manner the true costs and terms of consumer credit. Although the name of the act itself has played a role in making bankers hostile to it (since the name implies that banks had previously lied to their customers), the complexities of the Federal Truth-in-Lending regulations now run to more than 100 pages. Rather than further antagonize their constituents over a problem that bankers and regulators alike generally assume to be of minor interest, the agencies have given only a nod at compliance. The Senate Banking Committee concluded in a 1976 study that

*in some instances enforcement seemed to be non-existent; in most areas the apparent attitude of the federal agencies has been one of grudging acceptance of its consumer protection responsibilities.... Violations once discovered have been settled on the most amicable basis possible with the offending banks. Few formal enforcement actions have been brought, and little consumer education has been attempted.*[12]

The lack of interest by the bank regulatory agencies in consumer protection legislation is clearly illustrated by the Federal Reserve's unwillingness to issue regulations proscribing unfair or deceptive banking practices. In the first eighteen months after receiving this authority, the Board issued no regulations, nor did it institute rule-making proceedings.

The most glaring defect in Truth-in-Lending enforcement was the failure to seek restitution or other reimbursement for consumers injured by bank violations. When violations were discovered, through complaints or through the examination proc-ess, the agencies tended to seek only informal corrective action by the banks. They were notified of the violations and advised to change their forms or procedures for the future. Seldom were formal enforcement proceedings commenced. From 1969 to 1976, the FDIC issued one cease and desist order, the Comptroller of the Currency three (plus three formal consent orders), and the Federal Reserve none.[13] With some few exceptions in the case of the Comptroller, none of the agenices had seen fit to seek restitution for consumers injured by bank violations. As Rep. Benjamin Rosenthal concluded, after his subcommittee's investigation into Truth-in-Lending compliance,

*the agencies are thwarting the self-enforcing nature of the Truth-in-Lending Act by not notifying borrowers of the violations found by Federal bank examiners.*[14]

The banking agencies have also failed in their responsibility to educate consumers about their rights under the Act. Truth-in-lending regulation is an area where most state regulators have been supremely indifferent, but a few have been path-breakers. Five states actually applied for exemptions under the Act allowing their own state banking agencies to enforce more stringent Truth-in-Lending laws.[15] Massachusetts, in fact, passed the first Truth-in-Lending law in the nation in 1967, and the Massachusetts act had been a model for the federal statute. In Maine, Connecticut, and Massachusetts, the bank regulators in the mid-1970s revolutionized Truth-in-Lending enforcement by showing that requiring borrower notification and bank restitution for substantive violations were very effective means of getting self-enforcement of the Act by financial institutions. The experimentation with enforcement programs in these states was "invaluable in reviewing Federal enforcement programs," according to Rep. Benjamin Rosenthal, chairman of the Subcommittee on Commerce, Consumer and Monetary Affairs.[16]

Until 1976, federal banking agencies had been reporting very few Truth-in-Lending violations. Rather than indicating general compliance, though, these findings were the result of perfunctory and inadequate Truth-in-Lending examinations. To obtain an evaluation of federal regulatory agencies' thoroughness, the House Commerce, Consumer and Monetary Affairs Subcommittee asked the Connecticut, Maine, and Massachusetts banking departments to prepare special reports on Truth-in-Lending compliance in their states. A comparison of these findings with those of the FDIC, which examined the same banks in these states, revealed that state examiners found far more violations than the FDIC did, as Table II shows. If one doesn't look, of course, one won't find violations. The following statement by John Quinn, then Superintendent for Consumer Protection in Maine, illustrates, federal examiners weren't really looking:

*As an example, in June of this year [1976] our field examiner uncovered 345 substantive TIL [truth-in-lending] violations in loans granted by a single Maine bank during the preceding twelve-month period. In each of these loans the bank had disclosed only one month's finance change as the total finance charge. Despite the fact that the bank had been warned about such practices in both 1970 and 1972, the bank had returned to the practice and virtually all of its consumer loans had been written in this manner since January 1, 1975. While our Bureau did not conduct a TIL examination of this bank during 1975, the bank was, however, examined for compliance with TIL by the FDIC in November of 1975.*

TABLE II COMPARISON OF CONNECTICUT, MASSACHUSETTS,
MAINE, AND FDIC TRUTH-IN-LENDING COMPLIANCE FINDINGS

Banks with Violations as a Percent of Banks Examined

| | Type of Violation | | |
| --- | --- | --- | --- |
| | Annual Percentage Rate | Finance Charge | Rescision Notification |
| I. COMMERCIAL BANKS | | | |
| Connecticut | | | |
| FDIC | 17% | 7% | 12% |
| State Banking Dept. | 90% | 25% | 15% |
| Maine | | | |
| FDIC | 18% | 9% | 5% |
| State Banking Dept. | 69% | 56% | 50% |
| Massachusetts | | | |
| FDIC | 13% | 0% | 2% |
| State Banking Dept. | 41% | 26% | 11% |
| II. SAVINGS BANKS | | | |
| Connecticut | | | |
| FDIC | 3% | 0% | 3% |
| State Banking Dept. | 72% | 41% | 34% |
| Maine | | | |
| FDIC | 3% | 0% | 0% |
| State Banking Dept. | 37% | 63% | 30% |
| Massachusetts | | | |
| FDIC | 0% | 0% | 0% |
| State Banking Dept. | 26% | 22% | 17% |

Source: Opening statement of Congressman Benjamin S. Rosenthal,
Chairman, Commerce, Consumer and Monetary Affairs Subcommittee,
Sept. 15, 1976.

It is evident that the FDIC examiners could not, in fact,
have reviewed a single consumer loan issued by this bank in 1975.
Had they done so, the violations could have been recognized
immediately. Even the most inexperienced examiner should be
able to detect an apparent violation when, for example, a three-
year car loan discloses a total finance charge of only twenty-eight
dollars ($28).[17]

In Massachusetts, examination of banks by specialized Truth-in-
Lending examiners, rather than regular bank examiners, resulted in

far more violations being uncovered. In the period February through June 1976 forty-six savings banks and twenty-seven commercial banks were examined by the specialized teams. They noted 2,254 individual violations at the savings banks and 2,855 individual violations at the commercial banks. In 1975, when these same institutions had been examined by the regular bank examiners, only 168 and 39 violations, respectively, had been cited.[18] There was not a sudden decline in compliance between 1975 and 1976; there were simply meaningful examinations.

In Maine, Connecticut, and Massachusetts, the state authorities in charge of Truth-in-Lending in the mid-1970s began reversing the regulatory approach to Truth-in-Lending which had made these examinations nothing more than internal audits provided to the banks at the banks' and their customers' expense. These state authorities informed the banks that substantive violations of Truth-in-Lending uncovered in future examinations would be treated "as violations of law and not merely as 'errors.'"[19] Enforcement was not punitive. In all three states there was an attempt to limit requirements of restitution to borrowers to nontechnical violations—that is, to those violations which prevented consumers from effectively shopping for credit. Failure to make proper disclosure of the annual percentage interest rate or the total finance charge were the major categories of substantive violations.

But when a substantive violation of Truth-in-Lending was found, the bank would be asked to refund any overcharge. For example, if the creditor understated the annual percentage rate, the creditor was asked to refund the difference between the stated finance charge and the actual finance charge. In Massachusetts, such overcharges in 1977 on loans made within the prior year exceeded a million dollars.

In Connecticut, Commissioner of Banks Lawrence Connell added to the arsenal of enforcement actions the threat of publishing the names of creditors who were significant violators.

Fair and effective enforcement of Truth-in-Lending requires that violations of the Act be penalized in accordance with the Act's provisions and that those who have been disadvantaged by non-compliance be indemnified. The threat of civil liability included in the statute was the inducement for self-enforcement. If the creditor refused to refund the overcharge, the banking department would pursue the matter through the state attorney general's office. In addition the borrower would be notified of his right to seek a civil penalty. The latter step was rarely needed.

This new regulatory approach greatly increased the level of compliance, while reducing the cost of state examinations. As John Quinn told a House Committee:

> *Larger banking systems which may have required a two-week examination just two years ago, may now be examined in a few days by one examiner. This is due simply to the fact that the banks themselves have finally instituted internal safeguards and review procedures to prevent TIL violations.*[20]

Congressional criticism, given the ammunition provided by pro-consumer enforcement actions in a few states, prodded the federal regulatory agencies to redesign their enforcement programs. But even at this late moment, the agencies showed their great discomfort about their consumer protection role. The Federal Reserve Board recommended to the Senate Banking Committee in July of 1977 that liability be removed from a creditor if he complied with the requirements of the statute within thirty days of being shown the error of his ways, in writing by a regulatory agency. This generosity created a "heads I win (if I'm not caught), and tails I don't lose (if I am caught, but then do what I was supposed to have done in the first place)" situation. (Congress, in 1980, gave the banks 60 days to correct errors brought to their attention through bank examinations without incurring any liability.)

In 1977, the agencies began special training programs for Truth-in-Lending examiners. In 1978, they finally implemented a program requiring lenders to rebate overcharges to borrowers and to make restitution for Truth-in-Lending violations. But, just as the federal bank regulatory agencies began to require reimbursements to borrowers for Truth-in-Lending violations, the Federal Reserve was able to get passed, as part of the Depository Institutions Deregulation and Monetary Control Act of 1980, provisions that essentially tied the regulator's hands and considerably diminished the consumer protection provisions of Truth-in-Lending. The omnibus banking reform act amended the restitution provisions of Truth-in-Lending so that the enforcing agencies were limited to requiring reimbursements only when creditors inaccurately disclosed annual percentage rates or finance charges, and only where the errors resulted from a clear and consistent pattern of violations, gross negligence, or willfulness. These are almost impossible standards for a regulator to prove. It makes it most unlikely that the bank regulatory agencies will now be able to require any reimbursements for violations.

Under the guise of simplifying the Act, the amendments also removed many of the Act's safeguards. The borrower's three-day right of recision (the 72 hours to reconsider a credit purchase without penalty) was revoked for credit purchases involving real estate. One can still change one's mind about buying a washing machine on credit, but not a home! Banks were also given additional leeway in the accuracy of their stated interest charges. If they are not more than a quarter of a percent off, they will not now be violating the law. One would have thought that with the widespread availability of pocket calculators, less, rather than more latitude in interest calculations would be expected.

To this day, all the federal banking agencies have "failed in their responsibility to educate consumers about their rights under the Act and the importance of credit costs in clear dollars-and-cents terms."[21] In 1977, Congress urged the agencies immediately to undertake meaningful educational programs, to begin notifying borrowers of substantive Truth-in-Lending violations and to support comparative loan-rate advertising.[22] The agencies' efforts have been devoted almost entirely to creditor rather than borrower education.

In order for the full benefits of the Truth-in-Lending Act to be realized, consumers must be aware of the meanings of credit costs and the variations in charges among lenders. In contrast to the creditor emphasis at the federal agencies, the Maine Consumer Protection Bureau developed a pamphlet which effectively did this. This small pamphlet, entitled, *Down Easter's Pocket Credit Guide,* contained a simple statement of benefits of knowing the cost of credit, the address and telephone number of the Maine Consumer Protection Bureau, a straightforward explanation of credit cost terms, and a handy set of tables showing the amount financed, monthly payment, and finance charge at various percentage rates for all kinds of consumer installment credit. A similar pamphlet was developed by the Massachusetts Banking Department. (An adaptation of the *Down Easter's Credit Guide* is included in this book as Appendix 1.)

In 1977, the House and Senate Banking Committees considered Truth-in-Lending bills which would have mandated that the Federal Reserve Board "semiannually collect, publish and disseminate to the public the annual percentage rates charged for credit ... by all creditors extending or offering to extend such credit in each Standard Metropolitan Statistical Area with populations in excess of 500,000."[23] The bills did not pass, and the federal agencies ignored the hint. (Similar legislation, requesting the Federal Reserve to experiment with publishing consumer interest rates in a sample of SMSAs did pass in 1980.)

I, however, thought it was a worthwhile project for a bank regulatory agency, and so in November of 1977, the Massachusetts Banking Department began publishing "The Shopper's Credit Guide." Each month we collected information from every depository institution in the Boston, Springfield, and New Bedford-Fall River SMSA's on interest rates charged for automobile loans, personal loans, and mortgages, and then sent this information to all newspapers in the area. To make the information complete, we also included data on rates at finance companies and from a representative sample of automobile finance agencies, like GMAC. The result, in a partial reproduction, was a handy and up-to-date reference guide which could easily be clipped out of the paper. Interestingly, only the *Boston Globe* regularly published the Shopper's Credit Guide. It became a regular feature in the Sunday paper.

That it was used was evident. Creditors with the lowest rates were soon swamped with loan applications from out-of-area applicants, and those with higher rates quickly dropped them to the industry average. Given clearly understandable and useful information, consumers *will* shop for credit. As the press release for the guide pointed out, lenders charge different rates. Shopping for a better loan rate can save consumers as much as they might knock off the price of the car by bargaining with a dealer. For a $5,000, four-year new-car loan, for example, a 1978 issue of the guide showed interest rates in the Boston area ranging from 8.26 percent at a savings bank to 18.63 percent at a finance company. The 4 percent spread between a 9 percent rate and a 13 percent rate makes a $466 difference on a forty-eight-month $5,000 loan! The consumer is likely to pay more than necessary for financing unless he is able to refer to a source of comparative loan information. For a mortgage, borrowing from the lower cost lenders can save families $5,000 over the life of just a $40,000 mortgage! It pays to shop for credit.

If the federal agencies took the intent of Truth-in-Lending legislation seriously, they would not wait to be ordered to help borrowers shop for credit; they would be developing similar guides

The Boston Globe   Wednesday, November 16, 1977

# The rates you can get on car and personal loans

Loan rates, available at these financial institutions during November, according to a shoppers credit guide, prepared by Carol S. Greenwald, commissioner of banks.

ANNUAL PERCENTAGE RATE

| BANKS | NEW CAR LOAN (terms: $5000, 20% down, 48 months to repay) | PERSONAL LOAN (terms: $2000, unsecured, 24 months to repay) |
|---|---|---|
| Abington Savings | 9.31 | 10.23 |
| Arlington Co-operative | — | 12.59 |
| Arlington Five Cents Savings | 11.40 *(25% down) | 13.26 |
| Arlington Trust | 9.68 | 13.50 |
| Assabet Savings | 9.24 | 11.13 |
| Atlantic Savings | 9.00 | 13.50 |
| Auburndale Co-operative | 10.11 | 12.91 |
| Barclays International | — | 10.00 |
| BayBank and Trust | 10.50 *(36 mos.) | 13.00 |
| BayBank/Harvard Trust | 11.00 | 13.00 |
| BayBank Middlesex, N.A. | 10.00 *(25% down) | 14.00 |
| BayBank/Newton-Waltham | 11.00 | 13.00 |
| BayBank/Norfolk County Trust | 11.00 *(25% down, 42 mos.) | 13.00 |
| BayBank/Winchester Trust | 10.00 | 12.50 |
| Beacon Co-operative | 10.16 *(25% down, 42 mos.) | 13.80 |
| Belmont Savings | 11.00 | 11.00 |
| Benjamin Franklin Savings | 9.68 | 12.02 |
| Beverly Savings | — | 14.00 |
| Boston Five Cents Savings | 10.25 *(36 mos.) | 13.50 |
| Braintree Co-operative | — | 12.91 |
| Braintree Savings | 9.62 *(25% down) | 13.33 |
| Brighton Co-operative | 12.00 | 13.50 |
| Broadway National | 10.50 | 13.00 |
| Brookline Co-operative | 11.00 | 12.35 |
| Brookline Savings | 10.50 *(30% down) | 12.00 |
| Brookline Trust | 9.30 *(25% down, 36 mos.) | 13.33 |
| Cambridge Savings | 9.75 *(30% down) | 12.00 |
| Cambridge Trust | 11.00 | 11.37 |
| Canton Inst. for Savings | 10.64 *(36 mos.) | 12.00 |
| Cape Anne Savings | — | 14.68 |
| Capitol Bank and Trust | 12.00 | 14.00 |
| Central Co-operative | 10.11 | 13.80 |
| Century Bank and Trust | 10.97 | 13.80 |
| Century North Shore Bank & Tr. | 10.97 | 13.80 |
| CharlesBank Trust | 11.08 *(33½% down, 36 mos.) | 13.80 |
| Charlestown Savings | 12.00 | 14.00 |
| Chelsea-Provident Co-op. | — | 12.00 |
| Chestnut Hill Co-operative | — | 12.00 |
| Citizens Bank and Trust | 9.25 | 12.02 |
| City Bank and Trust | 11.08 *(33½% down, 36 mos.) | 12.91 |
| Cohasset Savings | 10.20 *($4,500 max, 36 mos.) | 12.91 |
| Commercial Bank and Trust | 10.11 *(33% down) | 13.80 |
| Commonwealth Bank and Trust | | |
| Concord Co-operative | — | 12.50 |
| Coolidge Bank and Trust | 10.50 | 13.00 |
| Danvers Savings | 10.50 | 14.00 |
| Dedham Co-operative | — | 11.13 |
| Dedham Inst. for Savings | 10.11 | 12.91 |
| Depositors Trust | 9.24 | 14.68 |
| East Boston Savings | 10.08 *(25% down, 36 mos.) | 12.91 |
| East Bridgewater Savings | — | 16.21 |
| Foxboro Savings | 9.24 | 12.91 |
| Framingham Co-operative | 10.50 | 13.50 |
| Framingham Savings | 10.50 | 13.50 |
| Framingham Trust | 11.50 | 14.50 |
| Glendale Square Co-operative | — | 12.91 *($1.500 max.) |
| Granite Co-operative | — | 12.02 |
| Hancock Bank and Trust | 10.00 *(25% down, 36 mos.) | 14.75 |
| Hibernia Savings | 11.08 *(25% down, 36 mos.) | 13.35 |
| Hillside-Cambridge Co-op | — | 12.91 |
| Hingham Savings | 9.50 | 15.00 |
| Holbrook Co-operative | 10.11 | 12.02 |
| Home Savings | 9.50 | 13.00 |
| Hull Co-operative | 16.50 | 16.50 |
| Hyde Park Co-operative | 10.25 *($4,500 max, 36 mos.) | 14.75 |
| Hyde Park Savings | 11.92 | 12.35 |
| Lexington Savings | 9.17 | 13.33 |
| Liberty Bank and Trust | 10.20 *(33½% down, 36 mos.) | 14.68 |
| Lincoln Trust | 10.97 | 13.80 |
| Lynn Five Cents Savings | 10.00 | 13.50 |
| Malden Savings | 9.75 | 12.75 |
| Marblehead Bank and Trust | 10.11 | 13.00 |
| Marblehead Savings | 10.20 *(36 mos.) | 13.80 |
| Massachusetts Co-operative | — | 13.80 |
| Medford Co-operative | 10.20 *($4,000 max, 36 mos.) | 12.02 |
| Medford Savings | 9.75 | 12.00 |
| Medway Savings | 10.97 | 14.68 |
| Meeting House Hill Co-op. | — | 14.68 |
| Melrose Co-operative | 10.00 *(25% down) | 12.00 |
| Melrose Savings | 11.00 | 12.00 |
| Merchants Co-operative | 10.00 | 14.00 |
| Metrobank and Trust | 9.95 | 14.50 |
| Metropolitan Bank and Trust | 10.97 | 13.80 |
| Middlesex Family Co-op | | |
| Middlesex Inst. for Savings | 9.17 | 13.33 |
| Milton Co-operative | 10.16 *(42 mos.) | 12.02 |
| Milton Savings | 9.50 | 13.00 |
| Mt. Washington Co-operative | — | 12.02 |
| Mutual Bank for Savings | 10.23 *($4,500 max, 36 mos.) | 13.34 |
| Natick Five Cents Savings | 9.25 | 12.50 |
| Natick Trust | 8.41 *(33½% down, 36 mos.) | 12.91 *($1.500 max.) |
| National Grand Bank | 10.00 *(25% down) | 12.00 |
| Naumkeag Trust | 10.54 | 13.80 |
| Neponset Valley Bank and Tr. | | |
| Newton Co-operative | 9.68 | 12.91 |
| Newton South Co-operative | — | 13.80 |
| North Abington Co-operative | 10.11 | 12.91 |
| North Cambridge Co-operative | — | 12.02 |
| Norwood Co-operative | 10.75 *(42 mos.) | 14.00 |
| Old Colony Bank and Trust of Middlesex | 9.24 *(25% down) | 12.91 |
| Old Colony Bank and Trust of Suffolk | 10.54 | 12.91 |
| Old Stone Morris Plan of Suffolk | 11.00 | 15.00 |
| Peoples Savings | 10.16 *(25% down, 42 mos.) | 12.91 |
| Pilgrim Co-operative | — | 12.35 |
| Plymouth Savings | 9.24 | 12.91 |
| Presidential Co-operative | — | |
| Provident Inst. for Savings | 10.00 *(36 mos.) | 13.00 |
| Quincy Co-operative | 11.00 | 12.00 |
| Quincy Savings | 10.00 | 13.00 |
| Randolph Co-operative | — | 12.91 |

as part of their job. A recurring theme in nearly every discussion of Truth-in-Lending has been that the objective of providing consumers with sufficient information on the costs of credit has remained largely unfulfilled. The information contained in the detailed disclosure statements now required by Federal Reserve regulations is unavailable to the consumer until after he has decided to take out a loan and has contacted the creditor. One of the most critical decisions the consumer must make, however, is which institutions he should contact at the outset. Currently, there is very little information at his disposal on which to base this decision.

As part of the Depository Institutions Deregulation and Monetary Control Act of 1980, Congress finally directed the Federal Reserve Board to collect and publish on a demonstration basis in a number of metropolitan areas interest rates charged by creditors for consumer credit. It will be interesting to see whether the Fed will implement this provision in a manner most helpful to consumers, that is, by publishing interest rates by name of lender at least monthly, or whether it will only give lip service to the intent of the Act and publish area averages on a quarterly basis.

### Equal Credit Opportunity

On October 28, 1974, President Ford signed into law the Equal Credit Opportunity Act (ECOA). It became effective a year later. The purpose, as stated in the Act, is

> ...to make credit available with fairness, impartiality, and without discrimination on the basis of sex or marital status.[24]

The Act was amended to prohibit discrimination based on the applicant's age, race, national origin, religion, political affiliation, or receipt of welfare benefits. The driving force behind the enactment of ECOA was testimony presented before the National Commission on Consumer Finance and the Congress, which documented the widespread discrimination facing women in credit markets. Even the bankers admitted it: The President of the ABA at the time, Eugene Adams, stated, "I think we have to acknowledge that banks, along with the rest of the credit industry, do in fact discriminate against women when it comes to granting credit."[25]

The federal bank regulatory agencies' reaction to this new consumer protection law was their standard mild hostility. The Federal Reserve Board wrote the implementing regulations (Reg B) and then assigned enforcement responsibility to Governor Philip Jackson. In a speech to the Board of Directors of the Dallas Federal Reserve Bank in April of 1976, eighteen months after the Act was signed, Jackson openly questioned its value:

> *We cannot afford to risk the economic consequences of tactical mistakes in pursuing a goal of equal credit opportunity similar to those which have been experienced in our push for equality of civil rights....*
>
> *If the expansion of our anti-discriminatory features continues, is it not likely that we will ultimately reach the point where most creditors feel that they are not able to exercise personal judgment between applicants?...*
>
> *Sometimes we forget the passage of a law which assures the rights of one group at the same time limits or takes away the rights of another.... There are many in our country who feel that this pendulum of exchanging one right for another can swing too far and thus discourage the willingness on the part of one portion of our society to save and invest if they have too little discretion over how their savings or investments may be employed.*[26]

While the Fed has continued to drag its heels, the Comptroller and the Federal Home Loan Bank Board and the FDIC have imposed record-keeping requirements on banks so that the agencies could actually monitor compliance. The Comptroller and the FHLBB have in fact begun computer analysis of the collected data to try to detect discrimination in lending.

While this commitment of resources is essential, compliance examinations must be cost-effective. Preselection of banks, rather than random examination of all 14,000 commercial banks, would reduce costs and increase the likelihood of finding violations. Data from the Home Mortgage Disclosure program, collected since 1975 for the purpose of detecting redlining, would be one good source of preselection data. But for five years, this information has sat in bank files waiting for the federal agencies to analyze it. (In 1980, the Federal Home Loan Bank Board finally issued a report analyzing home mortgage disclosure data for three cities—and substantiated that banks redline.)

But another commitment to equal credit enforcement must be made by those who head the federal agencies: a conviction that this is important enough to be worth some antagonism from the banking community. There will be antagonism generated by effective enforcement because, as with Truth-in-Lending, there will not be effective self-enforcement unless there are damages assessed. The agencies must not only require restitution to borrowers who have been unfairly denied credit, but in addition assess penalties for violating the law.

The absolute refusal by regulatory agencies to notify individuals of their rights when the agencies' own examinations show those rights have been violated is clear evidence of the regulators' view of themselves as management consultants to banks. The Federal Reserve Board even refuses to tell a person whose consumer complaint they are investigating—even when the complaint is found to be valid—that he or she has another avenue of redress, in the courts, or that there are financial penalties in the act for violations.

In essence, the agencies are acting as a buffer between the law and the banks. When the agencies tell a consumer that they will handle his complaint and get him redress, what they mean is that if the consumer was discriminated against, the agency will see that the loan is made. They do not go on to say that there are civil penalties that could be levied. They won't say it until the federal bank regulatory agencies are reoriented so that consumerism stops seeming an annoying public relations obligation and is seen to be the essence of the agencies' purpose: to promote the public interest in banking.

### Deregulating Banking

"Safety and soundness" regulation is very expensive. To enforce their regulations in this area, the federal bank regulatory agencies spent $155 million in 1975. An untold additional amount was spent by banks to comply. What we should get for all this public and private spending is far more efficient financial markets. It is not clear that we will be getting our money's worth until both the agency structure and the philosophy of bank regulation is changed.

Banks now function in a highly restrictive regulatory framework. Government-imposed barriers restrict the geographic markets within which banks may compete, by means of stringent branching and market-entry regulations. Regulatory restrictions limit the products that financial institutions may offer; it is government, for example, that maintains commercial banks' monopoly on offering checking accounts. And regulators set the pricing of bank products. Deregulation is long overdue.

While the Bank Holding Company Act should be strengthened to control the areas into which banks can diversify, regulation is in many instances unnecessarily restricting the ability of the financial sector to perform. Much of the present regulation could be removed without creating the risk of unsound practices or widespread bank failures.

Many of the most restrictive forms of regulation are products of the Depression years. Some of these restrictions were intended to protect the strength of financial institutions, and others were designed as constraints on this strength: Financial institutions have alternately been viewed as helpless incompetents and as all-powerful moguls. While stability—the avoidance of either extreme—may have been the overriding need of the 1930s, increased competitiveness and responsiveness to public social and economic goals are clearly the needs of the 1980s.

### Government Price-fixing

The antitrust laws make private price-fixing agreements illegal. In banking, what private parties cannot lawfully do, the government does for them. Through regulations of a federal agency, the government sets the price at which banks may offer their deposit services, thus eliminating price competition for deposits. These regulations have not only been ineffective in serving their original purpose, they have been perverse in their results. Interest-rate ceilings have periodically caused depository institutions to experience extreme difficulty in attracting funds, as market rates have climbed above the deposit ceilings. They have caused small savers to receive less than they should for their funds. The prohibition of interest on demand deposits has reduced the flow of funds into banks, as businesses choose instead to utilize improved money management techniques to shift deposits into interest-bearing short-term instruments. Reductions in deposit flows has, in turn, created pressure on financial institutions to turn to other, more expensive sources of funds. Thus interest rate regulation has not been effective in stabilizing banking or housing finance—or, ultimately, in reducing the cost pressures on banking.

Furthermore, the original reasoning behind interest-rate regulation is no longer valid. Federal deposit insurance has reduced the significance of isolated bank failures. The demand-deposit interest prohibition is being gradually rendered meaningless by the use of such devices as NOW accounts, and by electronic funds transfer systems, which blur the distinction between savings and demand deposits.

For these reasons, interest-rate regulation should be eliminated.

### Government-created Cartels

A fundamental part of free enterprise is the right of each business to offer whatever products or services it can produce, to whatever customers it can reach. In the financial area, though, we let the bank regulatory agencies create restrictions that banks could not legally create themselves. As Thomas E. Kauper, a past assistant attorney general in charge of the Justice Department's antitrust division, stated in congressional testimony in 1976:

> *Limitations on the kinds of services financial institutions can offer are extensive in Federal and state regulatory schemes. These limitations could not be agreed to by private businessmen—such allocation of the product markets to be served by individual companies would clearly be per se unlawful under the Sherman Act. They are the kinds of restraints which the Supreme Court has described in the context of private agreements as "conclusively presumed to be unreasonable and therefore illegal. ...because of their pernicious effect on competition and lack of any redeeming virtue...." Northern Pacific Railway Co. v. United States, 356 U.S. 1,5 (1958). Thus, while private efforts to allocate financial markets would be felonies, public efforts to squeeze financial institutions into unyielding pigeonholes are legion."*[27]

The current regulatory scheme mandating specialization of bank services has frozen the financial intermediaries into their historical roles rather than allowing them to evolve in ways that best meet the needs of consumers and the economy. Commercial banks originated to serve the needs of business in trade and commerce; thrifts and credit unions developed to serve the needs of individual savers and consumers. Government regulation, however, has preserved and emphasized specialization, by imposing different restrictions on the deposit and lending powers of different kinds of financial institutions. This enforced specialization has been supported in large part by a desire to influence the allocation of credit to housing.

In fact, though, specialization has not succeeded in allocating the necessary funds for housing. The present regulatory system has certainly not redirected funds to those urban areas most in need of financing, as we saw in our discussion of redlining.

Only where the market has clearly broken down due to various forms of discrimination, as in redlining or in lending criteria biased against minorities or women, should government intervene to minimize market imperfections. There is a role for government regulation, but it is *not* to prevent financial institutions from competing with one another.

### Geographic Cartels

The same reasoning applies to restrictions on entry by financial institutions into new geographic markets. Such restrictions could not be agreed to by private parties; they should not be imposed by government unless the public interest clearly requires it. The public interest does not require nearly as limited an entry policy as is currently contained in state and federal regulations.

A basic goal of government restrictions on entry into banking is the preservation of the integrity of the financial system as a whole. Entry is properly limited to those who can demonstrate adequate capitalization and other financial backing, good management and organizational prospects, and various other qualifications which may support a judgment that the new institution will be worthy of a public trust. These requirements seem entirely reasonable.

It seems unwarranted, however, to require the applicant bank to prove that a given community needs its services. In practice, this is an exercise in determining the likely degree of competition between the banks. Regulators use such simple measures as population-to-banking-office ratios, adjusted for income levels, to determine an entrant's prospects and the effect of its entry on existing firms. The analysis is done on the premise that a given market contains only a finite amount of business, particularly funds for deposit, and that allowing too many competitors to seek deposits in a given market risks causing the failure of the less successful institutions. This situation, referred to as overbanking, is avoided by predicting the number of competitors which a community can support and regulating new entry accordingly. The burden is on the new entrant to justify his intrusion.

By contrast, in unregulated sectors of the economy, both entry and exit of firms from a market are regulated by the marketplace itself. Firms are free to enter a market and to try to take business away from existing firms; the less successful competitors withdraw. Since one type of exit—failure—has been viewed as unacceptable in banking, the free-market approach has been abandoned in banking. But failure is not the only exit: Weaker banks can be merged with stronger banks, or acquired by holding companies, through the good offices of bank regulators. As far as branch overextension is concerned, closing a branch which proves unprofitable is a reasonable alternative to the present system, in which (at least theoretically) every branch has its profitability certified in advance. Regulators must rethink the premise that every financial institution must be preserved if the system as a whole is to remain stable. Of course, failures should be avoided if possible. But regulatory procedures can be refined to regulate exit, instead of restricting entry as severely as it does now. The public would be better served by a system in which competition and efficiency are maximized. Society's basic goal, after all, is not the permanent preservation of any one financial institution but rather a safe and sound financial system.

Restrictions on entry, especially legal limitations on branching within states and the federal prohibition of branching across state lines, have also been defined as necessary to preserve small banks. Without these restrictions, it is claimed, smaller locally owned and controlled banks will be forced out of existence, and their markets will be taken over by distant and uninterested giants. The basic premise behind these arguments—the asserted inability of small banks to compete with branches of larger ones—is open to serious question. It is time to eliminate the regulator's subjective judgment on the question, and to let the market make that determination.

It is undeniable that absolute restrictions on branching have insulated protected markets from new competition. They have unnecessarily impeded the provision of banking services and effective competition. These adverse effects, and the questionable premises behind them, have been recognized by the Supreme Court, which noted in a 1974 decision that inflexible limitations on new entry into a market inhibit growth by internal expansion, and compel banks to resort to mergers and acquisitions in order to enter new markets.[28]

Deregulation of the competitive constraints on financial institutions are needed now. Unfortunately, unnecessary and pervasive regulation in banking has been with us for so long that it has become accepted as the natural order of things. It is not. It is an aberration. The question should not be, "Why should we abolish severe competitive restraints?" but rather "Why should we retain them?"

It should be clear that I am not maintaining that all regulation is wasteful. But in banking we have exaggerated the wasteful, inefficient regulations while hesitating to legislate or enforce useful ones. We have been eager, cheered on by the industry, to pass legislation and issue regulations which protect banks' markets and protect individual banks from competition; we have been derelict in promoting and protecting the interest of consumers of bank services.

### Changing the Regulatory Structure

If we are to have effective regulation, and regulators with the will to act in the public interest, the regulatory structure itself must be changed. The present fractured system—in which there are three federal regulators of commercial banks, a separate regulator for thrifts and another for credit unions, in addition to state supervisory agencies—leads to laxity in regulation and an unwillingness to act.

Moreover, it has led to just the kind of client-protector relationship discussed earlier. When different agencies oversee different fiefdoms, each regulator comes to see issues through the eyes of his constituency rather than those of the whole financial community, let alone the public. An excellent example of this narrowing of perspective was provided by a recent acting chairman of the Federal Home Loan Bank Board, which oversees savings and loan associations. According to the *American Banker*, when asked if he saw regulators as having the responsibility for acting as advocates for the institutions they regulate, he said he did see himself as an advocate for S&Ls. "Advocacy and regulation go hand-in-hand," he said to applause.

As things now stand, banks can pick their regulators, shopping around among agencies. They simply have to switch from state to national charters, or vice-versa, as several hundred banks (with assets totaling more than $11 billion[29]) have done in the 1970s. In periods when national bank status offers the opportuntiy to expand through mergers, or to engage in nonbanking activities not permitted by the Fed, there are conversions to national charters. When the Fed's reserve requirements start seeming too high, there are conversions to state-chartered, nonmember (of the Fed) status. (Though most of the 9,000 state-chartered commercial banks are insured by the FDIC, so that they are under that corner of the federal regulatory crazy quilt.) In addition to all the above-named agencies, one should add the Federal Home Loan Bank Board and the National Credit Union Administration, which have in their charge federally chartered S&Ls and credit unions (institutions that are rapidly coming to resemble commercial banks, from an individual consumer's point of view). Which is not even to mention the nation's mutual savings banks or its state-chartered S&Ls and credit unions.

It is hardly surprising that Senator Proxmire has described the present regulatory system as a "nightmare." Senator Abraham Ribicoff's Governmental Affairs Committee, speaking just of the federal level, could be more restrained. In its *Study on Federal Regulation*, the committee concluded that:

> *The structure of banking regulation is unique. In no other situation does a regulated industry have an opportunity to choose its regulatory agency. This ability to select a regulator through switching charters, joining the Federal Reserve System, or applying for Federal deposit insurance has led to forum-shopping among the banks. That is to say, banks can and do select a federal regulator which best suits their needs. In turn, forum-shopping has led to competition among the three agencies to attract members. The existence of three Federal bank regulatory agencies has led to inconsistent and often inefficient regulation.*[30]

In the wake of the largest bank failures in the nation's history, Arthur Burns, then chairman of the Federal Reserve, made his now famous speech to the ABA, which was read into the *Congressional Record* in which he charged the regulators with "competition in laxity" and described the present regulatory structure with unflinching clarity:

> *I must say to you, however, that I am inclined to think that the most serious obstacle to improving the regulation and supervision of banking is the structure of the regulatory apparatus.*

*That structure is exceedingly complex. At the Federal level, every bank whose deposits are insured is subject to supervision and regulation, but authority is fragmented. The Comptroller of the Currency charters and supervises national banks. The Federal Reserve System supervises State chartered member banks, regulates activities of Edge Act corporations, regulates all bank holding companies, and controls the reserves and other operating features of all member banks. The Federal Deposit Insurance Corporation insures nearly all banks, but supervises only State-chartered banks that are non-members of the Federal Reserve. The FDIC also has certain regulatory powers that apply to insured non-member banks.*

*Those of you who have been intimately concerned with regulatory matters will realize that I have oversimplified, that our system of parallel and sometimes overlapping regulatory powers is indeed a jurisdictional tangle that boggles the mind.*

*There is, however, a still more serious problem. The present regulatory system fosters what has sometimes been called "competition in laxity." Even viewed in the most favorable light, the present system is conducive to subtle competition among regulatory authorities, sometimes to relax constraints, sometimes to delay corrective measures. I need not explain to bankers the well-understood fact that regulatory agencies are sometimes played off against one another. Practically speaking, this sort of competition may have served a useful purpose for a time in loosening overly cautious banking restrictions imposed in the wake of the Great Depression. But at this point, the danger of continuing as we have in the past should be apparent to all objective observers.*

*I recognize that there is apprehension among bankers and students of regulation concerning over-centralized authority. Providing for some system of checks and balances is the traditional way of guarding against arbitrary or capricious exercise of authority. But this principle need not mean that banks should continue to be free to choose their regulators. And it certainly does not mean that we should fail to face up to the difficulties created by the diffusion of authority and accountability that characterizes the present regulatory system. Some will doubtless conclude that the proper approach lies in improved coordination among the multiple bank regulatory agencies, together with harmonization of divergent banking laws. My own present think-*

*ing, however, is that building upon the existing machinery may not be sufficient, and that substantial reorganization will be required to overcome the problems inherent in the existing structural arrangement.*[31]

In place of the present divided bank regulatory structure, all five federal bank and thrift regulatory agencies—the Federal Reserve, the Comptroller of the Currency, the Federal Deposit Insurance Corporation , the Federal Home Loan Bank Board, and the National Credit Union Administration—should be consolidated into one Federal Bank Commission. Regulatory restructuring has been recommended for almost half a century, and should be avoided no longer.

The ideal commission would be a completely consolidated federal agency regulating all depository institutions. The existing system, which separates jurisdiction of savings and loan associations and credit unions from the entire complex of bank regulation, provides an institutional mechanism that tends to perpetuate differences among depository institutions.

Consolidation is needed for equity and to avoid costly duplication. Uniformity of examination procedures, for example, is essential. The development of a common examination report and uniform examination standards is being worked on by the newly created Federal Bank Examination Council, which will make recommendations for uniformity in supervisory matters other than bank examinations. But the Council, created in 1978, can accomplish only the obvious and unobjectionable purpose of subjecting similar financial institutions to uniform examination standards. More comprehensive restructuring is required in order to achieve equity and more efficient regulation. And, at this point, where vested interests in the present fragmented system, bank constituencies and regulators' jobs are threatened, opposition to reform mounts. Objections to consolidation are as predictable as the endorsements of the Council's cosmetic and symbolic gains—which forestall more fundamental reforms. Bureaucratic ambition overcomes rationality at this point; the federal regulators have in the past made or supported some restructuring proposals, but only those that would expand their own jurisdictions.

It should be noted that in addition to offering gains in efficiency and equity from a government and public point of view, consolidation of federal bank regulatory agencies would benefit most financial institutions. Banks, S&Ls, and credit unions are now subject to overlapping jurisdiction involving different federal agencies for different regulatory purposes. Reporting requirements are sometimes unclear and inconsistent; communication is needlessly complicated.

The present federal bank regulatory structure assumed its basic form in 1934, and, proposals for consolidating it emerged almost immediately. In 1937, the Brookings Institution proposed that the responsibilities of the Comptroller of the Currency for bank examinations and supervision be assumed by the Federal Deposit Insurance Corporation, which would then regulate national banks as well as state-chartered banks. In 1938, the Federal Reserve Board's annual report responded to the challenge by suggesting that the Federal Reserve should be the sole federal bank regulatory authority. The basic outlines of the bureaucratic struggles for the next forty years emerged very early.

A variety of commissions studying the regulatory structure have all concluded that some form of consolidation is needed, but they have disagreed on which agency should be the survivor. The Hoover Commission in 1949 emerged with three different proposals from each of three different task forces: 1) merge the Comptroller into the Federal Reserve; 2) merge the FDIC into the Federal Reserve; 3) merge both the Comptroller and FDIC into the Federal Reserve. The 1961 Commission on Money and Credit concluded that all the agencies should be combined into the Federal Reserve, while the 1971 Hunt Commission report went in the opposite direction and suggested that the Federal Reserve get out of bank supervision and regulation, transferring its authority over state banks to the FDIC. The 1975 Financial Institutions and the National Economy (FINE) study, done for Rep. Henry Reuss's House Banking Committee, was the first to suggest that all financial regulatory authorities should be consolidated into one agency to be called the Federal Depository Institution Commission. It was to be composed of five commissioners: the deputy attorney general, a member of the Securities and Exchange Commission, the vice-chairman of the Federal Reserve Board, and two representatives of the public, one of whom would serve as chairman. A GAO study, done in 1977 at Senator Proxmire's request, concluded that there was a need for much greater inter-agency coordination. And in its study of federal regulation, Sen. Ribicoff's Committee on Government Affairs concluded in late 1977 (in the report quoted earlier) that there should be "consolidation of the three bank regulatory agencies along the lines of legislation proposing a Federal bank commission." Taken together, these proposals would seem to have raised every imaginable possibility for rearranging the functions of the three federal banking agencies. Their only common point was that some consolidation was desirable.

The failure of any of these plans to be implemented has its roots in both American ideology and agency politics. Americans have always, it seems, had an ideological distrust of concentrations of financial power. This emerged with the appearance of the first banks and most particularly with the chartering of the first public banks, the First and Second Banks of the United States, in the early 1800s. Concern has been with the concentration of financial power, whether in private or public hands. A massive federal agency regulating most of the institutions that make loans has been as distasteful to the public as a massive concentration of banking resources in five or six privately owned banks would be. The federal bank regulators and state bank commissioners have played on this historical antipathy to their advantage. Any proposal to consolidate all federal bank regulatory authority into a single agency was virtually certain to draw opposition from two of the three agencies involved—the only likely proponent being the agency designated as the recipient of the added authority and prestige. If the proposal was to create a brand-new agency, one could usually count on opposition from all three agencies. Finally, the state bank regulators have opposed the consolidation of the federal bank regulators, fearing that one powerful agency would overwhelm state regulation. The access of state bank regulators to their state's representatives in Congress has made them a formidable lobby.

Moreover, the banks do not want the federal bank regulatory agencies consolidated. They are more than happy to play one regulator off against the other and to maintain the competition in laxity among the agencies which is essential to each agency's constituency maximization. This bank power to keep your regulator in line would be lost if bankers were not free to choose their regulator and to change it at will.

Bankers have been quick to drape over the present divided regulatory structure the mantle of popular concerns about concentration of financial power. The present divided bank regulatory structure, the ABA told the Senate Banking Committee in 1976, is in the great democratic tradition of Jefferson and Jackson.[32] According to the testimony of the ABA,

> *To characterize the current structure of banking regulation as a "crazy quilt" or as the result of "piece-meal" legislation is to ignore fear of concentration of control of financial power as one of the major forces shaping the banking system and its regulation. The bank regulatory structure is the result of deliberate actions by previous congresses which found reason to limit the concentration of control at the Federal level. The regulatory structure reflects a view that concentrate [sic] of control through the political process is as objectionable as concentration of control through economic processes. The structure of banking regulation is, in fact, a microcosm of the broad concept that representative government should involve a system of checks and balances on the power of central authority. It is ironic that in a period of revelation of great abuse of central authority that senior Congressmen of the party of Jefferson and Jackson are proposing further concentration of control of financial power at the Federal level.[33]*

It is probably a surprise to many, as it was to Senator Proxmire, that the American Bankers Association was "a repository of latent populism."[34] But when the ABA was challenged to extend its concern about the concentration of bank regulation to concern about concentration in banking itself, the ABA demurred, as the following dialogue indicates:

> *The Chairman [Senator Proxmire]: So your populism and dispersion of concentration of power would stop at the regulators? It wouldn't apply to the banks themselves?*
> *Mr. Chisholm [testifying on behalf of the ABA]: I think it is something that should be monitored closely nationally. But I don't think it presents the threat presently that many people are led to believe.[35]*

### Benefits From Agency Consolidation

Consolidation of bank regulatory agencies into a single organization would achieve gains in equity and efficiency and reduce or eliminate weaknesses in the present system.

First, supervision would be more effective, since the danger of problems "slipping through the cracks" between current jurisdictions and responsibilities would be eliminated. At present, bank problems do indeed slip through. This is largely because problem bank situations or supervisory concerns at a less-than-critical stage—but requiring investigation or remedial action—often involve interbank relationships of one type or another, that is, correspondent balances, participation loans, bank stock loans, or interaffiliate transactions within a holding company system or banking chain. Under our fractured regulatory structure, a given regulator has direct access only to institutions with a particular charter status for the purpose of conducting an examination, investigating a particular question, or requiring reports. Interagency cooperation has indeed improved in recent years, but the coordination required before one agency can invade another's turf inevitably causes delays and inefficiency. Worse still, if one regulator is acting on a hunch or pursuing a relatively routine matter, it might not seem worthwhile to work out the necessary steps for an interagency exchange, and the matter may be dropped. Even the most effective cooperation between agencies is inherently inferior to a full consolidation of regulatory efforts.

A case in point: Much concern was expressed in 1977 over the possibility that some bankers were in the habit of using their banks' correspondent balances to obtain preferential loans for themselves. Even if the FDIC or Federal Reserve had included in their examination reports bank loans to officers of other banks, they would only be monitoring loans to bank officers from correspondent banks that are also state-chartered. If an officer of a state-chartered bank were cleverly abusing his trust in this area, the bank would maintain correspondent balances only at national banks, so that no federal agency would have data on both sides of the transaction. Similarly, the comptroller of the currency would have lacked authority to pursue his investigation of the Bert Lance case if the trail had gone outside national banks. He might well have gained the cooperation of the FDIC or the Federal Reserve, but the necessity to do so would certainly have impeded the investigation. There is always the possibility that he might not gain visitation rights for a national bank examiner on another agency's turf. And if the matter had been more routine, it might never have been thought worthwhile to take the time to work out all the interagency cooperation needed; the matter might not have been pursued.

### Piercing the Corporate Veil

A second major weakness of the present regulatory structure is its split of jurisdiction over banks and bank holding companies. Although so many banks have set up bank holding companies that such companies now control nearly two-thirds of the assets and deposits of commercial banks, the structure for regulating them remains fragmented. The Federal Reserve oversees the holding companies and their nonbank subsidiaries; the banks themselves are supervised by the Comptroller or by the FDIC and a state regulator if the bank is state-chartered.

To treat banks and their holding companies as separate entities is to ignore reality. In a particular situation, the Fed might find that the holding company is in satisfactory shape while in reality it is vulnerable to problems that are emerging at the level of the parent's bank subsidiaries, over which the Fed has no direct jurisdiction and about which it may actually possess only limited knowledge. Conversely, a problem at a subsidiary bank may be cleaned up, as far as the bank's supervisory authority is concerned, by a transaction that effectively shifts the problem up to the parent or sideways to another affiliate; in either case beyond the direct jurisdiction (and concern) of the bank's regulator. Only by consolidating responsibility for the holding company and its affiliates in a single agency will it be possible to get a clear picture of the soundness of the entire operation and to focus oversight effectively on any developing problems in the system.

In several cases in recent years, nonbank subsidiaries managed to dump soured assets onto the banks and caused the banks to collapse, literally between examinations of the Comptroller or the FDIC. The failure of Hamilton National Bank of Chattanooga, Tennessee, in 1976 is a notable example. Hamilton National, long considered a Rock of Gibraltar in its region, failed because of soured real estate loans dumped on the bank by its holding company. The financial decline of the bank was quite rapid. The bank joined its parent company in 1972. In 1972–73, the holding company acquired two or three mortgage companies, and beginning early in 1974 and continuing throughout the year, the loan portfolio of the bank became increasingly populated by real estate loans originated by those mortgage companies. When the real estate market collapsed in 1974, the loans became losses exceeding 200 percent of the bank's capital. Because of the divided supervision, the Federal Reserve was aware of the growing volume of real estate loans at the holding company, but the Comptroller was not aware of them until they appeared on the books of the bank. If one agency had examined both sets of books, the problem would have been spotted much earlier, possibly in time to have saved the bank.

In a 1977 speech before the Exchequer Club in Washington, D.C., George Le Maistre, then chairman of the Federal Deposit Insurance Corporation, stated, "Events of the past three years have demonstrated that the fragmentation of bank holding company supervision is a serious inadequacy of the present bank regulatory framework." Citing the problems leading to the failures of the Beverly Hills National Bank, the Hamilton National Bank, the American City Bank and Trust Co. (Milwaukee), and Palmer First National Bank and Trust Co. (Sarasota, Florida), Le Maistre concluded:

*These cases have demonstrated that one segment of a holding company organization cannot easily be insulated from the remainder of the system. These cases also have shown that because a holding company tends to be operated as an integrated enterprise, it is simply a form of self-deception to assume that the lead bank, or any other holding company banking affiliate for that matter, is in a safe and sound condition just because its last examination was satisfactory. The ease of transferring assets among affiliated companies can change a banking affiliates' soundness abruptly.*

Le Maistre suggested that many of the existing difficulties could be resolved by assigning to the federal agency responsible for a given "lead bank" primary supervisory responsibility for its entire holding company system. Le Maistre conceded that, on grounds of efficiency and supervisory uniformity, the appropriate resolution would be consolidation of all bank and bank holding company regulatory powers into a single federal agency. But that solution would do away with three federal banking bureaucracies. Better to redivide the pie, taking some power from the Federal Reserve and handing it to the FDIC. For obvious reasons, the Comptroller of the Currency agreed with the FDIC's proposal and the Federal Reserve disagreed.

### Mergers in the Public's Best Interest

The third point is that a fractured structure complicates resolution of problem bank situations, which can often be accomplished by an orderly acquisition before a crisis develops. Since no agency has complete, accurate, and unbiased information on all possible takeover candidates, any regulator's efforts to arrange this sort of resolution are necessarily impeded. Furthermore, since responsibility is divided, decisions may be made which protect the agency's position and that of its "client" bank but are damaging to the banking system as a whole and ultimately to the public.

The FDIC, acting like a private insurance company rather than a public regulatory agency, has argued that it must sell a failing bank to the highest bidder, disregarding the fact that acquisition by a bank that may have bid less would increase competition. In this case, the FDIC's concern with minimizing its losses overwhelmed its other concerns, to the public's detriment. On occasion, the FDIC has pushed a merger or forced a marriage between weak and stronger banks in order to avoid a bank failure, when in fact the merger was highly anticompetitive and a more competitive solution could have been worked out.

### One Law and Three Interpretations

The application of different regulatory policies to common situations can have deleterious effects far beyond confusion. It is simply bad government to have different agencies interpreting the same laws in different ways, especially when they give the governed their choice of agencies. For example, the Bank Merger Act of 1960 (amended in 1966) divided the responsibility for evaluating bank merger proposals among the three federal agencies. Agency differences have been quite pronounced at times in the weights given to competitive factors in approving or denying bank merger applications. For many years, a bank merger application filed with the Comptroller was virtually certain to gain approval. The differences have been clearly perceived by bankers, who have proven quite adept at structuring applications or even changing charters in order to come under the jurisdiction of the regulator most likely to approve their proposals.

Of all the federal regulatory agencies, the Comptroller's office has been most often criticized by the Justice Department for approving mergers that would have anticompetitive effects. Actions by Justice to stop anticompetitive mergers approved by the Comptroller support the view that the Comptroller's lax interpretation of competitive standards in fact violates congressional intent. Justice Department actions in the last few years have been extremely important in stopping mergers that had the Comptroller's prior approval. And in many cases this has produced significantly more competition in the long run. In some cases, one of the banks involved was subsequently acquired by another bank located outside the market, with the result that where the Comptroller would have permitted elimination of competition, new competition was actually fostered.

Federal regulators have also been inconsistent in their determination of "incidental powers" and the scope of nonbanking activities permitted to banking organizations. Among the federal bank regulators, the Comptroller, historically has been most permissive in this regard, a fact well known to bankers. As a result, it is possible for bank holding companies, through national bank subsidiaries, to engage in activities that are prohibited by the Federal Reserve as the primary regulator of bank holding companies. Again, congressional intent—as interpreted in this case by the Federal Reserve—has been frustrated by the Comptroller's leniency (though the courts have subsequently overturned some of the Comptroller's rulings).

One agency's less restrictive approach to regulation forces the other agencies, through pressure from the banks they regulate, into competition. No agency wants to lose constituents to less restrictive regulators (through charter conversions or dropping of Federal Reserve membership, as the case may be). So the agencies step up their competition in laxity.

### Do Monetary Policy, Lending, Insurance, and Bank Supervision Mix?

As a part of a more general reorganization, a unified federal bank regulatory agency could focus on bank supervisory activities alone, and ancillary activities of the present regulatory agencies could be operated in a more logical and consistent manner. There are no sound reasons for combining bank supervision with other functions such as monetary-policy formulation and implementation, extension of short-term credit to financial institutions, and deposit insurance. In fact, it can be argued that responsibility for these nonsupervisory functions, all of which are lodged in one or more of the present federal regulatory agencies, may pose conflicts of interest with purely supervisory objectives.

The Fed argues that its monetary-policy role is aided by information from its bank examination and supervision work. But it has never been demonstrated that the Federal Reserve draws on its examination staffs for information relevant to formulating monetary policy. On an informal basis, the Federal Reserve presidents and governors may well pick up a feeling for the state of the economy and of banking from their close contacts with bankers. The Fed need not examine banks, however, to maintain these contacts. Discussions with officers of member banks will continue if for no other reason than the bankers' need to have access to the discount window. But one may well question if those entrusted with monetary policy should have bankers as their principal contacts to discuss the effects of monetary policy. It may be advantageous to loosen these ties and to encourage the Fed to discuss the effects of monetary policy with a wider segment of society.

It is in fact the relationship between monetary policy and bank regulation that other commentators regard as the foundation of their concern about overconcentration of power at the Federal Reserve. The greater the Board's role as a regulator, the greater will be the temptation to use its regulatory authority as a means to secure objectives in monetary policy. The Fed already succumbs to this kind of temptation. According to Prof. Thomas Mayer, the exclusion of the Board from regulatory functions,

> ...*would eliminate the Federal Reserve's ability to use "arm-twisting" as a tool of monetary policy. The holding-company legislation has given the Fed great power to punish banks that refuse its "requests." Apparently the Fed has used this lever in 1973 to induce banks to hold down the prime rate, etc. On general political grounds one may well question whether the Federal Reserve, or any other government agency, should have such covert power over private firms when Congress has not granted it such powers overtly.*[36]

The Fed cannot justifiably let its power as a bank regulator become a tool of its monetary policy. Such a confusion of functions and objectives is inevitable as long as the Federal Reserve Board has both roles. Former vice-chairman Robertson expressed the same concern:

> *There should never be a possibility of utilizing the supervisory function to enforce a given monetary policy today and an*

*opposite one tomorrow, to look at bank loan portfolios through rose-colored glasses today and black ones tomorrow.*[37]

The Federal Reserve is supposed to act as a lender of last resort for the banking system. Historically, in fact, this function is the central bank's principal reason for being. As presently constituted, however, the Fed's lending facility, the discount window, is available only to *member* banks. It is ridiculous not to have a comparable short-term lending facility available to *all* banks. Without such a facility, banks may be forced into anticompetitive mergers or closings because of short-term liquidity problems; results clearly contrary to the public interest. The Fed now promotes the discount window as a major argument for maintaining or expanding its prime constituency, member banks. In the public interest, and as part of a rational reorganization plan, it would make good sense to establish a short-term lending facility that would be available to all depository institutions. Such an organization could consolidate bank-lending functions now lodged in the Fed, the Federal Home Loan Banks, and the National Credit Union Administration. The facility need not be combined with regulatory and supervisory functions but could act upon the recommendation or request of the primary regulator. This important step was taken in 1980 when the Federal Reserve received the authority to set reserve requirements on all transaction accounts at all depository institutions; all such financial institutions were granted access to the Fed's discount window.

Similarly, federal deposit and share insurance programs are now managed by three different agencies—FDIC, FSLIC, and NCUA. Here is an obvious possibility for gains in efficiency through consolidation. In order to avoid conflicts between supervisory goals and the insurance function, the insurance fund administration should be separate from the regulatory agency. It could act at the request of the regulatory agency, however, and the two organizations could collaborate to the extent that they have common concerns. (Models for such a relationship exist in Massachusetts, where three deposit-insurance funds, two of which predate the FDIC, successfully operate outside of but, subject to, the supervision of the Banking Department.)

### Arguments Against Consolidation

There have been a variety of arguments posed against consolidation. Some have argued that a single federal bank regulator would have a stultifying influence on banking, that innovation and progressive regulation would be inhibited under the heavy hand of a single agency. Bankers have argued that for all the difficulties of jurisdictional overlap. the present three-agency format is desirable precisely because it does not unify regulation in a single agency. As Walter Wriston, Chairman of Citicorp has stated:

> *One of the worst things that could happen to the banking industry would be to have a single regulator.*[38]

Bankers fear that "a single agency would have less reason to be responsive to the needs and reasonable aspirations of the banks and would be a more burdensome and inflexible bureaucracy"[39] than the present jumble.

The bankers' preference for the present system is quite understandable. It is banking's version of divide and rule: If you're going to fight anyone, always fight coalitions, because coalitions are usually characterized by indecision, irresolution, and inaction. The Federal bank-regulatory apparatus has clearly been characterized by this coalition syndrome, as well as by the peculiar pathology of bureaucracy, constituency maximization. The present fractured regulatory structure clearly meets the bankers' needs, if not the public's.

Within the financial sector, the existence of consolidated federal regulation of the savings and loan and credit union systems could logically demonstrate the viability of the dual state and federal systems with a single federal agency.

Some commercial bankers have opposed consolidation of the federal bank supervisors as a threat to the dual banking system. The dual banking system in this context may be defined as the existence of alternative entry routes into banking, and a corresponding choice of supervisors. Since every bank with federal deposit insurance is, however, subject to supervision by at least one of the federal banking agencies, the concept, in practice, implies a choice among different federal supervisors. For this choice to be meaningful, the dual banking system concept must rely on different federal regulators administering identical statutes in unequal manner. In other words, some effective competition in laxity is *required* on the part of the federal bank supervisors for choice to be meaningful. The Federal Bank Commission is not really a threat to the dual banking system from a state regulator's point of view. The main change is that it eliminates the opportunity for banks to play one federal regulator off against another.

The Federal Reserve has opposed the creation of the Federal Bank Commission with the argument that the Fed needs to engage in bank examination and supervision to conduct monetary policy. In his statement to the House Banking Committee, then Chairman Burns argued that if a new Federal Banking Commission were to assume the supervisory functions that now reside with the Board it "...could, either deliberately or inadvertently, frustrate monetary policy and destroy the effectiveness of the Federal Reserve in seeking to achieve the economic goals set by Congress."[40] Instead of stripping the Board of its bank-examination powers, Burns said that a strong majority within the Board supported the taking over by the Federal Reserve Board of the functions now assigned to the Office of the Comptroller of the Currency as necessary to the conduct of monetary policy. Paul A. Volcker, then president of the Federal Reserve Bank of New York and later Chairman of the Federal Reserve Board, agreed that bank supervision was an integral part of monetary policy. In a 1976 address to the American Bankers Association, Volcker stressed the value of firsthand information required by a bank regulator. "Monetary policy," he said, "works through the banking system and its effectiveness over time is dependent upon accurate understanding and appraisal of what is going on in banks and financial markets...."[41]

But as we have seen, there are strong arguments for separating the monetary policy and supervisory functions. And as for the "accurate understanding" necessary to formulating sound monetary policy, surely the Fed could obtain whatever information it needed from whichever governor served as one of the members of the new Federal Bank Commission.

There is, of course, no guarantee that the new regulators of a single Bank Commission (or, better yet, a single Deposit Institution Commission) would do a good job. Given the concerns outlined at the very beginning of this chapter, no one could promise that any bank regulator would be an improvement. But it is difficult to see how improvement can possibly occur without consolidation at the federal level.

### The State Bank Supervisors

State bank regulators have rarely been confused about their role: it is to represent the bankers' interests in order to ensure their longevity as bank commissioners or their future jobs as bankers. State bank commissioners are the primary regulators for approximately 12,200 state-chartered domestic commercial and mutual savings banks with assets of some $500 billion. At present, two-thirds of all banks are state-chartered, and these institutions hold approximately 43 percent of all bank assets. While the average state-chartered banks is smaller than the average national one, there are many very large state-chartered banks: Of the fifty largest banks in the United States, in fact, approximately half are state-chartered.

The "dual banking system" is another way of describing a structure of banking regulation whereby banks are chartered and supervised on the state as well as the federal level. This is States' Rights in the field of bank regulation. The National Banking Act of 1863 established the dual system; up to that time, all banks were chartered by the states, with the notable exceptions of the First Bank of the United States (chartered in 1790, but its charter expired in 1811, and the Second Bank of the United States, 1816–1836). Aside from these two institutions, banking in this country was state banking until the Civil War, when the federal government re-entered the banking scene in order to finance the war. Until the FDIC was created in 1934, the state and federal governments had equal powers in the system. The necessity of federal deposit insurance had the effect of reducing some of the states' authority in the area of granting charters, but the system essentially remained intact.

Despite the importance of state banks, state bank regulators are clearly the weakest link in the regulatory chain. A few states have regulatory structures comparable in quality to federal agencies, but most do not. The reality of the dual banking system is that the state systems do not provide an effective alternative to federal oversight. As a result, the grossest "competition in laxity" is not among the federal agencies but between the state regulators and the federal ones. To maintain their constituencies, state regulators have assumed the role of champion of state-chartered banks. They have achieved their constituency both by charging a lower price (no required idle reserves) and by supporting their bankers' legislative positions. The attraction of the state system has been lessened by the Depository Institutions Deregulation and Monetary Control Act of 1980 because all banks, even non-Fed members, will have reserve requirements set by the Fed. Thus, the state system will no longer offer a cheaper alternative than the federal system. To keep their constituency, state regulators may compete even more strenuously in regulatory laxity.

There is no bank lobby with a less progressive history than that of the Conference of State Bank Supervisors (CSBS). To attract bankers, it holds its meetings in bank-convention surroundings like Las Vegas and the Playboy Club at Great Gorge, New Jersey. CSBS officially states that it exists for one primary purpose, namely, "to assure the maintenance of a viable, decentralized Dual Banking System with its inherent checks and balances which protects all banks against the creation by the federal government of a bank regulatory monopoly."[42] CSBS derives over 90 percent of its multimillion-dollar operating budget from annual dues collected from state-chartered banks. State bank commissioners are supposed to, and do, send letters to the banks they regulate asking them to become associate members of CSBS—voluntarily, of course—and to send an assessment fee to support the organization. The letter assures the bank that state bank commissioners and state banks have many mutual concerns that can best be defended by the banks' regulators. The CSBS-suggested form letter, meant to be sent to state bankers by their state's bank commissioner, propounds that both the CSBS and state bankers are seeking the type of efficient, affirmative supervision that serves as an aid, not an obstacle, to enlightened bank management.[43] CSBS asserts in the suggested form letter that they are the only organization representing the entire state banking community and urges state bankers to join CSBS, citing the organization's record of daily support of common ideas.

Connecticut Bank Commissioner Lawrence Connell, Jr., and I both felt strongly enough about the clear conflict of interest created by this financial dependency to drop our states' memberships in CSBS, while in office. We argued that this financial dependence obstructed the association's ability to pursue a meaningful public interest role on issues where banker and consumer aims were at odds.

But criticism of state supervision need not be limited to the supervisor's bank-interest oriented approach to regulation; it is often incompetent supervision as well. Few state banking departments can claim parity with respect to the quality of their supervisory and examination procedures. The various federal agencies have thousands of well-paid and well-trained examiners with access to sophisticated support staff and the latest computer systems. While a few states have large staffs of adequately paid examiners, most states have too few examiners, who are poorly trained and poorly paid. There are over 4,300 bank examiners employed by the federal government, but only 1,900 employed by all state banking departments. Training and education programs are virtually nonexistent except in the largest departments, such as those in New York, California, Illinois, and Massachusetts. If states' rights and the dual banking system really are to be defensible, then the individual state banking departments must be able to stand on their own. The quality of their performance should at least equal that of federal regulators.

The real question at this point is whether it is worth the effort and cost to rescue and revive state bank regulation, or whether the federal government should not simply complete its takeover of this field. Those who support the continuation of a dual banking system argue that the present system fosters regulatory flexibility that is essential to the banking industry. These advocates argue that centralizing regulatory authority over the banking industry would destroy the checks and balances inherent in the dual system. While this argument tends to enshrine "competition in laxity" as a virtue of the bank regulatory structure, supporters of the dual banking system seriously argue that the ability of banks to choose their regulators is healthy for the banks and the country. As the past president of the Oregon Bankers Association, John R. Segerstrom, effectively stated:

> *Should banking fall under single regulatory control, we will lose the flexibility to change, and run a very high risk of following the railroads, and others, into decay. The true function of the dual banking system, and of the ebbs and flows of the conflict between conservatives and populists, has not been to perfect the industry under one or the other banners, but to maintain enough flexibility to allow evolution with the times. Historically, single, monolithic regulation has been the death knell of free enterprise, and banking has no right to expect a better fate. Who needs the dual banking system? We do. We all do. Our future depends on it.*[44]

An official publication of the Conference of State Bank Supervisors, entitled "Why State Banking?" echoes these themes by reiterating that the Dual Banking System, with its freedom of conversion between the two systems tends to reduce the degree of unnecessary regulation, for banks are inclined to seek the system which permits them to serve their communities, with a minimum of external interference. It tends to preserve local options and avoids a monolithic set of standards imposed from the Potomac on the banks in all states regardless of regional differences. Local and regional perspectives permit the people to become the conscience of banking and check the inclination of nationally centralized officials to assume the posture of arbiters of the public conscience.

There is merit in all these populist arguments, which is exactly why the present posture of state bank regulation is so painful. For the most part, state bank regulators have been an entrenched force for the status quo, opposing all competitive banking changes. Rather than acting as the conscience of banking and local concerns, state bank regulators have generally scorned consumer banking issues like Truth-in-Lending and redlining. As we saw, only five states ever applied for a state exemption under Truth-in-Lending on state-chartered banks. Other state regulators shied away from this consumer bank regulation because it interrupted their mutuality of views between the state bank regulators and their banks.

On the other hand, some bank regulators have been in the forefront of consumer banking regulation, and these state regulatory agencies have served as testing grounds for all of the federal consumer banking legislation of the 1970s.

As Rep. Thomas Corcoran of Illinois stated at a September 1978, oversight hearing of the Subcommittee on Commerce, Consumer and Monetary Affairs:

> ...*if you recall in the Truth-in-Lending area there were a couple of states that took the lead and really persuaded, based on their experience and on the excellence of their program, I recall particularly Massachusetts, that elevated the standards of the aggressive program of the Federal government in that respect.*"[45]

It is the promise of the dual banking system—its possibility for experimentation and local control—which makes the idea of state regulation so exciting. It is its actual performance which is so disheartening, because the ideal is so far from the reality. Much more so than the federal system, the state bank regulators are most often on the side of the industry, rather than the "conscience of banking." Yet the possibilities of the dual banking system are sometimes realized, as state bank regulators in California, New York, Michigan, Connecticut, Massachusetts, Maine, and New Jersey have demonstrated in the past decade. Without the innovations of these bank commissioners, it is unlikely that federal reforms in the areas of redlining, equal credit opportunity, Truth-in-Lending, and interest-bearing demand deposit accounts would have occurred. In the great tradition of experimentation on the state level before an idea is nationally adopted, these state bank regulators showed how bank regulation could be responsive to the needs of the public.

On balance, the possibilities for innovation and popular control presented by the state banking system make that system worth preserving. But the state system should be recognized for what it is—an opportunity for the states and local groups to shape their banks to meet their needs. To be worthwhile, the state bank commissioner must become an arm of the political process, in the best sense of that word—that is, he or she must become a means of furthering the political and economic goals of society. If state bank regulatory agencies are simply limited to examinations of the banks' books, then the state system is superfluous: Their federal counterparts are generally better equipped to do that work. The only justification for a state bank regulatory presence is if—in fact, rather than just in rhetoric—the state banking system preserves local options and control and permits, as the Conference of State Bank Supervisors states in its publication "Why State Banking?" "the people to become the conscience of banking."

# 9.

# How to Fight Back

### Start Your Own Bank

You are not as dependent on the Establishment banks as you think you are. It is not as difficult or as expensive as you think it is to start your own financial institution. The easiest to form is a credit union. Because they are locally owned, self-help financial cooperatives, credit unions can be a major factor in neighborhood revitalization. Power recently granted to federal credit unions—enabling them to make thirty-year mortgage loans and to participate, along with other financial institutions and credit union organizations, in making larger loans—enhances this role.

Credit unions can be formed by groups of people who share a common bond of occupation or association or, under certain conditions, live in a well-defined geographical area. In five states (Massachusetts, New Hampshire, Rhode Island, South Carolina, and Utah), any contiguous geographical area can serve as the basis for a community bond for a state-chartered credit union. For example, anyone living in the city of Boston could be eligible to join a newly formed Boston Peoples Credit Union. You will need a large potential membership base in order to grow large enough to satisfy the credit needs of your members. Under most state laws and federal regulations, the residential limitations are too narrow to make a community-based credit union viable. To get a federal charter for example, a community-based credit union would have to limit itself to serving an area whose population did not greatly exceed 25,000 people. That limits a community credit union to serving an urban neighborhood or a small town.

But there is another way. An association or club can be the basis for a credit union. The feminist credit unions are good examples. Members of feminist organizations, like the National Organization for Women (NOW), have used their associations as the basis for chartering credit unions in several cities. After the credit union has been formed, anyone who joins one of the associations becomes eligible to join the credit union. You need not be actively involved in women's issues to join a women's group like NOW as an entry into a credit union so that you can borrow at lower interest rates and receive higher interest on your savings. Federal law allows credit unions to pay up to 8 percent on passbook savings accounts and limits interest charges on all loans to a 15 percent maximum rate.

The potential for these kinds of credit unions and their growth are limitless. There are millions of bona fide clubs and associations in America. Any one of them, if it has a membership base of at least three hundred, could be a vehicle for your credit union.

One of the most attractive features of credit unions is that you don't need much money to start one—only enough to cover start-up costs. A representative from any regional office of the National Credit Union Administration (see Appendix 2 for the one nearest you) will gladly meet with a group that wants to start a credit union and help the organizers through the technical forms. Once a charter is granted by the NCUA, all deposits are insured up to $100,000 per account.

For groups in poorer urban areas, the government will provide the initial seed capital and technical assistance to set up Community Development Federal Credit Unions (CDFCUs). In addition to the traditional credit union goals to serve its members, CDFCUs have the additional mission of service to the total community. The NCUA, under the leadership of Lawrence Connell, Jr., formerly Connecticut Commissioner of Banks, has set up a Division of Community Development to develop prechartering training and chartering assistance for groups interested in starting a CDFCU. The NCUA also provides CDFCUs with instructions in accounting and operating procedure.

Similar help is provided new credit unions by the Credit Union National Association or by the Credit Union League of the USA, the credit union trade associations. If you're going to start a credit union, it's probably a good idea to call a representative of CUNA or CLUSA first. They will be happy to shepherd your group through the regulatory channels as well as providing technical counseling, including how to set up your books for sound financial practices.

Starting your own savings and loan association or savings bank is another option. Between 1934 and 1978, 2,000 federal savings and loan associations were started. Before 1933 there were no federal savings and loan associations; now S&Ls are the predominant mortgage lenders. Unlike starting a credit union, chartering an S&L or savings bank in a city does require a group to put together pledges from prospective depositors of $2 million dollars in deposits in savings accounts at the proposed S&L, of which about $400,000 would be pledges from the incorporators. While the numbers sound large, they are not as imposing as they might first seem. The incorporators' savings accounts are pledged as the start-up funds for the bank and cannot be withdrawn for up to five years. But these deposits do receive interest, so they resemble five-year term certificates. And while they're not explicitly insured, experience shows that this is virtually a riskless proposition. All depositors' funds which go toward the $2 million in pledges are, of course, federally insured up to the normal $100,000 per account. In essence, you have nothing to lose and only your neighborhood to save. Obviously, the incorporators do not need to know how to operate a savings and loan association; they will hire a professional banker to do that. But as the directors of the S&L, they will set the S&L's policies and can ensure that their neighborhood is not redlined.

### Join a Credit Union

If starting a financial institution appears to be more work than you were looking for, you might simply move your funds to a credit union. Credit unions are exempt from the federal regulations which mandate that banks pay not more than 5¼ percent on passbook savings accounts and that savings banks and savings and loan associations pay 5½ percent. Most credit unions pay 6 percent or more on passbook accounts. Many credit unions now offer "share draft" accounts, which are essentially interest-bearing checking accounts. Find a credit union you can join, and join. The rates on auto and personal loans are usually lower than at competing institutions. Federally chartered credit unions by law can never charge more than 15 percent on any loan, so if a lender quotes a higher rate, go join a credit union.

### Throw Them Out of Your Bank

A unique option is provided in Massachusetts, New Hampshire, and Vermont for a community group to take over a local financial institution. Cooperative banks are essentially state-chartered savings and loan associations in Massachusetts, New Hampshire, and

Vermont. Few people even in these states realize how demo-
cratically conceived these institutions are: Each depositor, regardless of the size of his account, gets one vote at the annual meeting of
share holders to elect the management and directors. In these states,
then, you can throw the bums out of your bank. If your cooperative
bank is redlining, doesn't offer student loans or charges exorbitant
rates, you and your friends and fellow victims should organize so
that a big group of depositor/shareholders comes to the sparsely
attended annual meeting and outvotes the ten to fifteen kin and
friends of management who came there for the ceremonial election.

This course could be open throughout the United States if
the Federal Home Loan Bank Board had not disenfranchised
shareholders of savings and loan associations by their regulations
allowing proxy voting by management and the signing away of
shareholder voting rights when accounts are opened. If you care
about economic democracy or just plain fairness, you should write
to the chairman of the Federal Home Loan Bank Board and tell him
that the present regulations are outrageous and that the Bank Board
should use its power to change them. (See Appendix 2 for address.)

### Know Your Legal Rights

The right to equal access to credit for women and minorities is now
protected by federal law. In order to exercise those rights, though,
you must know them. If you're rejected for a loan, you have a legal
right to a written, clear explanation of the denial within thirty days
of rejection. An application, under federal law, is not simply filling
out the form. If you call and ask for rates and then say you're
interested in a loan and the bank asks you for any further
information (that is, the address of the property, your income, your
name), you have filed an application. If the bank then says on the
phone, "Forget about the loan, your application has been rejected,"
they must give you a written reason for a credit denial, which you
will be able to contest.

It is against federal law for a creditor to discriminate in the
granting of credit because of sex, marital status, race, color,
religion, national origin, or age (marital status, in fact, cannot even
be asked about). A creditor may not discriminate because you
receive all or part of your income from a public-assistance program,
such as AFDC or food stamps, or from Social Security or unemployment compensation. Earnings in the form of alimony or income
from public assistance programs, cannot be discounted in deter-

mining credit-worthiness. Income, whatever its source, is to be treated as bona fide income. (It is illegal, for example, for a creditor to count a man's salary at 100 percent and a woman's at 75 percent.)

While the Equal Credit Opportunity Act does not give anyone an automatic right to credit, it does require that a creditor apply the same standards of credit-worthiness equally to all applicants. A creditor *cannot* legally *ask*:

1. Your sex, race, religion, or national origin, *except* as part of monitoring information collected by government agencies to analyze the disposition of home mortgage loan applications. Providing this information is totally voluntary on your part, but giving the requested information may well prevent discriminatory treatment of your application and will certainly help the regulatory agencies stop discrimination. You should not worry about the lender using this information to discriminate against you: After all, he already knows your race and sex. But, if you indicate your race and sex on the application form, then the regulatory agency will know too, and will be able to spot discriminatory practices and do something about them. (Also, if the lender knows that the agency will be able to check up on what it does, he may be less likely to discriminate against you.)

2. Your marital status, if you apply for your own account where there is no pledge of property for collateral, as in a personal loan. He cannot ask whether you are single, married, divorced, or widowed.

3. Information about your spouse unless a) your spouse is jointly applying with you, b) your spouse will be allowed to use the account, or c) you are relying on your spouse's income (or alimony or child support from a former spouse).

4. Your plans for having a family.

5. Whether you receive alimony, child support, or separate maintenance payments unless the creditor first tells you that you do not have to disclose this type of income unless you want to rely on it to get credit. (A creditor may ask, however, if you have to *pay* alimony, child support, or separate maintenance.)

6. The race or national origin of the people who live in the neighborhood where your property is located.

If the bank violates any of these prohibitions, you may well have grounds for a civil suit. The law allows for $10,000 in damages plus legal fees for an individual complaint, and up to $500,000 for a class action suit. Challenge any practice that seems to be unfair or discriminatory. You can do this by filing a complaint against the lender with the appropriate regulatory agency. To complain, you should write a short letter to the federal regulatory agency. The agency will then investigate the lender's policies and practices and require that fair lending laws be obeyed. If the lender is a savings and loan association, send a short letter explaining what happened to the Federal Home Loan Bank Board. (See Appendix 2 for address.) If the lender is a bank (either a commercial bank or a savings bank), send your letter to the Federal Deposit Insurance Corporation. (See Appendix.) If the lender is a finance company or retail store, send your letter to the Federal Trade Commission, Division of Credit Practices. (See Appendix.) These agencies will investigate your complaint. If you want to contact a regional office of these agencies, consult the Appendix for the address and telephone number of the nearest office.

### Truth-in-Lending

Truth-in-Lending laws require that you be fully informed about the terms and conditions of any credit transaction. You should have the following information before you sign the loan contract, and it should be explained so that you understand it completely.

For installment-type loans:
- the amount of the credit you will be using for the transaction;
- the finance charge, expressed in dollars, and the interest rate of the finance charge, expressed as an Annual Percentage Rate;
- an itemized list of all charges not included as part of the finance charge;
- the number, amount, and due dates of payments;
- the amount or method of computing charges if you are late with payments;
- the description of any property pledged as security for the credit being granted;
- a description of any prepayment penalties;
- a description of how any precomputed finance charge will be refunded to you if you prepay in full;
- the address and telephone number for you to use if you have any questions.

Lenders must quote only the annual percentage rate when telling you the cost of a loan. If someone quotes a very low rate, like 5½ percent for an auto loan, and you thought rates were about 12 percent, you were probably quoted a discounted rate, which is illegal. If you can get the creditor to put that discounted rate in writing on the loan disclosure form, you have the basis for obtaining a true 5½ percent loan and a lawsuit with up to $1,000 in damages or a class action suit of up to $500,000. The same is true if a mortgage lender quotes you a mortgage loan rate plus points and then does not translate that rate, including the points, into an annual percentage rate.

In fact, if any of the information listed above is missing from the loan disclosure statement that the lender was required to give you at the time the loan was consummated, you may well have the basis for suing the creditor for monetary damages. Check your loan disclosure form. Every blank space or line must be filled in by the lender before you sign the loan contract. If it is not, you probably have the basis for a civil suit.

To obtain restitution, you may not need to hire a lawyer. All the federal bank regulatory agencies and the bank commissioners of Maine, Massachusetts, Connecticut, Oklahoma, and Wyoming will require restitution to the borrower if the annual percentage rate was misstated or if the Truth-in-Lending laws were violated. So, if you feel that your rights have been violated under the Truth-in-Lending laws, contact the consumer assistance division of one of these bank regulatory agencies.

### Shop for Credit

Rates vary dramatically among lenders. Taking some time to call around can make a big difference in your credit costs. While shopping for credit can be a time-consuming, hit-or-miss technique of calling as many lenders as possible, a great deal of money can be saved. The interest rate tables in Appendix 1 show you how much you can save over the life of a loan. For example, you can save $1000 on the financing of a car by shopping for credit.[1] In the case of mortgages, the additional amount of interest a consumer pays over 25 years on a higher rate can be even larger. On a $50,000 mortgage, the interest cost is $91,600 for a 10½ percent rate and $107,986 for a 12 percent rate, or a difference of $16,386. That is worth a lot of phone calls.

As the Shopper's Credit Guide shows, differences in interest rate charges as great as those used in the above examples occur at any one time in a single market. Shopping for credit, of course, could be simplified if more government agencies followed the lead of the Massachusetts Banking Department and regularly published the rates charged by lenders for consumer loans. The Bureau of Consumer Protection in Maine is the only government agency which has so far followed the Massachusetts example, and has announced that it will start publishing comparative rate information. While legislation passed Congress in 1980 mandating that such information be collected and published by the Federal Reserve for a few SMSAs on an experimental basis, it is not clear yet in what form the Fed will disseminate this information.

If you want this kind of information available in your community, let your Congressman know that you want the Fed to collect and publish interest rate information monthly by name of lender.

### Shopping for the Best Banking Services

Financial institutions do differ in the price of their services. Do not settle for less than free checking with automatic transfers from savings, and, if you live in the Northeast, look for free NOW accounts. In 1981, when NOWs become available nationwide, everyone will have the option of a full NOW account.

Check out the credit unions. Many offer share drafts, which make a credit union account the functional equivalent of an interest paying checking account.

You may also want to know your bank's lending policies. Read your bank's Community Reinvestment Act Statement. It can be obtained free by asking. Legally, every federally insured financial institution must have one available for the public and must provide a file for comments received by the public. These comments will be read by the examiners and used in determining whether a bank should be allowed to branch, merge, or acquire another bank.

If you think your bank is redlining, or not providing student loans, or failing to meet your community's other credit needs, go with a couple of friends to file critical statements in the bank's public comment file, and get your friends to get a few of their friends to do the same thing. In fact, cram that public comment file. If you don't trust the bank, send copies of your letters to the appropriate bank regulator; if the bank examiner then comes and finds no comments in the bank's public file, the bank will certainly be in deep trouble.

### Support Your Local Activists

Neighborhood associations and consumer groups have forced bank regulators to deal effectively with problems they would never have heard about otherwise. These groups testify at congressional hearings. Who else is going to promote the public's interest on proposed banking legislation? Community groups and consumer groups have also gained a voice in the federal regulatory appointments process, a new but growing development. Gone is the day when a banker or bank lobbyist could be appointed to head a federal regulatory agency without some protest. To make that protest effective, the consumer groups must have clout, in terms of members and money. The protesters can have catalytic effects on the nominees.

When Robert McKinney, the President of an Indiana Savings and Loan Association, was nominated in August of 1977 by President Carter to head the Federal Home Loan Bank Board, protests from community groups stunned McKinney and increased his awareness of the issues. In his first speech to a trade industry group—in Dallas, Texas, in October of the same year—Chairman McKinney announced the Bank Board's new commitment to equal opportunity. He told the industry:

> *We also might as well face the hard cold fact the Federal Home Loan Bank Board often has been accused of being too close to its industry.... We will be vigorous in our enforcement, not only of our basic safety and soundness regulations but also of civil rights and consumer protection laws as well...Make no mistake, violators will not have a friend at the Federal Home Loan Bank.*[2]

When Anita Miller, a member of the Bank Board cited this speech in testimony before the House Subcommittee on Commerce, Consumers and Monetary Affairs, Rep. Rosenthal asked:

"Do you think the fact that the Senate gave Mr. McKinney such a difficult time caused him to respond in this fashion?"[3]

Mrs. Miller responded diplomatically:

"My personal analysis leads me to believe that Bob became far more aware of the importance of these issues to both the Congress and to consumers as a result of this hearing process."[4]

### Who Is Your State Bank Commissioner?

The states can do a great deal in the area of consumer protection and bank regulation. The appointment of the state bank commissioner should be one of the prime areas of concern for consumer groups. The next time your governor is up for election, community groups should press their views on who the next bank commissioner will be. Regulators are too important to let the banks choose their own.

What difference does it make? Here's what happened in one state when the banks *didn't* choose their regulator:

- The Banking Department published a Shopper's Credit Guide in the local newspapers each month, listing—by name of bank—the interest rates for auto loans, personal loans, and mortgages, so that the public could get the best deal.
- The Banking Department created a mortgage review board, so that mortgage applicants who believed they had been redlined could have their applications reviewed by an impartial body.
- The Banking Department pioneered in making the banks pay restitution for violations of Truth-in-Lending without the necessity of the borrower's going to court.
- The Banking Department created a complaint-handling service to aid consumers with their banking problems.
- The Banking Department allowed branches that would further competition, in the belief that competitive pressures best serve the public, and denied mergers and acquisitions that were anticompetitive. Both these policies were the exact reversal of the usual regulatory procedure, which allows a bank to branch only if no other bank objects.
- The Banking Department further tied new branches to affidavits of community service in the bank's present community, in some cases requiring dollar commitments of mortgage loans to be made in urban neighborhoods before approving new branches.
- The Banking Department held public hearings about employment discrimination in banks and collected data to prove that banks were violating the equal employment acts.
- The Banking Department published a free pocket credit guide so that consumers would have a handy reference to translate an 8¾ percent mortgage on a $40,000 loan into monthly payments, or a $5000 auto loan into monthly payments, so that they'd know whether they could afford the purchase, how much they'd pay in the end if they lengthened the term of the loan, and so on.

### Banking and Bank Regulation in the Age of Social Action

The Community Reinvestment Act of 1978 (CRA), one of the two most important banking laws passed in the 1970s,[5] dramatically illustrates the revolutionary developments of the decade. The significance of CRA is that it shifts the focus of regulatory decisions on bank structure—merger, branching, and holding-company acquisitions—from deposit services to credit availability. Before 1978, virtually the entire focus in regulatory decisions was on a given community's "convenience and needs"; the basic question was need for deposit services. Credit needs were rarely, if ever, discussed. It was new deposit services that banks outlined in their applications: Saturday banking hours, evening banking hours, a drive-up window at the new branch.

At that time, also, bank regulators were always concerned with "overbanking," so they would calculate what the deposit potential was in the primary service area, divide it by the population, and determine whether there was room for another bank, on the basis of whether the resulting deposit/population ratio was higher or lower than the state average or some other standard norm. While bank regulators had detailed data on deposits by bank branch, they had no data on loans for banks' market areas. Lending, as long as it was not risky or illegal, was not the regulator's concern.

CRA changes all of that. It defines the community's needs in terms of credit as well as deposit services; after all, communities not only need a safe repository for their funds and a reliable third-party-payments mechanism, they need access to credit. Credit need is further defined by making special reference to low- and moderate-income neighborhoods.

CRA is not credit allocation. The Act and implementing regulations leave it to each bank to determine its community, to define the community's credit needs, and to specify how it plans to meet those needs—subject to dispute by the local community. For the first time, community groups have been given a role in the bank regulatory process. Before CRA, community groups had no standing in this area. Public hearings were rarely, if ever, held; depositors were not notified of pending applications. CRA has brought the public into the regulatory process. Banks must prominently post in their lobbies pending applications, and they must keep community comment files which are to be read by examiners and reviewed in regulatory decisions.

The statute has clearly changed the focus of the bank regulatory agencies. It has also made bankers much more willing to talk with community groups. Previously, lending decisions were not seen as something to be reviewed by the community; they were solely management's affair, as long as they were legal. CRA has changed this, and it's a major philosophical, ideological change. A bank can now be denied an acquisition or branch if it refuses to make certain kinds of loans for which the community can prove there is an unmet need.

The revolution is also clear in the history of interest rate ceilings on savings accounts. The regulators and Congress, at the request of the banking and thrift industries, were maneuvered into a series of actions to prevent the average depositor from receiving a market rate of interest on his savings. The humor in the situation, if there is any, is that the market kept trying to innovate around the regulations and so the regulators and our elected representatives were caught in the unseemly spectacle of plugging holes in the regulatory dike. In 1966, when market interest rates first rose substantially above the interest rate ceilings, the regulators were not too concerned by their actions. It was the repetition of such actions that came to be very embarrassing, because it kept reminding the public who was preventing them from receiving the high market interest rates. It became more and more difficult to sell the argument that the public should subsidize the banks.

Market forces steadily ate away at all the rationales for keeping deposit rates under market rates. Each time the banks and thrifts felt secure in their regulators' protection, their security was attacked by a new market innovation. It was finally undermined by the money-market funds, which had indicated way back in 1973–1974 how important they were going to be. In 1978–1979, they really blossomed, growing from $4.5 billion to a $60 billion industry in two years. The irony of this development is that money-market funds actually increase the dominance of the largest commercial banks, a dominance the ceilings were designed to prevent in the first place. Because the funds place much of their money in CDs at the largest commercial banks, small savers' money is effectively siphoned out of the thrifts and smaller banks, and winds up in the very largest.

It was the plight of the elderly which finally ended the political support for interest rate ceilings on savings deposits. Hilda Cloud, a silver-haired seventy-eight-year-old woman, was a modern Joan of Arc, destroying the army of bank lobbyists. Congressmen were rightly embarrassed by regulations which denied those living on Social Security a fair return on their savings.

Consumer groups and community groups can make change happen. CRA was passed because of pressure from community groups across the nation, who were outraged by the redlining of their neighborhoods. Interest rate ceilings on savings accounts will be removed because the elderly organized and protested. The lessons are clear. You can make change happen. It's your money. You can make it serve your interests.

# Appendix 1
## Down Easter's Credit Guide*

Down Easters have a reputation of being good "horse traders," yet when it comes to credit, they spend millions of dollars each year in unnecessary interest charges. Their "horse-sense" has been "buffaloed" by the complexities of credit. This guide is designed to put you back behind the reins. By using it, you won't apply for credit with your hat in your hand; you'll bargain for credit with an eye toward saving money.

### SHOPPING FOR CREDIT

Imagine that you need to borrow $5,000 for a new car. If financed through a car dealer, you could pay as much as 13 percent. But the same amount could probably be obtained through a bank or credit union at, say, 11 percent.

Let's say you need to borrow $15,000 for a mobile home. Compare the total Finance Charge at 13 percent for ten years vs. 12 percent. (Use the tables.)

$11,876 vs. $10,825 means a savings of $1,051!

Before signing the dotted line, call several lenders to find out about their Annual Percentage Rate. Then use this Guide to compare the costs. You'll notice that the lower the Annual Percentage Rate, the lower the total Finance Charge, and the lower the monthly payments. You'll be able to make an unhurried decision at home, away from the busy loan officer or salesperson.

*Adapted from the Down Easter's Pocket Credit Guide, 2nd Edition, by arrangement with the Bureau of Consumer Protection, Department of Business Regulation, State House, Station 35, Augusta, Maine 04333.

**269**

### Credit Shopping Tips

Put some pressure on the lender. Many lenders think that consumers are only interested in how much the monthly payments are. Let them know you're a Credit Shopper. Your first question should be, "What's the Annual Percentage Rate?" Those who never ask usually end up paying the long dollar.

Look for "simple interest" loans. You'll pay no more nor less than you should. And if you make some payments ahead of schedule, you can reduce the total Finance Charge.

Explore all sources of credit. Loans secured by the cash surrender value of insurance policies, and loans secured by savings or share accounts are usually the cheapest. Insurance policy loans can be obtained from your insurance company; call your agent.

Most Bank Credit Cards carry the maximum Annual Percentage Rate the law allows, 18%. Additionally, banks get a commission from merchants on all goods and services purchased with their cards. This extra charge, usually 2–5 percent, is of course, passed on to the consumer. You'll need to do some shopping to find one, but a few banks offer cards which reduce the APR to 12 or 14 percent after the first $500. Many offer this lower rate after the first $2,000.

DEALER RESERVE: Mobile home and car dealers usually get a certain percentage of the Finance Charge on contracts they arrange. This "commission" is called Dealer Reserve, and can result in higher interest rates. Lower rates can usually be found by going directly to a Bank or Credit Union for financing.

The lower the Annual Percentage Rate, the more you can afford to buy on credit. A $4,000 loan for 3 years at 18 percent costs $145 per month. But, for the same payment and length of time, you can borrow $4,400 at 12 percent; that's $400 more! A $10,000 loan for 15 years at 14 percent costs $133 per month. But, for the same payment and length of time, you can borrow $11,100 at 12 percent; that's $1,100 more!

Credit Shopping might mean that you can afford those little extras that seemed just out of reach before.

Many lenders offer package deals such as "free" gifts if you take out a loan, lower rates in return for opening a checking or savings account, or "free" life insurance. A wise credit shopper looks at the total cost. How much is the "free" gift worth? Are the checking and savings accounts competitive? Is the life insurance really free?

## INDEX TO TABLES

*Table I:* Use for auto loans, furniture and appliance loans, etc.
*Table II:* Use for mobile home loans, home improvement loans, etc.
*Table III:* Use for mortgages.

### Notes

1. All figures have been rounded to the nearest dollar.
2. Amounts within the same column may be added together to find payments and finance charges for loan amounts not listed.
3. Great care has been taken to make these tables correct, but there is no warranty of accuracy.

## Table I

### 8% Annual Percentage Rate

| Amount Financed | 1 YEAR | | 2 YEARS | | 3 YEARS | | 4 YEARS | |
|---|---|---|---|---|---|---|---|---|
| | Monthly Payment | Total Finance Charge | Monthly Payment | Total Finance Charge | Monthly Payment | Total Finance Charge | Monthly Payment | Total Finance Charge |
| $ 100 | 9 | 4 | 5 | 9 | 3 | 13 | 2 | 18 |
| 500 | 44 | 22 | 23 | 43 | 16 | 64 | 12 | 86 |
| 1,000 | 87 | 44 | 45 | 86 | 31 | 128 | 24 | 172 |
| 1,500 | 130 | 66 | 68 | 128 | 47 | 192 | 37 | 258 |
| 2,000 | 174 | 88 | 90 | 171 | 63 | 256 | 49 | 344 |
| 2,500 | 217 | 110 | 113 | 214 | 78 | 321 | 61 | 430 |
| 3,000 | 261 | 132 | 136 | 257 | 94 | 384 | 73 | 516 |
| 3,500 | 304 | 154 | 158 | 299 | 110 | 448 | 85 | 602 |
| 4,000 | 348 | 176 | 181 | 342 | 125 | 513 | 98 | 688 |
| 4,500 | 391 | 197 | 204 | 385 | 141 | 577 | 110 | 773 |
| 5,000 | 435 | 219 | 226 | 427 | 157 | 640 | 122 | 859 |
| 5,500 | 478 | 241 | 249 | 470 | 172 | 705 | 134 | 945 |
| 6,000 | 522 | 263 | 271 | 513 | 188 | 769 | 146 | 1,031 |

### 8½% Annual Percentage Rate

| Amount Financed | 1 YEAR | | 2 YEARS | | 3 YEARS | | 4 YEARS | |
|---|---|---|---|---|---|---|---|---|
| | Monthly Payment | Total Finance Charge | Monthly Payment | Total Finance Charge | Monthly Payment | Total Finance Charge | Monthly Payment | Total Finance Charge |
| $ 100 | 9 | 5 | 5 | 9 | 3 | 14 | 2 | 19 |
| 500 | 44 | 23 | 23 | 46 | 16 | 68 | 12 | 92 |
| 1,000 | 87 | 47 | 45 | 91 | 32 | 137 | 25 | 183 |
| 1,500 | 131 | 70 | 68 | 137 | 47 | 205 | 37 | 275 |
| 2,000 | 174 | 93 | 91 | 182 | 63 | 273 | 49 | 366 |
| 2,500 | 218 | 117 | 114 | 227 | 79 | 341 | 62 | 458 |
| 3,000 | 262 | 140 | 136 | 273 | 95 | 410 | 74 | 550 |
| 3,500 | 305 | 163 | 159 | 318 | 110 | 478 | 86 | 641 |
| 4,000 | 349 | 187 | 182 | 364 | 126 | 546 | 99 | 733 |
| 4,500 | 392 | 210 | 205 | 409 | 142 | 614 | 111 | 824 |
| 5,000 | 436 | 233 | 227 | 455 | 158 | 682 | 123 | 916 |
| 5,500 | 480 | 257 | 250 | 500 | 174 | 751 | 136 | 1,007 |
| 6,000 | 523 | 280 | 273 | 546 | 189 | 819 | 148 | 1,099 |

## Table I

### 9% Annual Percentage Rate

| Amount Financed | 1 YEAR | | 2 YEARS | | 3 YEARS | | 4 YEARS | |
|---|---|---|---|---|---|---|---|---|
| | Monthly Payment | Total Finance Charge | Monthly Payment | Total Finance Charge | Monthly Payment | Total Finance Charge | Monthly Payment | Total Finance Charge |
| $ 100 | 9 | 5 | 5 | 10 | 3 | 14 | 2 | 20 |
| 500 | 44 | 25 | 23 | 48 | 16 | 72 | 12 | 98 |
| 1,000 | 87 | 50 | 46 | 97 | 32 | 145 | 25 | 195 |
| 1,500 | 131 | 74 | 69 | 145 | 48 | 217 | 37 | 292 |
| 2,000 | 175 | 99 | 91 | 193 | 64 | 290 | 50 | 389 |
| 2,500 | 219 | 124 | 114 | 241 | 80 | 362 | 62 | 487 |
| 3,000 | 262 | 148 | 137 | 289 | 95 | 434 | 75 | 584 |
| 3,500 | 306 | 183 | 160 | 338 | 111 | 507 | 87 | 681 |
| 4,000 | 350 | 198 | 183 | 386 | 127 | 579 | 100 | 778 |
| 4,500 | 394 | 222 | 206 | 434 | 143 | 652 | 112 | 876 |
| 5,000 | 437 | 247 | 228 | 482 | 159 | 724 | 124 | 973 |
| 5,500 | 481 | 272 | 251 | 530 | 175 | 796 | 137 | 1,070 |
| 6,000 | 525 | 297 | 274 | 579 | 191 | 869 | 149 | 1,167 |

### 9½% Annual Percentage Rate

| Amount Financed | 1 YEAR | | 2 YEARS | | 3 YEARS | | 4 YEARS | |
|---|---|---|---|---|---|---|---|---|
| | Monthly Payment | Total Finance Charge | Monthly Payment | Total Finance Charge | Monthly Payment | Total Finance Charge | Monthly Payment | Total Finance Charge |
| $ 100 | 9 | 5 | 5 | 10 | 3 | 16 | 3 | 21 |
| 500 | 44 | 26 | 23 | 51 | 16 | 77 | 13 | 103 |
| 1,000 | 88 | 52 | 46 | 102 | 32 | 153 | 25 | 206 |
| 1,500 | 132 | 78 | 69 | 153 | 48 | 230 | 38 | 309 |
| 2,000 | 175 | 104 | 92 | 204 | 64 | 307 | 50 | 412 |
| 2,500 | 219 | 131 | 115 | 255 | 80 | 383 | 63 | 515 |
| 3,000 | 263 | 157 | 138 | 306 | 96 | 460 | 75 | 618 |
| 3,500 | 307 | 183 | 161 | 357 | 112 | 536 | 88 | 721 |
| 4,000 | 351 | 209 | 184 | 408 | 128 | 613 | 101 | 824 |
| 4,500 | 395 | 235 | 207 | 459 | 144 | 689 | 113 | 927 |
| 5,000 | 438 | 261 | 230 | 510 | 160 | 766 | 126 | 1,030 |
| 5,500 | 482 | 287 | 253 | 560 | 176 | 843 | 138 | 1,133 |
| 6,000 | 526 | 313 | 275 | 612 | 192 | 919 | 151 | 1,236 |

### Table I

#### 10% Annual Percentage Rate

| Amount Financed | 1 YEAR | | 2 YEARS | | 3 YEARS | | 4 YEARS | |
|---|---|---|---|---|---|---|---|---|
| | Monthly Payment | Total Finance Charge | Monthly Payment | Total Finance Charge | Monthly Payment | Total Finance Charge | Monthly Payment | Total Finance Charge |
| **$ 100** | 9 | 6 | 5 | 11 | 3 | 16 | 3 | 22 |
| **500** | 44 | 28 | 23 | 54 | 16 | 81 | 13 | 109 |
| **1,000** | 88 | 55 | 46 | 108 | 32 | 162 | 25 | 218 |
| **1,500** | 132 | 83 | 69 | 161 | 48 | 243 | 38 | 326 |
| **2,000** | 176 | 110 | 92 | 215 | 65 | 323 | 51 | 435 |
| **2,500** | 220 | 137 | 115 | 269 | 81 | 404 | 63 | 544 |
| **3,000** | 264 | 165 | 138 | 323 | 97 | 485 | 76 | 652 |
| **3,500** | 308 | 193 | 162 | 376 | 113 | 566 | 89 | 761 |
| **4,000** | 352 | 220 | 185 | 430 | 129 | 647 | 101 | 870 |
| **4,500** | 396 | 248 | 208 | 484 | 145 | 728 | 114 | 979 |
| **5,000** | 440 | 275 | 231 | 538 | 161 | 808 | 127 | 1,087 |
| **5,500** | 484 | 302 | 254 | 591 | 177 | 889 | 140 | 1,196 |
| **6,000** | 528 | 330 | 277 | 645 | 194 | 970 | 152 | 1,305 |

#### 10½% Annual Percentage Rate

| Amount Financed | 1 YEAR | | 2 YEARS | | 3 YEARS | | 4 YEARS | |
|---|---|---|---|---|---|---|---|---|
| | Monthly Payment | Total Finance Charge | Monthly Payment | Total Finance Charge | Monthly Payment | Total Finance Charge | Monthly Payment | Total Finance Charge |
| **$ 100** | 9 | 6 | 5 | 11 | 3 | 17 | 3 | 23 |
| **500** | 44 | 29 | 23 | 57 | 16 | 85 | 13 | 115 |
| **1,000** | 88 | 58 | 46 | 113 | 33 | 170 | 26 | 229 |
| **1,500** | 132 | 88 | 70 | 170 | 49 | 260 | 39 | 350 |
| **2,000** | 176 | 116 | 93 | 226 | 65 | 340 | 51 | 458 |
| **2,500** | 221 | 146 | 116 | 284 | 82 | 434 | 64 | 584 |
| **3,000** | 264 | 173 | 139 | 339 | 98 | 510 | 77 | 687 |
| **3,500** | 309 | 204 | 162 | 398 | 114 | 608 | 90 | 818 |
| **4,000** | 353 | 231 | 186 | 452 | 130 | 680 | 102 | 916 |
| **4,500** | 397 | 263 | 208 | 511 | 146 | 781 | 116 | 1,051 |
| **5,000** | 441 | 289 | 232 | 565 | 163 | 851 | 128 | 1,145 |
| **5,500** | 485 | 321 | 255 | 625 | 179 | 955 | 141 | 1,285 |
| **6,000** | 529 | 347 | 278 | 678 | 195 | 1,021 | 154 | 1,374 |

### Table I

#### 11% Annual Percentage Rate

| Amount Financed | 1 YEAR | | 2 YEARS | | 3 YEARS | | 4 YEARS | |
|---|---|---|---|---|---|---|---|---|
| | Monthly Payment | Total Finance Charge | Monthly Payment | Total Finance Charge | Monthly Payment | Total Finance Charge | Monthly Payment | Total Finance Charge |
| **$ 100** | 9 | 6 | 5 | 12 | 3 | 18 | 3 | 24 |
| **500** | 44 | 30 | 23 | 59 | 16 | 89 | 13 | 121 |
| **1,000** | 88 | 61 | 47 | 119 | 33 | 179 | 26 | 241 |
| **1,500** | 133 | 91 | 70 | 178 | 49 | 268 | 39 | 361 |
| **2,000** | 177 | 121 | 93 | 237 | 65 | 357 | 52 | 482 |
| **2,500** | 221 | 152 | 117 | 296 | 82 | 447 | 65 | 602 |
| **3,000** | 265 | 182 | 140 | 356 | 98 | 536 | 78 | 722 |
| **3,500** | 309 | 212 | 163 | 415 | 115 | 625 | 90 | 842 |
| **4,000** | 354 | 242 | 186 | 475 | 131 | 715 | 103 | 963 |
| **4,500** | 398 | 273 | 210 | 534 | 147 | 804 | 116 | 1,083 |
| **5,000** | 442 | 303 | 233 | 593 | 164 | 893 | 129 | 1,203 |
| **5,500** | 486 | 333 | 256 | 652 | 180 | 983 | 142 | 1,324 |
| **6,000** | 530 | 363 | 280 | 712 | 196 | 1,072 | 155 | 1,444 |

#### 11½% Annual Percentage Rate

| Amount Financed | 1 YEAR | | 2 YEARS | | 3 YEARS | | 4 YEARS | |
|---|---|---|---|---|---|---|---|---|
| | Monthly Payment | Total Finance Charge | Monthly Payment | Total Finance Charge | Monthly Payment | Total Finance Charge | Monthly Payment | Total Finance Charge |
| **$ 100** | 9 | 6 | 5 | 13 | 3 | 19 | 3 | 25 |
| **500** | 44 | 32 | 23 | 62 | 16 | 94 | 13 | 126 |
| **1,000** | 89 | 63 | 47 | 124 | 33 | 187 | 26 | 252 |
| **1,500** | 133 | 97 | 70 | 188 | 50 | 282 | 39 | 378 |
| **2,000** | 177 | 127 | 94 | 249 | 66 | 375 | 52 | 504 |
| **2,500** | 222 | 161 | 117 | 314 | 83 | 470 | 65 | 632 |
| **3,000** | 266 | 190 | 141 | 373 | 99 | 561 | 78 | 757 |
| **3,500** | 310 | 225 | 164 | 440 | 116 | 658 | 91 | 885 |
| **4,000** | 354 | 254 | 187 | 497 | 132 | 749 | 104 | 1,009 |
| **4,500** | 399 | 290 | 211 | 565 | 149 | 846 | 117 | 1,138 |
| **5,000** | 443 | 317 | 234 | 621 | 165 | 936 | 130 | 1,262 |
| **5,500** | 488 | 354 | 258 | 691 | 182 | 1,034 | 144 | 1,390 |
| **6,000** | 532 | 380 | 281 | 745 | 198 | 1,123 | 157 | 1,514 |

## Table I

### 12% Annual Percentage Rate

| Amount Financed | 1 YEAR | | 2 YEARS | | 3 YEARS | | 4 YEARS | |
|---|---|---|---|---|---|---|---|---|
| | Monthly Payment | Total Finance Charge | Monthly Payment | Total Finance Charge | Monthly Payment | Total Finance Charge | Monthly Payment | Total Finance Charge |
| $ 100 | 9 | 7 | 5 | 13 | 3 | 20 | 3 | 27 |
| 500 | 44 | 33 | 24 | 65 | 17 | 98 | 13 | 132 |
| 1,000 | 89 | 66 | 47 | 130 | 33 | 196 | 26 | 264 |
| 1,500 | 133 | 99 | 71 | 195 | 50 | 294 | 40 | 396 |
| 2,000 | 178 | 132 | 94 | 260 | 66 | 391 | 53 | 528 |
| 2,500 | 222 | 166 | 118 | 325 | 83 | 489 | 66 | 660 |
| 3,000 | 267 | 199 | 141 | 390 | 100 | 587 | 79 | 792 |
| 3,500 | 311 | 232 | 165 | 454 | 116 | 685 | 92 | 924 |
| 4,000 | 355 | 265 | 188 | 519 | 133 | 783 | 105 | 1,056 |
| 4,500 | 400 | 298 | 212 | 584 | 149 | 881 | 119 | 1,188 |
| 5,000 | 444 | 331 | 235 | 649 | 166 | 979 | 132 | 1,320 |
| 5,500 | 489 | 364 | 259 | 714 | 183 | 1,076 | 145 | 1,452 |
| 6,000 | 533 | 397 | 282 | 779 | 199 | 1,174 | 158 | 1,584 |

### 12½% Annual Percentage Rate

| Amount Financed | 1 YEAR | | 2 YEARS | | 3 YEARS | | 4 YEARS | |
|---|---|---|---|---|---|---|---|---|
| | Monthly Payment | Total Finance Charge | Monthly Payment | Total Finance Charge | Monthly Payment | Total Finance Charge | Monthly Payment | Total Finance Charge |
| $ 100 | 9 | 7 | 5 | 14 | 3 | 21 | 3 | 28 |
| 500 | 45 | 35 | 24 | 68 | 17 | 102 | 13 | 138 |
| 1,000 | 89 | 69 | 47 | 135 | 33 | 205 | 27 | 276 |
| 1,500 | 134 | 104 | 71 | 206 | 50 | 309 | 40 | 415 |
| 2,000 | 178 | 138 | 95 | 271 | 67 | 409 | 53 | 552 |
| 2,500 | 223 | 173 | 119 | 344 | 84 | 515 | 67 | 692 |
| 3,000 | 267 | 207 | 142 | 406 | 100 | 613 | 80 | 828 |
| 3,500 | 312 | 242 | 166 | 482 | 117 | 721 | 93 | 967 |
| 4,000 | 356 | 276 | 189 | 542 | 134 | 818 | 106 | 1,103 |
| 4,500 | 401 | 311 | 213 | 619 | 151 | 927 | 120 | 1,246 |
| 5,000 | 445 | 345 | 237 | 677 | 167 | 1,022 | 133 | 1,379 |
| 5,500 | 490 | 381 | 261 | 757 | 184 | 1,133 | 146 | 1,522 |
| 6,000 | 535 | 414 | 284 | 812 | 201 | 1,226 | 159 | 1,655 |

## Table I

### 13% Annual Percentage Rate

| Amount Financed | 1 YEAR | | 2 YEARS | | 3 YEARS | | 4 YEARS | |
|---|---|---|---|---|---|---|---|---|
| | Monthly Payment | Total Finance Charge | Monthly Payment | Total Finance Charge | Monthly Payment | Total Finance Charge | Monthly Payment | Total Finance Charge |
| $ 100 | 9 | 7 | 5 | 14 | 3 | 21 | 3 | 29 |
| 500 | 45 | 36 | 24 | 71 | 17 | 107 | 13 | 144 |
| 1,000 | 89 | 72 | 48 | 141 | 34 | 213 | 27 | 288 |
| 1,500 | 134 | 109 | 71 | 214 | 51 | 320 | 40 | 437 |
| 2,000 | 179 | 144 | 95 | 282 | 67 | 426 | 54 | 576 |
| 2,500 | 224 | 182 | 119 | 356 | 84 | 533 | 67 | 728 |
| 3,000 | 268 | 216 | 143 | 423 | 101 | 639 | 80 | 864 |
| 3,500 | 313 | 255 | 167 | 499 | 118 | 746 | 94 | 1,019 |
| 4,000 | 357 | 287 | 190 | 564 | 135 | 852 | 107 | 1,151 |
| 4,500 | 402 | 327 | 214 | 641 | 152 | 959 | 121 | 1,310 |
| 5,000 | 447 | 359 | 238 | 705 | 168 | 1,065 | 134 | 1,439 |
| 5,500 | 492 | 400 | 262 | 783 | 185 | 1,173 | 148 | 1,602 |
| 6,000 | 536 | 431 | 285 | 846 | 202 | 1 278 | 161 | 1,727 |

### 13½% Annual Percentage Rate

| Amount Financed | 1 YEAR | | 2 YEARS | | 3 YEARS | | 4 YEARS | |
|---|---|---|---|---|---|---|---|---|
| | Monthly Payment | Total Finance Charge | Monthly Payment | Total Finance Charge | Monthly Payment | Total Finance Charge | Monthly Payment | Total Finance Charge |
| $ 100 | 9 | 8 | 5 | 15 | 3 | 22 | 3 | 30 |
| 500 | 45 | 38 | 24 | 73 | 17 | 111 | 14 | 150 |
| 1,000 | 90 | 75 | 48 | 147 | 34 | 222 | 27 | 300 |
| 1,500 | 134 | 113 | 72 | 221 | 51 | 336 | 41 | 451 |
| 2,000 | 179 | 149 | 96 | 293 | 68 | 444 | 54 | 600 |
| 2,500 | 224 | 188 | 120 | 368 | 85 | 560 | 68 | 752 |
| 3,000 | 269 | 224 | 143 | 440 | 102 | 665 | 81 | 899 |
| 3,500 | 314 | 263 | 167 | 515 | 119 | 784 | 95 | 1,053 |
| 4,000 | 358 | 299 | 191 | 587 | 136 | 887 | 108 | 1,199 |
| 4,500 | 403 | 338 | 215 | 662 | 153 | 1,008 | 122 | 1,354 |
| 5,000 | 448 | 373 | 239 | 733 | 170 | 1,108 | 135 | 1,499 |
| 5,500 | 493 | 414 | 263 | 810 | 187 | 1,232 | 149 | 1,654 |
| 6,000 | 537 | 448 | 287 | 880 | 204 | 1,330 | 162 | 1,798 |

### Table I

#### 14% Annual Percentage Rate

| Amount Financed | 1 YEAR Monthly Payment | Total Finance Charge | 2 YEARS Monthly Payment | Total Finance Charge | 3 YEARS Monthly Payment | Total Finance Charge | 4 YEARS Monthly Payment | Total Finance Charge |
|---|---|---|---|---|---|---|---|---|
| $ 100 | 9 | 8 | 5 | 15 | 3 | 23 | 3 | 32 |
| 500 | 45 | 39 | 24 | 76 | 17 | 115 | 14 | 156 |
| 1,000 | 90 | 77 | 48 | 152 | 34 | 230 | 27 | 312 |
| 1,500 | 135 | 116 | 72 | 232 | 51 | 347 | 41 | 473 |
| 2,000 | 180 | 155 | 96 | 305 | 68 | 461 | 55 | 624 |
| 2,500 | 225 | 194 | 120 | 386 | 86 | 578 | 69 | 788 |
| 3,000 | 269 | 232 | 144 | 457 | 103 | 691 | 82 | 935 |
| 3,500 | 314 | 272 | 168 | 540 | 120 | 809 | 96 | 1,103 |
| 4,000 | 359 | 310 | 192 | 609 | 137 | 922 | 109 | 1,247 |
| 4,500 | 404 | 349 | 216 | 695 | 154 | 1,040 | 123 | 1,418 |
| 5,000 | 449 | 387 | 240 | 762 | 171 | 1,152 | 137 | 1,559 |
| 5,500 | 494 | 427 | 265 | 849 | 188 | 1,272 | 151 | 1,734 |
| 6,000 | 539 | 465 | 288 | 914 | 205 | 1,383 | 164 | 1,870 |

#### 14½% Annual Percentage Rate

| Amount Financed | 1 YEAR Monthly Payment | Total Finance Charge | 2 YEARS Monthly Payment | Total Finance Charge | 3 YEARS Monthly Payment | Total Finance Charge | 4 YEARS Monthly Payment | Total Finance Charge |
|---|---|---|---|---|---|---|---|---|
| $ 100 | 9 | 8 | 5 | 16 | 3 | 24 | 3 | 32 |
| 500 | 45 | 40 | 24 | 79 | 17 | 120 | 14 | 162 |
| 1,000 | 90 | 80 | 48 | 158 | 34 | 239 | 28 | 324 |
| 1,500 | 135 | 122 | 72 | 239 | 52 | 363 | 41 | 487 |
| 2,000 | 180 | 161 | 97 | 316 | 69 | 479 | 55 | 648 |
| 2,500 | 225 | 203 | 121 | 398 | 86 | 605 | 69 | 812 |
| 3,000 | 270 | 241 | 145 | 474 | 103 | 718 | 83 | 972 |
| 3,500 | 315 | 284 | 169 | 557 | 121 | 847 | 97 | 1,137 |
| 4,000 | 360 | 321 | 193 | 632 | 138 | 957 | 110 | 1,295 |
| 4,500 | 405 | 365 | 217 | 716 | 155 | 1,089 | 124 | 1,462 |
| 5,000 | 450 | 401 | 241 | 790 | 172 | 1,196 | 138 | 1,619 |
| 5,500 | 496 | 447 | 266 | 876 | 190 | 1,331 | 152 | 1,786 |
| 6,000 | 540 | 482 | 290 | 948 | 207 | 1,435 | 165 | 1,943 |

### Table I

#### 15% Annual Percentage Rate

| Amount Financed | 1 YEAR Monthly Payment | Total Finance Charge | 2 YEARS Monthly Payment | Total Finance Charge | 3 YEARS Monthly Payment | Total Finance Charge | 4 YEARS Monthly Payment | Total Finance Charge |
|---|---|---|---|---|---|---|---|---|
| $ 100 | 9 | 8 | 5 | 16 | 3 | 25 | 3 | 34 |
| 500 | 45 | 42 | 24 | 82 | 17 | 124 | 14 | 168 |
| 1,000 | 90 | 83 | 49 | 164 | 35 | 248 | 28 | 336 |
| 1,500 | 135 | 125 | 73 | 246 | 52 | 374 | 42 | 509 |
| 2,000 | 181 | 166 | 97 | 328 | 69 | 496 | 56 | 672 |
| 2,500 | 226 | 209 | 121 | 410 | 87 | 623 | 70 | 848 |
| 3,000 | 271 | 249 | 145 | 491 | 104 | 744 | 84 | 1,008 |
| 3,500 | 316 | 293 | 170 | 574 | 121 | 872 | 98 | 1,187 |
| 4,000 | 361 | 332 | 194 | 655 | 139 | 992 | 111 | 1,344 |
| 4,500 | 406 | 376 | 218 | 738 | 156 | 1,121 | 126 | 1,526 |
| 5,000 | 451 | 416 | 242 | 819 | 173 | 1,240 | 139 | 1,680 |
| 5,500 | 497 | 460 | 267 | 902 | 191 | 1,371 | 153 | 1,865 |
| 6,000 | 542 | 499 | 291 | 982 | 208 | 1,488 | 167 | 2,016 |

#### 15½% Annual Percentage Rate

| Amount Financed | 1 YEAR Monthly Payment | Total Finance Charge | 2 YEARS Monthly Payment | Total Finance Charge | 3 YEARS Monthly Payment | Total Finance Charge | 4 YEARS Monthly Payment | Total Finance Charge |
|---|---|---|---|---|---|---|---|---|
| $ 100 | 9 | 9 | 5 | 17 | 4 | 26 | 3 | 35 |
| 500 | 45 | 43 | 24 | 85 | 17 | 129 | 14 | 174 |
| 1,000 | 91 | 86 | 49 | 170 | 35 | 257 | 28 | 348 |
| 1,500 | 136 | 129 | 73 | 257 | 53 | 390 | 42 | 523 |
| 2,000 | 181 | 172 | 97 | 339 | 70 | 514 | 56 | 696 |
| 2,500 | 226 | 215 | 122 | 428 | 88 | 650 | 70 | 872 |
| 3,000 | 271 | 258 | 146 | 508 | 105 | 771 | 84 | 1,044 |
| 3,500 | 317 | 301 | 171 | 599 | 123 | 910 | 98 | 1,221 |
| 4,000 | 362 | 344 | 195 | 678 | 140 | 1,027 | 112 | 1,292 |
| 4,500 | 407 | 387 | 220 | 770 | 158 | 1,170 | 126 | 1,570 |
| 5,000 | 452 | 430 | 244 | 847 | 175 | 1,284 | 140 | 1,741 |
| 5,500 | 498 | 473 | 268 | 942 | 193 | 1,430 | 155 | 1,918 |
| 6,000 | 543 | 516 | 292 | 1,016 | 209 | 1,541 | 169 | 2,088 |

### Table I

#### 16% Annual Percentage Rate

| Amount Financed | 1 YEAR | | 2 YEARS | | 3 YEARS | | 4 YEARS | |
|---|---|---|---|---|---|---|---|---|
| | Monthly Payment | Total Finance Charge | Monthly Payment | Total Finance Charge | Monthly Payment | Total Finance Charge | Monthly Payment | Total Finance Charge |
| $ 100 | 9 | 9 | 5 | 18 | 4 | 27 | 3 | 36 |
| 500 | 45 | 44 | 24 | 88 | 18 | 133 | 14 | 181 |
| 1,000 | 91 | 89 | 49 | 175 | 35 | 266 | 28 | 361 |
| 1,500 | 136 | 134 | 74 | 264 | 53 | 401 | 43 | 545 |
| 2,000 | 181 | 178 | 98 | 350 | 70 | 532 | 57 | 721 |
| 2,500 | 227 | 224 | 123 | 440 | 88 | 668 | 71 | 908 |
| 3,000 | 272 | 266 | 147 | 525 | 105 | 797 | 85 | 1,081 |
| 3,500 | 318 | 314 | 172 | 616 | 123 | 935 | 99 | 1,271 |
| 4,000 | 363 | 355 | 196 | 701 | 141 | 1,063 | 113 | 1,442 |
| 4,500 | 409 | 403 | 221 | 792 | 158 | 1,202 | 128 | 1,634 |
| 5,000 | 454 | 444 | 245 | 876 | 176 | 1,328 | 142 | 1,802 |
| 5,500 | 499 | 493 | 270 | 968 | 194 | 1,470 | 156 | 1,997 |
| 6,000 | 544 | 532 | 294 | 1,051 | 211 | 1,594 | 170 | 2,162 |

#### 16½% Annual Percentage Rate

| Amount Financed | 1 YEAR | | 2 YEARS | | 3 YEARS | | 4 YEARS | |
|---|---|---|---|---|---|---|---|---|
| | Monthly Payment | Total Finance Charge | Monthly Payment | Total Finance Charge | Monthly Payment | Total Finance Charge | Monthly Payment | Total Finance Charge |
| $ 100 | 9 | 9 | 5 | 18 | 4 | 27 | 3 | 37 |
| 500 | 46 | 46 | 25 | 90 | 18 | 137 | 14 | 186 |
| 1,000 | 91 | 92 | 49 | 181 | 35 | 274 | 29 | 373 |
| 1,500 | 137 | 138 | 74 | 271 | 53 | 412 | 43 | 559 |
| 2,000 | 182 | 184 | 98 | 362 | 71 | 549 | 57 | 746 |
| 2,500 | 228 | 230 | 123 | 452 | 89 | 686 | 72 | 932 |
| 3,000 | 273 | 276 | 148 | 542 | 106 | 823 | 86 | 1,118 |
| 3,500 | 319 | 322 | 172 | 633 | 124 | 960 | 100 | 1,305 |
| 4,000 | 364 | 368 | 197 | 723 | 142 | 1,098 | 114 | 1,491 |
| 4,500 | 410 | 414 | 221 | 814 | 159 | 1,235 | 129 | 1,678 |
| 5,000 | 455 | 460 | 246 | 904 | 177 | 1,372 | 143 | 1,864 |
| 5,500 | 501 | 506 | 271 | 994 | 195 | 1,509 | 157 | 2,050 |
| 6,000 | 546 | 552 | 295 | 1,085 | 212 | 1,646 | 172 | 2,237 |

### Table I

#### 17% Annual Percentage Rate

| Amount Financed | 1 YEAR | | 2 YEARS | | 3 YEARS | | 4 YEARS | |
|---|---|---|---|---|---|---|---|---|
| | Monthly Payment | Total Finance Charge | Monthly Payment | Total Finance Charge | Monthly Payment | Total Finance Charge | Monthly Payment | Total Finance Charge |
| $ 100 | 9 | 10 | 5 | 19 | 4 | 29 | 3 | 39 |
| 500 | 46 | 47 | 25 | 94 | 18 | 142 | 14 | 193 |
| 1,000 | 91 | 95 | 49 | 187 | 36 | 284 | 29 | 385 |
| 1,500 | 137 | 143 | 74 | 282 | 54 | 428 | 43 | 581 |
| 2,000 | 182 | 189 | 99 | 373 | 71 | 567 | 58 | 771 |
| 2,500 | 228 | 239 | 124 | 470 | 89 | 713 | 72 | 968 |
| 3,000 | 274 | 283 | 148 | 560 | 107 | 851 | 87 | 1,155 |
| 3,500 | 320 | 335 | 173 | 658 | 125 | 998 | 101 | 1,355 |
| 4,000 | 365 | 378 | 198 | 746 | 143 | 1,134 | 115 | 1,541 |
| 4,500 | 411 | 430 | 223 | 846 | 161 | 1,283 | 130 | 1,742 |
| 5,000 | 456 | 472 | 247 | 933 | 178 | 1,418 | 144 | 1,925 |
| 5,500 | 502 | 526 | 272 | 1,034 | 196 | 1,569 | 159 | 2,130 |
| 6,000 | 547 | 567 | 297 | 1,120 | 214 | 1,701 | 173 | 2,311 |

#### 17½% Annual Percentage Rate

| Amount Financed | 1 YEAR | | 2 YEARS | | 3 YEARS | | 4 YEARS | |
|---|---|---|---|---|---|---|---|---|
| | Monthly Payment | Total Finance Charge | Monthly Payment | Total Finance Charge | Monthly Payment | Total Finance Charge | Monthly Payment | Total Finance Charge |
| $ 100 | 9 | 10 | 5 | 19 | 4 | 29 | 3 | 40 |
| 500 | 46 | 48 | 25 | 96 | 18 | 146 | 15 | 198 |
| 1,000 | 91 | 97 | 50 | 193 | 36 | 292 | 29 | 397 |
| 1,500 | 137 | 145 | 75 | 289 | 54 | 439 | 44 | 595 |
| 2,000 | 183 | 194 | 99 | 386 | 72 | 585 | 58 | 794 |
| 2,500 | 229 | 242 | 124 | 482 | 90 | 731 | 73 | 992 |
| 3,000 | 274 | 290 | 149 | 578 | 108 | 877 | 87 | 1,190 |
| 3,500 | 320 | 339 | 174 | 675 | 126 | 1,023 | 102 | 1,389 |
| 4,000 | 366 | 387 | 199 | 771 | 144 | 1,170 | 116 | 1,587 |
| 4,500 | 411 | 436 | 224 | 868 | 162 | 1,316 | 131 | 1,885 |
| 5,000 | 457 | 484 | 249 | 964 | 180 | 1,462 | 146 | 1,984 |
| 5,500 | 503 | 532 | 273 | 1,060 | 197 | 1,608 | 160 | 2,182 |
| 6,000 | 548 | 581 | 298 | 1,157 | 215 | 1,754 | 175 | 2,381 |

### Table I
#### 18% Annual Percentage Rate

| Amount Financed | 1 YEAR | | 2 YEARS | | 3 YEARS | | 4 YEARS | |
|---|---|---|---|---|---|---|---|---|
| | Monthly Payment | Total Finance Charge | Monthly Payment | Total Finance Charge | Monthly Payment | Total Finance Charge | Monthly Payment | Total Finance Charge |
| $ 100 | 9 | 10 | 5 | 20 | 4 | 30 | 3 | 41 |
| 500 | 46 | 50 | 25 | 99 | 18 | 151 | 15 | 205 |
| 1,000 | 92 | 100 | 50 | 198 | 36 | 302 | 29 | 410 |
| 1,500 | 138 | 151 | 75 | 300 | 54 | 455 | 44 | 617 |
| 2,000 | 183 | 200 | 100 | 396 | 72 | 603 | 59 | 820 |
| 2,500 | 229 | 251 | 125 | 500 | 91 | 758 | 74 | 1,028 |
| 3,000 | 275 | 300 | 150 | 595 | 108 | 905 | 88 | 1,230 |
| 3,500 | 321 | 351 | 175 | 700 | 127 | 1,061 | 103 | 1,439 |
| 4,000 | 367 | 401 | 200 | 793 | 145 | 1,206 | 118 | 1,640 |
| 4,500 | 413 | 452 | 225 | 900 | 163 | 1,364 | 132 | 1,850 |
| 5,000 | 458 | 501 | 250 | 991 | 181 | 1,508 | 147 | 2,050 |
| 5,500 | 504 | 552 | 275 | 1,100 | 199 | 1,667 | 162 | 2,262 |
| 6,000 | 550 | 601 | 300 | 1,189 | 217 | 1,809 | 176 | 2,460 |

#### 18½% Annual Percentage Rate

| Amount Financed | 1 YEAR | | 2 YEARS | | 3 YEARS | | 4 YEARS | |
|---|---|---|---|---|---|---|---|---|
| | Monthly Payment | Total Finance Charge | Monthly Payment | Total Finance Charge | Monthly Payment | Total Finance Charge | Monthly Payment | Total Finance Charge |
| $ 100 | 9 | 10 | 5 | 20 | 4 | 31 | 3 | 42 |
| 500 | 46 | 51 | 25 | 102 | 18 | 155 | 15 | 210 |
| 1,000 | 92 | 103 | 50 | 205 | 36 | 310 | 30 | 421 |
| 1,500 | 138 | 154 | 75 | 307 | 55 | 466 | 44 | 631 |
| 2,000 | 184 | 206 | 100 | 410 | 73 | 621 | 59 | 842 |
| 2,500 | 230 | 257 | 126 | 512 | 91 | 776 | 74 | 1,052 |
| 3,000 | 276 | 308 | 151 | 614 | 109 | 931 | 89 | 1,262 |
| 3,500 | 322 | 360 | 176 | 717 | 127 | 1,086 | 104 | 1,473 |
| 4,000 | 368 | 411 | 201 | 819 | 146 | 1,242 | 118 | 1,683 |
| 4,500 | 414 | 463 | 226 | 922 | 164 | 1,397 | 133 | 1,894 |
| 5,000 | 460 | 514 | 251 | 1,024 | 182 | 1,552 | 148 | 2,104 |
| 5,500 | 505 | 565 | 276 | 1,126 | 200 | 1,707 | 163 | 2,314 |
| 6,000 | 551 | 617 | 301 | 1,229 | 218 | 1,862 | 178 | 2,525 |

### Table I
#### 19% Annual Percentage Rate

| Amount Financed | 1 YEAR | | 2 YEARS | | 3 YEARS | | 4 YEARS | |
|---|---|---|---|---|---|---|---|---|
| | Monthly Payment | Total Finance Charge | Monthly Payment | Total Finance Charge | Monthly Payment | Total Finance Charge | Monthly Payment | Total Finance Charge |
| $ 100 | 9 | 11 | 5 | 21 | 4 | 32 | 3 | 44 |
| 500 | 46 | 53 | 25 | 105 | 18 | 161 | 15 | 118 |
| 1,000 | 92 | 106 | 50 | 210 | 37 | 321 | 30 | 435 |
| 1,500 | 138 | 160 | 76 | 314 | 55 | 482 | 45 | 653 |
| 2,000 | 184 | 213 | 101 | 419 | 73 | 642 | 60 | 870 |
| 2,500 | 231 | 266 | 126 | 524 | 92 | 803 | 75 | 1,088 |
| 3,000 | 277 | 319 | 151 | 629 | 110 | 964 | 90 | 1,306 |
| 3,500 | 323 | 372 | 176 | 734 | 128 | 1,124 | 105 | 1,523 |
| 4,000 | 369 | 426 | 202 | 838 | 147 | 1,285 | 120 | 1,741 |
| 4,500 | 415 | 479 | 227 | 943 | 165 | 1,445 | 135 | 1,958 |
| 5,000 | 461 | 532 | 252 | 1,048 | 184 | 1,606 | 150 | 2,176 |
| 5,500 | 507 | 585 | 277 | 1,153 | 202 | 1,766 | 164 | 2,393 |
| 6,000 | 553 | 638 | 302 | 1,258 | 220 | 1,927 | 179 | 2,611 |

#### 19½% Annual Percentage Rate

| Amount Financed | 1 YEAR | | 2 YEARS | | 3 YEARS | | 4 YEARS | |
|---|---|---|---|---|---|---|---|---|
| | Monthly Payment | Total Finance Charge | Monthly Payment | Total Finance Charge | Monthly Payment | Total Finance Charge | Monthly Payment | Total Finance Charge |
| $ 100 | 9 | 11 | 5 | 22 | 4 | 33 | 3 | 45 |
| 500 | 46 | 54 | 25 | 108 | 18 | 164 | 15 | 225 |
| 1,000 | 92 | 109 | 51 | 217 | 37 | 328 | 30 | 450 |
| 1,500 | 139 | 163 | 76 | 325 | 55 | 493 | 45 | 674 |
| 2,000 | 185 | 218 | 101 | 434 | 74 | 657 | 60 | 899 |
| 2,500 | 231 | 272 | 127 | 542 | 92 | 821 | 76 | 1,124 |
| 3,000 | 277 | 326 | 152 | 650 | 111 | 985 | 91 | 1,349 |
| 3,500 | 323 | 381 | 177 | 759 | 129 | 1,149 | 106 | 1,574 |
| 4,000 | 370 | 435 | 203 | 867 | 148 | 1,314 | 121 | 1,798 |
| 4,500 | 416 | 490 | 228 | 976 | 166 | 1,478 | 136 | 2,023 |
| 5,000 | 462 | 544 | 254 | 1,084 | 185 | 1,642 | 151 | 2,248 |
| 5,500 | 508 | 598 | 279 | 1,192 | 203 | 1,806 | 166 | 2,473 |
| 6,000 | 554 | 653 | 304 | 1,301 | 221 | 1,970 | 181 | 2,698 |

## Table I
### 20% Annual Percentage Rate

| Amount Financed | 1 YEAR | | 2 YEARS | | 3 YEARS | | 4 YEARS | |
|---|---|---|---|---|---|---|---|---|
| | Monthly Payment | Total Finance Charge | Monthly Payment | Total Finance Charge | Monthly Payment | Total Finance Charge | Monthly Payment | Total Finance Charge |
| $ 100 | 9 | 11 | 6 | 22 | 4 | 34 | 3 | 46 |
| 500 | 46 | 56 | 25 | 111 | 19 | 170 | 15 | 230 |
| 1,000 | 93 | 111 | 51 | 222 | 37 | 339 | 30 | 459 |
| 1,500 | 139 | 167 | 76 | 332 | 56 | 509 | 46 | 689 |
| 2,000 | 185 | 222 | 102 | 443 | 74 | 678 | 61 | 918 |
| 2,500 | 232 | 278 | 127 | 554 | 93 | 848 | 76 | 1,148 |
| 3,000 | 278 | 334 | 153 | 665 | 112 | 1,018 | 91 | 1,378 |
| 3,500 | 324 | 389 | 178 | 776 | 130 | 1,187 | 106 | 1,607 |
| 4,000 | 370 | 445 | 204 | 886 | 149 | 1,357 | 122 | 1,837 |
| 4,500 | 417 | 500 | 229 | 997 | 167 | 1,526 | 137 | 2,066 |
| 5,000 | 463 | 556 | 255 | 1,108 | 186 | 1,696 | 152 | 2,296 |
| 5,500 | 509 | 612 | 280 | 1,219 | 205 | 1,866 | 167 | 2,526 |
| 6,000 | 556 | 667 | 305 | 1,330 | 223 | 2,035 | 182 | 2,755 |

## Table II
### 9% Annual Percentage Rate

| Amount Financed | 8 YEARS | | 10 YEARS | | 12 YEARS | | 15 YEARS | |
|---|---|---|---|---|---|---|---|---|
| | Monthly Payment | Total Finance Charge | Monthly Payment | Total Finance Charge | Monthly Payment | Total Finance Charge | Monthly Payment | Total Finance Charge |
| $ 100 | 1 | 41 | 1 | 52 | 1 | 64 | 1 | 84 |
| 1,000 | 15 | 407 | 13 | 520 | 11 | 640 | 10 | 827 |
| 5,000 | 73 | 2,033 | 63 | 2,601 | 57 | 3,195 | 51 | 4,130 |
| 10,000 | 147 | 4,065 | 127 | 5,202 | 114 | 6,389 | 101 | 8,257 |
| 15,000 | 220 | 6,097 | 190 | 7,802 | 171 | 9,582 | 152 | 12,385 |
| 20,000 | 293 | 8,129 | 253 | 10,403 | 228 | 12,776 | 203 | 16,515 |

### 9½% Annual Percentage Rate

| Amount Financed | 8 YEARS | | 10 YEARS | | 12 YEARS | | 15 YEARS | |
|---|---|---|---|---|---|---|---|---|
| | Monthly Payment | Total Finance Charge | Monthly Payment | Total Finance Charge | Monthly Payment | Total Finance Charge | Monthly Payment | Total Finance Charge |
| $ 100 | 2 | 44 | 1 | 56 | 1 | 68 | 1 | 89 |
| 1,000 | 15 | 432 | 13 | 553 | 12 | 680 | 10 | 881 |
| 5,000 | 75 | 2,158 | 65 | 2,764 | 58 | 3,398 | 52 | 4,400 |
| 10,000 | 149 | 4,315 | 129 | 5,528 | 117 | 6,796 | 104 | 8,797 |
| 15,000 | 224 | 6,472 | 194 | 8,292 | 175 | 10,194 | 157 | 13,195 |
| 20,000 | 298 | 8,629 | 259 | 11,056 | 233 | 13,592 | 209 | 17,593 |

### 10% Annual Percentage Rate

| Amount Financed | 8 YEARS | | 10 YEARS | | 12 YEARS | | 15 YEARS | |
|---|---|---|---|---|---|---|---|---|
| | Monthly Payment | Total Finance Charge | Monthly Payment | Total Finance Charge | Monthly Payment | Total Finance Charge | Monthly Payment | Total Finance Charge |
| $ 100 | 2 | 46 | 1 | 60 | 1 | 73 | 1 | 94 |
| 1,000 | 15 | 457 | 13 | 586 | 12 | 722 | 11 | 935 |
| 5,000 | 76 | 2,284 | 66 | 2,930 | 60 | 3,605 | 54 | 4,673 |
| 10,000 | 152 | 4,568 | 132 | 5,859 | 120 | 7,209 | 107 | 9,345 |
| 15,000 | 228 | 6,852 | 198 | 8,788 | 179 | 10,815 | 161 | 14,016 |
| 20,000 | 303 | 9,135 | 264 | 11,717 | 239 | 14,419 | 215 | 18,687 |

## Table II
### 10½% Annual Percentage Rate

| Amount Financed | 8 YEARS | | 10 YEARS | | 12 YEARS | | 15 YEARS | |
|---|---|---|---|---|---|---|---|---|
| | Monthly Payment | Total Finance Charge | Monthly Payment | Total Finance Charge | Monthly Payment | Total Finance Charge | Monthly Payment | Total Finance Charge |
| $ 100 | 2 | 49 | 1 | 62 | 1 | 77 | 1 | 100 |
| 1,000 | 15 | 483 | 14 | 620 | 12 | 764 | 11 | 991 |
| 5,000 | 77 | 2,412 | 67 | 3,098 | 61 | 3,814 | 55 | 4,949 |
| 10,000 | 154 | 4,823 | 135 | 6,193 | 122 | 7,628 | 111 | 9,897 |
| 15,000 | 232 | 7,235 | 202 | 9,289 | 184 | 11,443 | 166 | 14,846 |
| 20,000 | 309 | 9,646 | 270 | 12,384 | 245 | 15,256 | 221 | 19,794 |

### 11% Annual Percentage Rate

| Amount Financed | 8 YEARS | | 10 YEARS | | 12 YEARS | | 15 YEARS | |
|---|---|---|---|---|---|---|---|---|
| | Monthly Payment | Total Finance Charge | Monthly Payment | Total Finance Charge | Monthly Payment | Total Finance Charge | Monthly Payment | Total Finance Charge |
| $ 100 | 2 | 52 | 1 | 66 | 1 | 81 | 1 | 105 |
| 1,000 | 16 | 508 | 14 | 654 | 13 | 806 | 11 | 1,047 |
| 5,000 | 79 | 2,541 | 69 | 3,266 | 63 | 4,026 | 57 | 5,229 |
| 10,000 | 157 | 5,081 | 138 | 6,531 | 125 | 8,052 | 114 | 10,459 |
| 15,000 | 236 | 7,620 | 207 | 9,796 | 188 | 12,078 | 170 | 15,688 |
| 20,000 | 314 | 10,160 | 276 | 13,061 | 251 | 16,104 | 227 | 20,918 |

### 11½% Annual Percentage Rate

| Amount Financed | 8 YEARS | | 10 YEARS | | 12 YEARS | | 15 YEARS | |
|---|---|---|---|---|---|---|---|---|
| | Monthly Payment | Total Finance Charge | Monthly Payment | Total Finance Charge | Monthly Payment | Total Finance Charge | Monthly Payment | Total Finance Charge |
| $ 100 | 2 | 54 | 1 | 69 | 1 | 86 | 1 | 111 |
| 1,000 | 16 | 534 | 14 | 687 | 13 | 849 | 12 | 1,104 |
| 5,000 | 80 | 2,670 | 70 | 3,436 | 64 | 4,240 | 58 | 5,514 |
| 10,000 | 160 | 5,341 | 141 | 6,872 | 128 | 8,481 | 117 | 11,028 |
| 15,000 | 240 | 8,011 | 211 | 10,308 | 193 | 12,720 | 175 | 16,541 |
| 20,000 | 320 | 10,681 | 281 | 13,744 | 257 | 16,960 | 234 | 22,055 |

## Table II

### 12% Annual Percentage Rate

| Amount Financed | 8 YEARS Monthly Payment | 8 YEARS Total Finance Charge | 10 YEARS Monthly Payment | 10 YEARS Total Finance Charge | 12 YEARS Monthly Payment | 12 YEARS Total Finance Charge | 15 YEARS Monthly Payment | 15 YEARS Total Finance Charge |
|---|---|---|---|---|---|---|---|---|
| $ 100 | 2 | 56 | 1 | 73 | 1 | 90 | 1 | 118 |
| 1,000 | 16 | 561 | 14 | 722 | 13 | 892 | 12 | 1,162 |
| 5,000 | 81 | 2,802 | 72 | 3,609 | 66 | 4,458 | 60 | 5,802 |
| 10,000 | 163 | 5,603 | 143 | 7,218 | 131 | 8,914 | 120 | 11,604 |
| 15,000 | 244 | 8,405 | 215 | 10,825 | 197 | 13,371 | 180 | 17,405 |
| 20,000 | 325 | 11,206 | 287 | 14,434 | 263 | 17,827 | 240 | 23,207 |

### 12½% Annual Percentage Rate

| Amount Financed | 8 YEARS Monthly Payment | 8 YEARS Total Finance Charge | 10 YEARS Monthly Payment | 10 YEARS Total Finance Charge | 12 YEARS Monthly Payment | 12 YEARS Total Finance Charge | 15 YEARS Monthly Payment | 15 YEARS Total Finance Charge |
|---|---|---|---|---|---|---|---|---|
| $ 100 | 2 | 59 | 1 | 76 | 1 | 94 | 1 | 123 |
| 1,000 | 17 | 587 | 15 | 757 | 13 | 936 | 12 | 1,219 |
| 5,000 | 83 | 2,934 | 73 | 3,783 | 67 | 4,677 | 62 | 6,093 |
| 10,000 | 165 | 5,868 | 146 | 7,566 | 134 | 9,352 | 123 | 12,187 |
| 15,000 | 248 | 8,802 | 220 | 11,348 | 202 | 14,028 | 185 | 18,278 |
| 20,000 | 331 | 11,736 | 293 | 15,131 | 269 | 18,704 | 247 | 24,372 |

### 13% Annual Percentage Rate

| Amount Financed | 8 YEARS Monthly Payment | 8 YEARS Total Finance Charge | 10 YEARS Monthly Payment | 10 YEARS Total Finance Charge | 12 YEARS Monthly Payment | 12 YEARS Total Finance Charge | 15 YEARS Monthly Payment | 15 YEARS Total Finance Charge |
|---|---|---|---|---|---|---|---|---|
| $ 100 | 2 | 62 | 2 | 80 | 1 | 99 | 1 | 129 |
| 1,000 | 17 | 614 | 15 | 793 | 14 | 980 | 13 | 1,279 |
| 5,000 | 84 | 3,068 | 75 | 3,959 | 69 | 4,899 | 63 | 6,389 |
| 10,000 | 168 | 6,136 | 149 | 7,918 | 137 | 9,796 | 127 | 12,775 |
| 15,000 | 252 | 9,203 | 224 | 11,876 | 206 | 14,693 | 190 | 19,162 |
| 20,000 | 336 | 12,270 | 299 | 15,836 | 275 | 19,590 | 253 | 25,549 |

## Table II

### 13½% Annual Percentage Rate

| Amount Financed | 8 YEARS Monthly Payment | 8 YEARS Total Finance Charge | 10 YEARS Monthly Payment | 10 YEARS Total Finance Charge | 12 YEARS Monthly Payment | 12 YEARS Total Finance Charge | 15 YEARS Monthly Payment | 15 YEARS Total Finance Charge |
|---|---|---|---|---|---|---|---|---|
| $ 100 | 2 | 64 | 2 | 84 | 1 | 103 | 1 | 134 |
| 1,000 | 17 | 641 | 15 | 828 | 14 | 1,025 | 13 | 1,338 |
| 5,000 | 85 | 3,203 | 76 | 4,137 | 70 | 5,122 | 65 | 6,686 |
| 10,000 | 171 | 6,405 | 152 | 8,274 | 141 | 10,244 | 130 | 13,371 |
| 15,000 | 256 | 9,608 | 228 | 12,410 | 211 | 15,364 | 195 | 20,055 |
| 20,000 | 342 | 12,810 | 305 | 16,546 | 281 | 20,486 | 260 | 26,741 |

### 14% Annual Percentage Rate

| Amount Financed | 8 YEARS Monthly Payment | 8 YEARS Total Finance Charge | 10 YEARS Monthly Payment | 10 YEARS Total Finance Charge | 12 YEARS Monthly Payment | 12 YEARS Total Finance Charge | 15 YEARS Monthly Payment | 15 YEARS Total Finance Charge |
|---|---|---|---|---|---|---|---|---|
| $ 100 | 2 | 67 | 2 | 87 | 1 | 107 | 1 | 141 |
| 1,000 | 17 | 668 | 16 | 864 | 14 | 1,071 | 13 | 1,398 |
| 5,000 | 87 | 3,339 | 78 | 4,317 | 72 | 5,348 | 67 | 6,986 |
| 10,000 | 174 | 6,677 | 155 | 8,632 | 144 | 10,696 | 133 | 13,972 |
| 15,000 | 261 | 10,016 | 233 | 12,948 | 216 | 16,042 | 200 | 20,959 |
| 20,000 | 347 | 13,354 | 311 | 17,265 | 287 | 21,390 | 266 | 27,943 |

### 14½% Annual Percentage Rate

| Amount Financed | 8 YEARS Monthly Payment | 8 YEARS Total Finance Charge | 10 YEARS Monthly Payment | 10 YEARS Total Finance Charge | 12 YEARS Monthly Payment | 12 YEARS Total Finance Charge | 15 YEARS Monthly Payment | 15 YEARS Total Finance Charge |
|---|---|---|---|---|---|---|---|---|
| $ 100 | 2 | 70 | 2 | 91 | 1 | 112 | 1 | 147 |
| 1,000 | 18 | 695 | 16 | 900 | 15 | 1,115 | 14 | 1,459 |
| 5,000 | 88 | 3,476 | 79 | 4,498 | 73 | 5,577 | 68 | 7,290 |
| 10,000 | 177 | 6,952 | 158 | 8,995 | 147 | 11,152 | 137 | 14,581 |
| 15,000 | 265 | 10,427 | 237 | 13,493 | 220 | 16,728 | 205 | 21,869 |
| 20,000 | 353 | 13,902 | 317 | 17,990 | 294 | 22,303 | 273 | 29,160 |

## Table II

### 15% Annual Percentage Rate

| Amount Financed | 8 YEARS | | 10 YEARS | | 12 YEARS | | 15 YEARS | |
|---|---|---|---|---|---|---|---|---|
| | Monthly Payment | Total Finance Charge | Monthly Payment | Total Finance Charge | Monthly Payment | Total Finance Charge | Monthly Payment | Total Finance Charge |
| $ 100 | 2 | 73 | 2 | 94 | 1 | 117 | 1 | 152 |
| 1,000 | 18 | 723 | 16 | 937 | 15 | 1,161 | 14 | 1,520 |
| 5,000 | 90 | 3,614 | 81 | 4,680 | 75 | 5,807 | 70 | 7,596 |
| 10,000 | 179 | 7,228 | 161 | 9,361 | 150 | 11,613 | 140 | 15,193 |
| 15,000 | 269 | 10,842 | 242 | 14,041 | 225 | 17,420 | 210 | 22,789 |
| 20,000 | 359 | 14,455 | 323 | 18,720 | 300 | 23,226 | 280 | 30,386 |

### 15½% Annual Percentage Rate

| Amount Financed | 8 YEARS | | 10 YEARS | | 12 YEARS | | 15 YEARS | |
|---|---|---|---|---|---|---|---|---|
| | Monthly Payment | Total Finance Charge | Monthly Payment | Total Finance Charge | Monthly Payment | Total Finance Charge | Monthly Payment | Total Finance Charge |
| $ 100 | 2 | 76 | 2 | 98 | 2 | 122 | 1 | 159 |
| 1,000 | 18 | 751 | 16 | 974 | 15 | 1,209 | 14 | 1,581 |
| 5,000 | 91 | 3,753 | 82 | 4,865 | 77 | 6,040 | 72 | 7,906 |
| 10,000 | 182 | 7,507 | 164 | 9,730 | 153 | 12,080 | 143 | 15,812 |
| 15,000 | 274 | 11,260 | 247 | 14,594 | 230 | 18,119 | 215 | 23,718 |
| 20,000 | 365 | 15,013 | 329 | 19,460 | 307 | 24,158 | 287 | 31,624 |

### 16% Annual Percentage Rate

| Amount Financed | 8 YEARS | | 10 YEARS | | 12 YEARS | | 15 YEARS | |
|---|---|---|---|---|---|---|---|---|
| | Monthly Payment | Total Finance Charge | Monthly Payment | Total Finance Charge | Monthly Payment | Total Finance Charge | Monthly Payment | Total Finance Charge |
| $ 100 | 2 | 79 | 2 | 102 | 2 | 126 | 1 | 165 |
| 1,000 | 19 | 779 | 17 | 1,011 | 16 | 1,255 | 15 | 1,644 |
| 5,000 | 93 | 3,894 | 84 | 5,051 | 78 | 6,275 | 73 | 8,219 |
| 10,000 | 185 | 7,788 | 168 | 10,102 | 157 | 12,549 | 147 | 16,438 |
| 15,000 | 278 | 11,682 | 251 | 15,152 | 235 | 18,823 | 220 | 24,656 |
| 20,000 | 371 | 15,576 | 335 | 20,204 | 313 | 25,096 | 294 | 32,875 |

## Table II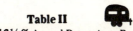

### 16½% Annual Percentage Rate

| Amount Financed | 8 YEARS | | 10 YEARS | | 12 YEARS | | 15 YEARS | |
|---|---|---|---|---|---|---|---|---|
| | Monthly Payment | Total Finance Charge | Monthly Payment | Total Finance Charge | Monthly Payment | Total Finance Charge | Monthly Payment | Total Finance Charge |
| $ 100 | 2 | 81 | 2 | 105 | 2 | 130 | 2 | 171 |
| 1,000 | 19 | 807 | 17 | 1,048 | 16 | 1,302 | 15 | 1,707 |
| 5,000 | 94 | 4,036 | 85 | 5,239 | 80 | 6,511 | 75 | 8,534 |
| 10,000 | 188 | 8,071 | 171 | 10,477 | 160 | 13,022 | 150 | 17,067 |
| 15,000 | 282 | 12,107 | 256 | 15,716 | 240 | 19,533 | 226 | 25,601 |
| 20,000 | 376 | 16,142 | 341 | 20,954 | 320 | 26,044 | 301 | 34,134 |

### 17% Annual Percentage Rate

| Amount Financed | 8 YEARS | | 10 YEARS | | 12 YEARS | | 15 YEARS | |
|---|---|---|---|---|---|---|---|---|
| | Monthly Payment | Total Finance Charge | Monthly Payment | Total Finance Charge | Monthly Payment | Total Finance Charge | Monthly Payment | Total Finance Charge |
| $ 100 | 2 | 84 | 2 | 109 | 2 | 136 | 2 | 177 |
| 1,000 | 19 | 836 | 17 | 1,086 | 16 | 1,350 | 15 | 1,772 |
| 5,000 | 96 | 4,179 | 87 | 5,428 | 82 | 6,750 | 77 | 8,853 |
| 10,000 | 191 | 8,357 | 174 | 10,856 | 163 | 13,501 | 154 | 17,704 |
| 15,000 | 287 | 12,536 | 261 | 16,284 | 245 | 20,250 | 231 | 26,555 |
| 20,000 | 382 | 16,713 | 348 | 21,712 | 326 | 27,000 | 308 | 35,406 |

### 17½% Annual Percentage Rate

| Amount Financed | 8 YEARS | | 10 YEARS | | 12 YEARS | | 15 YEARS | |
|---|---|---|---|---|---|---|---|---|
| | Monthly Payment | Total Finance Charge | Monthly Payment | Total Finance Charge | Monthly Payment | Total Finance Charge | Monthly Payment | Total Finance Charge |
| $ 100 | 2 | 86 | 2 | 112 | 2 | 140 | 2 | 183 |
| 1,000 | 19 | 864 | 18 | 1,123 | 17 | 1,398 | 16 | 1,834 |
| 5,000 | 97 | 4,322 | 88 | 5,619 | 83 | 6,991 | 79 | 9,171 |
| 10,000 | 194 | 8,644 | 177 | 11,237 | 167 | 13,982 | 157 | 18,342 |
| 15,000 | 291 | 12,966 | 265 | 16,856 | 250 | 20,972 | 236 | 27,513 |
| 20,000 | 388 | 17,288 | 354 | 22,474 | 333 | 27,964 | 315 | 36,684 |

## Table II

### 18% Annual Percentage Rate

| Amount Financed | 8 YEARS | | 10 YEARS | | 12 YEARS | | 15 YEARS | |
|---|---|---|---|---|---|---|---|---|
| | Monthly Payment | Total Finance Charge | Monthly Payment | Total Finance Charge | Monthly Payment | Total Finance Charge | Monthly Payment | Total Finance Charge |
| $ 100 | 2 | 90 | 2 | 117 | 2 | 145 | 2 | 192 |
| 1,000 | 20 | 893 | 18 | 1,162 | 17 | 1,446 | 16 | 1,900 |
| 5,000 | 98 | 4,468 | 90 | 5,812 | 85 | 7,234 | 81 | 9,495 |
| 10,000 | .197 | 8,935 | 180 | 11,623 | 170 | 14,468 | 161 | 18,989 |
| 15,000 | 296 | 13,402 | 270 | 17,434 | 255 | 21,701 | 242 | 28,483 |
| 20,000 | 394 | 17,869 | 360 | 23,246 | 340 | 28,936 | 322 | 37,976 |

### Table III

#### 6% Annual Percentage Rate

| Amount Financed | 15 YEARS | | 20 YEARS | | 25 YEARS | | 30 YEARS | |
|---|---|---|---|---|---|---|---|---|
| | Monthly Payment | Total Finance Charge | Monthly Payment | Total Finance Charge | Monthly Payment | Total Finance Charge | Monthly Payment | Total Finance Charge |
| $1,000 | 8 | 519 | 7 | 721 | 6 | 935 | 6 | 1,160 |
| 10,000 | 84 | 5,190 | 72 | 7,196 | 64 | 9,332 | 60 | 11,586 |
| 15,000 | 127 | 7,784 | 107 | 10,793 | 97 | 13,995 | 90 | 17,378 |
| 20,000 | 169 | 10,380 | 143 | 14,390 | 129 | 18,661 | 120 | 23,171 |
| 25,000 | 211 | 12,975 | 179 | 17,986 | 161 | 23,324 | 150 | 28,960 |
| 30,000 | 253 | 15,569 | 215 | 21,583 | 193 | 27,990 | 180 | 34,753 |
| 35,000 | 295 | 18,163 | 251 | 25,182 | 226 | 32,653 | 210 | 40,546 |
| 40,000 | 338 | 20,759 | 287 | 28,779 | 258 | 37,319 | 240 | 46,339 |
| 45,000 | 380 | 23,353 | 322 | 32,376 | 290 | 41,982 | 270 | 52,128 |
| 50,000 | 422 | 25,947 | 358 | 35,973 | 322 | 46,648 | 300 | 57,921 |

#### 6½% Annual Percentage Rate

| Amount Financed | 15 YEARS | | 20 YEARS | | 25 YEARS | | 30 YEARS | |
|---|---|---|---|---|---|---|---|---|
| | Monthly Payment | Total Finance Charge | Monthly Payment | Total Finance Charge | Monthly Payment | Total Finance Charge | Monthly Payment | Total Finance Charge |
| $1,000 | 9 | 570 | 7 | 790 | 7 | 1,028 | 6 | 1,279 |
| 10,000 | 87 | 5,682 | 75 | 7,894 | 68 | 10,259 | 63 | 12,756 |
| 15,000 | 131 | 8,521 | 112 | 11,842 | 101 | 15,387 | 95 | 19,135 |
| 20,000 | 174 | 11,361 | 149 | 15,789 | 135 | 20,515 | 126 | 25,511 |
| 25,000 | 218 | 14,200 | 186 | 19,736 | 169 | 25,643 | 158 | 31,887 |
| 30,000 | 261 | 17,041 | 224 | 23,683 | 203 | 30,771 | 190 | 38,266 |
| 35,000 | 305 | 19,880 | 261 | 27,630 | 236 | 35,899 | 221 | 44,643 |
| 40,000 | 348 | 22,721 | 298 | 31,575 | 270 | 41,027 | 253 | 51,019 |
| 45,000 | 392 | 25,560 | 336 | 35,522 | 304 | 46,167 | 284 | 57,398 |
| 50,000 | 436 | 28,401 | 373 | 39,470 | 338 | 51,283 | 316 | 63,774 |

### Table III

#### 7% Annual Percentage Rate

| Amount Financed | 15 YEARS | | 20 YEARS | | 25 YEARS | | 30 YEARS | |
|---|---|---|---|---|---|---|---|---|
| | Monthly Payment | Total Finance Charge | Monthly Payment | Total Finance Charge | Monthly Payment | Total Finance Charge | Monthly Payment | Total Finance Charge |
| $1,000 | 9 | 618 | 8 | 862 | 7 | 1,121 | 7 | 1,398 |
| 10,000 | 90 | 6,180 | 78 | 8,607 | 71 | 11,204 | 67 | 13,954 |
| 15,000 | 135 | 9,269 | 116 | 12,912 | 106 | 16,806 | 100 | 20,928 |
| 20,000 | 180 | 12,359 | 155 | 17,214 | 141 | 22,408 | 133 | 27,905 |
| 25,000 | 225 | 15,448 | 194 | 21,519 | 177 | 28,010 | 166 | 34,879 |
| 30,000 | 270 | 18,537 | 233 | 25,822 | 212 | 33,612 | 200 | 41,856 |
| 35,000 | 315 | 21,626 | 271 | 30,126 | 247 | 39,214 | 233 | 48,830 |
| 40,000 | 360 | 24,717 | 310 | 34,428 | 283 | 44,816 | 266 | 55,807 |
| 45,000 | 404 | 27,806 | 349 | 38,734 | 318 | 50,418 | 299 | 62,780 |
| 50,000 | 449 | 30,896 | 388 | 43,036 | 353 | 56,017 | 333 | 69,758 |

#### 7½% Annual Percentage Rate

| Amount Financed | 15 YEARS | | 20 YEARS | | 25 YEARS | | 30 YEARS | |
|---|---|---|---|---|---|---|---|---|
| | Monthly Payment | Total Finance Charge | Monthly Payment | Total Finance Charge | Monthly Payment | Total Finance Charge | Monthly Payment | Total Finance Charge |
| $1,000 | 9 | 670 | 8 | 934 | 7 | 1,217 | 7 | 1,520 |
| 10,000 | 93 | 6,688 | 81 | 9,334 | 74 | 12,170 | 70 | 15,175 |
| 15,000 | 139 | 10,031 | 121 | 14,002 | 111 | 18,255 | 105 | 22,760 |
| 20,000 | 185 | 13,374 | 161 | 18,669 | 148 | 24,340 | 140 | 30,346 |
| 25,000 | 232 | 16,717 | 201 | 23,336 | 185 | 30,425 | 175 | 37,932 |
| 30,000 | 278 | 20,060 | 242 | 28,003 | 222 | 36,510 | 210 | 45,517 |
| 35,000 | 324 | 23,403 | 282 | 32,670 | 259 | 42,595 | 245 | 53,103 |
| 40,000 | 371 | 26,746 | 322 | 37,338 | 296 | 48,680 | 280 | 60,688 |
| 45,000 | 417 | 30,089 | 363 | 42,005 | 333 | 54,765 | 315 | 68,274 |
| 50,000 | 464 | 33,432 | 403 | 46,672 | 370 | 60,350 | 350 | 75,860 |

## Table III

### 8% Annual Percentage Rate

| Amount Financed | 15 YEARS Monthly Payment | Total Finance Charge | 20 YEARS Monthly Payment | Total Finance Charge | 25 YEARS Monthly Payment | Total Finance Charge | 30 YEARS Monthly Payment | Total Finance Charge |
|---|---|---|---|---|---|---|---|---|
| $1,000 | 10 | 721 | 8 | 1,009 | 8 | 1,316 | 7 | 1,642 |
| 10,000 | 96 | 7,203 | 84 | 10,076 | 77 | 13,157 | 73 | 16,417 |
| 15,000 | 143 | 10,803 | 125 | 15,113 | 116 | 19,734 | 110 | 24,625 |
| 20,000 | 191 | 14,405 | 167 | 20,150 | 154 | 26,311 | 147 | 32,834 |
| 25,000 | 239 | 18,006 | 209 | 25,189 | 193 | 32,888 | 183 | 41,042 |
| 30,000 | 287 | 21,606 | 251 | 30,226 | 232 | 39,465 | 220 | 49,247 |
| 35,000 | 334 | 25,206 | 293 | 35,262 | 270 | 46,042 | 257 | 57,455 |
| 40,000 | 382 | 28,809 | 335 | 40,299 | 309 | 52,619 | 294 | 65,664 |
| 45,000 | 430 | 32,409 | 376 | 45,336 | 347 | 59,196 | 330 | 73,872 |
| 50,000 | 478 | 36,009 | 418 | 50,375 | 386 | 65,773 | 367 | 82,080 |

### 8½% Annual Percentage Rate

| Amount Financed | 15 YEARS Monthly Payment | Total Finance Charge | 20 YEARS Monthly Payment | Total Finance Charge | 25 YEARS Monthly Payment | Total Finance Charge | 30 YEARS Monthly Payment | Total Finance Charge |
|---|---|---|---|---|---|---|---|---|
| $1,000 | 10 | 773 | 9 | 1,083 | 8 | 1,418 | 8 | 1,768 |
| 10,000 | 98 | 7,726 | 87 | 10,830 | 81 | 14,159 | 77 | 17,684 |
| 15,000 | 148 | 11,590 | 130 | 16,243 | 121 | 21,237 | 115 | 26,522 |
| 20,000 | 197 | 15,451 | 174 | 21,657 | 161 | 28,315 | 154 | 35,364 |
| 25,000 | 246 | 19,314 | 217 | 27,070 | 201 | 35,393 | 192 | 44,203 |
| 30,000 | 295 | 23,177 | 260 | 32,484 | 242 | 42,477 | 231 | 53,045 |
| 35,000 | 345 | 27,039 | 304 | 37,898 | 282 | 49,558 | 269 | 61,883 |
| 40,000 | 394 | 30,902 | 347 | 43,311 | 322 | 56,636 | 308 | 70,725 |
| 45,000 | 443 | 34,765 | 391 | 48,727 | 362 | 63,717 | 346 | 79,567 |
| 50,000 | 492 | 38,627 | 434 | 54,141 | 403 | 70,795 | 384 | 88,406 |

## Table III

### 9% Annual Percentage Rate

| Amount Financed | 15 YEARS Monthly Payment | Total Finance Charge | 20 YEARS Monthly Payment | Total Finance Charge | 25 YEARS Monthly Payment | Total Finance Charge | 30 YEARS Monthly Payment | Total Finance Charge |
|---|---|---|---|---|---|---|---|---|
| $1,000 | 10 | 827 | 9 | 1,160 | 8 | 1,520 | 8 | 1,898 |
| 10,000 | 101 | 8,257 | 90 | 11,595 | 84 | 15,176 | 80 | 18,969 |
| 15,000 | 152 | 12,385 | 135 | 17,390 | 126 | 22,764 | 121 | 28,452 |
| 20,000 | 203 | 16,515 | 180 | 23,188 | 168 | 30,352 | 161 | 37,935 |
| 25,000 | 254 | 20,643 | 225 | 28,986 | 210 | 37,940 | 201 | 47,418 |
| 30,000 | 304 | 24,770 | 270 | 34,781 | 252 | 45,528 | 241 | 56,900 |
| 35,000 | 355 | 28,900 | 315 | 40,578 | 294 | 53,116 | 282 | 66,383 |
| 40,000 | 406 | 33,028 | 360 | 46,376 | 336 | 60,704 | 322 | 75,866 |
| 45,000 | 456 | 37,156 | 405 | 52,171 | 378 | 68,292 | 362 | 85,352 |
| 50,000 | 507 | 41,285 | 450 | 57,969 | 420 | 75,880 | 402 | 94,835 |

### 9½% Annual Percentage Rate

| Amount Financed | 15 YEARS Monthly Payment | Total Finance Charge | 20 YEARS Monthly Payment | Total Finance Charge | 25 YEARS Monthly Payment | Total Finance Charge | 30 YEARS Monthly Payment | Total Finance Charge |
|---|---|---|---|---|---|---|---|---|
| $1,000 | 10 | 881 | 9 | 1,239 | 9 | 1,622 | 8 | 2,028 |
| 10,000 | 104 | 8,797 | 93 | 12,373 | 87 | 16,211 | 84 | 20,272 |
| 15,000 | 157 | 13,195 | 140 | 18,557 | 131 | 24,318 | 126 | 30,407 |
| 20,000 | 209 | 17,593 | 186 | 24,743 | 175 | 32,422 | 168 | 40,545 |
| 25,000 | 261 | 21,991 | 233 | 30,930 | 218 | 40,529 | 210 | 50,679 |
| 30,000 | 313 | 26,389 | 280 | 37,114 | 262 | 48,633 | 252 | 60,814 |
| 35,000 | 365 | 30,786 | 326 | 43,300 | 306 | 56,740 | 294 | 70,948 |
| 40,000 | 418 | 35,184 | 373 | 49,486 | 349 | 64,844 | 336 | 81,086 |
| 45,000 | 470 | 39,584 | 419 | 55,670 | 393 | 72,951 | 378 | 91,220 |
| 50,000 | 522 | 43,982 | 466 | 61,857 | 437 | 81,055 | 420 | 101,355 |

## Table III

### 10% Annual Percentage Rate

| Amount Financed | 15 YEARS | | 20 YEARS | | 25 YEARS | | 30 YEARS | |
|---|---|---|---|---|---|---|---|---|
| | Monthly Payment | Total Finance Charge | Monthly Payment | Total Finance Charge | Monthly Payment | Total Finance Charge | Monthly Payment | Total Finance Charge |
| $1,000 | 11 | 935 | 10 | 1,318 | 9 | 1,727 | 9 | 2,161 |
| 10,000 | 107 | 9,345 | 97 | 13,162 | 91 | 17,264 | 88 | 21,594 |
| 15,000 | 161 | 14,016 | 145 | 19,742 | 136 | 25,893 | 132 | 32,390 |
| 20,000 | 215 | 18,687 | 193 | 26,322 | 182 | 34,525 | 176 | 43,187 |
| 25,000 | 269 | 23,359 | 241 | 32,902 | 227 | 43,154 | 219 | 53,984 |
| 30,000 | 322 | 28,030 | 290 | 39,482 | 273 | 51,786 | 263 | 64,781 |
| 35,000 | 376 | 32,702 | 338 | 46,062 | 318 | 60,415 | 307 | 75,578 |
| 40,000 | 430 | 37,373 | 386 | 52,642 | 363 | 69,047 | 351 | 86,371 |
| 45,000 | 484 | 42,044 | 434 | 59,222 | 409 | 77,676 | 395 | 97,168 |
| 50,000 | 537 | 46,716 | 483 | 65,805 | 454 | 86,308 | 439 | 107,964 |

### 10½% Annual Percentage Rate

| Amount Financed | 15 YEARS | | 20 YEARS | | 25 YEARS | | 30 YEARS | |
|---|---|---|---|---|---|---|---|---|
| | Monthly Payment | Total Finance Charge | Monthly Payment | Total Finance Charge | Monthly Payment | Total Finance Charge | Monthly Payment | Total Finance Charge |
| $1,000 | 11 | 989 | 10 | 1,395 | 9 | 1,832 | 9 | 2,294 |
| 10,000 | 111 | 9,890 | 100 | 13,952 | 94 | 18,320 | 92 | 12,940 |
| 15,000 | 166 | 14,835 | 150 | 20,928 | 142 | 27,480 | 137 | 34,410 |
| 20,000 | 221 | 19,780 | 200 | 27,904 | 189 | 36,640 | 183 | 45,880 |
| 25,000 | 276 | 24,725 | 250 | 34,880 | 236 | 45,800 | 229 | 57,350 |
| 30,000 | 332 | 29,670 | 300 | 41,856 | 283 | 54,960 | 275 | 68,820 |
| 35,000 | 387 | 34,615 | 349 | 48,832 | 330 | 64,120 | 320 | 80,290 |
| 40,000 | 442 | 39,560 | 399 | 55,808 | 378 | 73,280 | 366 | 91,760 |
| 45,000 | 497 | 44,505 | 449 | 62,784 | 425 | 82,440 | 412 | 103,230 |
| 50,000 | 553 | 49,450 | 499 | 69,760 | 472 | 91,600 | 458 | 114,700 |

## Table III

### 11% Annual Percentage Rate

| Amount Financed | 15 YEARS | | 20 YEARS | | 25 YEARS | | 30 YEARS | |
|---|---|---|---|---|---|---|---|---|
| | Monthly Payment | Total Finance Charge | Monthly Payment | Total Finance Charge | Monthly Payment | Total Finance Charge | Monthly Payment | Total Finance Charge |
| $1,000 | 11 | 1,046 | 10 | 1,479 | 10 | 1,943 | 10 | 2,431 |
| 10,000 | 114 | 10,459 | 103 | 14,773 | 98 | 19,403 | 95 | 24,286 |
| 15,000 | 170 | 15,688 | 155 | 22,159 | 147 | 29,105 | 143 | 36,426 |
| 20,000 | 227 | 20,918 | 206 | 29,546 | 196 | 38,806 | 190 | 48,569 |
| 25,000 | 284 | 26,147 | 258 | 36,932 | 245 | 48,508 | 238 | 60,712 |
| 30,000 | 341 | 31,376 | 310 | 44,318 | 294 | 58,209 | 286 | 72,852 |
| 35,000 | 398 | 36,606 | 361 | 51,705 | 343 | 67,911 | 333 | 84,995 |
| 40,000 | 455 | 41,835 | 413 | 59,092 | 392 | 77,612 | 381 | 97,135 |
| 45,000 | 511 | 47,065 | 464 | 66,478 | 441 | 87,314 | 429 | 109,278 |
| 50,000 | 568 | 52,294 | 516 | 73,864 | 490 | 97,016 | 476 | 121,421 |

### 11½% Annual Percentage Rate

| Amount Financed | 15 YEARS | | 20 YEARS | | 25 YEARS | | 30 YEARS | |
|---|---|---|---|---|---|---|---|---|
| | Monthly Payment | Total Finance Charge | Monthly Payment | Total Finance Charge | Monthly Payment | Total Finance Charge | Monthly Payment | Total Finance Charge |
| $1,000 | 12 | 1,104 | 11 | 1,559 | 10 | 2,050 | 10 | 2,568 |
| 10,000 | 117 | 11,028 | 107 | 15,594 | 102 | 20,495 | 99 | 25,651 |
| 15,000 | 175 | 16,541 | 160 | 23,391 | 152 | 30,744 | 149 | 38,478 |
| 20,000 | 234 | 22,056 | 213 | 31,188 | 203 | 40,990 | 198 | 51,302 |
| 25,000 | 292 | 27,568 | 267 | 38,986 | 254 | 51,236 | 248 | 64,125 |
| 30,000 | 350 | 33,083 | 320 | 46,782 | 305 | 61,485 | 297 | 76,952 |
| 35,000 | 409 | 38,595 | 373 | 54,579 | 356 | 71,731 | 347 | 89,780 |
| 40,000 | 467 | 44,110 | 427 | 62,379 | 407 | 81,977 | 396 | 102,603 |
| 45,000 | 526 | 49,622 | 480 | 70,173 | 457 | 92,226 | 446 | 115,425 |
| 50,000 | 584 | 55,135 | 533 | 77,970 | 508 | 102,470 | 495 | 128,250 |

### Table III

#### 12% Annual Percentage Rate

| Amount Financed | 15 YEARS | | 20 YEARS | | 25 YEARS | | 30 YEARS | |
|---|---|---|---|---|---|---|---|---|
| | Monthly Payment | Total Finance Charge | Monthly Payment | Total Finance Charge | Monthly Payment | Total Finance Charge | Monthly Payment | Total Finance Charge |
| $1,000 | 12 | 1,160 | 11 | 1,643 | 11 | 2,159 | 10 | 2,704 |
| 10,000 | 120 | 11,604 | 110 | 16,426 | 105 | 21,599 | 103 | 27,030 |
| 15,000 | 180 | 17,405 | 165 | 24,641 | 158 | 32,397 | 154 | 40,548 |
| 20,000 | 240 | 23,207 | 220 | 32,853 | 211 | 43,195 | 206 | 54,063 |
| 25,000 | 300 | 29,008 | 275 | 41,067 | 263 | 53,993 | 257 | 67,578 |
| 30,000 | 360 | 34,810 | 330 | 49,279 | 316 | 64,791 | 309 | 81,092 |
| 35,000 | 420 | 40,611 | 385 | 57,494 | 369 | 75,589 | 360 | 94,607 |
| 40,000 | 480 | 46,413 | 440 | 65,706 | 421 | 86,387 | 411 | 108,122 |
| 45,000 | 540 | 52,211 | 495 | 73,918 | 474 | 97,188 | 463 | 121,630 |
| 50,000 | 600 | 58,016 | 551 | 82,132 | 527 | 107,986 | 514 | 135,150 |

#### 12½% Annual Percentage Rate

| Amount Financed | 15 YEARS | | 20 YEARS | | 25 YEARS | | 30 YEARS | |
|---|---|---|---|---|---|---|---|---|
| | Monthly Payment | Total Finance Charge | Monthly Payment | Total Finance Charge | Monthly Payment | Total Finance Charge | Monthly Payment | Total Finance Charge |
| $1,000 | 12 | 1,219 | 11 | 1,729 | 11 | 2,271 | 11 | 2,842 |
| 10,000 | 123 | 12,187 | 114 | 17,269 | 109 | 22,712 | 107 | 28,423 |
| 15,000 | 185 | 18,278 | 170 | 25,903 | 164 | 34,068 | 160 | 42,632 |
| 20,000 | 247 | 24,372 | 227 | 34,535 | 218 | 45,424 | 213 | 56,846 |
| 25,000 | 308 | 30,465 | 284 | 43,170 | 273 | 56,777 | 267 | 71,055 |
| 30,000 | 370 | 36,557 | 341 | 51,804 | 327 | 68,133 | 320 | 85,265 |
| 35,000 | 431 | 42,650 | 398 | 60,436 | 382 | 79,489 | 374 | 99,478 |
| 40,000 | 493 | 48,742 | 454 | 69,070 | 436 | 90,845 | 427 | 113,684 |
| 45,000 | 555 | 54,835 | 511 | 77,705 | 491 | 102,198 | 480 | 127,895 |
| 50,000 | 616 | 60,929 | 568 | 86,339 | 545 | 113,554 | 534 | 142,107 |

### Table III

#### 13% Annual Percentage Rate

| Amount Financed | 15 YEARS | | 20 YEARS | | 25 YEARS | | 30 YEARS | |
|---|---|---|---|---|---|---|---|---|
| | Monthly Payment | Total Finance Charge | Monthly Payment | Total Finance Charge | Monthly Payment | Total Finance Charge | Monthly Payment | Total Finance Charge |
| $1,000 | 13 | 1,279 | 12 | 1,813 | 11 | 2,384 | 11 | 2,985 |
| 10,000 | 127 | 12,775 | 117 | 18,118 | 113 | 23,837 | 111 | 29,823 |
| 15,000 | 190 | 19,162 | 176 | 27,178 | 169 | 35,754 | 166 | 44,735 |
| 20,000 | 253 | 25,549 | 234 | 36,237 | 226 | 47,671 | 221 | 59,646 |
| 25,000 | 316 | 31,938 | 293 | 45,296 | 282 | 59,588 | 277 | 74,558 |
| 30,000 | 380 | 38,324 | 351 | 54,355 | 338 | 71,508 | 332 | 89,470 |
| 35,000 | 443 | 44,711 | 410 | 63,414 | 395 | 83,425 | 387 | 104,381 |
| 40,000 | 506 | 51,098 | 469 | 72,474 | 451 | 95,342 | 442 | 119,293 |
| 45,000 | 569 | 57,485 | 527 | 81,530 | 507 | 107,259 | 498 | 134,204 |
| 50,000 | 633 | 63,873 | 586 | 90,590 | 564 | 119,176 | 553 | 149,116 |

#### 13½% Annual Percentage Rate

| Amount Financed | 15 YEARS | | 20 YEARS | | 25 YEARS | | 30 YEARS | |
|---|---|---|---|---|---|---|---|---|
| | Monthly Payment | Total Finance Charge | Monthly Payment | Total Finance Charge | Monthly Payment | Total Finance Charge | Monthly Payment | Total Finance Charge |
| $1,000 | 13 | 1,338 | 12 | 1,899 | 12 | 2,498 | 11 | 3,126 |
| 10,000 | 130 | 13,371 | 121 | 18,978 | 117 | 24,971 | 115 | 31,238 |
| 15,000 | 195 | 20,055 | 181 | 28,466 | 175 | 37,455 | 172 | 46,855 |
| 20,000 | 260 | 26,741 | 241 | 37,955 | 233 | 49,939 | 229 | 62,472 |
| 25,000 | 325 | 33,424 | 302 | 47,444 | 291 | 62,426 | 286 | 78,090 |
| 30,000 | 390 | 40,110 | 362 | 56,933 | 350 | 74,910 | 344 | 93,707 |
| 35,000 | 454 | 46,796 | 423 | 66,422 | 408 | 87,394 | 401 | 109,324 |
| 40,000 | 519 | 53,479 | 483 | 75,908 | 466 | 99,878 | 458 | 124,941 |
| 45,000 | 584 | 60,165 | 543 | 85,397 | 525 | 112,365 | 515 | 140,558 |
| 50,000 | 649 | 66,849 | 604 | 94,886 | 583 | 124,849 | 573 | 156,176 |

## Table III

### 14% Annual Percentage Rate

| Amount Financed | 15 YEARS Monthly Payment | Total Finance Charge | 20 YEARS Monthly Payment | Total Finance Charge | 25 YEARS Monthly Payment | Total Finance Charge | 30 YEARS Monthly Payment | Total Finance Charge |
|---|---|---|---|---|---|---|---|---|
| $1,000 | 13 | 1,398 | 12 | 1,986 | 12 | 2,612 | 12 | 3,266 |
| 10,000 | 133 | 13,972 | 124 | 19,846 | 120 | 26,114 | 118 | 32,656 |
| 15,000 | 200 | 20,959 | 187 | 29,767 | 181 | 39,171 | 178 | 48,986 |
| 20,000 | 266 | 27,943 | 249 | 39,690 | 241 | 52,228 | 237 | 65,313 |
| 25,000 | 333 | 34,929 | 311 | 49,614 | 301 | 65,285 | 296 | 81,639 |
| 30,000 | 399 | 41,915 | 373 | 59,534 | 361 | 78,339 | 355 | 97,969 |
| 35,000 | 466 | 48,900 | 435 | 69,458 | 421 | 91,396 | 415 | 114,296 |
| 40,000 | 533 | 55,886 | 497 | 79,378 | 482 | 104,453 | 474 | 130,622 |
| 45,000 | 599 | 62,872 | 560 | 89,302 | 542 | 117,510 | 533 | 146,952 |
| 50,000 | 666 | 69,858 | 622 | 99,225 | 602 | 130,567 | 592 | 163,278 |

### 14½% Annual Percentage Rate

| Amount Financed | 15 YEARS Monthly Payment | Total Finance Charge | 20 YEARS Monthly Payment | Total Finance Charge | 25 YEARS Monthly Payment | Total Finance Charge | 30 YEARS Monthly Payment | Total Finance Charge |
|---|---|---|---|---|---|---|---|---|
| $1,000 | 14 | 1,459 | 13 | 2,072 | 12 | 2,729 | 12 | 3,410 |
| 10,000 | 137 | 14,581 | 128 | 20,720 | 124 | 27,266 | 122 | 34,086 |
| 15,000 | 205 | 21,869 | 192 | 31,080 | 186 | 40,899 | 184 | 51,128 |
| 20,000 | 273 | 29,160 | 256 | 41,440 | 248 | 54,532 | 245 | 68,171 |
| 25,000 | 341 | 36,448 | 320 | 51,800 | 311 | 68,165 | 306 | 85,210 |
| 30,000 | 410 | 43,739 | 384 | 62,160 | 373 | 81,795 | 367 | 102,253 |
| 35,000 | 478 | 51,027 | 448 | 72,520 | 435 | 95,428 | 429 | 119,296 |
| 40,000 | 546 | 58,318 | 512 | 82,880 | 497 | 109,061 | 490 | 136,339 |
| 45,000 | 614 | 65,606 | 576 | 93,240 | 559 | 122,694 | 551 | 153,382 |
| 50,000 | 683 | 72,897 | 640 | 103,600 | 621 | 136,327 | 612 | 170,421 |

## Table III

### 15% Annual Percentage Rate

| Amount Financed | 15 YEARS Monthly Payment | Total Finance Charge | 20 YEARS Monthly Payment | Total Finance Charge | 25 YEARS Monthly Payment | Total Finance Charge | 30 YEARS Monthly Payment | Total Finance Charge |
|---|---|---|---|---|---|---|---|---|
| $1,000 | 14 | 1,520 | 13 | 2,161 | 13 | 2,843 | 13 | 3,554 |
| 10,000 | 140 | 15,193 | 132 | 21,603 | 128 | 28,427 | 126 | 35,522 |
| 15,000 | 210 | 22,789 | 198 | 32,405 | 192 | 42,639 | 190 | 53,281 |
| 20,000 | 280 | 30,386 | 263 | 43,206 | 256 | 56,851 | 253 | 71,040 |
| 25,000 | 350 | 37,982 | 329 | 54,008 | 320 | 71,063 | 316 | 88,803 |
| 30,000 | 420 | 45,578 | 395 | 64,810 | 384 | 85,275 | 379 | 106,562 |
| 35,000 | 490 | 53,175 | 461 | 75,611 | 448 | 99,490 | 443 | 124,322 |
| 40,000 | 560 | 60,771 | 527 | 86,413 | 512 | 113,702 | 506 | 142,081 |
| 45,000 | 630 | 68,368 | 593 | 97,214 | 576 | 127,914 | 569 | 159,840 |
| 50,000 | 700 | 75,964 | 658 | 108,016 | 640 | 142,126 | 632 | 177,603 |

# Appendix 2
## Who to Contact for Help in Dealing with a Bank

### Directory of Federal Bank Regulatory Agencies

Federal Home Loan Bank Board
1700 G Street, N.W.
Washington, D.C. 20552

Regional Offices—write to or call:

General Counsel's Office
c/o Federal Home Loan Bank eitner in D.C., 202-377-6000 or at the appropriate office listed below:

Post Office Box 2196
Boston, Massachusetts 02106
617-223-5300 (Connecticut, Maine, Massachusetts, New Hampshire, Rhode Island, Vermont)

11 Stanwix Street, 4th Floor
Gateway Center
Pittsburgh, Pennsylvania 15222
412-288-3400
(Delaware, Pennsylvania, West Virginia)

One World Trade Center
Floor 103
New York, New York 10048
212-432-2000
(New Jersey, New York, Puerto Rico and Virgin Islands)

Post Office Box 56527
Atlanta, Georgia 30343
404-522-2450
(Alabama, District of Columbia, Florida, Georgia, Maryland, North Carolina, South Carolina and Virginia)

Post Office Box 598
Cincinnati, Ohio 45201
513-852-7500
(Kentucky, Ohio and
Tennessee)

2900 Indiana Tower
One Indiana Square
Indianapolis, Indiana 46204
317-269-5371
(Indiana and Michigan)

111 East Wacker Drive
Chicago, Illinois 60601
312-565-5700
(Illinois and Wisconsin)

907 Walnut Street
Des Moines, Iowa 50309
515-243-4211
(Iowa, Minnesota, Missouri,
North Dakota and South
Dakota)

1400 Tower Building
Little Rock, Arkansas 72201
501-372-7141
(Arkansas, Louisiana,
Mississippi, New Mexico and
Texas)

Post Office Box 176
Topeka, Kansas 66601
913-233-0507
(Colorado, Kansas, Nebraska
and Oklahoma)

Post Office Box 7948
San Francisco, California 94120
415-393-1000
(Arizona, Nevada and
California)

Seattle, Washington 98101
206-624-3980
(Alaska, Hawaii and Guam,
Idaho, Montana, Oregon, Utah,
Washington and Wyoming)

---

Office of the Comptroller of the Currency
490 L'Enfant Plaza East, S.W.
Washington, D.C. 20219

Regional Offices—write to or call:

Deputy Comptroller for Customer and Communtiy Programs
c/o Office of the Comptroller either in D.C., 202-447-0934
or at the appropriate office listed below:

3 Center Plaza, Suite P-400
Boston, Massachusetts 02108
617-223-2274
(Connecticut, Rhode Island,
Vermont, New Hampshire,
Massachusetts and Maine)

1211 Avenue of the Americas
Suite 4250
New York, New York 10036
212-399-2997
(New York and New Jersey)

3 Parkway, Suite 1800
Philadelphia, Pennsylvania
19102
215-597-7105
(Pennsylvania and Delaware)

One Erieview Plaza
Cleveland, Ohio 44114
216-522-7141
(Ohio, Indiana, Kentucky)

F & M Center, Suite 2151
Richmond, Virginia 23277
804-643-3517
(West Virginia, Virginia,
Maryland, District of
Columbia, North Carolina)

Peachtree Cain Tower, Suite
2700
229 Peachtree Street, N.E.
Atlanta, Georgia 30303
404-221-4926
(Georgia, South Carolina,
Florida)

Sears Tower, Suite 5750
Chicago, Illinois 60606
312-353-0300
(Illinois and Michigan)

165 Madison Avenue, Suite 800
Memphis, Tennessee 38103
901-521-3376
(Mississippi, Alabama,
Tennessee, Arkansas,
Louisiana)

800 Marquette Avenue
1100 Midwest Plaza, East
Building
Minneapolis, Minnesota 55402
612-725-2684
(Minnesota, North Dakota,
South Dakota, Wisconsin)

911 Main Street, Suite 2616
Kansas City, Missouri 64105
816-842-1648
(Iowa, Missouri, Nebraska,
Kansas)

1201 Elm Street, Suite 3800
Dallas, Texas 75270
214-655-4000
(Texas and Oklahoma)

1405 Curtis Street, Suite 3000
Denver, Colorado 80202
303-837-4883
(Wyoming, Utah, Colorado,
Arizona, New Mexico)

707 Southwest Washington
Street
Room 900
Portland, Oregon 97205
503-221-3091
(Montana, Idaho, Oregon,
Washington, Alaska)

One Market Plaza
Steuart Street Tower, Suite 2101
San Francisco, California 94105
415-556-6619
(Nevada, California, Hawaii)

Federal Deposit Insurance Corporation
550 17th Street, N.W.
Washington, D.C. 20429

Regional Offices—write to or call:

Director
Office of Consumer Affairs and Civil Rights
c/o Federal Deposit Insurance Corporation
either in D.C., 202-289-4668
or at the appropriate office listed below:

233 Peachtree Street, N.E.
Suite 2400
Atlanta, Georgia 30303
404-221-6631
(Alabama, Florida, Georgia)

60 State Street, 17th Floor
Boston, Massachusetts 02109
617-223-6420
(Connecticut, Maine,
Massachusetts, New
Hampshire, Rhode Island,
Vermont)

233 S. Wacker Drive, Suite 6116
Chicago, Illinois 60606
312-353-2600
(Illinois, Indiana)

1 Nationwide Plaza, Suite 2600
Columbus, Ohio 43215
614-469-7301
(Kentucky, Ohio, West
Virginia)

300 North Ervay Street
Suite 3300
Dallas, Texas 75201
214-749-7691
(Colorado, New Mexico,
Oklahoma, Texas)

2345 Grand Avenue, Suite 1500
Kansas City, Missouri 64108
816-374-2851
(Kansas, Missouri)

1 South Pinckney Street
Room 813
Madison, Wisconsin 53703
608-252-5226
(Michigan, Wisconsin)

1 Commerce Square, Suite 1800
Memphis, Tennessee 38103
901-521-3872
(Arkansas, Louisiana,
Mississippi, Tennessee)

730 Second Avenue South
Suite 266
Minneapolis, Minnesota 55402
612-725-2046
(Minnesota, Montana, North
Dakota, South Dakota,
Wyoming)

345 Park Avenue, 21st Floor
New York, New York 10022
212-826-4762
(New Jersey, New York, Puerto
Rico, Virgin Islands)

1700 Farnam Street, Suite 1200
Omaha, Nebraska 68102
402-221-3366
(Iowa, Nebraska)

5 Penn Center Plaza, Suite 2901
Philadelphia, Pennsylvania
19103
215-597-2295
(Delaware, Maryland,
Pennsylvania)

908 E. Main Street, Suite 435
Richmond, Virginia 23219
804-643-6716
(District of Columbia, North
Carolina, South Carolina,
Virginia)

44 Montgomery Street, Suite
3600
San Francisco, California 94104
415-556-2736
(Alaska, Arizona, California,
Guam, Hawaii, Idaho, Nevada,
Oregon, Utah, Washington)

---

Federal Reserve Board
21st and Constitution Avenue, N.W.
Washington, D.C. 20551

Regional Offices—write to or call:

Director
Division of Consumer and Community Affairs
c/o Federal Reserve Bank either in D.C., 202-452-2631
or at the appropriate office listed below:

600 Atlantic Avenue
Boston, Massachusetts 02106
617-973-3000
(Maine, New Hampshire,
Vermont, Massachusetts,
Connecticut, Rhode Island)

100 North Sixth Street
Philadelphia, Pennsylvania
19109
215-574-6000
(Delaware, parts of
Pennsylvania and New Jersey)

33 Liberty Street
New York, New York 10005
212-791-5000
(New York and part of New
Jersey)

1455 East Sixth Street
P.O. Box 6387
Cleveland, Ohio 44101
216-293-9800
(Ohio, Kentucky, parts of
Pennsylvania and West
Virginia)

100 North Ninth Street
Richmond, Virginia 23261
804-649-3611
(Virginia, North Carolina,
Maryland, South Carolina,
District of Columbia, and part
of West Virginia)

104 Marietta Street, N.W.
Atlanta, Georgia 30303
404-231-8500
(Georgia, Tennessee, Alabama,
Florida, Louisiana, Mississippi)

230 South LaSalle Street
P.O. Box 834
Chicago, Illinois 60690
312-380-2320
(Iowa and parts of Illinois,
Indiana, Wisconsin and
Michigan)

411 Locust Street
P.O. Box 442
St. Louis, Missouri 63166
314-444-8444
(Arkansas and parts of Illinois,
Indiana, Missouri, Kentucky,
Mississippi, and Tennessee)

250 Marquette Avenue
Minneapolis, Minnesota 55480
612-783-2345
(Minnesota, North Dakota,
South Dakota, Montana, and
parts of Michigan and
Wisconsin)

925 Grand Avenue
Federal Reserve Station
Kansas City, Missouri 64198
816-881-2000
(Kansas, Colorado, Wyoming,
Oklahoma, Nebraska and parts
of Missouri and New Mexico)

400 South Akard Street
Station K
Dallas, Texas 75222
214-651-6111
(Texas, parts of Oklahoma,
New Mexico and Louisiana)

400 Sansome Street
San Francisco, California 94120
415-450-2000
(California, Hawaii, Nevada,
Arizona, Idaho and Oregon)

---

Federal Trade Commission
Equal Credit Opportunity
Washington, D.C. 20580

Regional Offices—write to or call:

**Atlanta Regional Office**
1718 Peachtree Street, N.W.
Suite 1000
Atlanta, Georgia 30309

**Boston Regional Office**
1301 Analex Building
150 Causeway
Boston, Massachusetts 02114

**Chicago Regional Office**
Suite 1437
55 East Monroe Street
Chicago, Illinois 60603

**Denver Regional Office**
Suite 2900
1405 Curtis Street
Denver, Colorado 80202

**Cleveland Regional Office**
Room 1339
Federal Office Building
1240 East 9th Street
Cleveland, Ohio 44199

**Los Angeles Regional Office**
11000 Wilshire Blvd.
Room 13209
Los Angeles, California 90024

**Dallas Regional Office**
2001 Bryan Street
Suite 2665
Dallas, Texas 75201

**New York Regional Office**
22nd Floor, Federal Building
26 Federal Plaza
New York, New York 10007

---

National Credit Union Administration
Office of Consumer Affairs
1776 G Street, N.W.
Washington, D.C. 20456

Regional Offices—write to or call:

Director
Office of Consumer Affairs
c/o National Credit Union Administration
either in D.C., 202-357-1080
or at the appropriate office listed below:

**Region I**
Regional Director
State Street South Building,
Room 3E
1776 Heritage Drive
Boston, Massachusetts 02171
(617) 223-6807

**Region III**
Regional Director
1365 Peachtree Street, Suite 500
Atlanta, Georgia 30309
(404) 881-3127

**Region II**
Regional Director
Federal Building
228 Walnut Street, Box 926
Harrisburg, Pennsylvania 17108
(717) 782-4595

**Region IV**
Regional Director
New Federal Building, Room 704
234 N. Summit Street
Toledo, Ohio 43604
(419) 259-7510

**Region V**
Regional Director
515 Congress Avenue, Suite
1400
Austin, Texas 78701
(512) 397-5131

**Region VI**
Regional Director
Two Embarcadero Center, Suite
1830
San Francisco, California 94111
(415) 556-6277

# Notes

## Chapter 1. The Banking Fraternity

1. Edwin Kiester, Jr., *The Case of the Missing Executive*, American Jewish Committee, New York, 1972, p. 6.
2. Arnold Foster, executive director of the Anti-Defamation League of B'nai B'rith, Dec. 2, 1974, memo.
3. Testimony of Richard Davinos, Chairman, Committee on Social Discrimination, The American Jewish Committee, and Israel A. Laster, Executive Director of the New York Regional Task Force on Executive Suite Discrimination of the Federal Employment and Guidance Service and the American Jewish Committee, Hearing before the Committee on Banking, Housing and Urban Affairs, U.S. Senate, 96th Congress, July 13, 1979, p. 9.
4. Ibid., p. 10.
5. Stephen L. Slavin and Mary A. Pradt, "Anti-Semitism in Banking," *Bankers Magazine*, July/August 1979, p. 20.
6. Report of the Comptroller General of the United States, "More Action Needed to Insure that Financial Institutions Provide Equal Employment Opportunity," June 24, 1976; the cover of the report.
7. Theodore Cross and Paul London, "It Makes a Difference Where You Bank Your Money," *Business and Society Review*, 1974, p. 25.
8. Council on Economic Priorities, *Shortchanged: Minorities and Women in Banking*, Sept./Oct. 1972, p. 5.
9. Martin Mayer, *The Bankers*, Weybright and Talley, 1974, p. 11.
10. Quoted in CEP, op. cit., p. 21.
11. Federal Guidelines on Discrimination Because of Religion or National Origin, Part 60-50 of Chapter 60 of Title 41 of the Code of Federal Regulations, 1973.
12. Office of Senator William Proxmire, Press Release, July 1, 1976.
13. U.S. Senate, Committee on Banking, Housing and Urban Affairs, "Report on the Treasury Department's Contract Compliance Program for Financial Institutions," 94th Congress, 1977, pp. 3–4.
14. Ibid., p. 5.
15. Ibid., p. 25.
16. Quoted in *The Boston Globe*, December 15, 1978, p. 50, reprinted courtesy of *The Boston Globe*.
17. Ibid.
18. Letter from James D. Henry, associate solicitor for labor relations and civil rights, quoted in the *American Banker*, April 21, 1976, p. 15.
19. Quoted in the *American Banker*, May 10, 1976, p. 24.
20. United States Senate, Committee on Banking, Housing and Urban Affairs, *Committee Report*, op. cit., p. 2.
21. Senator Proxmire, *Press Release*, July 1, 1976, p. 3.
22. See, Department of Housing and Urban Development, *Women and Housing: A Report on Sex Discrimination in Five American Cities*, 1975.
23. Ibid.

24. James F. Smith, "The Equal Credit Opportunity Act of 1974: A Cost/Benefit Analysis," paper presented to the Annual Meeting of the American Finance Association, Atlantic City, New Jersey, September 17, 1976, p. 6.
25. Ibid., p. 25.
26. The three agencies were the Federal Home Loan Bank Board, Comptroller of the Currency, and the Federal Deposit Insurance Corporation. The Federal Reserve Board did not agree to settle out-of-court.
27. Quoted in "The Mutual Savings Banks of New York City," a survey conducted by the N.Y. Chapter of the American Jewish Committee Institute of Human Relations, 165 East 56th St., N.Y., N.Y. 10022, October 1965, p. 5.
28. A. D. Danziger, *Proceedings of the U.S. League*, April 29–30, 1921, p. 91.
29. Ibid., p. 115.
30. Edward S. Herman, "Conflict of Interest in the Savings and Loan Industry," a part of *The Study of the Savings and Loan Industry*, directed by Irwin Friend for the Federal Home Loan Bank Board, 1969, p. 803.

## Chapter 2. Unarmed Robbery

1. Edward Herman, "Conflicts of Interest in the Savings and Loan Industry," in *The Study of the Savings and Loan Industry* directed by Irwin Friend, Univ. of Penn., and submitted to the Federal Home Loan Bank Board, Washington, D.C., 1969, p. 812.
2. Ibid., p. 850.
3. Ibid., p. 849.
4. Federal Reserve System, Comptroller of the Currency, Federal Deposit Insurance Corporation, Statement of Policy Concerning Improper and Illegal Payments by Banker and Bank Holding Companies, January 17, 1978, p. 3.
5. Herman, op. cit., p. 880.
6. Ibid., p. 880.
7. Statement by George Le Maistre, Chairman FDIC on the Safe Banking Act of 1977 before the Subcommittee on Financial Institutions Supervision, Regulation and Insurance, House of Representatives, September 28, 1977, p. 4.
8. Martin Mayer, *The Bankers*.
9. CSBS (Conference of State Bank Supervisors), *Memorandum Re: H.R. 9086—The Safe Banking Act of 1977*, October 3, 1977, p. 2.
10. Ibid.
11. Ibid.
12. Ibid., p. 3.
13. Ibid.
14. Ibid., p. 5.
15. Ibid, p. 5.
16. Ibid., p. 6.
17. Ibid., p. 9.

18. *American Banker*, "St Germain Files 'Safe Banking Bill' on Disclosure, Self-Dealing", September 14, 1979, p. 1.
19. Herman, op. cit., p. 887.
20. Kansas City *Times* "Bankers Protest Loan Law", March 26, 1979.
21. Ibid.
22. CSBS, op. cit. p. 1.
23. Kansas City *Times*, op. cit.

### Chapter 3. Where Have All the Bond Buyers Gone?

1. Jack Newfield and Paul Dubrul, *The Abuse of Power*, Viking Press, 1977, p. 175.
2. Ibid., pp. 171–172.
3. Securities and Exchange Commission Staff Report on Transactions in Securities of the City of New York prepared for the Subcommittee on Economic Stabilization of the Committee on Banking, Finance and Urban Affairs, House of Representatives, 95th Congress, August 1977, pp. 3, 4, 8.
4. Ibid., Chapter 3, pp. 1, 2, 3.
5. Ibid., Chapter 3, p. 22.
6. Ibid., Chapter 4, p. 31.
7. Letter from G. Lamar Crittendon, Executive V.P., First National Bank of Boston, dated April 3, 1975, to Governor Michael Dukakis, quoted in Harriet Tee Taggart, "Look Out, Massachusetts: Another Look at the State Debt Crisis, 1975–1976," Doctoral Seminar paper, MIT, March 27, 1978, p. 23.
8. Memo to Governor from J. Bailey and D. Taylor, dated January 24, 1976, ibid.
9. When the state did refinance their bonds in August 1978 at 6.42 percent, it could only be done for the final portion of the bond payments due after 1987.
10. Harriet Tee Taggart, op. cit.
11. U. S. House of Representatives, Staff Study of the Committee on Banking, Finance and Urban Affairs, "The Role of Commercial Banks in the Finances of the City of Cleveland," June 1979, p. 240.
12. Roldo Bartimole, "Troubled Cleveland", *The New York Times*, Sunday, February 11, 1979, p. E17.
13. Ibid.
14. U.S. House of Representatives, Staff Study, op. cit., p. 230.

### Chapter 4: Banks Are Dangerous to Your Wealth

1. See "U.S. Bars Bank Critic from E&H Bond Sales," *American Banker*, May 1, 1970, pp. 3, 6.
2. Ibid.
3. Bill O'Keefe, "AT&T Defers Low-Denomination Bond; Will Sell Record $500 Mill. Issue in Conventional Way," *American Banker*, October 22, 1970, p. 1, quoting John D. DeButts, AT&T Vice Chairman.

4. *The Wall Street Journal*, July 5, 1974, p. 13.
5. *American Banker*, July 10, 1974, p. 24.
6. *The Wall Street Journal*, March 11, 1974, p. 5.
7. Ibid.
8. Edward J. Kane, *United States Investor/Eastern Banker*, April 5, 1976, p. 35.
9. FDIC, [1 C.F.R. Part 329] Interest on Deposits, February 25, 1977.
10. Ibid.
11. Robert M. Bleiberg, "No More Wild Cards," April 22, 1974, p. 7, reprinted by courtesy of *Barron's National Business & Financial Weekly*.
12. House Banking Currency and Housing Committee, Hearings on Financial Reform, U.S. Congress, 1976, p. 1638.
13. Federal Reserve Bulletin, 60 (April 1974), p. 254.
14. Judith Miller, "Rate Ceilings Under Fire," *The New York Times*, March 25, 1978.
15. *American Banker*, "Mass. Town Is Offering Small Denomination Bonds," March 6, 1976, p. 16.
16. *The Wall Street Journal*, "A Matter of Interest," March 30, 1979.
17. Depository Institutions Deregulation & Monetary Control Act of 1980, House of Representatives, 96th Congress, Report No. 96-842, March 21, 1980, p. 12.
18. Edward J. Kane, "Expanded Powers for Thrift Institutions: Superthrift vs. Superlobbyist" in *Proceedings of a Conference on Bank Structure and Competition*, May 6 and 7, 1976, Federal Reserve Bank of Chicago.

### Chapter 5: Redlining: So You Want to Buy a House in the City

1. Michael Kramer, *The City Politic*, "Borrower Trouble: The Bank's Mortgage Cop-out," *New York* magazine, Feb. 2, 1975, p. 10. Copyright ©1975, by News Group Publications, Inc. Reprinted with permission of the *New York* magazine.
2. Jack Newfield and Paul Dubrul, *The Abuse of Power*, Viking Press, 1977, p. 98.
3. Report of the Governor's Commission on Mortgage Practices to Governor Dan Walker of Illinois, "Home Ownership in Illinois: The Elusive Dream," p. i.
4. Quoted by Tee Taggart, "Red-Lining," *Planning*, December 1974, p. 14.
5. Ibid., p. 15.
6. Ibid., p. 15.
7. Quoted in "Confrontation in the Communities," *Savings and Loan News*, June 1974, p. 41.
8. Ibid.
9. "Home Mortgage Lending Patterns in Metropolitan Boston," 1977.
10. Robert Schafer, "Mortgage Lending Decisions: Criteria and Constraints," Executive Summary, p. xxii. (Cambridge, MA: MIT-Harvard Joint Center for Urban Studies, 1978.)
11. *The Appraisal of Real Estate*, Sixth Edition, Textbook Committee, American Institute of Real Estate Appraisers, 1974, p. 40.
12. *Single Family Residential Appraisal Manual*, Jerome Knowles, Jr., American Institute of Real Estate Appraisers, 1974, pp. 8, 131. Also see

*An Introduction to Appraising Real Property*, Society of Real Estate Appraisers, 1975, pp. 6–16.

13. Ibid., Knowles, p. 26 and *An Introduction*, p. 6–16.
14. U.S. Commission on Civil Rights, *Understanding Fair Housing*, Washington, D.C., U.S. GPO, Feb. 1973, p. 4.
15. Ibid., p. 11.
16. Urban-Suburban Investment Study Group, Center for Urban Affairs, Northwestern University, "Regulation of Federally Chartered Savings & Loan Associatons: Chartering, Branching, Relocation, Redesignation of the Home Office" (Working Paper), 1974, pp. 31–40.
17. *Home Ownership in Illinois*, op. cit., p. 24.
18. *American Banker*, "Appraisal Disclosure Rule Proposed in Connecticut," April 11, 1977.
19. Schafer, op. cit., p. viii.
20. *The Village Voice*, May 2, 1977, p. 14.
21. New York State Banking Department, *Mortgage Financing and Housing Markets in New York State: A Preliminary Report*, May 10, 1977, p. iv–3.
22. Schafer, op. cit.
23. Home Mortgage Lending Patterns in Metropolitan Boston, op. cit.
24. Taggart, op. cit., p. 15.
25. "Coping With Confrontation: A Case History," *Savings and Loan News*, June 1974, p. 51.
26. *Boston Globe*, editorial, June 13, 1975, reprinted courtesy of *The Boston Globe*.
27. Boston *Herald American*, "State Bankers Brand Deposit and Loan Edict as $1 Million Extravagance," June 13, 1975, p. 5.
28. Taggart, op. cit., p. 15.
29. Ibid.
30. Op. cit., *Savings and Loan News*, p. 43.
31. Kramer, op. cit., p. 10.
32. Ibid.
33. Robert M. Bleiberg, "The Thin 'Redline,'" June 23, 1975. Reprinted by courtesy of *Barron's National Business & Financial Weekly*.
34. *The Sacramento Bee*, "Redlining the Poor," June 13, 1975, p. 1.
35. *American Banker*, "California Orders Redlining Hearings," June 12, 1975, p. 1.
36. *The Sacramento Bee*, "Redlining the Poor," June 13, 1975, p. 1.
37. *Los Angeles Times*, "Redlining Action," June 17, 1975, Part III, p. 20.
38. Ibid.
39. *Los Angeles Times*, "Erasing the Red Line," June 18, 1975, Part II, p. 6. Copyright © 1975, *Los Angeles Times*. Reprinted by permission.
40. Press release from the Office of the Governor, dated August 28, 1975.
41. *American Banker*, June 26, 1975, p. 14, "Illinois Senate Passes Anti-redline Disclosure Bills."
42. Senate Committee on Banking, Housing and Urban Affairs, 94th Congress, 1st Session 1179 (1975), "Home Mortgage Disclosure Act: Hearing on S. 1281," Senate report, p. 1.
43. "Home Mortgage Lending Patterns in Metropolitan Boston," op. cit., p. 6 and Table 3.
44. *Business Week*, "The Philadelphia Solution to Redlining," May 9, 1977, p. 54.

45. Ibid.
46. New York State Banking Dept., "Reinvesting in the Community," April 1979, p. 12.
47. Ibid.
48. Senate Committee on Banking, Housing and Urban Affairs, Report on Fair Lending Enforcement by the Four Federal Financial Regulatory Agencies, S. Rep. No. 930, 94th Congress, 2d Session (1976), pp. 2–4.
49. Kramer, op. cit., p. 11.

---

### Chapter 6: The Bank Branch as Hostage

1. Statement of Ralph Nader and Jonathan Brown on the Community Reinvestment Act of 1977 before the Federal Reserve Board, Comptroller of the Currency, Federal Deposit Insurance Corp., Federal Home Loan Bank Board, Washington, D.C., March 16, 1978, p. 1.
2. *American Banker*, March 29, 1973, p. 1.
3. Statement submitted by Richard W. Golden for the New York Public Interest Group, Inc., before the Banking Board of the State of New York on "Whether Mortgage and Home Improvement Loan Activity in Existing Service Areas Should Be A Factor When Passing Upon Branch Applications," October 7, 1977.
4. Ira O. Scott, "Required Reading," September 22, 1977, pp. 4, 5, 10. Reprinted with permission from the *American Banker.*
5. *Wall Street Journal*, "California to Crack Down on Redlining," August 26, 1975, p. 13.
6. Petition of New York Public Interest Group, Inc., et al., to New York State Banking Department, April 6, 1977, p. 4.
7. Hearings before the Committee on Banking, Housing and Urban Affairs, United States Senate, 95th Congress, first session on S. 406, March 23–25, 1977, p. 1.
8. Ibid., p. 2.
9. Ibid., p. 10.
10. Ibid., p. 17.
11. Ibid., p. 133.
12. Ibid., p. 153.
13. Ibid., p. 277.
14. Ibid., pp. 324–325.
15. Statement of New York Bankers Association on the Development of Regulations to Implement the Community Reinvestment Act before the Federal Reserve System, Federal Deposit Insurance Corporation, Comptroller of the Currency, and the Federal Home Loan Bank Board, March 20, 1978, p. 2.
16. Federal Reserve Board, "Summary of Public Comments on the Community Reinvestment Act," June 28, 1978.
17. Testimony of James Carras, Co-chairperson, Boston Mortgage Review and Hugh MacCormack, President, Jamaica Plain Banking and Mortgage Committee before the FDIC, Comptroller of the Currency, Federal Home Loan Bank, Federal Reserve Board regarding the Community Reinvestment Act of 1977, March 28, 1977, p. 4.

18. Testimony of Richard Golden, Esq., before the Federal Reserve Board, Comptroller of the Currency, FDIC, Federal Home Loan Bank regarding the Community Reinvestment Act of 1977, Washington, D.C., March 16, 1978, p. 8.
19. *American Banker*, November 27, 1978, p. 1.
20. *Congressional Record*—Senate, June 6, 1977, p. S 8959.
21. *The Boston Globe*, "City Investment Plan Wins Bankers but Not Consumers," by Jonathan Fuerbringer, July 7, 1978.
22. Hearings, op. cit., pp. 74, 84.
23. *Banker and Tradesman*, William A. Mallard, editor, "A Squeeze Play..." April 26, 1978, p. 1 and ff.
24. Ibid.
25. *American Banker*, "NYS Delays Rules on Mutual Branching," November 9, 1978, p. 1.
26. *American Banker*, "Agencies Weigh Stipulating Conditions for Granting Some CRA-Protested Plans," April 2, 1979.
27. *American Banker*, "COC Defends 'Yes' on CRA Vote," May 3, 1979.

---

### Chapter 7: The Great Checking Account Robbery

1. Massachusetts Bankers Association and New Hampshire Bankers Association, "Petition for Relief With Respect to Third Party Withdrawal Orders Offered by Mutual Savings Banks," October 20, 1972, pp. 25–26.
2. Ibid., p. 26.
3. Letter from Frank Morris, President of the Federal Reserve Bank of Boston, to David C. Melnicoff, Deputy Executive Director, Board of Governors, August 17, 1973, p. 1.
4. Testimony of the Honorable Robert Carswell, Deputy Secretary of the Treasury, before the House Subcommittee on Financial Institutions Supervision, Regulation & Insurance, June 14, 1979, p. 7.
5. Ibid.
6. Ibid., p. 8.
7. Testimony of Ron Hazelton for the Savings Bank Association of Massachusetts at the Hearings of the Senate Sub-Committee on Financial Institutions, Worcester, Mass., September 11, 1975, p. 2.
8. Ibid., pp. 2–3.
9. *The Impact of the Payment of Interest on Demand Deposits*, a study of the staff of the Board of Governors of the Federal Reserve System, directed by Stephen H. Axelrod, January 31, 1977, p. 21.
10. Statement of John G. Heimann, Comptroller of the Currency, before the Commerce, Consumer and Monetary Affairs Subcommittee, March 22, 1979, p. 11.
11. Federal Reserve Bank of Boston, *Functional Cost Analysis: 1972 Average Banks*, Boston, 1973.
12. *Report on the Committee of Banking, Housing and Urban Affairs*, United States Senate, No. 95-407, August 18, 1977, p. 13.
13. Ibid.

14. Statement of Wilson Brunel, Chairman of the Board of the Massachusetts Bankers Association before the Senate Subcommittee on Financial Institutions, Worcester, Mass., September 11, 1979, p. 12.
15. Federal Reserve Board, Staff Economic Study #88, "Effects of 'NOW' Accounts on Costs and Earnings of Commercial Banks in 1974–1975," 1976.
16. Alan S. McCall and Lee C. Jone, "Commercial Bank Earnings and NOW Accounts: the Evidence from Massachusetts," FDIC, Division of Research, Working Paper No. 77-6, 1978.
17. Edward S. Herman, letter in *American Banker*, January 12, 1977, p. 4.
18. *United States Investor Eastern Banker*, "Can NOW Accounts Make a Profit," February 14, 1980, p. 51.
19. *The Boston Globe*, October 29, 1979, p. 18.
20. Bureau of National Affairs, Current Developments, May 21, 1979, A-28 (No. 20).
21. Ibid.
22. Letter to Senator William J. Proxmire, Chairperson, Committee on Banking, Housing and Urban Affairs from Jonathan Brown, staff attorney for the Public Interest Research Group, August 8, 1977, p. 1.
23. Quoted in Golembe Associates, Inc. *Golembe Reports*, "Of Restaurants and Central Banks," Vol. 1978—8, p. 5.
24. Joseph D. Hutnyan, "NOW-Reserve Bill Is Pro-Consumer But Is Unlikely to Pass Congress," *American Banker*, July 22, 1977, p. 4.
25. *American Banker*, "Fragile Coalition Behind NOWs Seen Periled by 'Christmas Syndrome,'" June 31, 1977, p. 1.
26. Norman Strunk, Vice President of the U.S. League, in a letter to Arthur Burns, Chairman of Federal Reserve, *American Banker*, April 19, 1976, p. 1.
27. Statement of J. Alvin George, Chairman, Credit Union National Association before the Senate Subcommittee on Financial Affairs in Hearings on Depository Institutions Deregulation Act of 1979, July 18, 1979, p. 5.
28. Ibid.
29. Statement of the Independent Bankers Association of American on S. 1347, The Depository Institutions Deregulation Act of 1979 before the Subcommittee on Financial Institutions of the Senate Committee on Banking, Housing and Urban Affairs, July 18, 1979, pp. 4–5.
30. Testimony of the Honorable W. Michael Blumenthal, Secretary of the Treasury, before the Subcommittee on Financial Institutions of the Senate Committee on Banking.
31. *Banker and Tradesman*, December 14, 1977, p. 1.
32. Ibid.
33. A million dollars in a NOW account paying 5 percent interest would earn $50,000 annually for the trust beneficiary.
34. Meinhard v. Salmon, 249, N.Y. 458, 464, 164 N.E. 545, 546 (1928).

### Chapter 8: Who's Regulating the Regulators?

1. *The New York Times*, "Ability and Will of Bank Regulators to Monitor Industry Is Questioned," Dec. 18, 1977, p. 56.

2. Ibid.
3. Hearings before the Committee on Banking, Housing and Urban Affairs, U.S. Senate, 94th Congress on S2298, Feb. 3, March 1 and 19, 1976, p. 89.
4. Ibid.
5. *The New York Times*, "Banks Lobby Called Strongest in Capital," Dec. 22, 1977, p.A1.
6. Ibid., p. D3.
7. Ibid.
8. Ibid.
9. *American Banker*, "COC Check Uncovers Consumer Violations at 88% of 1400 Banks," Dec. 9, 1977, p. 1.
10. Ibid.
11. U.S. Senate, "Report on Consumer Protection Enforcement Activities by the Three Commercial Bank Regulatory Agencies," Committee on Banking, Housing and Urban Affairs, 94th Cong., 2d Session, Report No. 94-1388, Oct. 9, 1976, p. 2.
12. Ibid., p. 4.
13. Ibid., p. 7.
14. News release, Sept. 9, 1976, "Subcommittee to Examine and Release Data on Truth-in-Lending Compliance," 94th Congress, Committee on Government Operations, Commerce, Consumer & Monetary Affairs Subcommittee.
15. The five states were Maine, Massachusetts, Connecticut, New York, and Oklahoma.
16. Benjamin S. Rosenthal, "Consumer Protection Legislation: Its Economic and Regulatory Dimensions," an address before the 38th Annual Convention of the National Association of State Savings and Loan Supervisors, New Orleans, Louisiana, May 2, 1977, p. 7.
17. Testimony of John E. Quinn, Superintendent, Bureau of Consumer Protection, before the Commerce, Consumer and Monetary Affairs Subcommittee, Sept. 15, 1976, p. 4.
18. Testimony of Carol S. Greenwald, Commissioner of Banks, Commonwealth of Massachusetts before the Commerce, Consumer and Monetary Affairs Subcommittee, Sept. 15, 1976, p. 2.
19. Ibid., p. 2.
20. Quinn, op. cit., p. 3.
21. "The Truth-in-Lending Act: Federal Banking Agency Enforcement and the Need for Statutory Reform," Third Report by the Committee on Government Operations, May 10, 1977, p. 4.
22. Ibid.
23. S1312 95th Congress, section 15.
24. Title V Public Law 93-495, section 502.
25. Eugene Adams, "Speech before the Florida Bankers Association," reprinted in *American Banker*, June 25, 1973, p. 22.
26. Philip C. Jackson, Jr., member Board of Governors of the Federal Reserve System to the Joint Meeting of the Board of Directors of the Federal Reserve Bank of Dallas and the El Paso Branch, El Paso, Texas, April 17, 1976.
27. Congressional testimony of Thomas E. Kauper, assistant attorney general in charge of the Justice Department's antitrust division,

reprinted as "Required Reading," *American Banker*, January 29, 1976, p. 5.

28. United States v. Marine Bancorporation, 418 U.S. 602, 612 (n.8)(1974).

29. Committee on Governmental Affairs, "Banking Regulation" in 95th Cong., 1st Session, *Study on Federal Regulation*, U.S. Senate, Vol. V on "Regulatory Organizations," U.S. Government Printing Office, December 1977, p. 227.

30. "Study on Federal Regulation," Committee on Governmental Affairs, U.S. Senate, Dec. 1977, Vol. V, "Regulatory Organization," Ch. Six, p. 222.

31. *Congressional Record*, 94th Congress, September 5, 1975, Vol. 121, No. 129, p. 1.

32. Hearings before the Committee on Banking, Housing and Urban Affairs, U.S. Senate, 94th Cong., 2nd Session on S2298, Feb. 3, March 1 & 19, 1976, p. 186.

33. Ibid., p. 195.

34. Ibid., p. 212.

35. Ibid., p. 213.

36. *Bank Stock Quarterly*, "Who Should Regulate the Banks?" April 1976, p. 24.

37. Ibid., p. 24.

38. Ibid., p. 20.

39. Ibid.

40. Statement by Arthur Burns, Chairman, Board of Governors of the Federal Reserve System, before the Subcommittee on Financial Institutions Supervision, Regulation and Insurance of the Committee on Banking, Currency and Housing, March 18, 1976, p. 4.

41. *Bank Stock Quarterly*, op. cit., p. 24, quoting from Volcker's address to the American Bankers Association National Credit Conference, Atlanta, Georgia, March 9, 1976.

42. CSBS, "Why State Banking?" Washington, D.C.

43. Attachment B, included with November 5, 1976, letter from Lawrence E. Kreider, Executive Vice President of CSBS to Carol S. Greenwald, Commissioner of Banks.

44. Quoted in *The Supervisor*, Vol. 15, No. 8, Oct. 1978, p. 8.

45. House of Representatives, Hearings before the Committee on Government Operations (Subcommittee on Commerce, Consumers and Monetary Affairs), "Banking Regulatory Agencies Enforcement of the Equal Credit Opportunity Act and the Fair Housing Act," Sept. 14, 1978, p. 92 of transcript.

---

### Chapter 9: How to Fight Back

1. A four-year auto loan for $5000 at 10 percent has a total finance charge of $1,087, while the same loan at 17½ percent, a rate commonly charged by finance companies, would cost $1,984, a difference of $897.

2. Quoted in testimony by Anita Miller, Member, Federal Home Loan Bank Board in Hearings before the Subcommittee on Commerce, Consumers and Monetary Affairs, September 14, 1977, p. 67.

3. Ibid., pp. 67–68.
4. Ibid.
5. The other, in my opinion, was the amendment to the Bank Holding Co. Act of 1970 which closed a loophole in the Bank Holding Co. Act of 1956 and allowed the Federal Reserve to supervise all bank holding companies and to rule on the propriety of all their acquisitions.

# Index

Adams, Eugene, 229
*Abuse of Power, The* (Dubrul and Newfield), 70-71
American Bankers Association, 167, 169
    "contact bankers" of, 218
    opposition to NOW accounts by, 198, 205-7
    "Project Unravel" of, 178
American City Bank and Trust Company of Milwaukee, 245
American Civil Liberties Union, 14
American Institute of Real Estate Appraisers, 133, 135
American Telephone and Telegraph, 100-1
Appraisal, redlining and, 132-36
Atkins, Chester G., 81
Automatic transfer service (ATS), 206

Bailey, Jim, 75, 79
Baltimore, redlining in, 127, 136
Bank Marketing Association, 199
Bank Merger Act (1960), 246
Bank of California, 180
"Bank on Brooklyn," 164
*Bankers, The* (Mayer), xxii, 8, 57-58
Banking Act (1933), 188, 194
Banking Act (1935), 188, 194
Barclays Bank, 110
Barnett, Robert, 111
*Barron's*, 114, 144-45
*Beacon Hill Update* (periodical), 157
Beame, Abraham, 69, 71, 72
Becker Research Corporation, 154
Bergin, Kay, 6
Beverly Hills National Bank, 245
Blumenthal, Michael, 9, 209
Bodine, James F., 152
Bond market
    breakdown of, 85-86
    broadening of, 86-88
    government financial crises and, *see specific cities and states*
Boston
    financial crisis of, 73-76
    redlining in, 127, 128, 130, 136-39, 141
Boston Five Cents Savings Bank, 144, 146-47
*Boston Globe*, 22, 81, 142, 155, 157, 227
*Boston Herald American*, 182
Boston Mortgage Review Board, 153-57, 173
Boston Redevelopment Authority (BRA), 137

Boston Safe Deposit and Trust Company, 110
Branches of banks, 158-85
    activist bank commissioners and, 160-65, 179-83
    Community Reinvestment Act and, 165-85
Brandeis, Louis, 66
Brecht, Warren F., 24
Brooke, Edward, 148
Brooklyn, redlining in, 138-39
Brown, General George S., 4
Brown, Jonathan, 176, 203, 217-18
Brown, Nelson, 134
Brown, William H., III, 7
Brown Brothers Harriman & Co., 110
Bronx, redlining in, 132
Brunel, Wilson, 195
Buckley, John, 75, 78
Burns, Arthur, 70, 89, 104, 166
    Regulation Q and, 117
    on NOW accounts, 201, 205
Burns, Donald, xiii, xvi, 148, 160, 162-63

California Business and Transportation Agency, 162-63
California Department of Savings and Loan, xiii-xiv, 142
    "Fair Lending" regulations of, 163
Calhoun First National Bank, 59
Cardozo, Benjamin, 210-11
Carey, Hugh, 71
Carr, Elliot, 155, 182
Carras, James, 173
Cartels
    geographic, 234-36
    government-created, 233-34
Carter, Jimmy, 12, 27, 122, 172, 215
Catholics, discrimination against, 5
Certificates of deposit, interest rate ceilings and, 105-8
Chase Manhattan Bank
    Labor Department settlement with, 12
    mini-bonds issued by, 103-4
Checking accounts
    interest-bearing, 97-99
    *See also* NOW accounts
Chicago, redlining in, 128, 130-32, 134-35
Cincotta, Gale, 131, 140, 167-68, 170, 171, 185

**307**

Citicorp
  capital funds of, 119
  mini-bonds issued by, 103-4
Citizen State Bank of Carrizzo Springs,
  Texas, 56
Citizens Action Program (Oak Park),
  143
Civil Rights Act (1964), 7
Civil Rights Act (1968), 130, 157
Civil Rights Commission, U.S., 132
Cleveland
  default by, 83-85
  redlining in, 132
Cleveland Electric Illuminating
  Company (CEI), 84, 85
*Cleveland Plain Dealer*, 85
Cleveland Trust Company, 83, 85
Cloud, Hilda, 118
Commerce Bankshares, 184
Commercial banks
  opposition to NOW accounts from,
    187-88
  *See also* American Bankers
    Association; Independent Bankers
    Association; *specific banks*
Committee of the Judiciary, 132
Community Development Federal
  Credit Unions (CDFCUs), 258
Community Reinvestment Act (1977),
  xiii-xvi, 165-85, 219
  implementation of, 175-85
Comptroller of the Currency, xiv, xvi,
  31
Conference of State Bank Supervisors
  (CSBS), 66, 253-56
Connecticut
  branching of banks in, 161
  Truth-in-Lending legislation in,
    222-24
Connecticut Banking Department, xiv
Connell, Lawrence, Jr., xiii, xvi, 160-61,
  170, 207, 253
Consumers Bankers Association, 30
Consumers' Savings Bank of Worcester,
  Mass., 186
Consumers Union, 118
"Contact bankers," 218
Cooke, M. Todd, 152, 153
Corcoran, Thomas, 255-56
Council on Economic Priorities, 8, 10
Council on Urban Life, 129
County Bank of Santa Cruz, Cal.,
  179-80
Crane (Mass. Treasurer), 75
Credit unions, 259
Credit Union League of the USA, 258
Credit Union National Association, 207

Dennis, Warren, 30
Depository Institutions Deregulation

and Monetary Control Act (1980),
  122, 225, 229, 252
Deregulation of banking, 231-32
Disclosure, mortgage, 142-52
  *See also* Redlining
Disinvestment, urban, *see* Branches of
  banks; Redlining
Dubrul, Paul, 70-72, 128
Dukakis, Michael, x, 12, 15, 74-78,
  81-82, 89, 157, 182

Eisenmenger, Robert, 188
Electronic fund transfer system (EFTS),
  xviii, 233
Emergency Debt Restructuring Act
  (Mass.), 82
Emergency Financial Control Board
  (New York), 71-72
Employees Retirement Insurance Safety
  Act (ERISA), 124
Eliot Savings Bank, 180-82
Equal Credit Opportunity Act (1974 and
  1976), xiii, 28-31, 167, 219, 220,
  229-31, 261
Equibonds, 114

Fair Credit Billing Act, 219
Fair Housing Act (1968), xiii, xvii, 31,
  135, 157
"Fair Lending" regulations (Cal.), 163
Federal Bank Examination Council, 239
Federal Deposit Insurance Corporation
  (FDIC), xiv, xvi
  creation of, 97, 252
  interest rate ceilings and, 106, 108
  Morris Plan banks and, 108-11
  $20,000 maximum coverage of, 105
Federal Deposit Insurance Corporation
  Act (1934), 167
Federal Home Loan Bank Board
  (FHLBB), xiv, xv, xviii, xix, 67, 121
  authorization of POW accounts by,
    206
  elimination of Regulation Q and, 125
  racial bias and, 134-35
Federal Housing Administration, 136-37
Federal National Mortgage Association
  $5,000 debentures of, 105
  racial bias and, 134
Federal Open Market Committee, xix
Federal Reserve Act (1914), 167
Federal Reserve Bank of Boston, 188
Federal Reserve Board (FRB), xiv, xvii,
  xix-xx
  interest rate ceilings and, 105-6
  NOW accounts and, 200-9
  Regulation Q and, 117
  regulations issued by, 219
Federal Reserve System, membership
  problem of, 202-4

Federal Savings League, 177
Feminist credit unions, 257-58
Fiduciary Trust Company, 110
Financial Institutions and the National Economy (FINE) study, 240
Financial Institutions Regulation Act (1978), 60-66
First Bank of the United States, 241, 252
First National Bank of Boston, 139
First Pennsylvania Banking and Trust Company, 119
"Inflation Fighter" plan of, 114
First Pennsylvania Corporation, 152
Fishbein, Allan, 185
Foley, Paul, 15
Ford, Gerald, 19, 30, 70-71, 229
Francis, Richard, 160
Friedman, Milton, 97

Garn, Jake, 170
Gelder, Ralph, 160
Geographic cartels, 234-36
Gnaizda, Robert, 111
Golden, Harrison, 72
Golden, Richard W., 159
Goldman Sachs, 82
Gray, William, 153
Gray Panthers, 111-12, 118-20
Great Depression, myths of causes of, 97
Greater New York Savings Bank of Brooklyn, 164-65, 184-85

Hamilton National Bank of Chattanooga, Tennessee, 54, 244, 245
Harris Trust Company of Chicago, 12
Hazelton, Ron, 186-87, 191
Heimann, John, 54-55, 116, 160, 172, 185, 192, 207, 220
Helding, Frederick, 152
Helms, Jesse, 18-19
Herman, Edward S., 34, 48, 197
Holding companies, mini-bonds issued by, 103-4
Home Mortgage Disclosure Act (1975), xiii, 150-51, 167, 171, 219
non-extension of, 178
Home mortgages
interest rates on, 37-38, 95-99
See also Redlining
Home Owners' Loan Act (1933), 128
Homer Sidney, 101
House of Representatives, U.S.
Subcommittee on Commerce, Consumer and Monetary Affairs, 96
Subcommittee on Financial Institutions, 98

Housing and Urban Development Act (1968), 68-69

I. G. Farbenindustrie, 197
Illinois, mortgage disclosure laws in, 144
Illinois Federal Savings and Loan of Chicago, 134
Independent Bankers Association of America, 26-27, 200, 208
Interest-bearing checking accounts, 97-99
See also NOW accounts
Interest rates
on home mortgages, see Redlining
on savings accounts, see Regulation Q
Internal Revenue Service, 100
Isaac, William M., 184-85

Jackson, Philip, 230
Jamaica Plains Community Council, Banking and Mortgage Committee of, 130, 159, 173
Jaycees, 22
Jews, discrimination against, 4-5
John Hancock, 82
Johnson, Tom L., 84

Kane, Edward J., 106-8
Kauper, Thomas E., 233
Kidder Peabody, 80
King, Edward, 22
Kiwanis, 22
Klaman, Saul B., 119-20
Kniffin, William H., 32
Koplow, Freyda, 143
Kucinich, Dennis, 84-85
Kuhn, Maggie, 119
Kuttner, Robert, 153

Lance, Bert, xiii, 58-61, 63
Labor Department, U.S., 12
guidelines on religious discrimination of, 11
Lee, Inez, 8, 11
Leighton, George N., 135
Le Maistre, George, 49, 245
Life insurance companies, 125
Lindsay, John V., 69
Lombard, Joe, 76
Long, Virginia, 160
Lorber, Lawrence Z., 19
Los Angeles Times, 149

McCormack, Hugh, 173
McIntyre, Thomas, 117, 189, 204, 205
McKinney, Robert H., 121, 172, 179, 216
Maine Consumer Protection Bureau, 226

Maine, Truth-in-Lending legislation in, 222-24
Martinek (bank president), 141
Massachusetts
    financial crisis of, 76-83
    first Truth-in-Lending legislation in, 222-24
Massachusetts Anti-Defamation League, 14, 17
Massachusetts Bankers Association, 195
Massachusetts Banking Department
    Boston Mortgage Review Board and, 153-57
    branching of banks in, 161-62, 180-83
    employment survey of, 13-18, 20-21, 24
    Morris Plan banks and, 108-11
    mortgage disclosure and, xii-xiv, 144-48
    NOW accounts and, 187
    "Shopper's Credit Guide" of, 226-27
Massachusetts Bay Transit Authority (MBTA), 80, 81, 83
Massachusetts Commission Against Discrimination, 14
Massachusetts Housing Finance Agency (MHFA), 79-81, 83
Massachusetts Savings Bank Association, 16, 21
Mayer, Martin, xxii, 8, 57-58
Mayer, Thomas, 248
Meany, George, 104
Merrill Lynch, 82
Milwaukee, redlining in, 128-30
Mini-bonds, 102-4
Minneapolis-St. Paul, redlining in, 128
Mitchell, George, 70, 89
Money-market certificates (MMCs), 117-22
Money market funds, 99
Morgan Guaranty Trust of New York, 210
Morris, Frank, 79, 188, 201
Morris Plan banks, 108-11
Mortgage market
    discrimination in, 28-31
    See also Redlining
Mortgage review boards, 153-55
Moscovitch, Edward, 77
Municipal Assistance Corporation (New York), 71-72

NAACP, 14
Nader, Ralph, xi-xx, 167, 170, 217
National Association of Federal Credit Unions, 207
National Association of Mutual Savings Banks, 104
National Bank of Georgia, 59
National Bank of North America, "Supreme Interest" plan of, 114

National Banking Act (1863), 252
National City Bank of Cleveland, 84
National Commission on Consumer Finance, 229
National Committee Against Discrimination in Housing, 132
National Credit Union Administration (NCUA), xiv
National Organization of Women, 118, 257-58
National People's Action on Housing, 131, 140, 143
National Urban League, 132, 159
New England Merchants National Bank of Boston, 9
New York City
    financial crisis of, 69-73, 81
    redlining in, 138-39
*New York Daily News,* 70
New York Public Interest Research Group, Inc. (PIRG), 159, 163-65, 173
New York State
    NOW accounts in, 189-90
    study of redlining in, 132, 137, 139
New York State Bankers Association, 172
New York State Banking Department
    branching of banks and, 159, 161, 164-65
    disclosure and, 143-44
*New York Times, The,* 146
Newfield, Jack, 70-72, 128
9 to 5, 9, 14
Nixon, Richard M., 30, 68-69, 216
Non-interest-paying checking accounts (NINOWs), 205
Northern Pacific Railway Co. *v.* United States (1958), 233
NOW accounts xxiii
    charges on, 198-99
    consumer benefits from, 191-92
    effects on commercial banks of, 194-97
    Federal Reserve Board and, 200-9
    origins of, 186-87
    savings and loan associations and, 199-200
    spread of, 188-91
    supposed disadvantages of, 192-94
    trust funds and, 209-11

Office of Contract Compliance, U.S. Department of Labor, 9
Ohio, mortgage disclosure laws in, 144
Old Stone Corporation, 109, 111

Palmer First National Bank and Trust Company of Sarasota, Fla., 54, 245
Passbook savings accounts, interest rates on, 93-99

"Payment order of withdrawal"
accounts (POWs), 206-7
Pension funds, stock market and,
124-25
Perpetual Federal Savings and Loan
Association, 178-80
Philadelphia Mortgage Plan, 152-53
Philadelphia National Bank, 152
Philadelphia Partnership, 152
Philadelphia Saving Fund Society, 152
Phillips, Almarin, 204
Pinck, Joan, 15
Pittsburgh, antiredlining laws in, 141
Porter, David S., 157
"Project Unravel," 178
Providence, redlining in, 128
Provident Institution for Savings, 144
Proxmire, William, xiii, 7, 9, 17-19, 22,
24, 28, 58
on Community Reinvestment Act,
165-67, 169
Regulation Q and, 117
Prudential, 82
Public Advocates, 100, 180

Quinn, John, 222-23, 225

Racial transition in neighborhoods,
131-35
Redlining, 127-57
appraisal and, 132-36
disclosure of, 142-52
fight against, 140-41
mortgage review boards and, 153-55
Philadelphia Mortgage Plan and,
152-53
race and, 131-35
underwriting and, 133
Regulation of banking
changing constituency of, 215-19
changing structure of, 236-42
as government price-fixing, 232-33
origins of, 215
struggle for pro-consumer, 219-31
See also Deregulation of banking;
specific laws
Regulation B, 219, 230
Regulation Q, xix-xx, 97, 102, 103, 171
abolition of, 122-26
applied to Morris Plan banks, 109-11
revisions of, 112-22
suits to remove, 111-12, 118
Regulation Z, 219
Report on Transactions in Securities of
the City of New York (SEC), 72-73
Republic Federal Savings of Chicago,
140-41
Reuss, Henry, 240
Ribicoff, Abraham, 237, 240
Robertson, Ross M., 204, 248

Rockefeller, Nelson, 71
Rohatyn, Felix, 69, 71
Rosenthal, Benjamin, xiii, 70, 89, 120,
216, 221, 222
Rotary International, 22

St. Germain, Ferdinand, 58, 60, 62, 63,
66, 98, 115-17, 183
St. Louis, redlining in, 132
Safe Banking Act, see Financial
Institutions Regulation Act
Salomon Brothers, 15, 82-83
San Francisco, redlining in, 128
Sargent, Frank, 76-77
Savings Bank Association of
Massachusetts, 181-82
Savings Bank Association of New York,
116, 160
Savings Bank and Its Practical Work,
The (Kniffin), 32
Savings banks, origins of, 32-34
Savings bonds, U.S., interest rates on,
99-100, 102
Savings and loan associations, NOW
accounts and, 199-200
Savings and Loan News, 141
Sawyer, Daniel A., 8
Saxon, John, 55
Schafer, Robert, 132, 137, 139
Schechter, Henry, 168
Schmidt, Carl, 160, 179
Schwartz, Anna, 97
Scott, Ira O., Jr., 160
Sears, Roebuck and Co., 119
Second Bank of the United States, 240,
252
Securities and Exchange Commission
(SEC), 72-73
Segerstrom, John R., 254
Senate, U.S.
Banking, Housing and Urban Affairs
Committee of, 17-19, 22, 27-28, 216
redlining studies by, 132
Series E. U.S. savings bonds, interest
rates on, 99-100
Shanker, Albert, 71
Short-changed: Minorities and Women
in Banking (Council on Economic
Priorities), 8
Siebert Muriel, 164, 183
Simon, William, 70
Smith, James E., 30, 205, 216, 217
Southwest Community Congress,
140-41
Sprague, Irvine, 207
State National Bank of Rockville, Md.,
119
Stone, James, 74-75
Strunk, Norman, 200
Sumitomo Bank, 180

Tax Reform Act (1976), 86

Taylor Dan, 74-76, 82
Tobler, Emmanuel, 143, 157
Tower, John, 168
Treasury Department, U.S.
  data collection and title inflation by,
    10-12
  Equal Opportunity Program of, 8
  $1,000 notes of, 104-5
  opposition to A. T. & T. bond plan
    by, 101-2
  opposition to mini-bonds plan by, 103
  undermining of affirmative action by,
    7-10, 17-20
Trust funds, 209-11
Truth-in-Lending Act (1968), xiii, xiv,
    167, 219-29, 262-63
Tuccillo, John, 96

Underwriting of mortgages, 133
United Federation of Teachers, 71
Urban Development Corporation, 69-70
Urban disinvestment, *see* Branches of
    banks; Redlining

U.S. League of Savings Associations,
    114-15, 117, 200, 208
U.S. National Bank of San Diego, xiii

Volcker, Paul A., 251

Walker, Dan, 150
*Wall Street Journal*, 121, 189
Washington, D.C., Public Interest
    Research Group, Inc. (PIRG), 176,
    178, 203
*Washington Financial Reports*
    (periodical), 103
Weir, Brock, 85
Weiss, Steven, 161, 188
Werner, Llewellyn, 148
White, Kevin, 73-74, 76
Winthrop Chemical, 197
Women, discrimination against, 5-7
Women's Equity Action League
    (WEAL), 8
Wriston, Walter, 71, 104, 250